The Experts Book of Garden Hints

Over 1,500 Organic Tips and Techniques from 250 of America's Best Gardeners

FERN MARSHALL BRADLEY, EDITOR

Contributing writers: **Lois Trigg Chaplin, George DeVault, Terry Krautwurst, Susan McClure, Lynn McGowan, Patricia S. Michalak, Jean M. A. Nick, Nancy J. Ondra, Sara Pacher, Sally Roth, Miranda Smith, Heidi A. Stonehill**

Illustrator: **Frank Fretz**

Rodale Press, Emmaus, Pennsylvania

Printed in the United States of America on acid-free ∞, recycled paper ♻, containing 20 percent post-consumer waste

Library of Congress Cataloging-in-Publication Data

The Experts book of garden hints : over 1,500 organic tips and techniques from 250 of America's best gardeners / Fern Marshall Bradley, editor ; contributing writers, Lois Trigg Chaplin . . . [et al.] ; illustrations by Frank Fretz.
     p.   cm.
   Includes bibliographical references (p.   ) and index.
   ISBN 0-87596-555-5   hardcover
   1. Organic gardening—Miscellanea.
2. Gardening—Miscellanea.   I. Bradley, Fern Marshall. II. Chaplin, Lois Trigg.
SB453.5.E96   1993
635.0484—dc20   93-2767
                       CIP

Distributed in the book trade by St. Martin's Press

2 4 6 8 10 9 7 5 3 1   hardcover

Executive Editor: **Margaret Lydic Balitas**

Managing Editor: **Barbara W. Ellis**

Editor: **Fern Marshall Bradley**

Contributing Editors: **Ellen Phillips, Nancy J. Ondra, and Joan Benjamin**

Copy Manager: **Dolores Plikaitis**

Copy Editor: **Laura Stevens**

Senior Research Associate: **Heidi A. Stonehill**

Office Manager: **Karen Earl-Braymer**

Editorial assistance: **Susan Nickol and Kimberly Moore**

Secretary: **Deborah Weisel**

Art Director: **Anita G. Patterson**

Cover and Book Designer: **Linda Jacopetti**

Cover Photographer: **Mitch Mandel**

Illustrator: **Frank Fretz**

Indexer: **Ed Yeager**

If you have any questions or comments concerning this book, please write:
   Rodale Press
   Book Readers' Service
   33 East Minor Street
   Emmaus, PA 18098

Contents

Introduction

Imagine the ultimate gardener's sweepstakes: The grand prize is an unlimited expense account for 30 days, along with a special pass allowing you to tour nurseries, organic farms, botanical gardens, and research gardens all over the United States and Canada. Show your pass to nursery managers, farmers, professors, extension agents, and you'll be granted exclusive interviews. You'll have the chance to ask these expert gardeners for all of their best ideas and gardening secrets.

Who's offering this sweepstakes? Unfortunately, no one. But it would certainly be a dream come true for me. And I was lucky enough to have the chance to arrange something rather like the sweepstakes while editing *The Experts Book of Garden Hints*. I worked with a group of garden writers who interviewed expert gardeners—more than 200 of them—and came up with a wonderful collection of new and exciting ideas for home gardeners.

Paging through *The Experts Book of Garden Hints* is like sampling from a mouth-watering tray of hors d'oeuvres. On your first sample, you might find a great new idea for making compost. Dabble in another chapter, and you'll discover a fast and easy way to plant small seeds. Perhaps you'll turn to the chapter on vegetables and find an illustration of a nifty way to trellis beans. Every page has a treat.

If you're not in a nibbling mood but want to feast on information on a specific topic, be sure to use the index. It will direct you to all of the tips on tomatoes or pruning shrubs, for example, quickly and efficiently.

Each time I read sections of *The Experts Book of Garden Hints*, I find interesting pointers or a variation on a gardening technique that I plan to try in my garden soon. As I read, I'm also overwhelmed with gratitude for the generosity of gardeners. I think most gardeners love to share their tips and tricks, and the gardening experts we consulted were true to gardening form. Everyone our writers talked to was delighted to answer questions and share secrets. We're sure you'll want to join us in thanking the creative gardening experts whose ideas fill this book. We also suspect that on every "visit" to their gardens, you'll find more new and exciting ideas for your own garden.

You'll find information about the experts at the end of each chapter under the heading "The Garden Professionals." If you're curious about any of the books or mail-order companies mentioned in those descriptions, you can find more information about many of them in the "Recommended Reading" and "Sources" sections in the back of the book.

So, in a way, you *are* a winner of my imaginary sweepstakes—without ever leaving your garden—when you tour the nurseries and meet the experts on every page of *The Experts Book of Garden Hints*. To collect your "prize," all you need to do is read on!

Fern Marshall Bradley
Editor

PART 1

IMPROVE YOUR SKILLS

Mastering new skills is one of the most exciting aspects of gardening. You probably don't realize how many special skills you've already acquired as a home gardener. Germinating seeds, planting and transplanting, pruning, and potting are among the things you've learned to do by reading, by watching others, and through lots of trial and error.

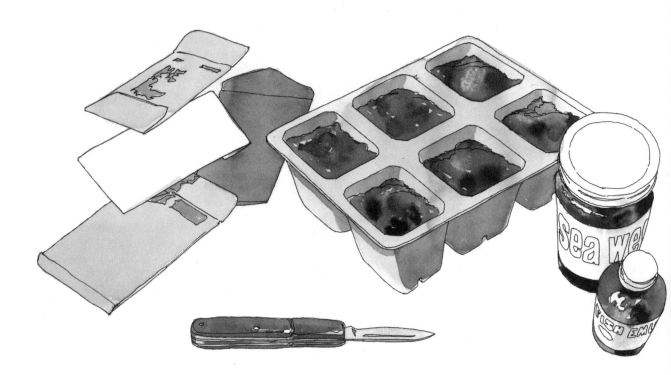

Growing from Seed

For many gardeners, growing plants from seed is the essence of gardening. It means nurturing a plant through all of its stages of growth, and it is often the most rewarding way to start vegetables, annuals, and perennials.

Sowing seed is an exacting procedure that can be made easier or harder by what you do (or don't) know. Disease, lack of light, and too much or too little fertilizer can result in poor growth. Providing seedlings with the light, temperature, and nutritional conditions that they need takes some experimentation. In this chapter, experienced gardeners share their hints for success and their cautions about the possible pitfalls of growing plants from seed.

Starting Seeds Indoors

There's nothing quite as soothing for the winter-weary gardener as preparing seed-starting mix and gently tucking seeds into a flat. We cheer on the green, young seedlings as they push through the soil mix and unfold their first leaves. But seed starting indoors can be tricky. Try some of these tips from the experts for getting the best and fastest seed germination.

PRE-SPROUT PRECIOUS SEEDS

If you're the type to worry while you wait for your valuable seeds to sprout, relax. By germinating your seeds in paper towels (as shown in the illustrations at left), you can pre-sprout your seeds and avoid the risks you encounter when sprouting seeds in soil mix. Also, with the paper-towel method, you can speed up the germination process.

Nancy Bubel, the author of *The New Seed-Starters Handbook,* suggests that you pre-sprout any seeds that are rare or especially precious to you. "Arrange them on a moistened paper towel in an alignment where they aren't touching each other. Cover them with a second moist towel to sandwich the seeds in between," she explains. "Then roll the whole thing up, and put it in a plastic bag." Nancy sets her bags of seeds on top of the hot water heater to keep them warm.

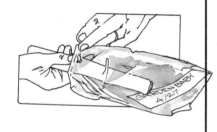

PRE-SPROUTING SEEDS

Check the seeds every two or three days, and remove them from the towels as soon as they've sprouted. Transplant them immediately to small pots. Rolling seeds in moist paper towels is also a good way to prepare dormant seeds for the cold/moist treatment called stratification. (See "Some Like It Cold" below for details.)

SOME LIKE IT COLD

Seeds of some plants need exposure to moist and cold to break dormancy and sprout. Dormancy keeps seeds from sprouting during cold winter weather when seedlings might freeze or be damaged. You can duplicate nature's moist winter chill with a process called stratification.

Place a layer of moistened growing mix in a plastic container. Scatter a layer of dormant seeds over the surface, then cover with more moist soil mix. Be sure to make the layer of seeds thick enough so that you can find them easily once the treatment is over. If necessary, add more layers of seed and mix until all the seeds are planted. Cover the container with a tight-fitting lid, and place it in the refrigerator.

Different seeds need different amounts of time in the refrigerator. Check "Recommended Reading" on page 333 for books that provide seed-starting requirements, or check seed catalogs. When the cold/moist treatment is finished, sow the seeds in flats and move them into a bright area to sprout. If you can't find out how long your seeds need stratification or whether they need it at all, you can try a general stratification technique developed by Elissa Steeves, a horticulture teacher at Pulaski County High School in Virginia. "In general, if it's a tree, shrub, or wildflower, I assume you have to stratify just to be safe," says Steeves. "All I do is sow the seeds, wrap the containers airtight in plastic wrap, and put them in the refrigerator in the vegetable keeper for a week." To prevent evaporation, make sure the wrap snugly seals the container, stretching tightly across the top of the container so that it doesn't sag. After the week in the refrigerator, let the container set at room temperature for a day or two. Then put it into the freezer for one week. The idea is to alternate between the refrigerator and the freezer at least twice. The warm-up period in between helps to satisfy the double dormancy needed by some seeds due to a natural dormancy requirement plus a tough seed coat.

SEED-STARTING BASICS

Most seeds need only moisture and warmth before they will sprout. But some seeds have a few additional requirements that you can easily supply.

Seeds may need darkness in order to germinate, or they may need light. Completely cover those that need darkness with a good seed-starting mix. If your seeds need light, just sprinkle them across the top of your seed-starting mix.

Seeds that are dormant or that have hard seed coats may need extra care. Mimic the cold/moist conditions of winter to break seed dormancy with a process called stratification. Place the seeds between layers of moist soil mix in a plastic container. Cover tightly with a lid, and refrigerate. (See "Some Like It Cold" at left for details.)

Break through tough seed coats with a process called scarification. Simply nick the seeds with a sharp knife or scratch them by rubbing them between pieces of sandpaper.

TWO SEEDS IN EVERY POT

If you sow seeds directly into cell packs, sow more than one seed in each cell; you'll be sowing insurance. If both seeds germinate, simply pull one seedling out or pinch it off at the soil level. This will save you the work of reseeding if one seed doesn't come up, and, because you won't have to reseed, all of the seedlings will be a uniform age.

A QUICK SEED COVER-UP

When starting seeds in a flat, simply lay them on top of the moistened soil mix and cover with a thin layer of dry soil mix. It's easier and faster than poking a hole in the seedbed, placing the seed, and then filling each hole. If you cover the flat with a plastic dome or layer of plastic wrap, the moisture in the flat will rain down from the cover and moisten the dry soil.

TESTING...TESTING...

If you're in doubt about the viability of seeds that you've stored for a while or that you've discovered in the kitchen drawer, use Nancy Bubel's paper towel method from "Pre-Sprout Precious Seeds" on page 2 to figure out how many good seeds you have. Place 10 seeds in the paper towels and count how many germinate. Multiply that figure by 10. That's your percentage of germination. If 8 out of 10 seeds germinate, the germination rate is 80 percent. Anything under 70 percent is considered poor for most seeds. That doesn't mean you can't use them; just sow more thickly to compensate for the ones that don't come up.

BACKHANDED SEEDING WORKS BETTER

The traditional method of seeding a flat (patting seeds in so that they make firm contact with the soil but aren't buried) can be a big task for the little fingers of children and a painstaking task for the bigger fingers of grown-ups. But there's a tip that helps children successfully complete the tricky job of seeding a flat—and the tip works just as well for adults. Bibby Moore, a registered horticultural therapist from North Carolina, has children use the backs of their fingers to press the seeds into the flat. "When the children turn their hands over, the backs of their fingers tend to operate as a uniform press," she says, "whereas with their fingertips they tend to punch holes." The technique is easy: Just turn your palms up with your fingers outstretched and press.

SURFACE-SOW SMALL SEEDS

Tiny seeds may disappear after planting, never to be seen again, if you cover or water them in the usual way. "Many small seeds like those of impatiens, begonias, and snapdragons must be sown right on the surface of the soil," says Nancy Bubel, the author of *The New Seed-Starters Handbook.* Bubel advises watering the seed flat before scattering the seeds on the soil. Otherwise, you'll slosh the seeds into corners or bury them. For subsequent watering, set the flat in a pan of water for bottom watering until the soil surface is dark and moist. Remove the flat, and repeat again as the soil begins to dry out. Take care when choosing your seed-starting container for small seeds: Make sure it will fit in a roasting pan or other shallow container to allow for bottom watering.

FUSSY SEEDERS SAVE TIME

Preparing seed flats efficiently can save you time when your seedlings are ready to transplant. "I tell my students that if they take an hour to carefully sow two or three flats of seeds, it will only take 20 minutes to transplant them," says Elissa Steeves, a horticulture teacher at Pulaski County High School in Virginia. Steeves finds that when seeds are broadcast, they're usually scattered too thickly. This makes it difficult to transplant and forces the seedlings to stretch to compete for light. For very small seeds like begonias, broadcasting works best, but larger seeds need more space. Here's the technique for sowing these larger seeds, as shown in the illustration below:

1. Fill the flat one-half to three-quarters full with your favorite seed-starting mix (without fertilizer). Thoroughly moisten the mix with water.

2. Spread your seeds on a paper towel.

3. To sow seeds, dip a sharpened pencil point in a bowl of water, and use the moist point to pick up a seed or two. The seeds will stick to the pencil point. Place them in rows by touching the point to the mix in the seed flat. The seeds will drop from the pencil point when they touch the

Seeding carefully in rows makes for easier transplanting after seedlings sprout and grow. Wrap the seed flats tightly with plastic wrap to keep the mix moist and promote germination.

EASY SEEDING STYLES

Seeds that germinate slowly can frustrate new and experienced gardeners alike. "Children need the easiest seeds to work with — those that germinate quickly and surely," says Bibby Moore, a registered horticultural therapist from North Carolina. "For youngsters just starting out, use marigolds, zinnias, four-o'clocks [*Mirabilis jalapa*], squash, tomatoes, and cucumbers. Don't use nasturtium seed. Even though the seeds are big and easy to handle, they have a poor germination rate." Moore doesn't use radishes because many children won't eat them.

Older adults with more patience and more-experienced palates can try a wider variety of seeds. But they often face different challenges: poor eyesight and shaky hands. In this case, sow seeds directly into a cell pack to eliminate the exacting job of transplanting.

A DUAL-PURPOSE DIBBLE

Transplanting seedlings from seed flats to individual pots requires agile fingers. There are little tools called dibbles made for this purpose, but you can use an ordinary metal nail file instead. The file makes it easy for you to work in the tiny spaces between seedlings to lift them from the flat rather than pull them. You can also use it to poke planting holes to slip the seedlings into.

mix. (Resist the temptation to poke the seeds into the mix; just rest them on top.)

4. To keep the flat moist, cover it with clinging plastic wrap. (For convenience, you can buy clear plastic domes to put over the top, but plastic wrap is cheaper.) To prevent evaporation, make sure the wrap snugly seals the container, stretching tightly across the top of the container so that it doesn't sag.

5. As soon as the seedlings show the first sign of growth (the white root tip emerges), it's time to remove the wrap and place the flat under lights or in the brightest window available. Steeves cautions against fertilizing until the seedlings develop their first two true leaves. Then apply fish emulsion diluted according to label instructions.

SLOW SEEDLINGS TO YOUR SCHEDULE

If spring finds you with too many seedlings and not enough time to transplant them, slow down the growth process. "People don't realize how much you can play with plants, using temperature and water to adjust them to your schedule," says Christina R. J. Pey, a supervisor for the production greenhouses at the Missouri Botanical Garden.

If you get behind on planting, withhold water a little and move the plants to a cooler place. This advice is especially helpful if a late cold snap forces you to keep your transplants indoors longer than expected. Indoors, moving plants to a cooler place might mean moving them from a spot in the sunroom to a place beside a basement window. This trick can buy you an extra week or so of time before you need to plant. However, don't ever let plants become so dry that they wilt, or you might stunt or kill them.

BRIGHT LIGHTS FOR BETTER SEEDLINGS

It's worth the effort to start seedlings indoors under lights, says Jim Wilson, a cohost of public television's "The Victory Garden." Wilson says he's surprised to find that only 5 to 10 percent of the gardeners he's polled start seedlings under fluorescent lights. "It's the best way to get stocky plants, especially in a cool garage or basement," Wilson says.

Wilson was one of the pioneers in experimenting with fluorescent lights for seedlings in cooperation with Sylvania back in the fifties. He found that the distance of the lights from the plants makes a big difference.

Start out with the lights no more than 2 inches from the seed flat. Light efficiency falls off exponentially as you increase distance. As the plants grow, raise the lights gradually to no more than 6 inches from the top of the plants. A garage or basement is an ideal place to start your seedlings. In a garage, shroud the setup with a large sheet of plastic during the early part of the season to help capture the small amount of heat given off by the lights and to shield plants from cold drafts. Wilson hangs his lights on dog chains from a ceiling beam.

CLEAN CONTAINERS CONTROL DISEASE

If you start seedlings indoors, be sure you're using clean containers. "If you reuse the same containers year to year for starting your seedlings, they've got to be clean or you increase the chances of plant disease," warns Christina R. J. Pey, a supervisor for the production greenhouses at the Missouri Botanical Garden. Pey recommends simply washing pots and flats in a mild dish detergent and then dipping them in a solution of 1 part bleach to 9 parts hot water. Use a big galvanized tub—or even the bathtub, if you don't have a vessel large enough to dip a flat in. Let the containers dry completely before filling them.

SPHAGNUM IS HER FUNGICIDE

Sphagnum moss can help fight fungus problems in seedling flats. Elissa Steeves, a horticulture teacher at Pulaski County High School in Virginia, sprinkles about ¼ inch of milled sphagnum moss in between the rows of seeds coming up in flats to help prevent damping-off, which is caused by a fungus that attacks sprouting seeds and very young seedlings. One type of damping-off fungus keeps seeds from germinating, but the type most troublesome to gardeners kills seedlings shortly after they've sprouted. The seedlings rot at their bases and fall over, or they just wither up and die.

"It's the acidity of the moss that keeps the fungus from developing," Steeves says. If you don't have milled sphagnum moss, mill it yourself by rubbing the unmilled moss between your fingers.

DON'T START—CONTINUED

Below, Nancy Plengey, the flower and herbs trial manager for Johnny's Selected Seeds in Maine, suggests just the right number of weeks that gardeners should allow for raising flower and herb transplants indoors.

Flower	Weeks until Transplant Time
Ageratum	6-8
Aster	6-8
Celosia	6-8
Centaurea	4-6
Cosmos	4-6
Marigold	4-6
Morning glory	4-6
Pinks	6-8
Snapdragon	8-10
Statice	8-10
Stock	6-8
Strawflower	6-8
Sweet pea	4-6
Zinnia	4-6

Herb	Weeks until Transplant Time
Basil	4-6
Chives	6-8
Dill	4-6
Lavender	8-10
Rosemary	8-10
Sage	6-8
Thyme	8-10

FILL FLATS TO THE BRIM

Fill seed flats right to the top with seed-starting mix, suggests Ed Hume, the owner of Ed Hume Seeds in Washington State. "You've got to have airflow across those seedlings to avoid damping-off," he says. A flat that is filled halfway doesn't get as much airflow.

TRY THE TOP OF THE FRIDGE

One of the best places to start seeds is on top of the refrigerator. Sow the seeds in a flat or other shallow container, and place it on top of the refrigerator. It's always warm there, and the refrigerator will supply bottom heat for your flat of seedlings. Immediately after the seeds sprout, move them under lights or to a bright window to keep the young seedlings from getting leggy. Try other warm household places to start seeds, such as the top of the hot water heater or under a swing-arm lamp.

◆ A LEAN-TO REFLECTOR FOR UPRIGHT SEEDLINGS

Seedlings grown on windowsills have a habit of stretching to reach the sunlight. You can turn the seed flats around each day for straighter seedlings, but one side is always pointed away from the sun. Jean M. A. Nick, a garden book editor for Rodale Press, fashioned a simple reflector that continually directs sunlight to the back side of seedlings and produces straighter, stockier plants. "All you need to make one is corrugated cardboard, aluminum foil, tape, glue, and two rubber bands," says Nick.

Here's how to assemble a reflector:

1. Cut out the cardboard pieces as shown in the illustration below. Make sure that the corrugations (the little channels) in the cardboard run lengthwise on the roof, otherwise it will tend to sag.

2. Cut slots for the roof tabs in the back section and rubber band holes in the roof section as shown.

3. Insert the rubber bands so that the ends stick out on the top side of the roof.

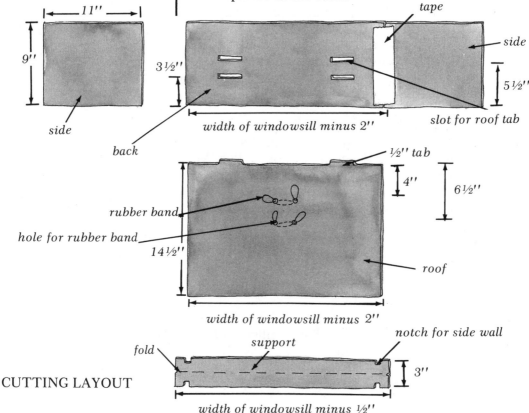

CUTTING LAYOUT

4. Cover the inside of the walls and the roof with aluminum foil, and fasten it with tape or glue.

5. Tape the sides and the back together. Leave about a ¼-inch gap between the cardboard pieces as you tape. This will allow you to fold the reflector up for storage.

6. Fold the support section in half lengthwise (first, score it with a utility knife to make this easier), and tape it closed. Set the back and side walls upright. Then hold the support centered above the side walls, and mark where it will rest on each side wall. Cut notches in the support at the places you've marked.

7. To assemble, slide the support piece through the loops of the rubber band closest to the center of the roof. Slip the roof tabs into the lower set of slots on the back wall. (The support should be on the top of the roof.) Slip the notches of the support over the top edges of the side walls, and adjust front to back until the roof is at a 45-degree angle. As the plants grow taller, you may want to raise the roof by switching the support piece to the other rubber band and moving the roof tabs into the higher slots in the back wall.

OVERALL VIEW

START SEEDS WITHOUT FERTILIZER

If the seed-starting mix you use contains fertilizer, you may end up with algae covering the surfaces of your flat or other containers. Algae can grow well in the warm, moist conditions present for seed starting. If you supply fertilizer, the algae gets a boost and may become a serious problem. Algae growth is worst in greenhouses and cold frames where the humidity stays high. It's easy to avoid the algae problem, though. Since seeds don't need fertilizer until they have sprouted, all you have to do is make sure that you don't buy a mix with fertilizer. And don't add fertilizer until after you've transplanted your seedlings.

EASY THINNING WITH A SNIP

An easy way to thin new seedlings in flats or in the garden is by cutting them off at ground level with a pair of nail scissors. "It's fast, and you avoid disturbing the roots of the seedlings you leave behind," says Nancy Bubel, the author of *The New Seed-Starters Handbook,* who starts nearly all of the seedlings for her garden and flower beds. Just be sure to use a small pair of scissors with a sharp point so you can maneuver around the seedlings easily. A large pair would be too awkward.

STAND UP AND SOW

All too often, the excitement of sowing seeds outdoors is dimmed by the back-bending work of it. For more comfortable planting, make a stand-up dibble: Cut a piece of 1-inch-diameter PVC pipe to a length of 3 feet—or whatever length will be comfortable for you. Cut one end at a steep angle. Then mark your rows and start planting: Jab the dibble's pointed end into the soil, and rock it back slightly to make a hole. Drop a seed down the pipe and into the hole, and move on to sow the next seed. As you work, cover the holes with your heel, or, when you're finished sowing seeds, go back and cover them using a hoe or rake.

Starting Seeds Outdoors

Starting seeds outdoors is a simple and satisfying process, but there are still decisions to make about seeding methods and timing. In the following sections, you may find some new ideas about this age-old activity.

HOMEMADE SEED TAPES

When you need to space seeds uniformly or if you want to avoid thinning seedlings, try homemade seed tapes. "You can buy seed tapes, but they are expensive and there aren't many types of seeds or cultivars available," says Jean M. A. Nick, a garden book editor for Rodale Press. She recommends making seed tapes, using cornstarch and paper towels, as shown in the illustrations below.

In a small saucepan, dissolve 1 tablespoon of cornstarch in 1 cup of cold water. Cook over medium heat, stirring constantly to prevent the mixture from becoming lumpy. Once the mixture boils and turns translucent and gel-like, remove the saucepan from the heat, and let it cool to room temperature.

Tear off 4- or 5-foot-long sections of paper towels. Leave the towels attached to each other, and cut them into long strips that are ½ to ¾ inch wide. Nick prefers using unbleached, recycled paper towels.

At this point, check the seed packet or some other source to determine the correct seed spacing for the seeds you're using. If you're making a tape of large seeds, the proper technique is to put dots of cornstarch at the proper spacing on the paper towels, and then dab one seed onto each dot.

To do this, begin by putting a few spoonfuls of the cornstarch mix in a plastic bag. Twist the bag until the gel is squeezed into one corner; snip off the tip of that corner. Using the bag as you would a pastry bag, squeeze out dots of cornstarch gel down the length of the paper towel. Place one seed on each cornstarch dot, and let the seed tape dry

for about 1 hour, or until it is no longer sticky. Then, roll up the seed tape, and place it in a plastic bag until you are ready to use it. Write the type of seed and the cultivar name in ink on each seed tape, or you may end up with mystery plantings, says Nick.

For the best results with small seeds, mix the seeds and cornstarch mixture together in the plastic bag. Then, as before, cut a small hole in one corner of the bag, and squeeze dots of the seed-and-cornstarch mixture onto paper towel strips with the correct amount of space between them. One teaspoon of cornstarch mixture and ¼ teaspoon of small seeds will cover 15 to 20 feet of seed tape. It may take practice to get just one seed to come out with each dot of mixture. Don't let the seed-and-cornstarch mixture set before making the tapes, or the seeds will become too moist and may sprout. Let the finished seed tapes dry, label them, roll them up, and store them in a plastic bag.

When planting time arrives, check the proper planting depth for each crop, then dig furrows of the appropriate depth in your garden. Unroll the seed tapes, place one in each furrow, and cover the tapes with soil. The cornstarch and paper towels will decompose in the damp earth, and the seeds will sprout evenly spaced along the row.

SOME SEEDS SHOULDN'T BE BURIED

Conventional wisdom has us bury seeds when sowing them directly in the garden. However, "most species that we direct-seed in the garden actually need light to germinate and will sprout better if just sprinkled on the ground," says Sara Groves, a flower garden designer in Georgia. Groves explains, "Nature doesn't bury seeds, she just drops them." (For a list of seeds that need light to germinate, see "Some Seeds Like It Light" at right.)

Groves's method requires leaving the ground slightly lumpy after working in soil amendments such as compost. This creates little pockets to hold the seeds, yet lets them receive light. Lay a piece of plywood over the seeded area, and walk on it to press the seeds into firm contact with the soil. Then remove the board and water thoroughly (and daily) with a fine spray. Use a mist nozzle to create a soft spray that won't disturb the seedbed.

BROADCAST SEED EVENLY

Here's a nifty technique for sowing seed evenly over large areas devised by Bill McDorman, the founder of High

---

SOME SEEDS LIKE IT DARK

Cover these vegetable seeds for surefire germination:

Beets	Cucumbers
Broccoli	Melons
Cabbage	Onions
Carrots	Parsley
Cauliflower	Peas
Celery	Radishes
Chard	Spinach

SOME SEEDS LIKE IT LIGHT

Sow these seeds on top of the soil for best germination:

Flowers

Achillea spp. (yarrows)
Brassica oleracea, Acephala group (ornamental kale)
Capsicum spp. (ornamental peppers)
Chrysanthemum × *superbum* (Shasta daisy)
Coleus × *hybridus* (coleus)
Coreopsis grandiflora (large-flowered tickseed)
Helichrysum bracteatum (straw-flower)
Impatiens spp. (impatiens)
Matthiola incana (stock)
Petunia × *hybrida* (common garden petunia)
Platycodon grandiflorus (balloon flower)
Tithonia rotundifolia (Mexican sunflower)

Vegetables and Herbs

Dill
Lettuce
Savory

UPDATE FOR SEED PACKETS

"The recommendations for planting depth written on some seed packets is outdated," says Ed Hume, the owner of Ed Hume Seeds in Washington State. As a rule, seeds should not be buried any deeper than their diameter. Forget those ¼-inch planting depths for all but the biggest seeds, such as peas and beans.

ROW COVERS FOR RELIABLE GERMINATION

"Row covers are really handy for boosting germination rates," says Janet Bachmann, a co-owner of a small organic farm in Arkansas. "Not only do they keep the soil warmer, they also retain a little extra moisture and keep the soil from crusting." Bachmann uses row covers over most of her direct-seeded crops and says that they are invaluable for slow germinators like carrots.

WHOLE LOT OF SHAKIN' GOIN' ON

An empty seasoning jar with a plastic lid that has large holes in it makes a perfect tool for broadcasting seeds in the garden. Tops with ¼-inch holes are perfect for small to medium-size, round seeds such as poppies, radishes, onions, and members of the cabbage family.

Altitude Gardens, an Idaho mail-order seed company that blends, tests, and sells wildflower seed mixtures. "This works for any broadcast crop—grass, green manures, or cover crops," says McDorman. Divide the area into equal-size blocks, making certain that no block exceeds 200 square feet. Then, divide the seed into as many piles as there are blocks. If you are seeding an area that measures 50×100 feet, divide it into 25 separate blocks, then divide your seed into 25 equal piles. Sow each small block with its measured amount of seed.

THE GARDEN PROFESSIONALS

Janet Bachmann is the coordinator for the Mid-South Farmers Network for the Rodale Institute. She and Jim Lukens are joint owners of a home-scale farm near Fayetteville, Arkansas.

Nancy Bubel, a Pennsylvania garden writer, is the author of *The New Seed-Starters Handbook* and *52 Weekend Garden Projects*.

Sara Groves is the owner and flower garden designer for FloraScapes, a garden design company in Oxford, Georgia.

Ed Hume is the owner of Ed Hume Seeds, Inc., in Kent, Washington, a company that specializes in untreated vegetable seeds. He also hosts "Gardening in America," a nationally syndicated gardening television program.

Rob Johnston is the president of Johnny's Selected Seeds in Albion, Maine. The company's seed catalog offers an innovative selection of vegetables, herbs, and flowers.

Bill McDorman is the founder and president of High Altitude Gardens in Ketchum, Idaho. The mail-order seed company tests and sells seeds for high altitudes, cold climates, and short seasons.

Bibby Moore is a registered horticultural therapist and is the former director of horticultural therapy at the North Carolina Botanical Garden in Chapel Hill.

Jean M. A. Nick is an associate editor of garden books for Rodale Press, Inc. She has extensive experience in the commercial greenhouse industry and currently raises vegetables and small fruits on 1 acre in her home garden.

Christina R. J. Pey is a supervisor for the production greenhouses at the Missouri Botanical Garden in St. Louis, Missouri. Her specialty is the aquatic collection, which includes tropical water lilies.

Nancy Plengey is the flower and herbs trial manager for Johnny's Selected Seeds, a mail-order seed company in Albion, Maine.

Elissa Steeves is a horticulture teacher at Pulaski County High School, a vocational school in Dublin, Virginia.

Jim Wilson is a cohost of public television's "The Victory Garden." He is the author of *Landscaping with Container Plants*, *Masters of the Victory Garden*, and *Landscaping with Wildflowers*.

Planting and Transplanting

Planting and transplanting are at the heart of gardening. To build a garden, change a garden, or move a garden, you must plant or transplant. This chapter shares the experience of expert gardeners on what works and what doesn't and presents the basics of planting and transplanting properly to ensure success. Some of what you read here may surprise you by offering a new way to look at an old practice. Try a few new techniques, and see what works best for you.

Planting the Small Stuff

You'll find a bounty of tips to help you get seeds started in "Growing from Seed," beginning on page 2. In this chapter, the experts offer special techniques for hardening off vegetable and flower seedlings and planting them out, as well as tips on how to get perennials off to a great start in the big outdoors.

HARDENING OFF FOR THE 9-TO-5 SET

Gardeners who have an office job and also have seedlings started indoors are in a bind when it's time to harden off the seedlings to prepare them for life outdoors. Although you can move them out in the morning when you leave for work, who will take care of the seedlings an hour or two later when it's time to bring them in? Heather Will-Browne, a bedding plant specialist at Walt Disney World in Florida, has found a way to let the seedlings take care of themselves. Put the flats or pots either on the porch or under the north eaves of your house so they are protected from the sun. (You don't need much room—even the stoop outside one of your doors will do.) "It's great because they're also protected from hard rains that will destroy tiny seedlings in just a few minutes," Will-Browne says. If they're on a porch, move the flats gradually toward the outer edge of the covered area so they'll be exposed to a bit more sun each day until they are conditioned for the garden.

RING AROUND THE TRANSPLANT

A little ring in the soil around new transplants creates a small basin to collect water so it goes right down to the roots. "Use your finger to draw a 4-inch-diameter circle around transplants in the soil," says Bibby Moore, a registered horticultural therapist from North Carolina. The rings don't need to be deep; just draw in the soil with enough pressure to make an indentation as you do when you write in the sand at the beach. This is also very helpful when applying fish emulsion. To fertilize, Moore waters thoroughly first, then applies 2 cups of fish emulsion per transplant. The emulsion is diluted at the rate of 1 tablespoon of emulsion per 1 gallon of water.

Planting in blocks rather than rows increases yields per square foot. Some crops seem to perform better with this treatment, and once leaves are big enough to shade the growing bed, block-planted crops require much less weeding than row plantings. The following table lists appropriate equidistant spacing distances in a good soil. The spacing listed is meant as final spacing. With crops such as kale, beets, and radishes, for example, initial spacing can be closer. Thin alternate plants as they grow, and use the thinnings in salads.

Crop	Spacing (inches)
Beets	3–5½
Broccoli	15–18
Bush beans	6
Cabbage	15–18
Carrots	2–4½
Celery	6–11
Corn	15–18
Cucumbers	12
Kale	15
Lettuce	6–12
Melons	15
Onions	2½–5
Peas	3–4
Potatoes	9–16
Radishes	1–2
Spinach	4–6
Squash	30
Tomatoes	18–24

A TANGLED TALE OF TRANSPLANT ROOTS

You can help bedding plants that are growing in cell packs and small pots make the transition to garden soil by untangling the roots before transplanting. "I have literally set annuals in a hole and dug them up at the end of the year to find that the roots had circled around and around in the hole. That's due to two things: the original root formation and the interface between the soil mix and the native soil," says Jim Wilson, a cohost of public television's "The Victory Garden." Plants that don't stretch roots out into the garden soil aren't going to grow well, and they're more likely to dry out. To prevent this, Wilson gently pries some of the transplants' roots loose from the potting soil at planting time to open up the root ball and keep roots from spiraling.

TEAR THE TOPS OFF PEAT POTS

Peat pots are handy, but they need careful transplanting for best growth. "We like peat pots because they make it so easy to deal with large numbers of transplants," says Christina R. J. Pey, a supervisor for the production greenhouses at the Missouri Botanical Garden. However, when planting peat pots, Pey cautions that you should tear off the top edge before planting to be sure it doesn't poke up through the soil. If the pot edge is higher than the soil surface, the peat will dry out and act as a wick, pulling moisture away from the roots. The gardeners at the Missouri Botanical Garden also break off sections of the sides and bottom of the containers to make it easier for the transplants' roots to make the transition to garden soil.

A SECOND CHANCE FOR SEEDLINGS

Most of us know the frustration of having a flat of seedlings or transplants turn out to be leggy, with stems flopping in a jumbled mess. Deep transplanting can give lanky cabbage, tomato, and other seedlings a second chance on life. "Once seedlings get leggy, they're pitiful," says Bibby Moore, a registered horticultural therapist from North Carolina. Moore revitalizes the sorry seedlings by burying their leggy stem right up to the bottom two leaves when she transfers them to individual pots. This technique works with seedlings of cabbage-family crops, as well as lettuce, tomato, and even marigold seedlings.

Moore cautions that this is not an ideal practice, it's just a salvage technique. "The next time you sow seeds, give them adequate light to begin with," she says. It's important to give the potted seedlings increased light so you don't end up with floppy transplants as well. Of course, if you do, you can resort to deep transplanting in the garden. Dig an angled planting trench, strip off lower leaves, and lay the floppy stem in the trench, as shown in the illustration below. The plant will form roots along the buried stem.

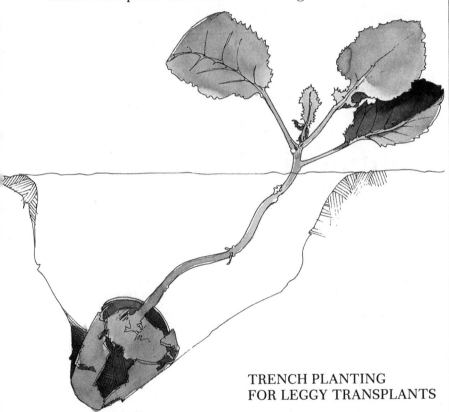

TRENCH PLANTING
FOR LEGGY TRANSPLANTS

SOIL CONES KEEP ROOTS GROWING

Cole Burrell, a Minnesota garden designer, has fine-tuned a method to set bareroot perennials quickly and effectively in their planting holes. "Don't straitjacket fibrous-rooted plants into narrow holes, or they'll produce new roots at the expense of top growth while the original roots slowly die off," says Burrell. You can try his special planting technique with your perennials.

NIX DRIED-OUT MIX

"One of the mistakes people make when they first set out bedding plants is to misjudge the need to water," says Heather Will-Browne, a bedding plant specialist at Walt Disney World in Florida. "Bedding plants are grown in a soil mix that dries out more quickly than the surrounding garden soil." Will-Browne recommends that gardeners test soil moisture by poking a finger into the ground right at the base of the transplant. This will reveal whether the soil mix around the roots is still moist enough for good plant growth. In three or four weeks, transplants should be rooting out into the surrounding soil, so this will no longer be a concern.

SQUASH IN THE LAWN

When space is short, try planting in the lawn. Bush squash, tomatoes, peppers, and eggplant all take to this system if you've prepared their planting holes properly. Two weeks before planting, dig a 2-foot-deep hole that is 1 foot square. Mix two shovelfuls of compost, a handful of bone-meal, and an ounce of rock phosphate with enough garden or lawn soil to fill the hole. After refilling the hole with this mix, water the area with a diluted seaweed/fish-emulsion mix. Let it sink in before planting or transplanting. Mulch around the plants with a thick layer of grass clippings to diminish competition from lawn grass.

MESQUITE TELLS TRANSPLANT TIME

"In Texas, lots of people plant mesquite trees. When the mesquite leafs out, it's safe to transplant your tender crops," says John Dromgoole, the host of PBS television's "The New Garden." In the Northeast, many people wait until oak leaves are the size of squirrels' ears, and some wait until half of the lilac blooms have browned. Every region has its own natural cues. Ask experienced gardeners in your neighborhood for their tips.

BEAT THE FEAR OF TRANSPLANTING

"Once and done" just doesn't apply to gardening. Every season, you'll see plants in your beds that look out of place—they're an awkward height or shape or their color clashes with the plants that it was supposed to complement. When these small disasters happen, take out your spade or trowel and transplant the plants. It's not difficult and generally won't harm the plants if it's done properly.

It's better not to move plants during stressful times of heat and drought, although as adventurous gardeners know, it can be done even then. Move the plants in early evening, water them well, and provide temporary shade until they perk up.

1. Mound a cone of soil inside the planting hole. The mound makes it easy to spread roots out evenly so they point in all directions.

2. Turn the plant upside down and let the roots fall open.

3. Put your hand on the roots to keep them spread out, then turn the plant over and place it on the cone.

4. Refill the hole, making sure that the plant's crown is just above ground level.

"Don't use this method for taprooted plants like purple coneflower [*Echinacea purpurea*], baptisias [*Baptisia* spp.], and butterfly weed [*Asclepias tuberosa*]," says Burrell. To plant these plants, prepare the planting site by loosening and amending the soil as needed, but don't dig planting holes. Instead, insert a shovel straight down into the soil and then push it forward to open a crevice. Line up the taproot in the crevice with the crown of the plant at soil level. Remove the shovel, and firm the soil in place.

Planting the Big Guys

Trees and shrubs are a great investment. They'll add beauty, shade, and privacy to your property for many years, increasing property value as they grow. But like most things, you get what you pay for—both in the initial cost of the plants and in the care you give them at planting time. Good planting practices are critical to the good health and longevity of trees and shrubs—and recent research has shown that a lot of the timeworn advice on planting is just plain wrong. In this section, you'll find accurate techniques, tips, and advice for giving these valuable plants the best possible start.

DON'T DIG TO CHINA

Old planting recommendations had you dig a hole twice as wide and twice as deep as the root ball of the tree or shrub you were planting. New research has shown that this advice could actually harm your plants. "The best way to plant is to dig the hole as wide as possible but no deeper than the root ball," says Bonnie Lee Appleton, Ph.D., an associate professor and extension horticulturist at Virginia Polytechnic Institute and State University. If the soil is dug too deep, the root ball can sink as the soil settles, so the plant eventually becomes too deeply buried. "We've found that the majority of roots stay within the top 8 to

12 inches of soil anyway," says Dr. Appleton. "Even the roots of big trees." It's okay to set the plant an inch or two shallower than the depth of the root ball. Apply mulch to cover the top of the ball, but don't let the mulch touch the base of the trunk.

SLICK HOLE SIDES MAKE BAD ROOT BINDS

How and when you dig a planting hole can be more important than how big it is. "Rough the surface of the planting hole by slicing the sides of the finished hole with the edge of the spade, or crack some of the soil off with a fork," advises Michael Maltas, the garden director of the organic showpiece garden for Fetzer Vineyards in California. "Then the roots will be able to find a crack and take off." Maltas also points out that you shouldn't dig planting holes in wet ground with a spade, or the sides will be smeared smooth. They'll harden, forming a barrier to the roots.

SITE PREP PAYS OFF

Tree planting involves much more than just digging a hole, says Tom Ranney, Ph.D., an assistant professor at the Mountain Horticultural Crops Research and Extension Center of North Carolina State University. "This is particularly true on urban or suburban sites where the soil is often compacted from heavy equipment and other factors," says Dr. Ranney.

Dr. Ranney recommends tilling the planting area before you dig. This will reduce compaction and encourage aeration and drainage. Since roots tend to stay in the top 1 foot of soil, tilling can make a real difference.

Adding soil amendments to backfill probably isn't necessary for typical plantings, says Dr. Ranney. But it may be appropriate for certain plants in particular sites. For example, if you're planting trees in raised beds or on berms, adding water-holding organic soil amendments can be very beneficial, Dr. Ranney says, since raised beds and berms tend to dry out faster than ground-level plantings.

It's important to maintain the planting site after planting as well. If grass grows in the area that will be covered by the mature spread of the tree's crown, it can compete with the tree's roots for nutrients and water. To prevent regrowth of grass after you've tilled and planted, spread mulch around the tree as far out as the drip line. Don't allow the mulch to touch the base of the tree, because this can encourage disease problems.

CHECK THE CROWNS

Before planting a balled-and-burlapped tree or shrub, brush off loose soil from the top of the ball, and find the uppermost roots. Extra soil can be pushed up around the crown of the plant when it is balled, so the top of the ball of soil isn't always a true indicator of the depth at which the plant was growing at the nursery. It's more reliable to set the plant so that the uppermost roots are just below ground level when you plant.

TRY A SPECIAL SPADE

Transplanting trees and shrubs is easier with the help of a spade specially designed for the task. A transplanting spade has a narrow, extra-long blade—up to 16 inches long. The shape makes it easier to probe deep into the soil to reach roots and lift the plant. This tool is also commonly called a tree-planting spade, drain spade, or a sharpshooter.

HIGHER AND DRIER

When drainage is less than perfect, try planting shrubs or trees 2 or 3 inches higher than they grew in the nursery. This helps to get the root ball up out of the quagmire.

PLANT THESE TREES IN SPRING

Fall is the best time to plant many trees, since they'll put out new roots until the ground freezes and get a jump-start in spring. But according to Bonnie Lee Appleton, Ph.D., an associate professor and extension horticulturist at Virginia Polytechnic Institute and State University, research shows that the trees listed below don't generate many new roots in fall. These trees all prefer spring planting:

'Bradford' Callery pear
Cherry
Dogwood
Japanese maple
Magnolia
Pin oak
White birch
Willow oak

PROPER TREE PLANTING

tree set at level at which it grew in the nursery

protective material on guy wire

slack in guy wire

stake driven through soil outside of root b

mulch doesn't touch tree trunk

burlap peeled back

mulch

3"

ropes or top of wire basket cut

root ball sits on cone of undisturbed soil

wide planting h
with angled side

The most important thing you can do for a new tree or shrub is to give it a good start by planting it correctly. Take time to dig a wide planting hole with rough sides, to set the plant at the proper level in the hole and loosen the root ball, to stake and mulch carefully, and to water the new plant in thoroughly.

WHEN TO AMEND PLANTING RULES

"Research on whether or not to amend soil when planting has been generalized too much," says Roger Funk, Ph.D., the vice president of human and technical resources at the Davey Tree Expert Company. If the soil on your site is similar to the soil in the root ball, there's no need to amend the soil in the planting hole. But if the soil in the root ball is significantly different from your local soil, your tree may grow better if you amend the soil before planting. In one trial, Dr. Funk planted balled-and-burlapped trees that had been grown in sandy clay loam in a landscape where the soil was a heavy clay. He didn't amend the soil and found that water pooled in the holes. "Since most nurseries are growing trees in sandy or loamy soil and lots of gardeners have clay soils—especially in new developments, where they may have subsoil—this can be a common problem," says Dr. Funk. "It's best to evaluate the specific conditions and decide what to do on a case-by-case basis."

TOP SCORES FOR TREE ROOTS

Many planting recommendations suggest that gardeners slice a root ball in half from its bottom surface to about halfway through the depth of the ball. This technique may work well on bedding plants, but don't try it on trees and shrubs. "It's a harsh, destructive technique, and you face the likelihood of splitting the root ball," says Bonnie Lee Appleton, Ph.D., an associate professor and extension horticulturist at Virginia Polytechnic Institute and State University. Instead, Dr. Appleton recommends this procedure: Score roots that have grown into a meshlike mat by making shallow vertical cuts through the matted roots, cutting through the outer roots but not into the root ball. Make the cuts on two or three sides of the root mass. If woody roots are circling the root ball, cut through them in two or three places to stop the circling. Make your cuts with a knife or a pair of pruners.

AVOID THE BURLAP ROOT TRAP

Trees and shrubs with roots that are wrapped in burlap can run into problems if you don't pull off the burlap when you plant them. "Many of today's wraps are synthetic

HOLD THE WATER

Often, plants that were growing in full sun at a nursery when you bought them are destined for a less-sunny site in your landscape. When you get them home, be careful not to overwater them—overwatering can rot their roots. According to Bonnie Lee Appleton, Ph.D., an associate professor and extension horticulturist at Virginia Polytechnic Institute and State University, boxwoods, azaleas, and Japanese hollies are especially affected by overwatering. Protect your plants from root rot by watering them just enough to keep the soil moist.

QUICK RELIEF FOR WIND-DRIED BUDS

Drying spring winds can be hard on newly planted bareroot fruit trees. Help keep the young buds and stems from drying out by spraying with an antitranspirant. An antitranspirant (sometimes called an antidesiccant), acts as a temporary sealer when sprayed on the stems, buds, and foliage to reduce the amount of moisture lost through the plant's pores. It is sold under brand names such as Wilt-Pruf and Cloud Cover. Spray right after you plant to evenly coat the bare branches.

and don't decompose like the old natural burlap did," says Bonnie Lee Appleton, Ph.D., an associate professor and extension horticulturist at Virginia Polytechnic Institute and State University. She recommends that after you set the plant into the hole, remove the ropes, pins, or wires on the wrap, then drop the wrap to the bottom of the hole and *leave it there*. Don't try to slide it out from beneath the plant—you might end up cracking the root ball, which can kill the tree or shrub. If the ball is in a wire basket, either cut away the top round of loops or cut the basket down opposite sides and push the wire down into the hole.

THE GARDEN PROFESSIONALS

Bonnie Lee Appleton, Ph.D., is an associate professor of horticulture, researcher, and extension nursery specialist at Hampton Roads Agricultural Experiment Station, Virginia Polytechnic Institute and State University, in Virginia Beach. She is the author of *Landscape Rejuvenation*.

C. Colston (Cole) Burrell, is a garden designer, author, photographer, and lecturer whose Minneapolis-based business, Native Landscapes, specializes in landscape restoration and innovative use of native plants and perennials in garden design. He is coauthor of *Rodale's Illustrated Encyclopedia of Perennials*.

John Dromgoole is a manager and part owner of Garden-Ville of Austin, a catalog and supply company located in Austin, Texas. He hosts a national television show dedicated to organic gardening on PBS called "The New Garden."

Roger Funk, Ph.D., is the vice president of human and technical resources at the Davey Tree Expert Company, a nationwide company headquartered in Kent, Ohio, that provides services for tree, lawn, and indoor plant care.

Michael Maltas is the garden director of the organic showpiece garden for Fetzer Vineyards in Hopland, California. Maltas grows acres of vegetables, flowers, and fruit at the Fetzer Valley Oaks Food and Wine Center.

Bibby Moore is a registered horticultural therapist and is the former director of horticultural therapy at the North Carolina Botanical Garden in Chapel Hill.

Christina R. J. Pey is a supervisor for the production greenhouses at the Missouri Botanical Garden in St. Louis, Missouri. Her specialty is the aquatic collection, which includes tropical water lilies.

Tom Ranney, Ph.D., is an assistant professor at the Mountain Horticultural Crops Research and Extension Center of North Carolina State University at Raleigh, Department of Horticultural Science.

Verlin Schaefer is an assistant mail-order manager for Stark Brothers Nurseries and Orchards Company in Louisiana, Missouri. The nursery offers fruit trees, grapes, ornamental trees and shrubs, and roses.

Heather Will-Browne is a horticulturist and bedding plant specialist at Walt Disney World in Orlando, Florida.

Jim Wilson is a cohost of public television's "The Victory Garden." He is the author of *Landscaping with Container Plants*, *Masters of the Victory Garden*, and *Landscaping with Wildflowers*.

Propagating Plants

Propagating is one of those gardening skills that seem a bit intimidating at first—until you try it. Once you see how easy it is to grow your own, you'll be taking snips and cuttings from plants all over your yard.

There's a method of propagating to suit any gardener's personality. You can start new plants in a downright lazy way, letting Mother Nature do the work for you through a technique called layering. Or you can experiment with soil mixes and rooting aids—even rig up a homemade fog propagator using a room humidifier.

Our experts offer innovative tips along with time-proven techniques for increasing your stock of flowers, shrubs, and fruits. If you're a beginner, start with the simple methods and the easiest plants. (Use the plant lists in this chapter to guide you.)

Enjoy Success with Cuttings

Cut a leafy stem off of a plant, and chances are you've got a cutting to root. Taking stem cuttings can be one of the simplest ways to propagate. Rooting woody cuttings can be a little trickier, but still easy enough that nearly everyone can succeed. Try the following tips for the best results with cuttings from every type of plant from houseplants to shrubs and trees.

A SIMPLE SHORTCUT FOR MORE PERENNIALS

Save money on perennials by growing your own from cuttings. "Take cuttings of soft but not too young growth, down to about the third leaf, in early to midsummer," recommends Dave Bowman, a co-owner of Crownsville Nursery in Maryland, which specializes in perennial flowers. Put them in a nursery bed or flat, and keep them out of direct sun until they develop their own root systems. You can cover the cuttings with plastic strawberry baskets or push leafy branches into the ground around them for temporary shade.

Cuttings may show new top growth without being rooted. To be sure new roots have formed, give your cuttings a slight tug, says Bowman. If they don't let go easily, they have rooted.

REVIVE GRANDMA'S ROSE JARS

Many old-time gardeners have successfully propagated rose cuttings with nothing more than an old canning jar. "I remember, when I was a child, my grandparents used to start roses readily. They'd just snip off a piece, stick it in the ground, and cover it with a fruit jar," says Dave Dunbar, a Penn State extension agent.

In the spring, take cuttings of succulent new growth. Push a cutting a few inches deep directly into good garden soil, then cover it with an upside-down glass jar as shown in the illustration below. The jar acts as a mini-greenhouse, keeping the cutting moist and humid. A spot between other plants in the garden makes a good nursery: You won't

forget about your cuttings when you see them frequently, they'll be watered along with the rest of the garden, and the taller plants will shade the sensitive cuttings from the sun. Your success rate won't be as high as with more advanced techniques, but it requires no special equipment and can be done on the spur of the moment—just like in Grandma's garden.

KEEP IT CLEAN

Diseases are hard to control in the warm, moist environment that cuttings need. To cut your losses, "start with sterile soil and sterile water," advises Steve Reynolds, a sales manager at Furney's Nursery in Washington State. "Boil the water and cool it before moistening your growing medium."

Be alert for the first signs of problems, such as curled or spotted leaves or visible fungal growth. Move quickly to remove the affected cuttings as well as neighboring cuttings. Air the flat, and try again. Reynolds takes the hard line if disease gets a toehold. "Once fungus is present, you may as well ditch it," Reynolds says. Start from the beginning with fresh medium, new cuttings, and a sterilized container. Be sure to make clean cuts to avoid ragged tissue that will decay and may cause disease problems.

TAKE CUTTINGS FROM MORE-WILLING WOOD

For the best success with cuttings, take them from young growth. "Cuttings of juvenile plants of any species root much more easily than cuttings of mature plants," states Kenneth W. Mudge, Ph.D., an associate professor of horticultural physiology at Cornell University in New York. How do you know if your forsythia or other parent plant is juvenile or mature? Flowers are the tip-off: Flowering growth is mature growth. Flowering, mature wood is usually found at the top or outside of the plant, while suckers and other low growth on the same plant are usually nonflowering, juvenile wood. As much as 90 percent of your cuttings should root if you take them from younger growth, says Dr. Mudge.

CUT 'EM LOW

Sprawling shrubs or trailing plants are usually easy to start from cuttings, but plants with a strong upright growth

TRY WILLOW WATER

The active ingredient of many commercial rooting preparations is indolebutyric acid (IBA), a natural plant hormone. Although store-bought rooting hormone powders now use a synthetic version of IBA, you can try the real thing by mixing up a batch of willow water.

Gather a handful of willow twigs (any *Salix* species will do) and snip them into pieces a few inches long. Soak the twigs in a few inches of water for a day or two, then remove the twigs. Use the willow water to soak cuttings in overnight or to water flats of newly started cuttings.

Since the making of willow water isn't an exact science, the strength of the mixture can vary depending on the time of year, the number of twigs, the concentration of hormones in the twigs, and the amount of time that the twigs were soaked.

TRY SUPER-EASY ROOTERS

Some obliging annuals and even a few perennials will root from cuttings stuck directly in the ground. Try ageratum, coleus, fuchsia, golden marguerite (*Anthemis tinctoria*), felicias (*Felicia* spp.), dahlia, impatiens, and wax begonia. Insert 2- to 4-inch cuttings directly in loose, rich soil where they are to grow. Water well until established.

MINIATURE
GREENHOUSE

habit, like many shrubs and trees, can be a little trickier. That's because these plants are hormonally programmed for top growth. "Upright growers like rhododendrons and photinias are easier to root from cuttings if you take clippings from lower branches, where the 'straight-up' hormone isn't as concentrated," notes Steve Reynolds, a sales manager at Furney's Nursery in Washington State.

GET THE TIMING RIGHT

Most softwood cuttings are easier to root if they're made in late spring or summer, after the first flush of growth. As Steve Reynolds, a sales manager at Furney's Nursery in Washington State, explains, "Spring growth is most vigorous, but at that time a plant's hormones are geared for new top growth, not for rooting."

Individual species have their own quirks regarding timing, which you may have to discover through trial and error. For example, cuttings of bearberry (*Arctostaphylos uva-ursi*) taken in spring won't root, Reynolds says. He suggests starting bearberry cuttings in July or August.

On the other hand, cuttings of burning bush (*Euonymus alata*) taken too late aren't successful. "As long as the leaves are green, it roots readily," says Kenneth W. Mudge, Ph.D., an associate professor of horticultural physiology at Cornell University in New York. "If you take cuttings when the leaves have turned pink, the cuttings will defoliate and will be hard to root."

MAKE A MINIATURE GREENHOUSE

Looking for ways to reuse clear-plastic soda bottles? You can turn them into miniature greenhouses for cuttings. John L. Creech, Ph.D., the former director of the U.S. National Arboretum, uses the improvised greenhouses to root azaleas and other plants. He cuts the bottom off of two bottles. He fills one bottom with moist sand, removes the colored-plastic bottom-rest from the other, and fits the two bottoms together as shown in the illustration at left.

"In July, I insert eight to ten cuttings, put the 'greenhouse' in a shady place, and keep the sand moist. It takes about six weeks for the plants to root," Dr. Creech explains. He then transplants the baby shrubs to pots filled with soil, keeps them in a protected place, and puts them out in the garden the following year.

KEEP CUTTINGS IN A FOG

Bathing cuttings in humid air is an essential step in getting them to take root. "The whole key to starting a softwood cutting," says Steve Reynolds, a sales manager at Furney's Nursery in Washington State, "is to keep the top of the cutting humid enough so it can live until the roots get established. Keep the humidity close to 100 percent."

Commercial growers use sophisticated fogging machines to supply humidity. Home gardeners can apply the same idea on a small scale, says Kenneth W. Mudge, Ph.D., an associate professor of horticultural physiology at Cornell University in New York. Dr. Mudge suggests using an ultrasonic cool-mist humidifier as part of a home fog propagator. (See the directions below for building a home fog propagator.) You can set up a fog propagator in a cool garage, on a shaded porch, or inside a greenhouse. Be sure that the propagator box isn't exposed to bright sunlight. "Shade is vitally important anytime you're rooting cuttings," Dr. Mudge points out.

You can find the materials to build the fog propagator at any lumberyard. Nails will work fine for fastening the parts together, although construction will be a little easier and a little sturdier (as well as slightly more expensive) if you use deck screws driven with a Phillips bit in your electric drill. Galvanized screws or nails are best because they won't rust in the propagator's humid environment. Also, galvanized nails grip better than "bright" nails. You can use untreated pine to build the frame, but it's best to coat it with flat black paint.

Here's how to construct the propagator frame:

1. Make the base. Cut 2 of the base sides to 34½ inches long. Cut the other 2 base sides to 21 inches long. Nail the longer pieces into the ends of the shorter pieces.

2. Make and install the uprights. Cut the uprights to 23¼ inches long. The key to making a sturdy propagator is to make all of the upright joints overlap the base joints. In other words, the seam where two uprights meet should never line up with the seam where two base pieces meet. Nail the uprights to the bases and then to their mating

---

START FROM THE ROOTS

Root cuttings are a reliable way to propagate plants with thick, fleshy roots. Slice off pencil-thick roots, and cut them into 2-inch pieces. Use a diagonal cut at the bottom of each piece so that you'll know which end is up. (They won't grow if you plant them upside down.) Pot up root cuttings in pots or cell packs filled with sterile, porous potting medium, such as half seed-starting mix and half perlite. Keep the cuttings barely moist, put them in a cold frame or unheated room, and give them bottom heat, if possible.

FOG PROPAGATOR MATERIALS

Cutting List

2 pcs. ¾'' × 5½'' × 34½'' (base sides)
2 pcs. ¾'' × 5½'' × 21'' (base sides)
8 pcs. ¾'' × 1½'' × 23¼'' (uprights)
1 pc. ¾'' × 1½'' × 33'' (top rail)
1 pc. ¾'' × 1½'' × 36'' (top rail)
2 pcs. ¾'' × 1½'' × 22½'' (top rails)

Hardware

3d galvanized common nails or 1¼'' galvanized deck screws, as needed

RELIABLE ROOT CUTTINGS

These plants propagate well from cuttings of their thick, fleshy roots. Dig deep to lift the mother plant, then cut roots into 2-inch pieces for propagating.

Acanthus spp. (bear's-breeches)
Anchusa spp. (bugloss)
Anemone spp. (anemones)
Asclepias tuberosa (butterfly weed)
Dicentra spectabilis (common bleeding heart)
Geranium spp. (cranesbills)
Gypsophila paniculata (baby's-breaths)
Papaver orientale (oriental poppy)
Salvia spp. (perennial salvias)
Verbascum spp. (mulleins)
Yucca filamentosa (Adam's-needle)

RECYCLE DRY-CLEANING BAGS

You can use very thin polyethylene, like dry-cleaning bags or inexpensive painters' ground-cloths, to hold in humidity for rooting cuttings, says Kenneth W. Mudge, Ph.D., an associate professor of horticultural physiology at Cornell University in New York. Lay the plastic directly over the flat of cuttings, touching the leaves. Secure at the corners with rubber bands.

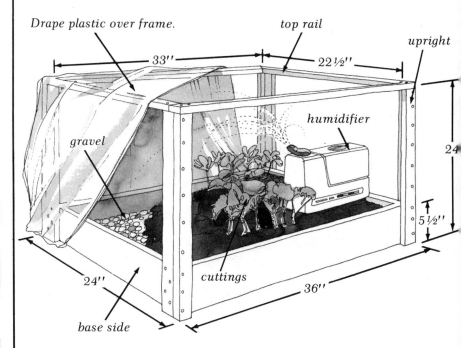

Drape plastic over frame. — *top rail* — *upright* — 33″ — 22½″ — *humidifier* — *gravel* — 24 — *cuttings* — 5½″ — 24″ — 36″ — *base side*

FOG PROPAGATOR

uprights as shown in the illustration above. Make sure the uprights are square to the bases.

3. Make and install the top rails. Cut 1 top rail to 33 inches long, 1 top rail to 36 inches long, and 2 top rails to 22½ inches long. Again, you want to tie the top of the box together with joints that overlap the upright joints as shown in the illustration.

You'll need to set up the propagator frame on a tray or greenhouse bench containing several inches of gravel for good drainage. Set the humidifier inside the frame, and fill the remaining area of the frame with several inches of a thoroughly moistened fifty-fifty mix of peat and perlite. Add the cuttings, and cover the frame with heavy-gauge polyethylene. Be sure the plastic hangs down past the top of the base sides to create a closed chamber.

Reap the Dividends of Division

Dividing one large plant into several smaller ones is another easy technique for creating new plants. We most commonly think of dividing perennials, but you can also divide bulbs and ornamental grasses.

MUM'S THE WORD

"You can easily make 100 plants out of 1 chrysanthemum," says Dave Bowman, a co-owner of Crownsville Nursery in Maryland. "And for best growth, it's actually better to divide them every year." Go out to the garden in spring, he advises, and start pulling up shoots. Replant directly in the garden, or set out in a nursery bed until later in the season.

You can also take cuttings from potted chrysanthemums. Cut back the plant after flowering, and wait for new growth. Then make as many cuttings as you can, clipping them off at the third set of leaves. Start the cuttings in a flat, cold frame, or nursery bed.

MAKE 100 DAYLILIES IN A DAY

If an established clump of daylilies is thriving in your garden, all you need is a sharp knife and a shovel to make a whole bed of these appealing perennials. "Do you know what a Ginsu knife is?" asks Chick Wasitis, laughing. Once ubiquitous on late-night television, those hard-working knives "make a terrific tool for slicing up clumps of daylilies," says Wasitis, a co-owner of Crownsville Nursery in Maryland, where he grows more than 1,000 kinds of perennials.

To divide an established daylily, lift the plant after it blooms, in mid- to late summer. Cut foliage back to 4 to 5 inches. Use a Ginsu knife, a handyman's razor-knife, or a butcher knife to separate the clump into divisions of at least a single fan with some roots attached. (Watch those fingers!)

GROW A HOST OF DAFFODILS

Shallow planting is the key to encouraging daffodils to divide. Brent Heath, a co-owner of the Daffodil Mart in

BEST BETS FOR DIVISION

Dividing established perennials is a fast and sure way to fill your yard with flowers. Plants with more than one tall stem, especially clump-forming ones like garden phlox or asters, are good candidates for dividing, says Dave Bowman, who grows over 1,000 perennials as a co-owner of Crownsville Nursery in Maryland. Or keep your eye open for ones that root as they wander along the ground, such as snow-in-summer (*Cerastium tomentosum*) and creeping phlox (*Phlox stolonifera*).

The plants listed below are easy to divide by digging up a clump and separating the roots into smaller sections. Some will pull apart by hand with a bit of gentle teasing; for others, you may need a sharp knife or trowel. Replant as soon as possible and water in well. Protect from direct sun for a few days until the roots recover.

Achillea spp. (yarrows)
Eupatorium coelestinum (hardy ageratum)
Geum spp. (avens)
Helianthus spp. (perennial sunflowers)
Hemerocallis spp. (daylilies)
Hosta spp. (hostas)
Iberis spp. (candytufts)
Iris spp. (irises)
Monarda didyma (bee balm)
Oenothera spp. (evening primroses)
Paeonia spp. (peonies)
Physostegia spp. (obedient plants)
Saponaria spp. (soapworts)
Tanacetum spp. (tansies)

AVOID DISEASE-CARRYING HITCHHIKERS

There are cases when propagating plants may cost you more than it saves in the long run. For example, strawberries and bramble fruits may often harbor viruses and other pest problems while still appearing healthy. Hidden aphids or root weevils can hitchhike along when you divide or take cuttings of infested older plants. To avoid the risk, start your planting from certified disease-free plants instead of accepting divisions or cuttings from a neighbor's row, advises Bernadine Strik, Ph.D., an Oregon State University extension specialist for grapes and berry crops.

Virginia, says that planting the bulbs 4 inches deep will spur bulb division. "But you're taking a risk with winter cold," Heath points out. "In winter, you may lose them."

Heath prefers to plant deep and let hybrid daffodils multiply naturally. In good growing conditions, daffodil bulbs planted deep will often double naturally in size each year, producing twice as many flowers the following season. "When you get up to 16, 32, or 64 flowers in a clump, the bulbs tend to stop multiplying. What you have is a big clump of little bulbs," Heath explains. This is the time to replant. In late May or early June, about eight to ten weeks after bloom, lift the clump, and gently shake off the dirt. Let the bulbs come apart naturally—don't pull them. Then plug the bulbs back into the soil. Plant the big bulbs 6 inches apart.

It's best to put small bulbs, called offsets, in a nursery bed, as shown in the illustration below, until they reach maturity. Keep in mind that even under optimum conditions it will take three years until these offsets come into bloom, says Bill Kennedy, a customer representative for Van Engelen,

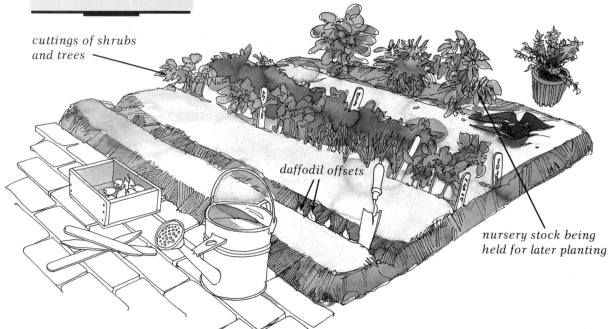

cuttings of shrubs and trees

daffodil offsets

nursery stock being held for later planting

A lightly shaded nursery bed of well-drained soil enriched with organic matter is the perfect place to start cuttings or grow young propagated plants until they near blooming size. You can also use a nursery bed to hold over container plants until you have time to plant them. To do this, dig a hole in the bed, line it with permeable landscape fabric, and set the root ball in the hole. Fill the lined hole with the soil you dug out, and fold over the excess fabric at the top.

a Dutch bulb nursery in Connecticut. Label the cultivars so it will be easy to move them into the garden as they mature. In fall of the following year, lift the bulbs, and move them to their homes in the bed or border.

SCALE A LILY BULB

If you love lilies, the good news is you can easily propagate enough of them to fill your yard. Bob and Diana Gibson, co-owners of B & D Lilies in Washington State, grow lilies by the acre, and they propagate many of their lilies by using scales from the mother bulb. The technique is shown in the illustration at right. "We sacrifice our bulbs, taking off the scales down to the pit," notes Bob Gibson. "But you can make four or five new bulbs every year by taking just the outer ring of scales. That way, you won't hurt the mother bulb at all."

Dig up the lily bulbs in fall after the foliage has nourished the bulb and died back. Mix up a bucket of potting medium for your scales. The Gibsons suggest 5 pounds of vermiculite, lightly moistened with 1 cup of water. Keep the mix barely moist so that a handful doesn't stick together. Remove the outer ring of scales from each bulb. Set the bulbs aside, and replant them in the garden as soon as possible, positioning them so that the top of the bulb is at least 6 inches below the soil surface. Let the scales dry in a shady place for one day so that a callus forms. Fill plastic sandwich-size bags with the moistened vermiculite, and use a pencil to poke several holes for ventilation in each bag. Add several scales to each bag, then store the bags in a warm (70° to 72°F), dark place.

At the end of three months, bulblets the size of green peas will have formed on each scale. Put the scales with bulblets in the refrigerator for 10 to 12 weeks, then plant out in a nursery bed, in light shade. In 3 to 4 weeks, the bulblets will put up a single leaf. By the end of the season, each plant will have three to four leaves. In another season, they'll grow a tall stem but no flowers. In fall, move them into the garden where they are to grow. At the end of the following year, they'll flower.

DON'T FEAR BOUNTIFUL BULBLETS

Lily bulbs form bulblets naturally in the garden. "A common panic of people who grow lilies in their garden," says Diana Gibson, a co-owner of B & D Lilies in Washing-

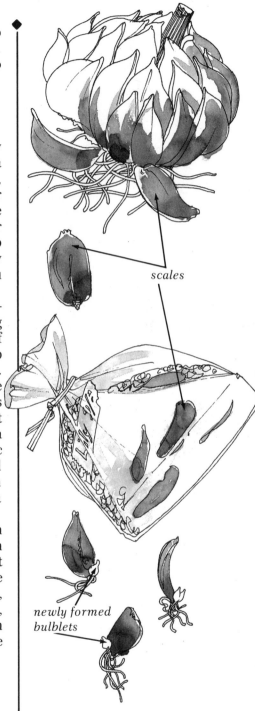

scales

newly formed bulblets

SCALING A LILY BULB

**ADVENTUROUS
ADVENTITIOUS ROOTS**

How do you know which of your plants are easy to root by layering? "Look for preformed adventitious roots," advises Kenneth W. Mudge, Ph.D., an associate professor of horticultural physiology at Cornell University in New York. Adventitious roots are roots occurring in other than their usual location, such as along stems. "At every node of the houseplant *Tradescantia albiflora*, wandering Jew, you'll see two little roots protruding from the stem. They're just sitting there waiting to grow out. *Hedera helix* [English ivy] and other ivies are easy to root, too, because of their adventitious roots," says Dr. Mudge.

ton State, "is the sight of 'suckers' coming up around the bottom of the plant, which they fear will sap the lily's strength." But lily suckers are really young plants growing from bulblets that form on the underground part of the stem. They will do just fine left where they are and will gradually mature into full-size bulbs, expanding the clump.

Let Your Plants Layer

Layering takes advantage of the natural tendency that many plants have to sprout roots along their stems. Try our experts' suggestions for using this technique to multiply herbs and shrubs or to regenerate a leggy houseplant.

BURY A BRANCH TO MAKE NEW PLANTS

Simple layering is one technique that really lives up to its name. You can propagate many of your favorites anytime during the growing season with this easy trick. "My lavender hedge all started with one plant," says Sally Roth, a garden writer from Indiana. "All I did was push a bit of soil over a low branch here and there in the spring. By the time I had the bed ready, a dozen new lavenders were rooted and ready to be snipped away from the mother plants."

Roth says she likes the fun of experimenting to see what will root. She merely bends a low branch to the ground and scoops a handful of soil over a short section of the stem, patting it down and sometimes weighting it with a stone if the branch is inclined to spring upward.

The herb garden is a good place to start experimenting, suggests Roth. Many herbs, including absinthe, anise hyssop, artemisias, bee balm, clary sage, culinary sage, lemon balm, rosemary, scented geraniums, and thymes of all types, are especially easy to propagate just by scuffing a bit of soil over a low stem.

The perennial border, too, is full of likely candidates, such as candytuft (*Iberis* spp.); catmint (*Nepeta* × *faassenii*); chrysanthemums; goldenrods (*Solidago* spp.); perennial asters; sweet William (*Dianthus barbatus*); thread-leaved coreopsis (*Coreopsis verticillata*), including the popular 'Moonbeam'; and periwinkles (*Vinca major* and *V. minor*). Vines such as English ivy, honeysuckle, jasmine, trumpet vine (*Campsis radicans*), and Virginia creeper (*Parthenocissus quinquefolia*) are also gratifyingly easy to propagate.

Herbs, perennials, and vines will usually root within several weeks, depending on the species. Even some woody shrubs can be propagated with this no-fuss method, though it may take a year or even two before they're ready to transplant. Try your hand with barberries (*Berberis* spp.), border forsythia (*Forsythia × intermedia*), rhododendrons and azaleas (*Rhododendron* spp.), rose-of-Sharon (*Hibiscus syriacus*), common lilac (*Syringa vulgaris*), pussy willows, willows (*Salix* spp.), viburnums, and weigelas (*Weigela* spp.). But don't limit yourself to these suggestions—experiment with whatever you like.

"Starting new plants this way appeals to the skinflint in me," admits Roth. "There's no investment in supplies, and it only takes a minute. If the plant doesn't root, I haven't lost a thing. And if it does . . . well, there's always room for one more."

SHORTEN YOUR HOUSEPLANTS

You can rejuvenate some overgrown, leggy houseplants by air layering, a layering technique that encourages roots to form on aboveground stems wrapped in sphagnum moss. This technique works well for tall houseplants such as schefflera (*Brassaia actinophylla*), croton (*Codiaeum variegatum*), dracaenas (*Cordyline* spp.), dumb canes (*Dieffenbachia* spp.), fatsias (*Fatsia* spp.), rubber plant (*Ficus elastica*) and other *Ficus* species, and Swiss-cheese plant (*Monstera deliciosa*). "This is a good way to make two shorter plants from one tall plant," notes Dave Dunbar, a Penn State extension agent. Dunbar uses air layering to keep his rubber plants and scheffleras in bounds. You can also experiment with air layering on plants outdoors that don't respond well to other types of propagation. Be sure you choose a healthy, vigorous stem for air-layering. Follow this technique, which is also shown in the illustration at right:

1. Using a razor blade or small, sharp knife, make a shallow, 2-inch-long slit in the stem anywhere from 6 to 18 inches behind the growing tip.

2. Sprinkle some rooting hormone on the cut, insert a wooden matchstick to keep the cut open, and then wrap with damp, long-fibered (unmilled) sphagnum moss.

3. Cover the moss with clear plastic, and secure the bundle at its top and bottom with masking tape.

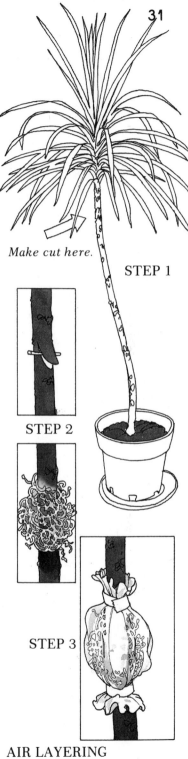

Make cut here.

STEP 1

STEP 2

STEP 3

AIR LAYERING
A HOUSEPLANT

4. When you see roots poking through the moss, cut off the new plant just below the new roots, and remove the tape and plastic. Soak the root ball of the new plant for 3 to 4 hours, and pot it up.

The Craft of Grafting

Many gardeners never venture to try grafting. It seems mysterious and tricky, and indeed it can be. If you'd like to try grafting, refer to a book on propagation for details on the technique. (You'll find some good references on propagation in "Recommended Reading" on page 333.) Here, we've included a few hints from the experts for gardeners who have taken the plunge. And if you're looking for a special grafting challenge, read "Craft a Five-Flavor Tree" on page 216.

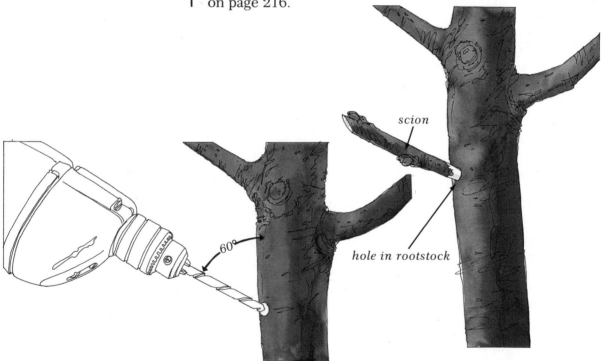

scion

60°

hole in rootstock

You can use a hand-held drill to make a hole of exactly the right size for a small scion. Select a drill bit with a diameter the same as or slightly smaller than your scion's. Drill a ½-inch-deep hole in the trunk of the rootstock. Use a sharp knife to shave off the bark from the bottom end (about 1 inch) of the scion. Insert the scion into the hole in the rootstock. It should fit snugly enough to make good contact with the stock wood, but you should be able to pull it out of the hole fairly easily. The scion and rootstock should form a permanent graft.

NAIL GRAFTING SUCCESS WITH PRACTICE

"Grafting is easy," says Doug Merkle, the operations manager for Indian Wells Orchard in Washington State, "but practice is the key." Merkle often uses a drywall nail to hold a graft on an apple tree together, then tightly wraps it with masking tape. Be sure that the two stems are joined cambium-to-cambium. (Cambium is a thin layer of actively growing tissue between the bark and the wood.)

"It takes manual dexterity to make good grafting cuts," says Juanita Popenoe, Ph.D., an assistant professor of plant and soil sciences at West Virginia University, "plus a lot of practice. The more you do it, the better you are at it." Inspired gardeners who are all thumbs may want to invest in a professional top-working tool, which is available from A. M. Leonard Nursery Supply Company. It's expensive, notes Dr. Popenoe, but very precise. The tool makes a V-cut in the rootstock and an exactly matching cut in the scion.

THE GARDEN PROFESSIONALS

Dave Bowman is co-owner of the Crownsville Nursery in Crownsville, Maryland. The nursery offers more than 1,000 kinds of perennials. Bowman is a frequent speaker at garden seminars and garden club meetings.

John L. Creech, Ph.D., is the former director of the U.S. National Arboretum in Washington, D.C. Among many other activities, he has also served as the program director for the conservation of plant genetic materials in the International Biology Program at the National Academy of Sciences.

Dave Dunbar is a county extension agent for the Penn State Cooperative Extension in Lehigh County, Pennsylvania. He is part of the team that answers home horticulture questions.

Bob and Diana Gibson are the co-owners of B & D Lilies in Port Townsend, Washington. This mail-order nursery offers a broad selection of hybrid and species lilies.

Brent Heath is a co-owner of the Daffodil Mart, which grows the largest selection of bulbs in the United States. It is located in Gloucester, Virginia. He and his wife, Becky, have written and edited materials on bulbs for several books and have written articles for gardening magazines such as *Fine Gardening*.

Bill Kennedy is a customer representative for Van Engelen, Inc., a Dutch bulb nursery in Litchfield, Connecticut. He also is the president of Stillbrook Supplies, Inc., which brokers horticultural supplies to private estates.

Doug Merkle is the operations manager for the four orchards and one vineyard that comprise Indian Wells Orchard. Merkle designed and developed the 1,500-acre property located in Mattawa, Beverly, and Zillah, Washington. Merkle also gives seminars on pruning, training, and grafting fruit trees.

Kenneth W. Mudge, Ph.D., is an associate professor of horticultural physiology in the Department of Floriculture and Ornamental Horticulture at Cornell University in Ithaca, New York.

PROPAGATION DATEBOOK

With so many options for propagating plants, it can be hard to decide what to do when. Layering can be done anytime in spring, summer, or autumn. In general, divide plants either in early spring, just as new growth begins, or in summer after bloom. Take cuttings after the flush of new spring growth is over. Propagate houseplants anytime. Here are some propagation suggestions to mark on your calendar:

• In early spring, divide asters, yarrows, and other perennials.

• In early to mid-summer, take softwood cuttings of ornamental shrubs.

• In July, take root cuttings of oriental poppies (*Papaver orientale*), bleeding hearts (*Dicentra* spp.), bugloss (*Anchusa* spp.), and other plants with thick, fleshy roots.

• In August, divide peonies, digging carefully so you don't damage any more eyes than is necessary. Replant with eyes not more than 2 inches below the soil's surface.

• In August, start cuttings of wax begonias, coleus, and geraniums for winter bloom indoors.

• In August, propagate groundcovers such as pachysandra and periwinkles (*Vinca* spp.) in cold frames.

• In August, start cuttings of subshrubs like lavender, santolina, sage, and thyme.

• In late summer, take cuttings of broad-leaved evergreens, such as boxwoods (*Buxus* spp.), arborvitaes (*Thuja* spp.), and hollies.

NEW GROWTH CAN FOOL YOU

You may think your grafts have been successful when you see signs of new growth on the scion wood, but wait before you celebrate. Scion wood can begin to grow even when the graft union has failed, although it will soon die back. Look for a callus that forms as the wound heals. That's a sure sign that the graft is successful, notes Juanita Popenoe, Ph.D., an assistant professor of plant and soil sciences at West Virginia University.

Juanita Popenoe, Ph.D., is an assistant professor in the Division of Plant and Soil Sciences at West Virginia University in Morgantown. She teaches plant propagation, small fruit production, and tree fruit production.

Steve Reynolds is a sales manager for wholesale ornamentals at Furney's Nursery in Seattle. He is a certified nurseryman in the state of Washington.

Sally Roth is a garden writer and editor in New Harmony, Indiana. She publishes a nature and gardening newsletter called *A Letter from the Country.*

Bernadine Strik, Ph.D., is an associate professor and extension grape and berry crop specialist at Oregon State University in Corvallis, Oregon.

Chick Wasitis is a co-owner of the Crownsville Nursery in Crownsville, Maryland. The nursery stocks more than 1,000 different kinds of perennials and grasses.

Pruning and Training

Pruning may seem like a mysterious art. The good news is that once you become familiar with pruning, it loses its baffling quality. If you learn how to make two basic pruning cuts—called heading cuts and thinning cuts—and understand how plants respond to those cuts, you can change pruning from a chore to a creative outlet.

Whenever you prune, evaluate which kind of pruning cuts will help control size or direction of growth, or produce better flowering or fruit production. These tips from top arborists and garden designers will get you started on a new, enlightened pruning routine.

Controlling Plant Size

We all love watching our landscape plants slowly grow and change with time. But sometimes growth can get out of hand. With regular pruning, you can prevent shrubs from turning the front walk into an obstacle course and keep that luscious fruit in the home orchard within easy reach.

PRACTICE SAFE PRUNING

With sharp shears, loppers, and a pruning saw, you can control the size and shape of most shrubs and small trees. But don't try to take on too much. Alex L. Shigo, the author of *Tree Pruning*, sets the following limits:

♦ If a branch is over 2 inches in diameter, don't try to cut through it.
♦ If you must use a ladder, the tree is too big for you to prune yourself.
♦ Never use a chain saw.
♦ Never prune near a utility line.

For limbs of large diameter or for tall trees, you can call upon another tool—a professional arborist. "If trees are of any size, the liability and safety issues are such that you'll want to have someone with experience handle the pruning," recommends Dan Neely, Ph.D., the editor of the *Journal of Arboriculture*.

RIGHT TOOL, RIGHT TASK

You wouldn't use a butcher knife to slice a loaf of bread or a paring knife to cut a watermelon in two. Likewise, you shouldn't cut tiny twigs with a pruning saw or large limbs with pruning shears. Pruning tools, like knives, come in graduated sizes and strengths for different diameters of wood. Pick the right model for whatever task lies ahead. Doing this allows you to make a clean cut every time and leave behind healthy, intact wood. Here are some suggestions on tools to choose and how to use them:

Hand-held pruners. Pruners are best for heading back or thinning out medium-size branches.

Hedge shears. Use these for manicuring formal hedges.

Long-handled loppers. These work well for pruning branches up to 1½ inches in diameter.

Pruning saws. These saws are good for cutting off limbs up to 2 inches in diameter. "Look for new Japanese blades on pole saws, which have revolutionized pruning," says Alex L. Shigo, the author of *Tree Pruning*. "The cut they make looks like it has been shaved with a razor."

Even if your pruning tools are not high-tech, they will work well if you keep the cutting blades sharp. "They must slice, not tear the wood," says Dan Neely, Ph.D., the editor of the *Journal of Arboriculture*.

SELECT STRATEGIC STEMS

The key to creating a sound strategy for pruning a deciduous or broad-leaved evergreen shrub is to first figure out how the plant is constructed. Just as a person's ankle bone is connected to the knee bone, which is connected to the leg bone, shrubs are networks of interconnected pieces. Each piece of the plant can have a unique reaction to pruning.

Some parts of a plant are better targets for pruning than others. Ken Miller, a principal of Ken Miller Horticultural Consultants in Missouri, looks for medium-size stems, such as those shown in the illustration at left. They resprout new growth readily, unlike larger branches or trunks. They aren't prone to producing an excess of surplus shoots, which is a common result when you shear small twigs. Usually, the best stems for pruning range from about ¼ to ⅝ inch in diameter. "They are slightly thinner than a fat Magic Marker," Miller says.

twiggy growth　　*medium-size branches*

PROPER STEM PRUNING

Once you find stems of the appropriate size, begin removing them one at a time. Look especially for long or overcrowded stems: Your goal is a compact shrub that maintains the original integrity and plant form of the species.

CORNER THE COLLAR

One cardinal rule in pruning woody plants is to not mess with the branch collar—the natural bulge at the base of the branch, as shown in the top illustration at right. This defies common practice of past decades, when pruning professionals routinely recommended cutting off limbs flush with the trunk. More recent research shows that cutting off the branch collar eliminates a natural barrier that keeps pests and diseases from infiltrating the core of the tree.

"Every woody plant has a collar," says Alex L. Shigo, the author of *Tree Pruning*. "This is true of shrubs, trees, even roses. Some people believe you can hack at will. Then cankers or other fungal diseases move in. People blame it on something else when the culprit is poor pruning."

Thus, when you see that a branch must go, prune carefully to keep the rest of the tree walled off from potential problems. Remove the bulk of the branch, leaving only a stub. Then carefully remove the stub, but leave the entire branch collar, as shown in the bottom illustration at right.

The branch collar swells slightly broader than the branch. It rings the branch base and protrudes slightly from the trunk. If you are in doubt about where the collar begins and ends, study wild trees that have lost branches. All that remains is the collar, perhaps enveloped in new wood or sealed with a complete, round doughnut of bark callus.

You want to achieve the same results after you prune. Cut just outside where the collar balloons out from the branch. The angle you take will vary with each tree, even with each branch. Proper cuts will heal round, not oval, and should seal by the following growing season.

TOPPING DOESN'T DO THE TRICK

One top tip that many tree professionals push is this: Don't top your trees. "A tree may respond vigorously when you whack off its head," says urban forester Dennis Lueck. "But it's an unhealthy choice for the tree and a hazard to the people beneath it."

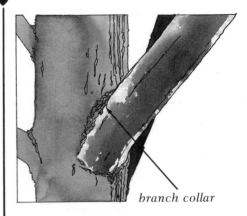

branch collar

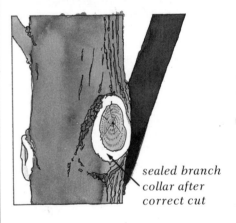

sealed branch collar after correct cut

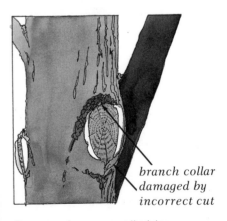

branch collar damaged by incorrect cut

Proper pruning preserves the integrity of the branch collar, the natural bulge where the tree branch connects to the trunk.

When a tree is pruned or wounded, there's a natural instinct to apply a bandage to the wound in the form of pruning paint. However, studies by Alex L. Shigo, the author of *Tree Pruning,* and others show that such paints are unnecessary. In fact, applying pruning paint to already-infected wood will seal in microorganisms and actually promote decay.

It's better, Shigo says, to help a wound seal naturally by encouraging callus tissue to form around its edge. To do this, use a sharp knife to remove any dead or injured bark from around the wound. Enlarge the wound as little as possible, making rounded edges. Cut any loose bark away to form a clean, smooth surface. The bark should be tight around the wound, so fasten it with small nails if necessary.

The big cuts made when a tree is topped, Lueck explains, are an open invitation to invasion by fungi and bacteria. Rot starts at the cuts, then extends down the trunk and enters the root system, debilitating the tree. Although the flush of new growth may be vigorous, most of it grows straight up. This results in a very weak branch union, creating a joint that is likely to snap when the branches get large and heavy or when a forceful wind or load of snow comes along.

"If you do top a tree," says Lueck, "top it at ground level." Then replace the "too big" tree with a species better suited to the location. And spread the word about topping. Too many homeowners—and arborists—still resort to this tactic to reduce tree size.

Maintaining Plant Form

Pruning also helps maintain and improve plant form. Plants need shaping and thinning to help light and air penetrate to all parts of the plant. This promotes good growth and helps minimize disease problems.

SELECTIVE PRUNING SIMPLIFIED

There's an art to directing the shape of trees and shrubs. Vaughn Banting, a Louisiana landscape designer and bonsai artist, has mastered that art while crafting exquisite miniature bonsai trees. He applies the same techniques to shape lush landscape plants. Simply put, he cuts stems back to a bud that will grow in the direction he wishes, as shown in the illustration on the opposite page.

"At the base of every leaf and stem on deciduous trees and broad-leaved evergreens, there is a dormant axillary bud. If you cut the stem just beyond that area, the leaf will give rise to an axillary shoot. If the leaf points left, so will the new shoot," says Banting.

Likewise, if the leaf is under the stem, the new branch will point down. If on the top, the shoot will point up. If the plant has opposite leaves like a maple, dogwood, or viburnum, you can't predict which bud will grow after pruning. Decide which bud you want to grow out, and damage the other bud with your thumbnail.

"This kind of attention to detail is the difference between training plants and just chopping them off," says Banting.

SELECTIVE PRUNING

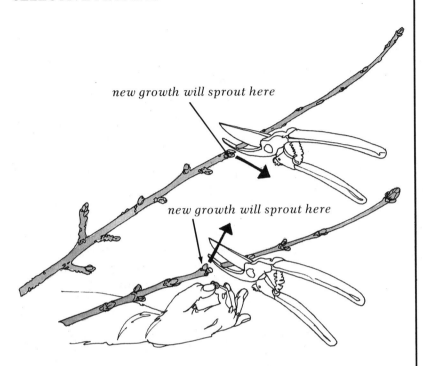

new growth will sprout here

new growth will sprout here

SHAPE TREES FROM THE START

For a young tree, the leader is the core of strength that supports lesser limbs. If a second branch arises that grows strongly upright, the union of that branch with the trunk could be weak. Years later, when the upright branch has grown large and heavy or when it is weighted down by ice or snow, the union may split. Take steps while trees are young to prevent this problem, advises Richard W. Harris, Ph.D., a professor emeritus of landscape horticulture at the University of California at Davis. "There is a key to keeping attractive and safe-structured trees. On any fork in the tree structure, one side should be smaller to prevent the danger of future splitting," says Dr. Harris.

For up to five years after you plant a young tree, keep a close eye on the branches that arise from the leader. You can manipulate them to keep the tree strong and healthy for decades. Here are a few factors to juggle:

Maintain the leader. If several upright shoots arise near the top of the main trunk, encourage the strongest to

FROM A BETTER ANGLE

Your finger can be your guide to deciding when the crotch angle—the angle between a lateral branch and a tree trunk—is too narrow. Crotch angles smaller than 45 degrees may be too weak to withstand high winds, ice, wet snow, or heavy fruiting. Strong angles are from 45 to 90 degrees. The best angle for maintaining a balance between fruiting and new growth for fruit trees is about 45 to 60 degrees.

Robert Kourik, a California landscape designer and consultant, tests for narrow crotch angles by putting his index finger between the branch and trunk. If your finger doesn't reach the bottom of the V and you see light below it, the crotch is too narrow. Try spreading the branch if it is young, or if the branch is crowding others or is unhealthy, prune it off.

become the leader by leaving it unpruned. Discourage others by removing their side branches and pinching off the top 2 inches of new growth or by heading the entire branch back by about one-quarter.

Develop strong attachments. Check all future side branches that emerge from the trunk. They should be one-half of the main limb's diameter or smaller.

Establish a branching framework. Lower on the trunk, you can pick the main framework of branches. Select branches that emerge from the trunk with a 45-degree or wider angle and radiate outward in different directions so they do not shade branches below. Be sure they are separated by 1 to 1½ feet of trunk. You can temporarily leave on other branches to strengthen the young tree, but retard their growth as detailed in "Maintain the Leader," on page 39. Once the tree has a sturdy trunk and enough branches to keep the trunk shaded, begin pruning away these temporary branches. Start with the largest, and remove a few each year for a two- to three-year period to reveal the finished structure of the tree.

PRUNE A PICTURESQUE PINE

Instead of relegating pines to their usual roles as screens or green backdrops, sculpt them into focal points with character. "You can prune and pinch young pines to give them a much older look, a sense of timelessness. You can reveal their inherent beauty and character," says David Slawson, Ph.D., an independent landscape designer from Kentucky who specializes in Japanese garden design.

Pinch soft new growth on pines with your fingers rather than with pruning tools, as shown in the illustrations on the opposite page. Grasp a candle—an infant branch tipped with buds—at the point you want to pinch. (Dr. Slawson usually leaves between one-third and one-half of the total length.) Bend until the end snaps off. Thin off unnecessary candles by grasping the base between your thumb and forefinger and snapping them off. If you must remove a branch, don't just head it back—you'll be left with an ugly stump that won't regrow. Make the cut at a point where two branches join, or where the branch emerges from a main stem—this kind of cut will be much less noticeable.

When pruning pines, your window of opportunity is limited. If you want new buds to form on a candle, you must pinch it while it is immature, before the needles form. This means you must pinch during a one- to two-week period in spring. If you pinch later, the candle will develop into a single branch, but it will not sprout sideshoots.

Watch for candle-break so you don't miss your chance to prune. The downy tan candles will emerge from the end of each branch and stretch out 3 to 6 inches long, or longer near the top of the tree. Pinch before the candle tissue hardens and begins to flush green with young needles. If you cut candles with pruning shears, you will remove the tips of the needles and the ends will turn brown. Which candles you remove or thin will vary according to your goals, which might include one or more of the following:

Size control. Use candling (pruning candles) to keep a pine compact without shearing. This is more subtle than shearing, because you are shaping individual branches, Dr. Slawson explains. To maintain a pine at a constant height, remove one or two of the longest candles on each branch. Then pinch the side candles back to one-third of their full height, or about ½ to 1 inch long.

More height. If you want more height, leave the longest candle on each branch tip and thin out the others. Don't pinch the remaining candles back until the tree reaches the height you want. However, continue to thin for shape.

An aged effect. If you want a gnarled tree with character, find a young tree in a nursery that has an interesting twist or S-curve to the trunk and branches. After planting, remove up to one-third of the branches to reveal the trunk line. On each remaining branch, remove the largest center candle if it emerges straight out of the branch. This will stimulate development of a zigzag branching pattern. Also remove some side candles, leaving two to three candles that point outward and one or two that point inward. Pinch those candles to create feathery clouds of foliage on the end one-third of the limb.

AN EASY ESPALIER

If you want to get double-duty out of a narrow space, you can train dwarf fruit trees to spread lengthwise along a trellis or a series of horizontal wires. The espalier can be freestanding or against a wall or fence. You will prune and direct the trees to drench the fruit with sunlight and shape the limbs in a bold geometric design. Espalier specialist Henry P. Leuthardt says a Belgian fence, a lattice-like series of foliage-framed diamonds, is the simplest espalier to make.

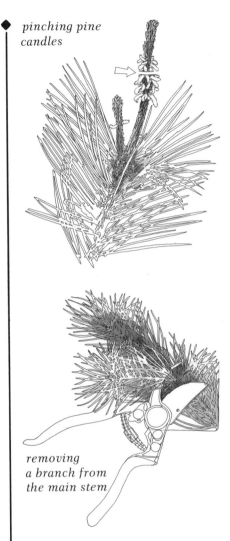

pinching pine candles

removing a branch from the main stem

PRUNE WHILE YOU CAROL

Hold off pruning your evergreens until a few weeks before Christmas. Then use the trimmings from arborvitaes (*Thuja* spp.), boxwoods (*Buxus* spp.), cedars (*Cedrus* spp.), firs (*Abies* spp.), pines (*Pinus* spp.), rhododendrons (*Rhododendron* spp.), and other evergreens for holiday wreaths and decorations.

In this pattern, shown in the illustration below, the key is to consistently secure the branches to the trellis as they grow. "The key word here is support," says Leuthardt. "Just because the branches start growing on an angle doesn't mean they won't go back to the vertical if left to their own devices."

Creating an espalier does take some attention and persistence. If you're up to the challenge, follow Leuthardt's recommended procedure:

1. Select three to five 1-year-old whips (unbranched nursery trees) of a spur-forming tree fruit like apples and pears. Plant them 2 feet apart along your trellis or other framework.

2. Head each tree back to 15 to 18 inches. This will encourage new branches to sprout just below the cut.

3. After new branches have appeared, prune off all but two strong branches. The two you keep should be on opposite sides of the tree. Train them to a 45-degree angle as soon as they need support. As the limbs continue to grow, tie each to the trellis at 1-foot intervals using either a flexible tie or something like cloth or raffia that will rot

CREATING A BELGIAN FENCE ESPALIER

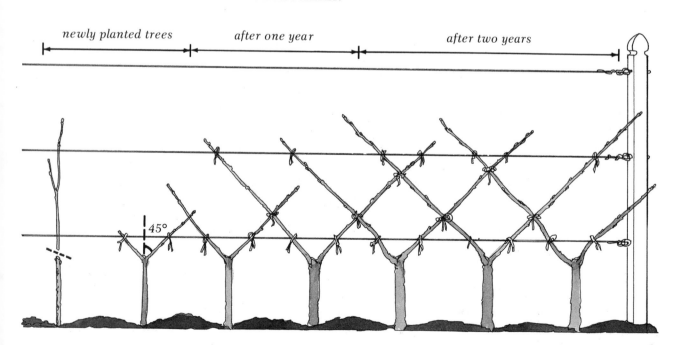

newly planted trees   *after one year*   *after two years*

45°

before cutting into the swelling branch. The limbs will cross neighboring tree limbs and create a latticework pattern.

4. From the second through the fourth year, the trees will sprout vertical branches. Head them back to 4 to 6 inches long so they don't compete with the main branch. They become short spur branches.

5. After about three years, the branches will stretch diagonally to the top of the trellis. At this point, cut back upright-growing branches and thin out excess growth to maintain the open diamonds between the branches.

6. To maintain your espalier, prune at least twice a year. After the first lush growth of the growing season, thin the new green growth as necessary. You may have to prune again during the growing season if the weather encourages abundant growth, Leuthardt warns. "However, don't prune after Labor Day so you won't encourage late growth that could freeze during winter," Leuthardt says. Wait until the dormant season to clear out late summer and fall growth or to heavily prune an older espalier.

Figuring Out the Timing

Once you've figured out *how* to prune properly, there's still the question of *when* to prune. In the sections below, our pruning specialists explain that removing part of the plant top stimulates growth at certain times of year and stifles it in other seasons.

THE WHYS AND WHENS OF PRUNING WELL

For most landscape plants, except conifers and disease-susceptible species, you have an almost endless choice of pruning times. You can juggle your pruning schedule to make your pruning most effective. See "Prune a Picturesque Pine" on page 40 for special instructions on timing and method for pruning pines and other conifers.

"Many errors are made in timing today," says Alex L. Shigo, the author of *Tree Pruning.* "A decade ago, correct pruning meant making a flush cut and a large trunk wound. We had to set the timing to minimize injury to a tree, not to doing the best job." Now, pruning experts recommend making a collar cut, which doesn't injure the tree. So timing considerations are different. "You should know why

PICK SMALL FRUITS TO GET BIG FRUITS

Once you've gone to the time and effort to establish an espalier, make sure that you're rewarded by more than its appearance. Thinning fruits will ensure that you get a good harvest. Large tree fruits such as apples need to be at least 2½ inches in diameter to be worth harvesting, says Henry P. Leuthardt, an espalier specialist from New York. If you leave too many fruits on your trees, they won't develop to that minimum size.

To encourage the growth of larger fruit, cut off smaller or damaged fruits when they're about the size of a marble. Leave about two pieces of fruit per spur or short fruiting branch, says Leuthardt.

I KNOW YOU, BUD!

When pruning trees and shrubs grown for flowers or fruits, it's important to be able to distinguish vegetative buds from flower buds. Vegetative buds—those forming leaves—are usually sharper, thinner, and longer than the plump flowering buds.

Terminal or apical buds, found at the tip of a twig, can be vegetative, flowering, or mixed, and they are usually plumper than lateral or axillary buds, which are found further down the twig.

For correct timing of pruning, it's important to know where flower buds form and when they open. See "The Whys and Whens of Pruning Well" on page 43 for suggestions on when to prune flowering shrubs and trees.

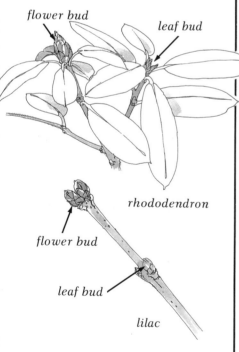

flower bud

leaf bud

rhododendron

flower bud

leaf bud

lilac

you are pruning, and start there," says Shigo. These are Shigo's timing guidelines:

♦ To stunt a tree, prune it in midsummer.

♦ For spring-flowering shrubs or trees, prune after the floral show is over. This group includes rhododendrons and azaleas (*Rhododendron* spp.), forsythias (*Forsythia* spp.), lilacs (*Syringa* spp.), and big-leaved hydrangea (*Hydrangea macrophylla*).

♦ Plants that flower on new growth should be pruned while they are dormant in early spring. This group includes most summer-flowering shrubs, everbearing raspberries, and floribunda and hybrid tea roses.

♦ To avoid leaving dead spots, shear a hedge after growth begins.

TO PRUNE OR NOT TO PRUNE

There are certain exceptions to your newfound pruning freedoms. Here are ways to avoid some pruning pitfalls:

Don't prune in the fall. "Avoid pruning living wood as a tree goes into dormancy. It's not equipped to produce callus until it reemerges from dormancy. The cut will remain open and susceptible much longer," says Alex L. Shigo, the author of *Tree Pruning.*

Watch slippery spring bark. "When trees are first breaking dormancy in spring, many have bark that is prone to slipping for a week or so. Avoid pruning at this time so you don't tear off more bark than you intended," advises Dan Neely, Ph.D., the editor of the *Journal of Arboriculture.*

Skip spring and early-summer pruning on disease-susceptible trees. If you grow American elms (*Ulmus americana*), which are prone to Dutch elm disease; oaks (*Quercus* spp.), which are susceptible to oak wilt; honey locusts (*Gleditsia* spp.) that are smitten with canker; or pears, apples, quinces, crab apples, pyracanthas (*Pyracantha* spp.), and cotoneasters (*Cotoneaster* spp.), all of which can get fire blight; avoid pruning during peak infection times.

"A lot of pathogens can enter wounds, but most diseases are limited to reproducing and infecting plants during a certain time period. If the wounds are fresh during that time, there could be big trouble," Dr. Neely says. Conditions in late spring and early summer often are favorable for infection to occur. "The temperature and humidity are relatively moderate and favor fungus sporing and bacterial division. Thus, the weather encourages their spread," says Dr. Neely.

Dr. Neely suggests pruning disease-susceptible trees in late winter, just before they emerge from dormancy. You can also prune trees in late summer, he says, but you risk having trees die back if dry weather follows pruning.

THE GARDEN PROFESSIONALS

Vaughn Banting is the president of Nicholas & Banting Horticultural Service in New Orleans. He is a landscape designer, bonsai artist, and licensed horticulturist.

Richard W. Harris, Ph.D., is a professor emeritus of landscape horticulture at the University of California at Davis. He is the author of *Arboriculture.*

Robert Kourik is a free-lance writer, publisher, consultant, and landscape designer in Occidental, California. He is the author of *Designing and Maintaining Your Edible Landscape Naturally.*

Scott Kunst is a landscape historian and owner of Old House Gardens in Ann Arbor, Michigan. He is a member of the adjunct faculty for the Historic Preservation Program at Eastern Michigan University and is a public school teacher in Ann Arbor.

Henry P. Leuthardt is an espalier specialist and the owner of Henry Leuthardt Nurseries, Inc., in East Moriches, New York. The nursery offers a selection of berries and grapes as well as dwarf, semidwarf, and espalier fruit trees.

Dennis Lueck is an urban forester and horticulturist in Eugene, Oregon. He works with public and private clients and gives talks at schools and universities. He is the author of *Trees for the Pacific Northwest.*

Ken Miller is a principal of Ken Miller Horticultural Consultants in St. Louis, Missouri. He designs "collector quality" gardens on both a residential and commercial scale, and he gives seminars on garden design around the country.

Dan Neely, Ph.D., is a retired plant pathologist from the state of Illinois's Natural History Survey and was a professor of plant pathology at the University of Illinois at Urbana. He is the editor of the *Journal of Arboriculture.*

Alex L. Shigo is the owner of Shigo and Trees Associates in Durham, New Hampshire, and a former chief scientist for the U.S. Forest Service. He is the author of *Tree Pruning, A New Tree Biology,* and *A New Tree Biology Dictionary.*

David Slawson, Ph.D., is an independent landscape designer from Kentucky. Dr. Slawson specializes in Japanese garden design and is the author of *Secret Teachings in the Art of Japanese Gardens.*

LEAVE LEAKY TREES TILL LATER

Sugar maple (*Acer saccharum*) and birch (*Betula* spp.) trees tend to leak watery sap if cut in spring. "They lose some nourishment that is moving up in the wood," says Dan Neely, Ph.D., the editor of the *Journal of Arboriculture.* "But the leaking usually does little harm. It's primarily a problem of appearances. Since nobody wants to look at a drippy pruning wound, it's best to wait to prune until later in the season."

Plant Breeding and Seed Saving

Plant breeding and seed saving combine art and science. They're activities that encourage us to experiment, study, and just simply enjoy unraveling the puzzle of plants. Trying to transfer a trait from one plant to another or discovering a way to make seed last longer in storage are tasks that appeal to our curiosity and creativity. They're also intrinsically linked. Obviously, you can't be a plant breeder without knowing about saving and storing seed. And seed savers often play a subtle role in shaping the crops they grow, just by planting seed from their best performers year after year. So dig in, learn from these experts in the field, decide what you'd like to experiment with, and enjoy!

Backyard Breeding

If you want to try your hand at home hybridizing, you'll need to decide what plant (or plants) you're going to work with. It's a good idea to start with a plant that you really like to eat or look at, since you'll be growing a lot of it. Read all you can to get familiar with its characteristics. You'll need to know what has already been done in the way of breeding the plant you've chosen so that you can decide what characteristics you want to develop.

GO FOR THE GOAL

All successful breeding programs start with a goal. While it may be fun to cross pretty flowers at random, "in the long run," advises Currier McEwen, M.D., an iris breeder from Maine, "if you want to develop something particular, you'll want to set your goals and work toward those." Look for parent plants that will lead you toward those goals, and cross them.

Your goals will depend on the plant you're working with, your likes and dislikes, and what characteristics the plants have to begin with. You may want to look for larger or more fragrant blooms or better insect or disease resistance. New or truer colors is another possibility. "We think of the iris as blue," states Dr. McEwen, "but if you hold an iris up against a delphinium, you see that we've still got some way to go. They've all got a little violet in them."

If you're new to plant breeding or have limited space, concentrate on one or two goals so you're not overwhelmed. But be on the lookout for plants you create that may lead you in a new direction. Who knows? Maybe you'll create a plant no one's ever dreamed of!

BEST BETS FOR BEGINNING BREEDERS

Tomatoes are a popular crop with amateur and professional breeders alike. "Tomatoes are easy to grow," points out Ken Ettlinger, the director of the Long Island Seed Company in New York. "And they're certainly easy to save seed from. Plus, the diversity of genetic material you have to work with is incredible."

For a more challenging project, Tim Peters, the research director for Territorial Seed Company in Oregon, suggests melons. "If home gardeners would work on combining the long-keeping characteristics of casaba- or Valencia-type melons into a cantaloupe, that would really be a valuable project. Then they wouldn't have to eat all of their melons in the space of a week—they could relax and enjoy them over a period of a month or two," says Peters.

MAKING HOMEMADE HYBRIDS

Making a cross is simple. You need to start with a pollen parent (male) and seed parent (female) that have characteristics you'd like to use. If the two parents flower at different times, choose the later-flowering parent as the seed parent. See "Callin' All Pollen" on page 49 for ways to save pollen for later use.

"If you're new at plant breeding, practice pollinating large-flowered plants like irises or daylilies. Their blooms have large floral parts, so it's easy to see the pollen and get it on the right place," advises Jean M. A. Nick, a garden book editor for Rodale Press. "When you cross a new plant, it's a good idea to take a minute and identify the flower parts before you begin." The illustration on page 48 may help you figure out which flower parts are which.

On most flowers, you'll have to remove the seed parent's stamens a few days before the flower opens to prevent

---

REACH FOR RECESSIVE

With plant breeding, what you see isn't always what you get. But that's what's so exciting about plant breeding.

Gregor Mendel, a nineteenth-century Austrian monk, opened Western eyes to the intricacies of plant breeding and genetics. Until he conducted his now-famous experiments with garden peas, scientists believed that crosses between similar plants always produced similar offspring.

Mendel crossed a yellow pea plant with a green pea plant—a cross that yielded yellow offspring. But when he crossed two of the yellow offspring, they produced one green pea plant for each three yellow pea plants. What Mendel discovered was that some genetic traits are recessive. That is, they're only expressed when the offspring receives the recessive gene from both parents.

So where did the green peas come from? Each of the yellow offspring from the first cross inherited a dominant yellow trait and a recessive green one from their parents. Most of their offspring expressed the yellow trait, but some received the green trait from both parents; with two recessives, the green color could be expressed.

As a plant breeder, you're often crossing parents that have both dominant and recessive genes. You're looking for offspring that inherit recessive traits from both parents and thus can express them. You just have to make enough crosses to discover what's hidden by the dominant traits.

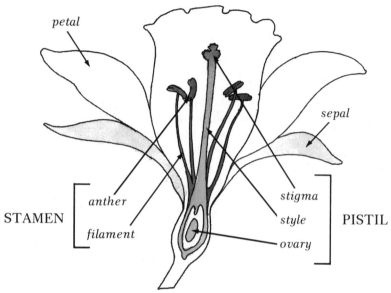

In a flower, male reproductive structures called stamens produce pollen. When pollen reaches the female reproductive structure, the pistil, the flower is fertilized and will produce seed.

CHOOSE YOUR COLOR

You can use selective pollination and selection to develop plants that have characteristics that appeal to you. Say you have a clump of pink cosmos, all of which are pale pink except one or two darker pink flowers, which you like better. Suzanne Ashworth, the author of *Seed to Seed*, suggests hand-pollinating flowers on the dark pink plants before they open and saving seed only from those crosses. Pull out plants with lighter pink flowers if they appear. "You keep on doing that over the course of several years, and you're going to end up with a pale pink one being the odd plant out," explains Ashworth.

X MARKS THE SPOT

No breeding program is complete without a good record-keeping system. You'll need a system for marking crosses on the plants as you make them. One way is to attach plastic tags with wires to the base of each flower — just be sure the tags are held securely.

You'll also need a logbook to record your crosses. The logbook is valuable for deciding which crosses to make next or for evaluating how successful a particular cross was.

Most breeders record the same information on both the tags and in the logbook. And they always list it in the same order. List the date, the seed parent, an ×, and the name of the pollen parent. You may want to number each cross made in a given year.

it from pollinating itself. (Plants like squash are an exception. For details on how to pollinate them, see "As Easy as One, Two, Three" below.)

To remove the pollen, carefully open the bud and pinch the anthers off with your fingers, a tweezers, or a small scissors. Removing the petals may make this easier. After you pinch off the anthers, you need to cover the stigma to prevent stray pollen from landing on it. If you have not removed the petals, fold them over the stigma and tape them shut. If you have removed the petals, use yarn to gently tie a brown paper bag over the flower.

When the seed parent's stigma is sticky and wet-looking, transfer the pollen with your finger or a clean utensil, or pick a flower from the pollen parent and brush the stigma with its pollen. Re-cover the stigma. Repeat the pollen transfer again the following day to increase your chances of success. If the cross was successful, the ovary will begin to swell in a week or two. You can remove the bag or tape at that time.

AS EASY AS ONE, TWO, THREE

Cucumbers, squashes, pumpkins, and other members of the gourd family, Cucurbitaceae, are among the easiest vegetables to experiment with. Squashes, especially, provide large flowers with easily identifiable parts. "With squashes and cucumbers, you need to know that there are male and female flowers," says Nancy Bubel, the author of *The New Seed-Starters Handbook*, "and it's the female flower that has the little swelling at the base that's going to produce the fruit." The differences between male and female squash flowers are shown in the illustration below. To cross gourd-family members, follow these steps:

1. Select a female (seed parent) and male (pollen parent) with characteristics that you'd like to select for.

2. Before the female flower opens, put a brown paper bag over it. This will prevent insects from pollinating the female flowers on the seed parent before you make your cross. Gently tie the bag closed with a rubber band or twist tie. Don't use a plastic bag because it may get too moist or hot inside. (Suzanne Ashworth, the author of *Seed to Seed*, actually tapes the tips of flowers closed with ¾-inch, extra-sticky masking tape when they are just showing a bit of color but haven't yet opened.)

3. When the female flower opens in its bag (or when taped flowers show full color), rub some pollen from the anther of the male flower onto a fine paintbrush. Transfer the pollen to the stigma of the female flower. Or pick the male flower and brush the anther's pollen onto the stigma of the female flower.

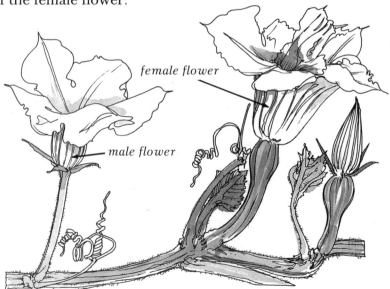

female flower

male flower

Some species, including squash and melons, bear male and female reproductive parts in different and distinct types of flowers.

CALLIN' ALL POLLEN

What if the pollen from your pollen parent is ready before the seed parent? Or vice versa? If the male parent is ready first, try to save the pollen. "If you're only going to save pollen a day or two," says Currier McEwen, M.D., an iris breeder from Maine, "you can just take the anthers off, put them in a dry dish, and cover it to protect them." If your seed parent is ready first, find a fellow gardener or breeder farther south who grows the pollen parent you want to use. He or she may be able to send you pollen before it would be ready in your garden.

Moisture can spoil pollen in a few hours, so dry storage is essential. If you have to store pollen for longer than a day or two, store it in a jar with a desiccating agent such as silica gel. Dr. McEwen stores pollen in gelatin capsules — the kind that pharmacists use for making pills. He opens up a capsule and pokes six tiny holes in one-half of it with a pin. Then he scrapes the ripe pollen grains into that capsule half and puts on the other half to close up the capsule. He places the capsule in a jar along with a desiccating agent and uses a rubber gasket when he screws on the lid to make it airtight. When stored this way, Siberian and Japanese iris pollen will last for weeks in the refrigerator and for months in the freezer.

4. Put the brown bag over the female flower again (or retape it) for about four or five more days to keep unwanted pollen away. Then, remove the bag or tape, and mark the stem with a label or string so you'll be able to recognize it when it's time to collect the fruit. Seeds from pumpkins and winter squash will be mature at traditional harvest time for the fruit. But with cucumbers and summer squash, let the fruits remain on the plant until they are overripe so that the seed has time to mature.

MAKE ROOM TO BE RECKLESS

Once you've made crosses and collected seed, the next steps are to get the seeds to germinate and to grow out the seedlings. For a wealth of great tips on germinating seed and caring for seedlings, refer to "Growing from Seed," beginning on page 2.

Once your seedlings are up, you'll need to mark out a plot to grow out seedlings. "Plant perennials like daylilies or irises in rows 12 inches apart, and space seedlings 6 inches apart in those rows," suggests Andre Viette, the owner of Andre Viette Farm and Nursery in Virginia. That means if you have 1,000 seedlings from one year's crosses, you'll need an area of about 20×25 feet to grow out the seedlings.

You'll also need the nerve to rogue out plants that don't measure up. From 1,000 seedlings, for example, Viette recommends selecting 100 plants that show the best potential. Toss the other 900 on your compost pile. Each year, cut your crop in half, until you have about 25 or 30 good plants. Most likely, you'll want to recross these plants to each other or their parents to bring out characteristics you're looking for.

How do you tell what measures up? Viette suggests growing a representative sample of the best cultivars available and measuring your creations against them.

Seed Collecting and Saving

Whether you want to cut down on spending for seeds, save seeds of a spectacular flower or vegetable, or help preserve heirloom seeds, seed saving is an activity you should try. It's an essential skill if you're a backyard breeder. The following sections will tell you what you need to know to be on your way to successful seed saving.

HANKERING FOR HYBRIDS?

If you're thinking of saving seed from a hybrid plant, think again. Nancy Bubel, the author of *The New Seed-Starters Handbook*, cautions, "There's really no point in saving seed from a hybrid plant; it wouldn't come true to the parent." Hybrid seed is created by crossing two highly inbred cultivars, which generally don't resemble their hybrid offspring. When the two inbred parents are crossed with each other, they yield F$_1$ hybrid seed. Seed companies have to repeat this cross each year to produce F$_1$ hybrid seed, such as the seed for 'Early Girl' and 'Celebrity' tomatoes, as well as many other popular vegetable and flower cultivars. These hybrids have more-desirable characteristics than either parent—they exhibit what we call hybrid vigor—but the seed they produce is likely to resemble the inbred grandparents. For some exceptions to this rule, see "Some Hybrids Do Come True" at right.

SEED SAVERS ARE PLANT BREEDERS, TOO!

You don't have to be out snipping stamens and pushing pollen around to develop great garden plants. "Seed savers are really plant breeders," maintains Ken Ettlinger, the director of the Long Island Seed Company in New York. "Any gardener that saves seed automatically follows a selection process. My parents and grandfather are all seed savers, and I've learned a lot by just watching what they do. They've always had a eye for selecting the biggest or the prettiest, or just something unusual." By saving seeds from your best crops season after season, you can develop a productive "new" plant that is well-adapted to your local conditions.

CAGED PEPPERS

Window screening can serve as a barrier to keep pollinating insects away from plants that you want to be purely self-pollinated. David Cavagnaro, a garden manager at Heritage Farm for Seed Savers Exchange in Iowa, encloses his seed-producing peppers in standard tomato cages wrapped with window screening. "The screening lets in the parasitic wasps that control aphids but excludes larger insects that carry pollen from one plant to another," Cavagnaro explains. In the spring, you can also wrap a layer of plastic or row cover material around the screening to give some cold protection.

SOME HYBRIDS DO COME TRUE

If you're looking for perennials to fill a new garden, don't let a tight budget keep you from getting high-quality plants. It's possible to get some hybrid perennials for seed-packet prices—you just need to know which ones to grow. The following perennials come true from seed. Common names are given in parentheses in the following list, but remember: You must ask for the particular species and/or cultivar named here to be sure you'll have a plant that will come true from seed.

Achillea 'Debutante' (yarrow)
Aquilegia × *hybrida* McKana hybrids (columbine)
Chrysanthemum × *superbum* 'Alaska' (Shasta daisy)
Coreopsis grandiflora 'Early Sunrise' (coreopsis)
Digitalis purpurea Excelsior hybrids (foxglove)
Echinacea purpurea 'Bravado' (purple coneflower)
Gaillardia × *grandiflora* 'Torchlight' (blanket flower)
Heuchera sanguinea 'Bressingham Mix' (coral bells)
Lupinus Russell hybrids (lupines)
Lychnis × *arkwrightii* 'Vesuvius' (Arkwright's campion)
Platycodon grandiflorus 'Fugi' series (balloon flower)
Veronica spicata 'Sightseeing' (spike speedwell)

Tie a piece of old panty hose around maturing seedpods to serve as a seed collector.

TIE A YELLOW RIBBON

"Once you've chosen a plant you want to save seed from," states Nancy Bubel, the author of *The New Seed-Starters Handbook,* "you'll want to identify it in some way." She suggests tying on a brightly colored ribbon or a tag. You can find weather-resistant ribbon, such as fluorescent surveyor's ribbon, through garden supply catalogs or at your local hardware store. Marking the plant reminds you and other family members to treat it with care. Most important, it will remind you not to eat it for dinner or cut it for your table centerpiece!

Don't depend on just a single tagged fruit or plant for your entire seed harvest. Tag several in case one gets damaged.

COLLECT ALL DAY WHILE YOU'VE GONE AWAY

What do you do if you'll be away when your seedpods mature? Some seedpods crack open when they're mature, and release the seeds. In some cases the seeds just tumble to the ground, but many wildflowers forcibly eject their seeds, scattering them in all directions. And the seeds of other plants simply float away. It's all too easy to lose those precious seeds if you don't take precautions. Take a tip from Currier McEwen, M.D., an iris breeder from Maine, and prevent such disasters before they occur. "If I've got to be away for a week or two," says Dr. McEwen, "I tie a piece of an old stocking around the pod, just in case it opens while I am away, so I won't lose the seeds." For best results, tie the nylon stocking in place with a piece of soft string or yarn, and take care not to damage the stem of the plant, as shown in the illustration at left.

TOMATOES: BREWED NOT STEWED

Seeds that are enclosed in fleshy pulp, like those of tomatoes and cucumbers, need special treatment before they'll dry and store properly. You need to separate the pulp from the seeds by fermenting the fully ripe or rotting vegetables, as shown in the illustrations on the opposite page. Suzanne Ashworth, the author of *Seed to Seed,* offers these instructions for fermenting seeds properly:

1. Slice the vegetable down the middle. Scoop out the seeds and pulp, and put them into a clean wide-mouthed glass jar, like a peanut butter or mayonnaise jar. Discard the shell.

2. Add about ¼ cup of water to the jar.

3. Let the jar sit in an out-of-the-way place for a few days at room temperature or higher—80° to 90°F is ideal. Stir the mixture once or twice daily. A layer of mold will form, and a strong odor will develop.

4. When you see bubbles rising, when the mold grows to a dense layer, or when most seeds have settled to the bottom, stop the fermentation process by adding water to double the mixture. Stir well. Good seeds will sink to the bottom, and pulp and plant debris will stay near the top. Skim off the debris on top. Then stir and skim repeatedly until only good seeds are left. Rinse the seeds and place them on a glass dish or window screen to dry.

"In fermentation, you have to be really careful that you don't go too far," warns Ashworth. "Once the pulp is separated from the seed, the chemical in the pulp that inhibits germination wears away. The warm, wet conditions present after fermentation are perfect for sprouting seed. So if you ferment your seed too long, you'll end up with sprouted seed."

DO TREAD ON ME

Threshing dry seeds to separate them from the seed heads or pods can be an activity for the whole family. Corn, carrot, and pea seeds are some of the common types of dry seed that require threshing.

Suzanne Ashworth, the author of *Seed to Seed*, suggests putting big pods in a bag, tying it shut, and having kids jump on the bag. Or roll the pods in a sheet and jog in place on top of it. "Kids think it's great fun to do that," says Ashworth. If the seeds are really hard and dry, you can have children ride tricycles over them. Ashworth even takes a hammer to seeds that are especially difficult to extract, like artichokes.

For more-fragile seeds, put your sack of seeds on top of a piece of old carpet for cushioning, close up the sack, jump on top, and start jogging. For very delicate seeds, roll the seedpods on top of a screen with a bucket underneath to catch any fallen seed and chaff.

BLOWIN' IN THE WIND

Winnowing is the all-important seed savers' technique used to separate seedpods and other plant debris from the seeds they protected. One way to winnow seed is to use the wind to carry the lighter chaff away. But the wind is often unpredictable—a sudden gust can completely blow away chaff *and* seed. A steady air current from a single direction is best. According to Suzanne Ashworth, the author of *Seed to Seed*, "You have good substitutes for wind. Hair dryers with the heating element removed, the blower from an old vacuum cleaner, or those little tiny computer fans—they work really well." Household fans also work if they are on a low setting.

Ashworth suggests that you cover your entire work area with a sheet before you start, in case a sudden gust of

tomato seeds and pulp

fermenting mixture

seeds drying

FERMENTING TOMATO SEEDS

WET VS. DRY

There are essentially two kinds of seeds: wet and dry. Wet seeds are those that are embedded in wet flesh, such as the seeds of melons. Eggplants, Jack-in-the-pulpits, magnolias, and dogwoods also have wet seed. To save wet seed, you need to extract it from the surrounding wet tissue. Some plants need to be fermented before you can do this. For information on how to ferment seeds, see "Tomatoes: Brewed Not Stewed" on page 52.

Dry seeds are those that are not embedded in wet flesh. They may be enclosed in pods, husks, or seed heads, instead. Dry seeds usually dry right on the plant. Dried seeds may need to be threshed and winnowed in preparation for storage. For information on threshing and winnowing, see "Blowin' in the Wind" on page 53.

wind or a too-strong blast from a fan scatters the seed as you winnow. Her winnowing technique is shown in the illustration below. Be sure to thoroughly shake out the sheet between batches to clean off all of the stray seed. She uses a sheet rather than a tarp because it is easier to fold and gather up in case some of the seeds spill.

WINNOWING WITH A FAN

A GREAT USE FOR GRAVITY

With round seeds, you can actually use gravity for winnowing. Suzanne Ashworth, the author of *Seed to Seed*, uses a small board on a slant as a "runway" for the seed. To winnow seed this way, you'll need a bowl and a smooth board of a size that's comfortable for you to lift and maneuver. Put some seed on one end of the board. Then lift the board and tilt it slightly, with the opposite end over the bowl. As the seed rolls down the board, direct a light air current up the board—your breath or a very small fan are ideal. "You'll have to adjust the angle of the board so that the seeds roll into the bowl, but most of the chaff blows away," Ashworth explains. Repeat the process until all of the chaff has been separated.

HAPPINESS IS A DRY SEED

Many seeds must be dried thoroughly before they will store properly. After collecting her seeds, Nancy Bubel, the author of *The New Seed-Starters Handbook,* spreads them on paper towels and lets them air-dry. A single layer of seeds works best. Suzanne Ashworth, the author of *Seed to Seed,* suggests using a ceramic or glass dish, screens, or even cookie sheets, which make it easy to scrape off stickier seeds after they've dried.

"Never dry in direct sunlight," says Ashworth. The drying surface may become too hot, especially if you've spread the seeds on a metal surface. For best results, monitor the temperature where you're drying—it shouldn't climb above 95°F. And don't dry seeds in the oven. If you plan to store the seed in airtight jars, Bubel recommends drying them for about a week. If you're going to briefly store them in envelopes that aren't airtight, then air-drying for a couple of days is fine.

THE UNSMUSHABLE SEED

How can you tell when your seed is dry enough? "I use the smush-mush technique," says Suzanne Ashworth, the author of *Seed to Seed.* If you can't bite into it or smush it, or if you hit it with a hammer and it shatters, the seed is dry enough to store. Smaller seeds are harder to judge, but they usually aren't as much of a problem as larger seeds, which you need to dry thoroughly before storing. When the seeds are unsmushable, store them in an airtight container as soon as possible so they won't reabsorb moisture.

STORAGE STRATEGY

"The most important things when saving seed are to keep them cool and to keep them dry," says Nancy Bubel, the author of *The New Seed-Starters Handbook.* Moisture and heat signal dry seed that it's time to get growing. They begin to use up their stored resources and lose a lot of their viability. Airtight glass jars with rubber gaskets, such as baby food jars, work well to keep out moisture. If you have enough jars, you can use one for each kind of seed you plan to save, placing the seeds directly in the jars. Or you can put different types of seeds in individual envelopes, plastic bags, or cloth bags and store them in a single jar.

Temperatures between 32° and 41°F are fine for storing most seeds, so your refrigerator is an ideal spot to keep

LET'S GET FRESH

Many wildflowers, perennials, and trees have seeds that rapidly lose their viability in storage. To get the best germination, sow these seeds outdoors in a nursery bed soon after you collect them. Here's a list of some seeds that germinate best when sown fresh:

Acer spp. (maples with spring-ripening seeds)
Aconitum spp. (monkshoods)
Aesculus spp. (horse chestnuts)
Alchemilla spp. (lady's-mantles)
Anemone spp. (spring-flowering anemones)
Arisaema triphyllum (Jack-in-the-pulpit)
Caltha palustris (marsh marigold)
Dicentra spp. (bleeding hearts)
Dodecatheon spp. (shooting-stars)
Eryngium spp. (sea hollies)
Fraxinus spp. (ashes)
Helleborus spp. (hellebores)
Linum spp. (flax)
Mertensia virginica (Virginia bluebells)
Quercus spp. (oaks)
Sanguinaria canadensis (bloodroot)
Stokesia spp. (Stoke's asters)
Tiarella spp. (foamflowers)

them. A cool, dry basement or root cellar may also work, if you don't have room in your refrigerator.

HOW DRY I AM

Desiccants are a great aid for controlling moisture that may have sneaked into your seed-storage jars. Suzanne Ashworth, the author of *Seed to Seed,* suggests putting a cupful of silica gel in a cloth bag and setting it in a 1- or 1½-gallon jar and then filling the rest of the jar with labeled envelopes of seeds. One of the best things about silica gel, which is available from craft stores that sell supplies for drying flowers, is that it's reusable. Most types contain indicator crystals that change from blue to pink as they absorb moisture. When the gel's indicator crystals turn pink, dry the gel for reuse by putting it in the oven at 200°F. When it's dry, the crystals will be blue again. Store the dry gel in an airtight container.

"One easy desiccant to use is powdered milk," says Nancy Bubel, the author of *The New Seed-Starters Handbook.* It's not as effective as silica gel, but it's cheaper. To use this desiccant, pour some powdered milk into a tissue or paper towel, and twist the ends together. Place it in the jar along with your seeds, as shown in the illustration at left. (It's best to use a jar with a rubber gasket seal.) If you're storing for several months, check the powder every two to four months, and change it if it's damp.

MOISTURE SAVES SOME SEEDS

Not all seed benefits from dry storage. In fact, Currier McEwen, M.D., an iris breeder from Maine, discovered that adding a tiny bit of moisture before storing iris seeds actually improves germination. When he harvests iris seeds, he opens the pods, empties the seeds into a dish, and removes any seeds that don't look plump and healthy. He puts the healthy seeds in a small plastic bag with three or four drops of water (depending on how many seeds per bag)—just enough to be moist but not wet. He then seals the bag airtight and puts it in the refrigerator. He stores the seeds above freezing and plants them in the spring. "If you live down South, you don't have to store the seeds," explains Dr. McEwen. "You could plant them right away if you wanted to." Dr. McEwen advises you not to store Siberian or Japanese iris seeds for more than a year. See "Wet and Wild" at left for a list of other plants that benefit from damp storage.

seeds

tissue filled with powdered milk

A "sachet" of powdered milk can serve as a desiccant in a jar of stored seeds.

WET AND WILD

Dry storage is the kiss of death to many wildflower seeds. If you can't sow the seeds listed below within a few weeks of collecting them, store them on a moist paper towel or in moist peat moss in a plastic bag in the refrigerator.

Anemonella thalictroides (rue anemone)
Claytonia virginica (spring beauty)
Corydalis spp. (corydalis)
Dicentra spp. (bleeding hearts)
Eranthis hyemalis (winter aconite)
Hepatica spp. (hepaticas)
Jeffersonia diphylla (twinleaf)
Sanguinaria canadensis (bloodroot)
Tiarella spp. (foamflowers)
Trillium spp. (trilliums)
Viola spp. (violets)

SHARE YOUR SEEDS

Want to join a group of enthusiastic gardeners interested in growing and preserving seeds? Then join a seed exchange. Seed exchanges will help you locate hard-to-find, rare, or unusual seeds and will give you a chance to share your own special seeds with other members.

Suzanne Ashworth, who is a member of the Seed Savers Exchange, says people usually first become members because they're interested in a vegetable that someone in their family grew at one time, or they're interested in unusual and different cultivars. "After that, they start to understand some of the reasons why the exchange exists. They can't get these unusual items anywhere else. If they, in fact, don't grow it and keep offering it, it could vanish," says Ashworth.

Each exchange functions a bit differently. In some cases, you pay a fee to have your seed listed in a catalog, and members write directly to you to get the seed. Other exchanges have a central address that accepts seed donations, packages them, and sends them to members. For a partial list of exchanges, see "Seed Exchanges" at right.

THE GARDEN PROFESSIONALS

Suzanne Ashworth is the author of *Seed to Seed*. She is a language specialist teacher for city schools in Sacramento, California, and teaches gardening and botany classes at American River College in Sacramento.

Nancy Bubel, a Pennsylvania garden writer, is the author of *The New Seed-Starter's Handbook* and *52 Weekend Garden Projects*.

David Cavagnaro is a garden manager in charge of preservation gardens at Heritage Farm for Seed Savers Exchange in Decorah, Iowa. In addition, he is a nature and horticultural photographer.

Ken Ettlinger is the director of the Long Island Seed Company in Flanders, New York, which offers vegetable seed blends and over 200 tomato cultivars.

Currier McEwen, M.D., a retired doctor of rheumatology, is an accomplished iris breeder at Seaways Gardens, located in South Harpswell, Maine. He has won many awards, including the Hybridizers Award from the American Iris Society.

Jean M. A. Nick is an associate editor of garden books for Rodale Press, Inc. She has extensive experience in the commercial greenhouse industry and currently raises vegetables and small fruits on 1 acre in her home garden.

Tim Peters is the research director for Territorial Seed Company, a mail-order company located in Cottage Grove, Oregon, that specializes in vegetables for the maritime northwest.

Andre Viette is the owner of Andre Viette Farm and Nursery in Fishersville, Virginia. The company sells over 3,000 species and cultivars of perennials wholesale and retail via mail order.

SEED EXCHANGES

Here are some organizations that have seed exchanges for members. Unless otherwise indicated, for membership information, send a self-addressed, stamped envelope to the address listed.

American Horticultural Society
7931 E. Boulevard Dr.
Alexandria, VA 22308
Society members receive an annual list for a wide variety of plants.

American Rock Garden Society
Jacques Mommens
P.O. Box 67
Millwood, NY 10546
Members receive an annual list, featuring rock garden plants and perennials.

The Flower and Herb Exchange
Route 3, Box 239
Decorah, IA 52101
Members can contribute or obtain seeds of rare flowers and herbs saved by other members.

Seed Savers Exchange
Route 3, Box 239
Decorah, IA 52101
Members share unusual or heirloom vegetable seeds saved by other members.

Southern Exposure Seed
    Exchange
P.O. Box 158
North Garden, VA 22959
This exchange offers hard-to-find seeds of vegetables, flowers, herbs, and grains to gardeners who contributed seeds.

Container Gardening

Growing plants in containers is one of the most rewarding types of gardening. You can let your imagination go wild—moving plants around as your mood or the seasons change or growing exotic specimens indoors that wouldn't survive the weather outside. With containers, you can group plants that have different soil requirements and can't be combined easily in the same garden bed. You can even use special training techniques to grow a dwarf version of a bamboo or a 20-foot tree.

But potted plants are the pets of the plant world, and if you want to be a successful container gardener, you have to take good care of them. A potted plant is dependent on you—for moisture, for the proper growing medium and sufficient nutrients, and for light, indoors or out. Even the container you choose can affect a plant's health.

The following tips will help you provide the care that your container-grown plants need to thrive, whether you are raising trees or forcing daffodil bulbs. You will also find handy hints on planting and design, as well as lists of plants that are best suited for certain conditions.

Making Mix and Choosing Containers

After you've decided what plants you want to grow, your first priority is choosing the right containers and potting soil. You can match your containers to your house style, personal taste, or the type of plant you're growing. (For example, a tropical-looking bamboo or vine would look at home in a wicker basket.) You'll be amazed at the variety of containers available—from standard clay and plastic to half-barrels and "found objects" like old teapots or watering cans. Here are some great tips for finding or making good soil mixes and containers.

DO YOU HAVE SOIL SAVVY?

If your garden soil produces luscious tomatoes or stunning roses, you may wonder whether it would work just as well for your potted plants. Definitely not, says Rita Buchanan, a Connecticut garden writer. "I think one of the most common mistakes container gardeners make is digging up soil from the garden and putting it in a pot," she says. "A pot is so little compared to the garden—moisture just doesn't drain through a pot like it does in the ground." That means you need a soil that won't pack down too easily or stay wet too long. Buy a commercial potting soil mix or make your own. Buchanan suggests mixing equivalent amounts of loamy garden soil, screened compost or peat moss, and perlite or coarse sand.

FACELIFT FOR PLASTIC POTS

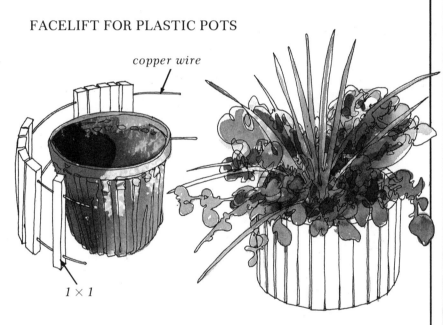

copper wire

1×1

Plastic pots are unquestionably useful because they're lightweight and reusable. But they don't make much of a show on the patio or deck. One alternative to repotting in a decorative container is to hide the plastic pot in an attractive "cover-up." This handsome wooden pot is really a shell of 1×1's. To make one, cut the 1×1's to the right length to cover your pot. Drill holes through each piece about 1 inch from the top and bottom, as shown. String the pieces together with copper wire.

COARSE MIX IS FINE FOR POTS

Check the heft on that bag of potting mix before you lug the sack home. Jim Wilson, a cohost of public television's "The Victory Garden," feels that the single most important thing about growing plants in containers is using a coarse-textured growing mix and avoiding dense, heavy

---

BYPASS PEAT

Many gardeners are discovering that peat moss isn't a perfect soil amendment. Not only is it hard to wet and rewet, but it has little nutrient value. And as more countries are moving to protect their native bogs, peat is becoming more expensive. So the next time you need a potting soil amendment, consider one of the following alternatives:

Finished compost. This amendment retains moisture, aerates, adds humus, and is a mild balanced fertilizer.

Composted manure. Manure that has been composted is a good source of nitrogen, potassium, and phosphorus.

Rice hull compost. This type of compost is an excellent aerator but has little nutrient value.

Cotton burr compost. This compost retains moisture easily, has a high nutrient content, and doesn't tie up nitrogen in the soil. Be sure that the product you purchase is chemical-free. It's a good idea to try germinating some seeds in the mix before using it in quantity to be sure it doesn't contain chemicals that might injure plants.

GIVE POTS A WINTER COAT

Pots made of clay or concrete are more likely to come through freezing winter weather without cracking if they're sealed on the inside. Coat the inside walls and bottom of the container with a paint-on roof coating (not to be confused with roofing bull). Use an inexpensive paintbrush with nylon bristles to apply the coating. Let dry thoroughly before filling coated pots with soil and plants.

MAKE YOUR OWN MOSSY POTS

Try this recipe for mossy pots from Kipp McIntyre, a co-owner of Mostly Moss, a Georgia business that specializes in sculptured moss gardens. First, collect mosses from around your yard. Finely chop them, and allow the bits to dry out. Then follow the recipe below to make a moss slurry in a deep bucket.

   1 c. flour
   2 c. buttermilk
   2 pkg. active dry yeast
   2 tbsp. corn syrup
1-1½ c. dried, crumbled moss

Mix together all ingredients in a bucket. Place the bucket in the sun for three days. When the mixture is really smelly, brush it liberally on the outsides of your clay pots. Then wrap the pots in plastic wrap and set them in the sun. "In two weeks, the pots will mold," says McIntyre. "In six to eight weeks, moss plants will be growing well."

potting soil. Wilson suggests that when you're buying potting soil in retail outlets you judge bags of similar volume by weight, because the label usually provides little information about contents. (Potting mixes don't have to list ingredients.) "If the bag is heavy, don't buy it," he says. "Some mixes contain sand to add weight, so you'll think you're getting more; if it's river sand of varying particle size, it just packs down in the pot. The other thing to watch for is bags where the soil is [made] wet to make it heavier and give it a rich, black color."

PICK A PERFECT POT

Not all containers are created equal—that's the word from Holly H. Shimizu, the acting assistant executive director at the U.S. Botanic Garden in Washington, D.C. If you're trying to decide which kind of container to use, she suggests keeping these points in mind:

◆ Clay and terra-cotta pots are porous, so you'll probably need to water plants in them more often than if you used plastic containers. But soil in these types of pots stays cooler than in plastic—a benefit in sunny sites and hot weather.
◆ Plastic pots hold heat and water better than clay pots. They're also lighter and less expensive, but they have a tendency to crack or break with age.
◆ Stone and concrete containers are extremely durable, but they're very heavy and relatively expensive.

Whatever kind of pot you choose, remember that any container used for plants should have holes for adequate drainage. Shimizu says that using old pots is fine, as long as you care for them properly. "When you recycle your pots, it's very important to make sure they're clean. A lot of people neglect to do that—and the pots can carry diseases that way," she says. She recommends removing old soil and plant debris, soaking the pot in water, then scrubbing it with a mild liquid detergent. Rinse the pot thoroughly, and dry it. Your container is now ready for a new plant!

Continuing Care

Choosing a pot and potting soil mix gives your plants a good start, but you can't stop there. Container plants need ongoing care—watering, feeding, grooming, watching for signs of pests and diseases, and if they stay outdoors all year, winterizing. Surprisingly, the biggest hurdle for most plant owners is watering. Here are some expert tips and tricks for handling watering and other routine chores.

HELP! THEY CAN'T SWIM!

Overwatering is the number one problem in container gardening, according to Tovah Martin, the staff horticulturist at Logee's Greenhouses in Connecticut. "When you're living with a plant intimately, you tend to baby it, and that usually means watering it too frequently," she says. "You have to remember that the soil does not go down to China." When you overwater, you are actually suffocating the roots, which can eventually die from lack of oxygen.

So when *should* you water? "When the soil is dry to the touch," says Martin. She suggests sticking your finger about ½ to 1 inch down into the soil; if it feels dry, it's time to get out the watering can. Don't let the soil become parched, however. If it gets too dry, it won't be able to absorb moisture, and the water will simply run down the sides of the container.

Sometimes the plant itself is your best moisture barometer. Martin lets her plants go into a slight wilt before watering them. "It usually does no harm to let plants wilt slightly," she says. "As a matter of fact, with many plants, such as bougainvilleas, it will promote bud formation."

How much water is enough? Martin recommends leaving about ¼ to ½ inch between the soil surface and the rim of the container when you're potting a plant. Then, each time you water, fill the pot to the rim once. Don't succumb to the temptation to refill it again and again, or you'll drown the roots.

PUT PANTY HOSE IN YOUR POTS

Old panty hose can be part of a handy system for watering houseplants and hanging baskets. Some houseplants, such as African violets, wood sorrels, and ferns, need more water than others. If you have trouble remembering to make those extra watering trips, try using a hidden water reservoir for passive irrigation. Barbara W. Ellis, the managing editor of garden books for Rodale Press, has rigged up a system using a plastic freezer container under each extra-thirsty plant in her office, as shown in the illustration

DOUBLE-POTTING BEATS THE HEAT

You can prevent the roots of sun-baked container plants from overheating by double-potting. Simply place the plant—pot and all—into a bigger pot. Then fill the space between the two containers with peat moss. The layer of peat surrounding the inner pot will help keep the roots cool and moist during the summer heat.

THE ROOT OF THE PROBLEM

When's the last time you looked at the roots of your potted plants? The last time you repotted them? Never? If your plants are looking peaked, inspect their root balls. Taking your plants out of their pots from time to time to inspect the roots won't hurt them. Simply turn the pots upside down and gently lift the plants out. If the roots look bright and shiny, you'll know they're healthy. But if they look soft, rotted, or discolored or if they smell bad, that's a sign of trouble. Cut away diseased or discolored roots and repot in a sterile soil mix.

◆

below. She pots up the houseplant in a shallow container, such as an azalea pot or bulb pan, that has a 1-inch-wide strip of panty hose inserted through the bottom drainage hole. The panty hose strip hangs down into the freezer container and wicks water up to the soil mix. She conceals the whole setup inside a larger decorative pot. "It's a really convenient system for plants that need more-frequent watering," says Ellis.

panty hose wick   *water reservoir*

A hidden water reservoir and a wick made from a strip of old panty hose are part of a nifty passive watering setup for a potted plant.

WINTERIZING POTTED TREES

If you garden in the North, take special precautions to make sure your hardy containerized trees and shrubs survive the winter outdoors. According to Christina R. J. Pey, a supervisor for the production greenhouses at the Missouri Botanical Garden, the most important thing is to check the size of the plant's root ball. "If the root ball is almost touching the container sides, chances are the plant will be affected by the cold and may even die," says Pey.

ROCKS IN YOUR POTS?

Contrary to what some gardeners may think, putting a layer of gravel or other similar material in the bottom of a container does not improve drainage. In fact, it can decrease plant growth, since the space occupied by rocks could hold soil and roots instead.

There is still a valid reason for putting rocks in pots, however: Pebbles, rocks, gravel, stone chips, or broken pottery can keep pots from blowing over.

HUMIDIFY YOUR HOUSEPLANTS

Keep your moisture-loving houseplants happy with a "pebble tray." To make one, spread a 1-inch-deep layer of pebbles in a waterproof tray. Then pour water into the tray until the water is about ½ inch deep. Set your plant pots on the pebbles. The water in the tray will evaporate slowly, humidifying the immediate area around the plant. To provide constant humidity, regularly refill the pebble tray with water.

SOIL WON'T PASS THIS SCREEN TEST

Does soil wash out of the bottom of your pots every time you water them? Try putting a screening material such as mesh wire over the drainage hole before potting your plants. Not only will the soil stay in, but you'll have fewer millipedes, insects, and other "undesirables" creeping in.

If the roots of any of your trees or shrubs are too near the sides of their container, consider moving the plant to a larger pot. If your plant is already in as large a pot as you want or have room for, you can prune the roots back. (When you root-prune, prune the top growth in the same proportion.)

Another way to winterize container-grown trees and shrubs is to move them to a protected site—against the side of a building or in a garage that gets lots of light. Clumping your plants together also provides protection against the cold. For larger containers that can't easily be moved, Pey suggests piling mulch up around them.

Creative Containers

Containers aren't just for houseplants or annual flowers. You can grow dwarf fruit trees, shrubs, flowering perennials and bulbs, ornamental grasses, vines, and just about any other plant in a container. You can have a container vegetable garden, herb garden—even water garden. So stretch your limits, and try something different. Here, the experts offer us some ideas for branching out into new areas with container gardening.

THEME GARDENS, CONTAINER-STYLE

The sky's the limit when it comes to container garden ideas. For something a bit out of the ordinary, try a garden with a lemon-fragrance theme, like the one on display one summer at the U.S. Botanic Garden in Washington, D.C. "All of the plants had some lemon flavor or golden flowers," says Holly H. Shimizu, the acting assistant executive director at the U.S. Botanic Garden. To start a similar container garden of your own, she suggests planting lemon-scented marigolds (*Tagetes tenuifolia*), golden lemon thyme (*Thymus × citriodorus* 'Aureus'), lemongrass (*Cymbopogon citratus*), lemon balm (*Melissa officinalis*), and lemon basil (*Ocimum basilicum* 'Citriodorum'). Don't forget lemon-scented geraniums (*Pelargonium crispum*), including 'Prince Rupert' and 'Mabel Gray', "the most lemony of all," according to Shimizu. "It's so lemony, your mouth waters," she says.

If a more formal design appeals to you, try a container knot garden. Shimizu recommends a figure eight com-

MULCH FOR MOISTURE

If your pots seem to dry out quickly between waterings, try mulching them. Rita Buchanan, a Connecticut garden writer, recommends using very fine gravel. (You can get it from a gravel quarry, a riverbed, or the seashore.) Wash the gravel thoroughly to remove dust or salt, then spread about a ¼- or ½-inch-thick layer on the surface of the soil.

LET THE SUN SHINE IN

Houseplants can generally tolerate more light than most people think. For example, rex begonias won't tolerate full sun outdoors, but in most parts of the country, they will do fine in a sunny south-facing window. Keep in mind, however, that your plant can get too much of a good thing. If the foliage starts to bleach out, move the plant to a shadier spot.

AN APPLE A DAY

To get bromeliads to bloom, you can put them—pot and all—inside a clear plastic bag with an apple for about a week. (Keep out of direct sun.) The ethylene gas given off by the fruit will induce the plants to flower. But beware: Ethylene has the opposite effect on bulbs, and it can actually destroy the developing buds. Before you put bulbs in the refrigerator for storage, be sure to remove apples and other fruit.

TROPICALS TAKE THE HEAT

Temperature has a critical effect on growth of tropical plants in containers indoors. Fred Saleet, the owner of The Banana Tree, a Pennsylvania company that specializes in uncommon tropical seeds, recommends the following temperature regimes:

• *Heliconia* spp. (heliconias): daytime—80°F or higher; nighttime—not below 70°F
• *Musa* spp. (bananas): daytime—75°F or higher; nighttime—at least 67°F
• *Strelitzia* spp. (bird-of-paradise): daytime—80°F or higher; nighttime—not below 68°F
• *Theobroma cacao* (chocolate-tree): daytime and nighttime—at least 70°F

Keep in mind that temperature requirements vary according to which species you're growing.

REUSABLE BULBS

Contrary to popular belief, if you've forced bulbs in pots for early spring bloom, you *can* get them to bloom in the garden again next spring. Just keep them well-watered, provide lots of light, and give them a few doses of fish emulsion, liquid seaweed, or other organic fertilizer as they're blooming. When the foliage starts to turn yellow, decrease watering. Wait until the foliage has withered completely, then put the pots in a warm, dry place where they can sit all summer. By fall, the bulbs will be ready to plant outdoors.

posed of clipped fragrant herbs and topiary—for example, silver and golden thyme to form the eight and a myrtle (*Myrtus communis*) topiary to fill the center of each of the circles. "The topiaries we used in our display had twisted stems and round heads, like lollipops," she says. "You can use any number of complementary plants—any other kind of topiary, if you want height, or another little filler in the middle of the eight. It depends on whether you like the open look or the closed look."

TRY THESE FOUR TROPICALS

If you're thinking about growing exotic plants indoors, you'll need to tend to their needs year-round, says Fred Saleet, the owner of The Banana Tree, a Pennsylvania company that specializes in uncommon tropical seeds. According to Saleet, four tropical plants that are relatively easy to grow and have the same general cultural requirements are bananas (*Musa* spp.), cacao or chocolate-tree (*Theobroma cacao*), the exotic bird-of-paradise (*Strelitzia* spp.), and heliconias (*Heliconia* spp.).

All four of these plants need a combination of warmth, bright light, and high humidity—and not just when it's sunny and warm outside. Says Saleet, "Many people grow them very well in the spring and summer. Then, in the winter, they ask, 'Why is it dying? It was growing so well!'" He suggests using a high-intensity light (100 watts or higher) when the weather turns dark and cold. "You want consistency in the climatic conditions," he says. "You don't want a break in the action."

Keep in mind that these tropical plants, particularly the banana, also require frequent fertilization. "If a plant is pushing out one flower after another, that means it's in need of a supply of nutrients," says Saleet. Don't make the mistake of fertilizing the plant if it looks sick, however. Although there's a chance that it's suffering from nutrient deficiency, more than likely there's something else, such as spider mite infestation, that's causing the problem.

DOUBLE YOUR BULBS, DOUBLE YOUR BLOOM

Ever wonder how exhibitors at flower shows get so many tulips or daffodils to bloom in one container? "The bulbs are planted one on top of the other," says Raymond J. Rogers, the garden editor for Dorling Kindersley in New York. "That's why the pots look like they're jam-packed—they *are* jam-packed." When the bulbs bloom, you'll have a pot that's bursting with color—a real showstopper on a gray winter day.

According to Rogers, who has won many awards for his bulb entries at the Philadelphia Flower Show, it's best to start with a soil mix composed of 2 parts good garden soil, 2 parts potting mix, 1 part perlite, and 1 part #3 grade (coarse) sand. Here's the method, which is also shown in the illustrations on this page:

1. Put the soil mix in the bottom one-third of the pot, then put in a layer of bulbs pointed-side-up. (How much mix you add depends on bulb size. For example, plant long-necked daffodils deeper than short-necked daffodils.)

2. Add mix until the tops of the bulbs just poke through the surface, then position a second layer of bulbs in between the tops of the first layer.

3. Add another layer of mix until you can barely see the tops of the bulbs poking through.

This method works best with tulips and daffodils, though some people have had success planting reticulated iris (*Iris reticulata*) in double layers. Rogers doesn't recommend double-planting for hyacinths, which tend to push each other out of the soil. Your potted bulbs will require an initial cold treatment and proper subsequent care to force them into bloom. For information on cold treatments and caring for potted bulb plants, refer to books on indoor gardening or perennials listed in "Recommended Reading" on page 333.

**MY, HOW SMALL
YOU'VE GROWN!**

The next time you start a
bonsai, plant a seedling of the
same species in the ground at
the same time. Within a few years,
you'll be amazed at the difference
in size between your miniature
containerized specimen and that
shady tree outside.

**TOP TEN HERBS
TO GROW INDOORS**

Here are ten herbs that are
excellent for indoor growing, recommended by Christina R. J. Pey,
a supervisor for the production
greenhouses at the Missouri
Botanical Garden:

Basil	Oregano
Dill	Parsley
Fennel	Sage
Marjoram	Tarragon
Mint	Thyme

◆ BE BOLD WITH BONSAI

"People don't realize how easy bonsai is," says John
Lennon, the owner of J. Lennon Landscaping in California.
"Everybody's afraid of them, and they shouldn't be." Lennon
feels that cultivating the exotic-looking dwarfed trees can
be every bit as easy as growing any other trees in containers.

Lennon suggests starting with Japanese maples (*Acer
japonicum* and *A. palmatum*) or junipers (*Juniperus* spp.),
both of which are "forgiving." You can buy the starters sold
in nurseries or simply start them from seedlings yourself.
Japanese maples like to be kept moist, so be sure to water
them frequently. They'll need a fair amount of sun, too.
Junipers like more light (preferably full sun) but less water
than maples do.

According to Lennon, one of the secrets of bonsai
success is repotting the plant on a regular basis, as you
would any containerized tree. It's best to perform this task
during the plant's dormant stage, usually in winter. Every
year or two, pull the bonsai tree out of its container, and
knock off about one-third of the root ball with a three-
pronged claw or other hand tool, as shown in the illustration below. (You can also use pruning shears to cut the
excess roots.) "You've got to be brutal," says Lennon. "If
you aren't vigorous with them, they won't come back vigorously." Repot the plant using fresh soil, then fertilize. The
plant should eventually respond with plenty of new growth.

Pruning is, of course, central to bonsai care. "That's
where practice comes in," says Lennon. He suggests taking
off about one-third of the plant each time you repot it. Keep

in mind that maples usually send out lots of new growth after they're pruned, so you'll need to prune the shoots regularly to keep the shape you have established. Junipers tend to produce most of their new growth all at once, so they won't need constant pruning.

According to Lennon, how you prune depends on the effect you want to achieve. For instance, if you want your maple to look as natural as possible, you'll need to round out the crown of the plant. Removing most of the branches from one side of a juniper can give it a kind of windswept look. Regardless of the style you choose, it's best to keep the center open to allow for good air circulation and prevent problems with pests.

THE GARDEN PROFESSIONALS

Rita Buchanan is a garden writer from Winsted, Connecticut, and an editor for Houghton Mifflin's Taylor's Guides. She is the author of *A Weaver's Garden* and is a former associate editor of *Fine Gardening* magazine.

Barbara W. Ellis is the managing editor of garden books at Rodale Press, Inc. She is a former publications director/editor for *American Horticulturist*.

John Lennon is the owner of J. Lennon Landscaping, a large-scale residential landscape maintenance company in San Anselmo, California. Lennon was formerly a gardener at George Lucas's Skywalker Ranch.

Frederick McGourty is a co-owner of Hillside Gardens in Norfolk, Connecticut. The nursery specializes in uncommon perennials and perennial garden design. He is the author of *The Perennial Gardener*.

Kipp McIntyre is a co-owner of Mostly Moss, located in Brushy Knob, Georgia, a business specializing in the design and installation of sculptured moss gardens.

Tovah Martin is the staff horticulturalist at Logee's Greenhouses in Danielson, Connecticut. She is the author of *Once Upon a Windowsill* and *The Essence of Paradise*.

Christina R. J. Pey is a supervisor for the production greenhouses at the Missouri Botanical Garden in St. Louis, Missouri. Her specialty is the aquatic collection, which includes tropical water lilies.

Raymond J. Rogers is the garden editor for Dorling Kindersley, Inc., in New York City, a branch of Dorling Kindersley Limited of London. He is a multiple ribbon winner in the bulb classes of the Philadelphia Flower Show.

Fred Saleet is the owner of The Banana Tree, Inc., a wholesale seed company in Easton, Pennsylvania, that specializes in uncommon tropical seeds.

Holly H. Shimizu is the acting assistant executive director at the U.S. Botanic Garden in Washington, D.C., and is a former curator of the National Herb Garden of the U.S. National Arboretum.

Jim Wilson is a cohost of public television's "The Victory Garden." He is the author of *Landscaping with Container Plants*, *Masters of the Victory Garden*, and *Landscaping with Wildflowers*.

BEST FOR HANGING BASKETS

For attractive indoor hanging baskets, try these plants recommended by Tovah Martin, the staff horticulturist at Logee's Greenhouses in Connecticut:

Aeschynanthus spp. (lipstick plants)
Begonia 'Tom Ment 1', 'Orange Rubra', and 'Elaine' (angel-wing begonia cultivars)
Columnea spp. (columneas)
Kalanchoe pumila, K. uniflora (kalanchoes)
Pelargonium peltatum (ivy geranium)

TOP FIVE FOR HOT POTS

If you need perennials that can stand hot, dry conditions in containers, try these five recommended by Frederick McGourty, a co-owner of Hillside Gardens, a Connecticut nursery that specializes in uncommon perennials:

Amsonia tabernaemontana var. *montana* (willow blue star)
Asclepias tuberosa (butterfly weed)
Gaillardia spp., especially *G. × grandiflora* 'Baby Cole' (blanket flowers)
Opuntia humifusa (prickly pear)
Yucca spp., especially *Y. filamentosa* 'Golden Sword' (yuccas)

PART 2

BE A SMART GARDEN MANAGER S

Smart garden management pays. It saves you money and allows you more time to relax—rather than work—in your yard and garden. Your plants will look beautiful, and you'll reap bountiful harvests of homegrown fruits and vegetables. It pays to select the best plants for your site and to take that extra measure of care to help them thrive. Improving your soil and making compost are two important first steps to creating a healthy garden. Preventing problems from insects and diseases, animal pests, and weeds will also result in happier plants and a happier gardener.

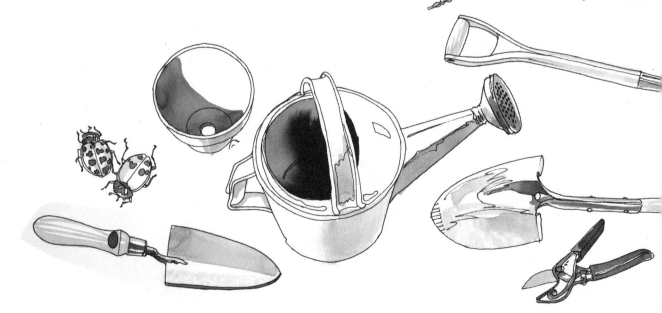

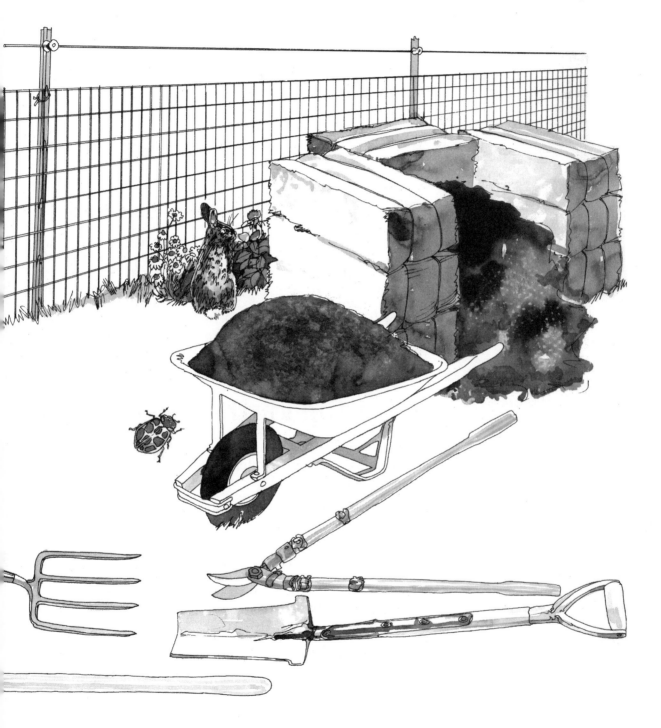

Planning and Shopping Smart

How can you improve your garden while doing less work? Plan in advance. Many of us never seem to find the time for it, but making a garden plan can actually save time, labor, and expense during the gardening season. Perhaps the following ideas from successful gardeners and designers on how to plan, make garden maps, and keep records can inspire you to really get organized ahead of time.

Once you've laid your garden plans, you'll be ready for one of the most exciting, yet most frustrating, aspects of gardening—the shopping. If you know exactly what plants or seeds you want, shopping is easy. But more often than not, you have to make decisions balancing what's best for the garden with what's best for the wallet. In this chapter, garden professionals share hints and insights that will help you be a smarter garden shopper whether you're shopping by mail order or at your local nursery or garden center.

Planning for the Big Picture

Planning can be extra-important for gardening the organic way. Having excellent-quality soil and using preventive techniques to keep pests from getting too pesky means thinking and doing before you plant. You'll find lots of helpful tips on improving your soil in "Balancing the Soil," beginning on page 89. And we've got great ideas for preventing pest problems in "Controlling Insect and Disease Problems," beginning on page 131.

But planning is a mix of the practical and the creative. We'll begin here with some of the big principles that you might want to mull over as you dream up your master garden plan.

DESIGN MANY GARDENS IN ONE

Don't be afraid to break free of traditional yard designs as you plan. Go beyond the typical rectangular plot for vegetables and fruit, flowers and shrubs around the foundation, and isolated shade trees dotting the lawn. The award-winning garden design of Kansas gardeners William and

Brenda Reid mixes and blends different types of edibles and ornamentals throughout the landscape. Their corner lot produces high yields of fruits, nuts, and vegetables, has imaginative play areas for the children, provides birds and wildlife with year-round habitat and food, and is beautiful from any aspect. William Reid says, "Brenda did most of the initial design work. Essentially, she started with the perimeters and worked herself inward, always leaving pathways and walks where they naturally fell."

Here are some of the Reids' unusual design ideas:

♦ A border of perennial wildflowers mixed with dwarf apples, dwarf pears, raspberries, and pecans surrounds the property.

♦ Apples and pears espaliered against a wall form a backdrop for perennials. Other fruit trees and native pecan trees are scattered throughout the yard.

♦ Many plants in the landscape attract birds, including Buffalo currants, gooseberries, a pawpaw tree, persimmons, mulberries, elderberries, and an edible viburnum.

♦ Beans grow up and over a bean tunnel to create a special play area for children. (You'll find details on erecting a tunnel in "Build a Bean Tunnel" on page 170.)

♦ Asparagus is planted in several places in the yard as a backdrop to other plantings.

PICK PLANTING SITES WITH PRECISION

The key to a successful planting is matching the plants to the site. This is especially true for plants that you are giving a more or less permanent home, like perennials, shrubs, and trees.

If you put a plant in a site that doesn't suit its growing needs, chances are it will suffer from pest problems or just not perform well. "People tend to put perennials where they want to see them, not where they will grow best," explains Dick Lighty, Ph.D., the director of Mount Cuba Center for the Study of Piedmont Flora in Delaware. "I often see people putting sun-loving plants in shade. Or if they put them in sun, as they should, they forget about whether the plants need water at the roots or not." You'll do your garden a favor if you research the needs of the plants you like. Be firm in weeding out plants that are simply not right for the site.

Cole Burrell, a Minnesota garden designer, explains

HOW HARDY ARE YOU?

There is no guarantee that the plant you buy will flourish in its new site. Mother Nature may work against you. Referring to the 1990 USDA Plant Hardiness Zone Map, shown on page 336, can help you choose appropriate plants. To find out which zone your home is in, find your state and the approximate location of your town on the map. Use the key in the bottom righthand corner of the map to determine which zone you are in.

When buying expensive plants or trees and shrubs, it's wise to choose those that are hardy *one zone farther north* than your location. For example, if you're in Zone 6, choose plants that are hardy to Zone 5. For less-prominent or inexpensive plants, you can choose those hardy to your zone as well.

Keep in mind that the 1990 zone map is a revision of a map dating from the 1960s. While each zone still represents the same range of average annual minimum temperature, where the zones fall has shifted on the new map. So if you thought you lived in Zone 7, for example, you may now find that you live in Zone 6.

NATIVE PLANT SOCIETIES

To find out more about native plants for your local area, contact your state native plant or wildflower society. The New England Wildflower Society can supply a broad range of information about native plants for the eastern United States. Their address is:

New England Wildflower Society
Garden in the Woods
Hemenway Rd.
Framingham, MA 01701

SIMPLIFY A SMALL YARD

To make a small yard look bigger, simplify the planting scheme, using broad sweeps of the same plants instead of 20 different ones, says Washington State garden designer Anne Janisse. Avoid limiting the landscape to perennials, she says, and get good bones in place first. Use a simple but strong design, aiming for year-round appeal. Use shrubs and trees to add structure and draw the eye.

Choosing plants that are the right size is a chronic problem, Janisse says, and it's an even greater problem in a small yard. Avoid impulse buying at the nursery, and research and plan your plantings ahead of time.

that while you can't change your basic climate or the exposure of a site, you can improve soil conditions before planting to suit the plants you want to grow. "In my own garden, I brought in a lot of compost and manure to improve the soil in one spot where I have lots of perennials," says Burrell. "As the garden moves out to the front, the soil gets sandy and dry." For poorer conditions like those, Burrell selects perennials that can tolerate dry soil, including rough gayfeather (*Liatris aspera*), dotted blazing-star (*Liatris punctata*), wild bergamot (*Monarda fistulosa*), and prairie coral bells (*Heuchera richardsonii*).

GO NATIVE BUT NOT WILD

There's no such thing as a *no-maintenance* landscape, but the wise use of native plants can help create a *low-maintenance* one. "Natives often have the advantage of being disease- and insect-resistant. Some are widely adaptable or tolerant of difficult landscape conditions," says Dick Bir, a North Carolina State University extension specialist. One example of a wide-ranging native tree that can be a wonderful addition to the home landscape is sourwood (*Oxydendrum arboreum*). Hardy to Zone 5, sourwood is native to the eastern and southeastern United States, has excellent form, flowers in late summer, and displays brilliant autumn color.

Bir also notes that there are as many poor-choice native plants as there are good ones. Natives, like other plants, may need fertilizing, watering, and weeding to become established. They may have occasional pest problems and require some pruning.

"And going native," Bir points out, "doesn't mean taking plants from the wild. Even when removing common plants in plentiful supply, you may unknowingly be disturbing other species that might not grow there again for a century. You also don't know what problems, such as poison ivy roots, you might bring back to your property."

BE YOUR OWN DESIGNER

Are you puzzled by the prospect of how to design an attractive and interesting bed of ornamentals? If you feel intimidated by the complexities of design, relax. Nancy DuBrule, the owner of Natureworks, an organic garden center in Connecticut, suggests that beginners work from four easy principles, which she explains here in everyday terms:

1. **Put plants with opposite texture, shape, and form next to each other.** "Contrasts show each other off better," says DuBrule. For example, think of the contrast between a clump of grassy-leaved Siberian iris (*Iris sibirica*) and the full form of a large-blossomed clump of peonies.

2. **Pay attention to which plants retain good foliage throughout the season, and use them.** "If you build an interesting framework of foliage, you don't notice the plants that get scraggly after they bloom," says DuBrule. She suggests that gardeners include some plants such as artemisias, meadow rues (*Thalictrum* spp.), and sages for their foliage rather than their blooms.

3. **Plan a focal point for each month.** "It can be striking in color or outrageous in shape and form. You want it to catch the eye and hold attention," DuBrule explains. For example, a bold mass of an ornamental grass such as feather reed grass (*Calamagrostis acutiflora* 'Stricta') turns a striking orange-brown in the fall.

4. **Allow adequate space for each plant.** "Leave a minimum of 1½ square feet for each plant. Some, such as daylilies, require much more," says DuBrule. "If the garden looks too sparse while you're waiting for the perennials to fill in, plant annuals between them. But even then, be careful. Annuals can grow pretty large, too."

Practical Planning Pointers

Once you've set general goals for your yard and garden, focus on specific sites. Planning for the vegetable garden, where you're worried about ease of harvest and crop rotation, is different from planning for other areas, where your biggest concern may be keeping maintenance low. Here, several of our specialists offer tips on dealing with specific planning considerations.

FANCY-UP A FRONT GARDEN WITH FLOWERS

Urban gardeners often have only a small patch of land between the sidewalk and the front of the house. Usually, a little lawn and a foundation planting fill the space, but Sarah Williams, an experienced urban gardener from Vermont, suggests that gardeners try a mixed ornamental planting instead. She offers several points to keep in mind when designing a small front garden:

Limit colors. "Too many colors in one spot are visually

GROUP LANDSCAPE PLANTS

If you have difficult soil, such as sand or clay, you've no doubt worked pretty hard to make it palatable to your shrubs and trees. "It makes sense then," says Kris Medic Thomas, a landscape manager and arborist for the city of Columbus, Ohio, "to plant other trees, shrubs, perennials, and annuals in that area, too. But there's more to it than just making use of well-prepared soil." Trees, shrubs, and other plants have a better chance of survival if they share space. They are protected from mower damage, and they create microclimates for each other. For example, they shade each other's roots, lower soil temperature, and break the force of harsh winds.

WANTED: SINGLE GARDENERS

Most people enjoy the solitary time they spend in the garden. But as any single gardener can tell you, having gardening company is also fun. Nancy Farrell, an innovative organic gardener from Vermont, found people with whom she could share plants, information, enthusiasm, and work by placing an ad in the personals section of the local newspapers, saying that she was looking for other single gardeners. This group now meets regularly to trade extra planting stock, have potlucks, compare catalogs, and share good ideas. Also, at the local hospice, they put in a garden that they tend together.

RESEARCH BEFORE YOU MOVE

Buy a book and find out what your new area will be like before you move, advises John Hancock, the owner of a fruit farm in Indiana. When Hancock moved to California, he suffered gardening culture shock. "I put the spade in the ground, and it broke off like it was adobe," he says. He was surprised, too, to find that lilacs wouldn't thrive without a cold winter.

Now Hancock gardens according to the California climate. He terraced a hillside for California poppies in three colors. They last for only two weeks, he says, "but it's a great two weeks!" He also plants in fall rather than spring to take advantage of winter rains. Hancock suggests doing a little "garden eavesdropping" when you move. "Look at what your neighbors are doing," he advises transplanted gardeners, "and do the same."

confusing," says Williams. "Stick to two or three—for instance, white, a range of blues, and a range of pinks—and be sure the major house color and any trim colors are repeated and complemented by the flowers in the front."

Keep plants in proportion. "You don't want to have to remove something because it has gotten too big or is giving too much shade," Williams explains.

Plan for continuous blooms throughout the season. You can have a gorgeous floral display from the first bulbs to the last chrysanthemums. Williams says, "A mixture of annuals, biennials, and perennials gives the largest visual variety and longest bloom time. Leaving spots for annuals varies the look every year and keeps the garden exciting."

Let low-maintenance be your watchword. Front gardens are highly visible, and you don't want them to end up as an embarrassment. "Bark mulch is a lifesaver," declares Williams. "It keeps weeding chores to a minimum, and its dark color contrasts nicely with the flowers."

REDUCE RENOVATION WOES

One daunting feature of an "inherited" yard can be an overgrown ornamental garden. If you face the task of renovating such a garden, you may appreciate these tips from Nancy DuBrule, the owner of Natureworks, an organic garden center in Connecticut. "First of all, find the plants that resist being moved," she suggests. "Design around them if possible." According to DuBrule, plants in this category include balloon flower (*Platycodon grandiflorus*) blue false indigo (*Baptisia australis*), false lupines (*Thermopsis* spp.), gas plant (*Dictamnus albus*), lupines (*Lupinus* spp. and hybrids), and peonies (*Paeonia* spp.).

Other plants will need dividing. DuBrule suggests that people lift and split plants such as daylilies, ornamental grasses, and irises. Before you replant the area, replenish the soil by adding organic matter and fertilizers. You may choose to select new plants or to replant some of the ones you lifted. "You can move them around to fit your new design. They're tough enough to take a transplant without being set back," DuBrule explains.

If the garden contains invasive plants, such as bee balm (*Monarda didyma*), coreopsis (*Coreopsis* spp.), feverfew (*Chrysanthemum parthenium*), and evening primroses (*Oenothera* spp.), now is the time to lift them, states DuBrule. You may want to keep some pieces, but think carefully before replanting or you may, in turn, pass along garden headaches to the next owner.

DEALING WITH DRAINAGE DILEMMAS

What can you do with wet spots on your property? "The first approach, and probably the most practical, is to choose plants that can take it, such as Japanese iris [*Iris ensata*], spotted Joe-Pye weed [*Eupatorium maculatum*], and perennial *Hibiscus* species," says Nancy DuBrule, the owner of Natureworks, an organic garden center in Connecticut. "The second approach is to raise the soil level." DuBrule likes to bring in topsoil when creating a raised area for a planting. "You can enclose the area with stone or wood, but you certainly don't have to," she adds. The most expensive and time-consuming approach is to correct the drainage by installing drainage tile.

DuBrule urges gardeners to be honest with themselves about the drainage characteristics of a site. In a poorly drained area, planting species that can't tolerate wet feet will just lead to headaches—and probably dead plants. So put up your umbrella, and take a long, slow walk around your yard next time it rains. Note where water settles in your garden beds or on the lawn. Make notes on your landscape plan, and follow through to deal with those drainage problems as you put your garden plan into effect.

THINK AHEAD TO SAVE LABOR LATER

Some simple advance planning can save precious time and energy during the rush and heat of the growing season. Oregon farming consultant Lynn Coody offers these examples of ways to plan for labor saving:

Assemble necessary supplies during the winter. You'll have more time for the catalog shopping that's needed to find many organic soil amendments and pest control supplies that aren't stocked in garden centers. It can be hard to order these materials in garden-size rather than farm-size quantities, so Coody seeks out other gardeners who are interested in placing a joint order and dividing up the materials.

Group crops by water requirements. This allows you to regulate watering needs more easily later in the season. For example, deep-rooted crops like lima beans and pumpkins need less water than shallow-rooted crops like

SAVE TIME, SAVE SPACE

Plan for crop combinations that will cut down on weeding and make good use of garden space. Stewart Hoyt, who operates a Community Supported Agriculture (CSA) operation in Vermont, gives some examples from his Vermont garden. "We always plant the first spinach in rows beside the early peas. By the time the peas are ready, the spinach is harvested, and we have room to harvest the peas. We use late corn and winter squash together, too. As long as you keep up with the cultivation before the squash begins to run, it's space- and time-conserving. The squash keeps down the late weeds."

GIVE A CHILD A GARDEN

Gardening is a great way to teach children about nature, and it provides lots of fun activities for them as well. If you'd like to include children in your garden plans, here are a few things you may want to think about:

Take the children into the garden while you work. Explain your activities, and share your feelings about gardening. Ask them questions, and encourage them to ask questions of you.

Give children simple, fun projects. Children love activity. They'll enjoy cutting pictures from seed catalogs and pasting them on a garden plan, or jumping on a bag to thresh seeds inside.

Provide children with their own garden plot. The child-size garden should create a private world where they can play. Let them make their own gardening decisions, with your guidance.

Show children the miracles of gardening. The more spectacular something is, the more it holds children's interest and encourages their willingness to learn. Help them build a vine teepee or grow giant sunflowers or huge pumpkins with their name engraved on the side. Give them tall, colorful, fast-growing, scented, fuzzy, or edible plants to grow.

Provide experiences first, and talk later. Experiences are often more memorable than words. Have children feel the soil, smell flowers, taste an herb, pull a carrot from the ground, or listen to leaves rustling. Talk to them about their discoveries after they've had the chance to explore.

cauliflower, lettuce, and spinach.

Divide the garden into weeding areas. Coody divides her garden into Areas 1, 2, and 3. "As soon as I plant, I begin to weed," she explains. "I thoroughly weed Area 1 first, letting the weeds grow in Areas 2 and 3. I move into Area 2 next, and finally, Area 3." Coody likes this approach because she never faces the overwhelming task of having to save her entire garden from the crush of overgrown weeds.

MADE IN THE SHADE

The shade cast by a vine-covered trellis may be just the twist that gardeners in hot-summer regions need to help their plants survive the heat. "If more people would use trellises and vines to shade some of their perennials and some of their vegetables, they'd get much longer show or yield from them," says Jim Wilson, a cohost of public television's "The Victory Garden." Wilson suggests planning for a fence on the western side of your vegetable garden or perennial beds, to block the sun from midafternoon on. "When Jane [his wife] and I were growing herbs at our farm, we had some of them backed up against the afternoon shade of trees, and they always held up two to three weeks longer than the ones in the baking sun," he says. Some shade also helps to extend the spring harvest of leafy vegetables such as lettuce.

GROW GRASS IN THE PATHS

Grass in the vegetable garden may not be a bad idea—if it's in the pathways. Janet Bachmann and partner Jim Lukens, who co-own a small organic farm in Arkansas, have discovered that keeping vegetable garden paths planted in permanent sod not only reduces maintenance but also benefits their crops. They grow vegetables in permanent beds, 4 × 50 feet. Three-foot-wide sod pathways composed of perennial ryegrass (*Lolium perenne*) and white clover (*Trifolium repens*) separate the beds. Bachmann explains the advantages of the system: "The sod provides a continuous supply of high-quality mulch material for the growing beds. When we mow, the lawn mower throws the clippings onto the beds, saving us a step. We can also concentrate our fertilizers this way; we don't spread them on the sod pathways, which don't need them. The sod allows us to walk in the garden after a rain. We don't have to worry about compacting our soils."

Bachmann and Lukens designed their beds and paths so that their tractor, which has a 7-foot span from wheel to wheel, travels on the sod when they till their beds. You may want to design your paths so that you can mow them in two passes with your lawn mower.

Getting the Plans on Paper

Does trying to draw a map of your yard or garden plot leave you tearing up endless sheets of paper—or tearing out your hair? If so, read the following sections for advice from the experts on hassle-free map making.

PLAY WITH POST-IT PLANNING

Those sticky squares of paper commonly known as Post-it notes are perfect for the trial-and-error process of planning the layout of your vegetable garden beds. North Carolina gardener and garden writer Bob Heltman stumbled across the idea for Post-it planning two seasons ago. "I was doing my second most favorite thing, armchair gardening, when I thought of it," Heltman remembers. "I started playing with the Post-its and found that using them was a quite pleasant and orderly way of planning my garden."

To try planning with Post-its, you'll need a smooth, hard surface to work on. Heltman made his own lap-size garden board out of a piece of tempered Masonite fiberboard. (You could also use a large erasable memo board like the one shown on page 78.) Decide the scale of your garden, such as 1 inch equals 1 foot. If your beds are 3 feet wide, you can use 3×5-inch Post-its. If they're 4 feet wide, you can snip an inch off of the 3×5-inch Post-its. Heltman also notes that you don't need a ruler with Post-it planning. "You can use the Post-it itself to measure spacing within and along a bed."

Write each crop name on a Post-it, and go to work. You can lift and restick each crop as many times as you like until you hit the arrangement you think is best. If you succession-crop, just layer Post-its one on top of another. For example, if you plan to follow an early crop of lettuce with beans, you can use two Post-its on that plot to show the succession.

TRY CROP SWAPPING FOR BETTER RESULTS

Rotating the position of crops in the garden makes best use of soil nutrients and can help reduce problems with some soilborne diseases. But it can be difficult to work out rotation schemes in small gardens. Oregon farming consultant Lynn Coody has come up with a novel and effective solution: She suggests planning rotations with friends who have gardens. "For instance," she says, "one year you can grow all the tomatoes, peppers, and eggplants and your friend can grow all the brassicas [cabbage-family crops] and squash. Then you can switch the following year. This system's good for your soil, but also it builds community."

MASTERING MAP-MAKING

You don't need professional skills to draw a map of your garden. Using lined graph paper, any gardener can make a usable garden map.

Your first step should be to measure the boundary lines of your property, using a flexible measuring tape that's 25 feet or longer. It's easiest to do this with a helper to hold one end of the tape. If you work alone, stick a pencil through the loop at the end of the tape, and push it into the ground to secure it.

You'll also want to take measurements of the size of your house and note its location with regard to the boundary lines. Make sure to note the size and location of existing garden beds and plantings as well.

Next, sit down with your list of measurements and your graph paper. Choose a scale, such as 1 square on paper equals 1 square foot of actual space. If you have a large property, you may need to tape a few sheets of paper together to work on that scale. Or you can choose a different scale, such as 1 inch on paper equals 5 feet of actual space.

Draw your boundaries, and then fill in the location of existing buildings and plantings. Double-check your counting to be sure you've drawn things accurately. With this skeleton map, you have a template to use when sketching in your plans and dreams for the ideal yard and garden.

Once you have the final layout of your garden, you can draw it up on a more permanent map (Post-its do tend to lose their stickiness over time), or you can encase the Post-it board in plastic wrap to keep the Post-its intact. This will also protect them from getting dirty or wet if you take the board out to the garden with you.

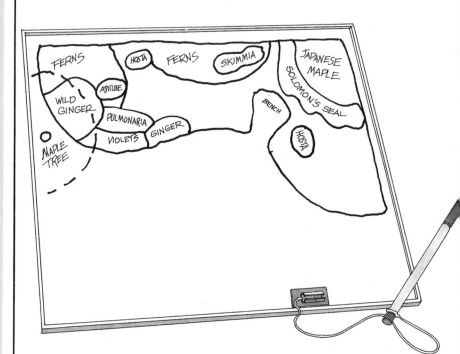

Try drawing on an erasable memo board when you're brainstorming garden plans or designs for flower beds and borders. You can quickly sketch in plant groupings and alter their size and shape by simply wiping them off and redrawing. Once you're satisfied with the general outlines of the plan or design, use it as a guide for creating a more detailed, formal drawing on paper.

MAKE MULTIPLE MAPS

Once you've drawn a general map of your property or the layout of your vegetable garden, save redrawing time by making photocopies. John Dromgoole, the host of PBS television's "The New Garden," makes 20 copies of his garden map each year and puts them in a notebook. "I try so many new things every year and do so much succession cropping that I need an efficient way to keep track of everything. The maps let me do this," says Dromgoole. He uses one map to plan out the first plantings of the year. As the season progresses, he records the placement and dates of following crops on separate copies. "I put notes on them, too," says Dromgoole. "For instance, I tried out a new kind of drip irrigation system last year. I really liked it in the beginning of the year, but by the end of the season, it developed leaks. I noted all the leaky spots on my maps."

Keeping Good Records

Keeping written notes on your garden is part of the ongoing process of making your plans a reality. Records help you know which of your new methods worked and which flopped. They help you decide which plants are best suited to your site. In the following tips, our veteran gardeners explain what they keep track of and the record-keeping styles that work best for them.

MARK THAT CALENDAR

If you're the gardener who's forever procrastinating about starting a record-keeping system, calendar record keeping may be just right for you. Stewart Hoyt, who operates a Community Supported Agriculture (CSA) operation in Vermont, says, "I've never been really good with record keeping. But now that we're doing a CSA, we have to keep track of things. So I've developed a simple system that I can stick to." Hoyt uses a calendar with "huge" daily spaces. When he comes in from the gardens each day, he notes everything he did that day along with the number of hours he spent on it. So post a calendar by the tool rack or just inside the back door, with a pencil on a string attached to it for maximum convenience. Take 3 minutes to note essentials. A calendar is a good place to record:

◆ Type and quantity of seed sown or number of transplants planted (including cultivar names)
◆ Rainfall or watering
◆ Areas weeded
◆ Pest control techniques used
◆ Harvest times and quantities

Then at the end of the season, sit down with the calendar and summarize the performance of your crops.

CUT TIME WITH TRACING PAPER

Bill McDorman, the founder of High Altitude Gardens, an Idaho mail-order seed company, tapes tracing paper over his garden maps each year. He says, "This saves me a lot of time. I work on the tracing paper during the planning phase, and I don't have to rewrite the map outlines."

TRY TO REMEMBER

Try to keep a year's worth of garden records *in your head,* and your memory may fail you. Write it down! Be sure that you:

List crop rotations. Changing the placement of crops within your garden each year is one way to outwit pests and fungi that attack certain plant families. Using a map or chart to record where you planted each crop last year will give you a visual reference for planning this year's crop placement. This will help ensure that you don't plant crops from the same family in the same spot year after year, making them more vulnerable to diseases and insects.

Maintain soil records. Keeping track of timing, type, and amount of fertilizer applications is important in avoiding mineral imbalances. Lack of nutrients can limit plant growth, and excesses of certain nutrients can also have detrimental effects. See "Balancing the Soil," beginning on page 89, to learn more about soil.

Keep a weather diary. Environmental disorders, such as water stress, sometimes cause symptoms that look very much like symptoms caused by insects or diseases. If you have data on weather conditions to refer to, it will help you make a better judgment about the underlying cause of the symptoms you see.

Compare cultivar records. Include jottings of how well your plants resisted heat and pests and also how well they were received on the dining room table! Perhaps you'll find some favorite cultivars or decide to choose new ones.

GET THE PICTURE

"Photographs are as useful as written records," says John Dromgoole, the host of PBS television's "The New Garden." "I can capture the whole garden in a few shots. I take pictures every few weeks during the growing season." Photographs refresh your memory and can answer questions about when and where things were planted if succession and intercropping plans get complicated.

KEEP THOSE RECORDS ON FILE

A handy way to keep track of crop performance in the vegetable garden is to make notes on file cards, as shown in the illustration below. New Hampshire organic farmer Rick Estes says, "File cards are the best record-keeping tool I've found." It's easy to separate cards into categories with dividers. Each year, you can drop in new notes just where you want them. Estes says, "I use the cards for keeping track of numbers and dates, how many of what crop I've seeded, and when." Estes also finds the cards effective for quick review and improvement of his techniques from year to year. "For example, the notes on my cards for tomatoes the year before last said 'leggy' next to the transplant date," he explains. "So I delayed seeding by a week, and last year's tomatoes weren't leggy."

Keeping garden records on file cards gives you quick access to information about specific crops or plantings.

IN-FIELD RECORD KEEPING

Thanks to plastic and indelible ink, you can keep year-to-year records right in your garden. Ken Ryan, an organic farmer and farm manager from New England, sticks an 8-inch plastic tag at the head of every bed as he plants it, noting the cultivar and planting date with a laundry marker. Rather than remove these tags at the end of the season or when a crop is finished, he leaves them in place. "I have years of tags at the head of every bed," says Ryan. "I have to touch up the writing every so often because it fades, but I keep up with that." Ryan likes this system because it helps him maintain good rotations if he has to deviate from his yearly plan.

Picking Perfect Plants

Do you feel overwhelmed when you page through garden catalogs or walk down endless aisles of plants at a nursery? How do you choose? We asked the experts for hints on how to get the most for your money and the best choices for your garden.

HINTS FOR HEALTHY BEDDING PLANTS

Don't make the assumption that all of the flats in the sea of plants at your garden center are equal. Inspecting plants before you buy can help you get the best quality for your money. Terry Humfeld, the executive director of the Professional Plant Growers Association, offers these four tips to help gardeners select top-quality bedding plants:

1. "Plants should have sturdy stems," Humfeld says. "Avoid any that are leggy or limp or whose leaves are curled, mottled, and yellowed. They may be infested by pests." Common pest problems for bedding plants include spider mites and aphids. Infested plants will have a harder time rebounding after being transplanted, and they may bring pest problems into your garden.

2. Stay away from plants whose lower leaves are turning yellow. It could be a sign that the flats were allowed to get too dry. Some roots may be permanently damaged.

3. Choose plants in packs that allow a larger root system and don't dry out quickly. These larger packs translate to 24 or 48 plants per flat. Flats may have as many as 72 cells

KEEP TRACK OF SOURCES

"People sometimes tend to forget to write down where they got something—seeds, good-quality transplants, fertilizers, or other supplies," says Larry Bass, a North Carolina extension horticultural specialist. Bass suggests keeping a file of sources. He says, "If something worked, you'll want to repeat it. But you can't do that unless you know where you got it."

MAKE A NOTEBOOK NOOK

Your garden notebook won't get used if it's not close at hand when you're in the garden. "My best garden tool is a notebook," says John Dromgoole, the host of PBS television's "The New Garden." "I use it to keep track of dates, when insects appear and where, what I did about them, fertility management—all kinds of things. But I can't go running in and out of the house every time I see something interesting." To keep his notebook handy, clean, and dry, Dromgoole installed a mailbox on a post in his garden. It is home for his garden notebook. "That way," he says, "I never put off taking notes."

(continued)

HOW MANY SEEDS PER OUNCE?

Many mail-order catalogs tell you how many seeds are in a packet. But some seed packets — especially those that are sold in stores — give the weight of the seed enclosed but not their numbers. Use the tables below and on the opposite page to translate weight into numbers so you can estimate the amount you'll need to buy. (If the weight of the contents is listed in grams, remember that 454 grams equals 1 ounce.)

Vegetable	Seeds per Ounce
Beets	1,600
Broccoli	9,000
Brussels sprouts	9,000
Cabbage	9,000
Carrots	23,000
Corn	120-180*
Cucumbers	1,100
Eggplant	6,500
Lettuce	25,000
Lima beans	25-75*
Onions	8,500
Peas	90-175*
Peppers	4,500
Pumpkins	100-300*
Radishes	2,500
Snap beans	100-125*
Spinach	2,800
Squash	120-400*
Tomatoes	11,500

*Some cultivars have larger seed than others.

per pack — an economical way to buy for large plantings. If you *do* choose flats with small cells, be sure to plant these plants immediately, before the roots become matted in the little cells.

4. Plants that aren't yet in bloom make a better transition to the garden than those in flower. When you have a choice, buy plants that aren't blooming. Sometimes that's not possible. Humfeld says, "If you can bring yourself to do it, pinch off the flowers and flower buds." Although most bedding plants are bred to flower in their packs, the plants will appreciate a chance to gain vegetative growth rather than flowering in their first days in the garden.

STUDY YOUR SEED CATALOGS

While an impulse buy of a seed packet from a store rack might inspire you to grow a new crop or a flashy flower you've never tried before, you're best off relying on mail-order buying for seed. "Don't be carried away by the glossy package in the store," says Simon Crawford, a technical services specialist for the PanAmerican Seed Company in Illinois. "Use the store to give you some ideas, but get some catalogs. Compare prices. Do a bit of research. It's worth doing and it's quite fun!" Crawford also offers the following words to the wise:

Check the date on the packet. If you do decide to buy off the rack instead of from a catalog, be sure the current year is stamped somewhere on the envelope. If it isn't, don't risk buying it. Fresh seed germinates more reliably than old seed.

Don't confuse pelleted seed with untreated seed. Pelleted seed is coated to make the seeds easier to handle and sow. Pelleted seed packets look bulky but may not contain that many seeds. Read catalogs or seed packets carefully so you'll know whether you're buying pelleted seed, or you may feel disappointed when you receive fewer seeds than expected.

Research disease resistance. If your zinnias or other favorites always suffer from powdery mildew but you don't want to give up growing them, check for a mildew-resistant cultivar. Compare several catalog offerings to find the best choices.

Know what special labels mean. Cultivars that carry the All-America Selections Winner label have received an award for excellence after testing at trial grounds throughout the United States and Canada. This doesn't always mean that it will be the best cultivar for your garden. To receive the All-America Selections Winner label, a cultivar must perform well around the *entire country;* you may find that other cultivars perform better in your particular region.

Seed packets may also carry other marks of quality, such as Burpee's "Gold Ribbon Selection." This mark indicates a professional-grade product, generally a high-priced hybrid, in a small packet for home gardeners.

Crawford's bottom-line advice is: "Any seed you buy should give good results if you follow the instructions that you're given. If it doesn't, you need to complain."

BUY BULBS BIG

What makes a bounteous bulb? "'Bigger is better' is the rule," says Sally Ferguson, the director of the Netherlands Flower Bulb Information Center in New York. "You get what you pay for." That means that the biggest bulbs will produce the biggest flowers, and they'll generally be priced accordingly. So if you want the best show possible, buy the biggest bulbs you can afford. Ferguson also notes that many people will mistakenly reject tulip bulbs with a torn tunic (the papery skin that covers them). "A healthy tulip without a tunic will grow as well as a healthy tulip with a tunic," she says. In fact, some research shows that removing the tunic may encourage rooting after the bulb is planted. You should avoid bulbs that are soft, mushy, or spotted with disease, as shown in the illustration below.

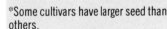

HOW MANY—CONTINUED	
Flower	*Seeds per Ounce*
Blanket flower	15,000
Calendula	3,500
Candytuft	9,500
Cleome	13,000
Coneflower	40,000
Cornflower	6,000
Cosmos	4,000–5,500*
Globe amaranth	10,000
Larkspur	8,000
Marigold	9,000
Mexican sunflower	3,000
Morning glory	800
Nasturtium	175
Periwinkle	20,000
Poppy	260,000
Portulaca	280,000
Stock	18,500
Strawflower	45,000
Summer cypress	28,000
Sunflower	500–700*
Zinnia	2,500–4,000*

*Some cultivars have larger seed than others.

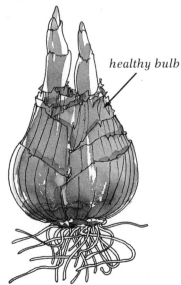

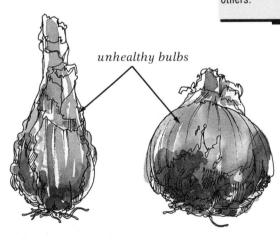

healthy bulb

unhealthy bulbs

SMALL BULBS STRETCH THE BUDGET

Although big bulbs yield the largest flowers, sometimes it pays to buy small bulbs in bulk, especially if they're daffodils. Daffodil bulbs multiply and grow larger each year, so if you can wait a year or two, small bulbs mean more for your money. Size doesn't indicate quality—it just means the bulbs are younger. Small bulbs are often the most affordable way to buy enough for naturalizing on a large lot. However, you never want to buy small tulips because they produce their biggest blossoms only in the first year.

◆ HAVE A ROOT PEER

Most gardeners look carefully at the leaves before buying a plant. But Andrew Schuerger, Ph.D., a senior plant pathologist at The Land Pavilion, an agricultural display at Epcot Center in Florida, says it's important to inspect the plant much more closely, not only to determine its general vigor but also to make sure it's not going to carry disease home to your garden.

"First," says Dr. Schuerger, "look at the base of the stem. If you see any rot, any soft black lesions, or other suspicious areas, don't buy that plant."

Bonnie Lee Appleton, Ph.D., an associate professor and extension horticulturist at Virginia Polytechnic Institute and State University, also suggests that gardeners inspect the roots of potential purchases. "I drive the retailers crazy, but I suggest that people take containers off of trees and shrubs before buying," Dr. Appleton says. Sometimes, bareroot nursery stock is potted just before sale. The only way to distinguish this newly potted stock from true container-grown stock is by checking roots. The roots of a bareroot plant will have less branching and be less well-developed than the roots of a container-grown plant. Why is this important? If you buy a bareroot plant thinking it was container-grown, you may not give it the extra care it needs after planting, and you could end up with a dead plant, explains Dr. Appleton.

To check roots without harming the plant, turn it upside down while holding the soil in place and supporting the base of the stem between two fingers. Now tap gently on the side of the plant's container. In most cases, the container will slip off enough for you to examine the root structure. Also check for root disease problems. "If the roots are nice and white and you don't see any rotted splotches, you can buy the plant," says Dr. Schuerger. "But sometimes I've pulled perfectly healthy-looking plants out, and their roots have been completely rotten." Verlin Schaefer, an assistant mail-order manager for Stark Brothers Nurseries and Orchards Company in Missouri, cautions gardeners that big doesn't always mean best when it comes to fruit-tree roots. "Look for a balance between the size of the root system and the size of the tree," says Schaefer. A 4- to 5-foot-tall, standard-size young fruit tree should have 10- to 12-inch-long roots. They should be well-formed with multiple roots coming out from the taproot. If you cut through the tip of a root, the inside tissue should be white. Brown or dirty-looking tissue is diseased.

As shown in the illustration below, the roots of dwarf trees will be different—shorter and fibrous, like the roots of an ornamental shrub—so don't be alarmed if the roots of your small trees don't measure up to those of the big ones. They aren't supposed to. According to Schaefer, the roots of dwarf fruit trees may be only 25 percent of the size of the roots of a standard-size tree. Semidwarfs will be about 50 to 75 percent of standard size.

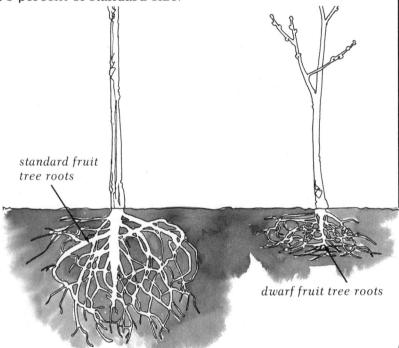

standard fruit tree roots

dwarf fruit tree roots

STEER CLEAR OF WILD-COLLECTED PLANTS

Native plants can be a wonderful choice for your yard and garden. But when you buy these plants, make sure they are nursery-grown, warns Kris Medic Thomas, a landscape manager and arborist for the city of Columbus, Ohio. Many nurseries can legally dig plants from the wild—a practice that disturbs delicately balanced ecosystems. In addition, Thomas has found that the wild-collected plants often have a slim chance of survival.

Bob McCartney, a co-owner of Woodlanders, a South Carolina nursery that specializes in southeastern native plants, concurs that nursery-grown plants have a much better chance in the garden. He warns that certain species are more likely to be wild-collected than others are. "I know

SEEK SMART SMALL BUYS

Is the biggest potted perennial the best bet for the garden? Not always, according to Bill Boonstra, a manager of Bluestone Perennials in Ohio.

That big, beautiful, lance-leaved coreopsis (*Coreopsis lanceolata*) in a 2-gallon container will probably bloom the first year. If you decide to save some money by buying a smaller specimen instead, you may have to wait until the following year to see flowers. However, the younger plant may offer some advantages other than lower price that make the wait for bloom worthwhile. Younger plants may have more-vigorous roots that are better able to adapt to and begin spreading in your garden soil. Boonstra explains, "When plants get older and sit around in large pots, they can stall out. A young plant that is actively growing doesn't have to be reawakened."

To verify root vigor before you buy, slide plants gently out of the pot. Fresh, active roots will be a soft, opaque white. (The color will vary on some species.) The root tips will be bristling with tiny, soft root hairs. On the contrary, when plants set in a container for too long, the young roots closest to the pot walls can be burned by heat or fertilizer salts or damaged by the physical constraint. They discolor and die, and the older roots may not rebound quickly.

KNOW WHAT YOU'RE ORDERING

Ignorance is bliss—but for gardeners ignorance can spell disaster. "Study and learn about what you're ordering," says Bob McCartney, a co-owner of Woodlanders, a South Carolina nursery that specializes in southeastern native plants. "One of my greatest frustrations is hearing from customers with a plant that is floundering or may have died because they didn't know its requirements." For example, customers in Zone 4 may wonder why their gorgeous new winter jasmine died in the winter instead of blooming. They failed to check and see that the plant is only hardy as far north as Zone 6. Or they may be frustrated because the hostas planted around the foundation in full sun look ghastly. If they'd done their homework, they would have planted them in moist shade instead.

McCartney also suggests that gardeners pay close attention to shipping information. Many people assume that they can order year-round, but most nurseries only ship during certain times of year. Before you set up your planting schedule, check to see when the nursery will ship your plants. Be sure your planned planting dates mesh with the nursery's projected shipping dates.

of no one propagating trilliums [*Trillium* spp.]," says McCartney. Others that fall into this category are native orchids such as lady's slipper orchids (*Cypripedium spp.*) and yellow fringed orchid (*Habenaria ciliaris*) and some of the native lilies (*Lilium superbum, L. grayi,* and *L. philadelphicum*). Others to question are native azaleas (*Rhododendron* spp.).

"One way to tell if a plant is nursery-grown is to inspect the root ball," Thomas says. "Most are planted in a clay-type soil, so the root balls will hold together well. The dirt surrounding the plants should be free of rocks and other natural debris." McCartney adds that nursery-propagated plants generally are uniform in size. "If you see odd, mixed sizes, oddly shaped plants, and native soil next to the roots, the plants probably were dug from the wild," he says.

A CHECK-UP FOR MAIL-ORDER ARRIVALS

Hurray! Your plants have just arrived in the mail! Lavish your energy and excitement on your plants to make sure they're in good health. "Unpack them immediately, and set them upright," says Bob McCartney, a co-owner of Woodlanders, a South Carolina nursery that specializes in southeastern native plants. Then examine them as explained below. Be sure the soil or roots are moist. If not, water right away.

Look for flexible, green stems. Check for live wood on dormant deciduous plants by scratching the bark slightly with your fingernail. You should see a layer of green wood underneath the bark you peeled up. If you can't find green wood, you need to let the nursery know immediately.

Be sure that plants in leaf aren't wilted. If they are, soak the pot or roots in water and mist the foliage. McCartney even suggests placing the plants in a closed shower or garment bag or other location where you can fashion a cool, humid environment until the leaves become turgid again. If they don't recover, contact the shipper right away.

Examine bulbs. They should be firm and free of mold.

If you can't plant right away, store the plants in a cool place such as a basement, a garage, or the shady side of your house. If the ground is frozen when plants arrive, pot them in containers and put them in a cool, dark place until the ground thaws. Water only enough to prevent them from drying out. You don't want to encourage topgrowth.

THE GARDEN PROFESSIONALS

Bonnie Lee Appleton, Ph.D., is an associate professor of horticulture, researcher, and extension nursery specialist at Hampton Roads Agricultural Experiment Station, Virginia Polytechnic Institute and State University, in Virginia Beach. She is the author of *Landscape Rejuvenation.*

Janet Bachmann is the coordinator for the Mid-South Farmers Network for the Rodale Institute. **Jim Lukens** is the program manager for Appropriate Technology Transfer for Rural Areas (ATTRA), a federally funded program that provides information to farmers about sustainable agriculture. They are joint owners of a home-scale farm near Fayetteville, Arkansas.

Larry Bass is a horticultural specialist with the North Carolina Cooperative Extension Service of North Carolina State University.

Dick Bir is an extension horticulture specialist at the Mountain Horticultural Crops Research and Extension Center of North Carolina State University at Raleigh. He is the author of *Growing and Propagating Showy Native Woody Plants.*

Bill Boonstra is a second-generation manager of Bluestone Perennials in Madison, Ohio. Established in 1972 by Richard Boonstra, the company sells perennials, by mail order only, for spring and fall planting seasons.

C. Colston (Cole) Burrell, is a garden designer, author, photographer, and lecturer whose Minneapolis-based business, Native Landscapes, specializes in landscape restoration and innovative use of native plants and perennials in garden design. He is coauthor of *Rodale's Illustrated Encyclopedia of Perennials.*

Lynn Coody is a farming consultant for Organic Agsystems Consulting in Cottage Grove, Oregon. She won second place in the 1984 Gardener of the Year contest, sponsored by *Organic Gardening* magazine.

Simon Crawford is a technical services specialist for the PanAmerican Seed Company in West Chicago, Illinois. Previously, he was a plant breeder with Asmer Seeds in England.

John Dromgoole is a manager and part owner of Garden-Ville of Austin, a catalog and supply company located in Austin, Texas. He hosts a national television show dedicated to organic gardening on PBS called "The New Garden."

Nancy DuBrule is the owner of Natureworks, an organic garden center specializing in perennials in Northford, Connecticut. She is a coauthor of *A Country Garden for Your Backyard.*

Rick Estes and Geri Veroneau grow certified organic vegetables and small fruit on 5 acres in Salisbury, New Hampshire. They run a Community Supported Agriculture (CSA) operation and sell to restaurants and grocery stores.

Nancy Farrell is an organic gardener in Burlington, Vermont, who enjoys experimenting with innovative methods.

Sally Ferguson is the director of the Netherlands Flower Bulb Information Center in Brooklyn, New York. The center provides information to U.S. consumers and horticulturists about the uses and culture of Dutch flower bulbs.

John Hancock is the owner of the John Hancock Fruit Farm in LaPorte, Indiana. He is also a film director. His credits include *Bang the Drum Slowly, Weeds,* and *Prancer.*

SIZING UP FRUIT TREES

Here's a quick rundown on what fruit-tree size terminology really means. A standard tree is full-size, while semidwarfs, as the name implies, are a little smaller. Dwarfs are smaller yet, and there is also a classification called miniature. Miniatures are even smaller than dwarfs and include cultivars especially suited to tiny patio gardens or containers. Actual sizes for any of these trees vary according to the species. Apples, for example, are sized as follows: standard, 25 feet tall; semidwarf, 14 to 18 feet; dwarf, 8 to 12 feet; and miniature, 4 to 8 feet. "Sometimes dwarf and semidwarf get lumped together in catalogs, and there is no way of knowing which is truly which," says Verlin Schaefer, an assistant mail-order manager for Stark Brothers Nurseries and Orchards Company in Missouri. "You must either trust your supplier or have had experience with them." So be forewarned: If you aren't sure, ask.

A PATENT SAYS A LOT

Verlin Schaefer, an assistant mail-order manager for Stark Brothers Nurseries and Orchards Company in Missouri, points out that if a plant carries a patent, there is something unique enough about it to make it worthwhile patenting. Patenting is an expensive procedure, and what the owner or company says about the plant is more likely to be based in substance than on marketing hoopla.

Bob Heltman is the president of Leading Edge Products and Services Company in Hendersonville, North Carolina, a manufacturers' agency representing inventors and product developers. He has written articles on gardening innovations for *National Gardening* magazine.

Stewart Hoyt is a market gardener and operates a Community Supported Agriculture (CSA) operation in Barnet, Vermont.

Terry Humfeld is the executive director of the Professional Plant Growers Association, which serves growers of all greenhouse crops, as well as members of related industries, and is located in Lansing, Michigan.

Anne Janisse is a garden designer for small urban residential gardens at the City People's Garden Store, a full-scale nursery and garden center in Seattle, Washington.

Dick Lighty, Ph.D., is the director of Mount Cuba Center for the Study of Piedmont Flora, located in Greenville, Delaware. He has written and lectured widely on native plants, naturalistic gardening, and garden maintenance.

Bob McCartney is a co-owner of Woodlanders, Inc., in Aiken, South Carolina. Woodlanders, Inc., specializes in southeastern native plants as well as rare and exotic species. He has lectured extensively throughout the United States.

Bill McDorman is the founder and president of High Altitude Gardens in Ketchum, Idaho. The mail-order seed company tests and sells seeds for high altitudes, cold climates, and short seasons.

William Reid is the director of the pecan experiment field at Kansas State University in Manhattan. **Brenda Reid,** his wife, is a research assistant in fruit breeding at the University of Arkansas in Fayetteville. The Reids live in Chetopa, Kansas; the design of their home landscape and garden has been recognized in the *National Gardening* competition.

Ken Ryan is the farm manager at Lookout Farm, which grows specialty vegetables, herbs, and edible flowers, in South Natik, Massachusetts. He is the former owner of Herban Gardens, a certified organic farm in Litchfield, New Hampshire.

Verlin Schaefer is an assistant mail-order manager for Stark Brothers Nurseries and Orchards Company in Louisiana, Missouri. The nursery offers fruit trees, grapes, ornamental trees and shrubs, and roses.

Andrew Schuerger, Ph.D., is a senior plant pathologist at The Land Pavilion, Epcot Center, in Orlando, Florida. The Land Pavilion is an agricultural display that includes 1½ acres of greenhouses that showcase world food crops.

Kris Medic Thomas is a landscape manager and arborist for the city of Columbus, Indiana. She is also a former staff horticulturist and trails manager at Callaway Gardens in Georgia.

Sarah Williams is is an elementary special education teacher in Colchester, Vermont. She is a lifelong gardener and currently gardens at her home in Burlington, Vermont.

Jim Wilson is a cohost of public television's "The Victory Garden." He is the author of *Landscaping with Container Plants, Masters of the Victory Garden,* and *Landscaping with Wildflowers.*

Balancing the Soil

Organic gardeners should get down to ground level before they launch their planting plans. Soil care is the heart of the organic method. Fortunately, organic soil care is just a matter of following a few simple principles. The most important one is to build the organic matter content of the soil. In this chapter, you'll find expert tips on just that, as well as on evaluating the soil, cultivating, and dealing with soil problems.

Sizing Up Your Soil

A good first step is to get to know the soil in your garden. Since it probably won't be too talkative, we asked the experts to explain how to get the most from professional soil tests and how to try simple do-it-yourself tests to learn more about your soil.

TAKE YOUR BEST SOIL TEST

If you opt for a professional soil test, keep in mind that the test will only be as good as the sample you submit for testing. "Collecting a good representative soil sample isn't as easy as it looks," claims Vernon Meints, Ph.D., a co-owner of Agri-Business Consultants, a Michigan independent crop consulting firm. Here are three suggestions from Dr. Meints to help you collect the best soil sample:

1. Divide your gardening space into sections according to what has been planted, then sample each section individually. For example, take separate samples from areas where you grew fruits, vegetables, or ornamental crops. You may need additional samples within each crop group if you've tried different fertilizer application methods or other practices within them. Dr. Meints has found that even simple practices, such as mulching with organic materials, can alter soil test results.

2. Sample only as deep as you till. Dr. Meints says, "Many gardeners think they're tilling deeper than they are, since rotary tillage fluffs the soil." According to Dr. Meints, rotary tillers generally till no more than 3 inches deep, so only take a sample from the top 3 inches.

3. Timing isn't critical. "It's more important that the job is done," says Dr. Meints. You may find that fall is the best time to sample, because soils are generally drier in fall than in spring. Also, soil-testing laboratories are less busy in the autumn, and you'll have several months to consider the results and plan a soil-improvement program.

SNIFF FOR SOUR-SMELLING SOIL

Taking a good whiff of your soil can help you judge whether or not you need to worry about having it tested. Shepherd Ogden, a co-owner of The Cook's Garden, a mail-order seed company in Vermont, uses a sniff test to monitor soil pH. Soil pH, which is a measure of the alkalinity or acidity of a soil, is important because it affects how easily nutrients in the soil can be absorbed by plant roots. Most garden plants do best when the soil is in the neutral range, at a pH between 6.0 and 7.0. "When the pH is not right, garden soil smells vinegary or sour, or the odor makes your nose tingle," Ogden explains. If the soil smells good and sweet, Ogden trusts that the pH is probably appropriate for good plant growth. When the soil smells sour, it's time to do a formal soil test.

BREAKING UP (HARDPAN) IS HARD TO DO

Digging deep can reveal hidden problems with your garden soil. If you use a rotary tiller frequently, your soil may have developed a hardpan. A hardpan is a compacted layer of soil below the surface. Water and plant roots can't penetrate a hardpan. Plant growth may suffer, and soil won't drain well. Your soil may also have this problem if it has been driven over by heavy equipment—during construction, for example.

Bill Wolf, the president of Necessary Trading Company, a Virginia company that manufactures and sells organic fertilizers, offers advice on how to detect a hardpan. "Using a trowel or shovel, examine the soil around perennial plants, in the root zone. Look for roots that suddenly turn sideways: That's where the compacted layer is," says Wolf. You can also insert a probe, such as a metal crowbar, into your garden soil. When you feel sudden pressure—it's usually at the depth of tillage—you'll know you hit the hardpan. Note the depth to compaction at several sites. If you find a hardpan layer, you can break it up by digging through it with a garden fork. For large areas with hardpans, plowing with a chisel plow is a more feasible solution.

SHOULD YOU SQUASH OR SAVE?

Turn a shovelful of garden soil or just scratch the surface, and you'll discover an underground living world. Thousands of insects and related creatures thrive in the dark, moist soil environment. Linda Gilkeson, Ph.D., the Integrated Pest Management Coordinator for the British Columbia Ministry of Environment, explains that soil animals can be beneficials you should save or pests you should destroy. Most beneficials either help control pests or help decompose organic matter. "Many gardeners don't know that soil-dwelling beneficials, like ground beetles, are standing guard between their garden plants and the pests," says Dr. Gilkeson.

You'll help your soil and your garden plants by encouraging a diverse population of organisms in your soil. You can encourage the good guys by minimizing soil disturbance and using organic mulches. Take the time to learn to tell pests from beneficials so you'll know which creatures to preserve and which to destroy when you're digging in the garden. Here's a short squash/save list of common garden soil inhabitants. (Some of these garden inhabitants are also illustrated at right.)

Squash armyworms. Armyworms are greenish brown caterpillars with white stripes on their sides and dark- or light-colored stripes on their back. They feed on garden plants at night. During the day, they hide in plant foliage or just beneath the soil surface.

Save centipedes and millipedes. These are serpentine creatures from ½ inch to 5 inches long, with many legs. Both are important predators and decomposers in the soil ecosystem. They consume dead plant materials. You'll find them among leaf litter or in any damp, dark spot.

Squash Colorado potato beetles. Adults have yellow wing covers with ten black stripes. Larvae are orangey, humpbacked grubs, with black spots on their sides. Larvae eat potato foliage, quickly defoliating potato plants. You'll find adults and pupae in soil where potatoes are grown.

Squash cutworms. These are fat, greasy-looking, gray or dull brown, 1- to 2-inch-long caterpillars with shiny heads. They are often confused with armyworms. They chew through stems of vegetable and flower seedlings at

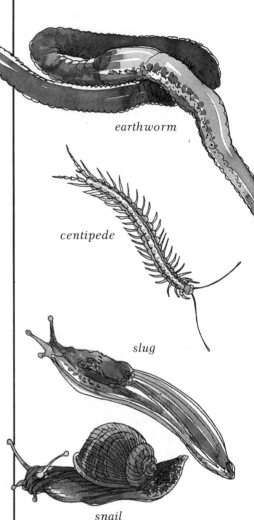

earthworm

centipede

slug

snail

night. During the day, they rest just below the soil surface.

Save earthworms. Most garden species are less than 5 inches long. Look for red, gray, and brown worms at and beneath the soil surface. Many feed upon decomposing organic matter, transporting it through their burrows and redistributing it throughout the soil.

Save ground beetles. Adults are blue-black or brown, ¾- to 1-inch-long beetles. Larvae are dark brown or black and grublike but slender. Adults and larvae prey on other insects and pests, including slugs. Some species eat weed and vegetable seeds. Spread organic mulches to attract them.

Squash grubs. Grubs are the larvae of Japanese beetles, June or May beetles, and other beetles. They are wormlike, fat, C-shaped, and most often white with a dark-colored head. They munch on both living and dead plant roots. You'll find them in soil beneath lawns.

Save rove beetles. These resemble earwigs without rear pincers. The hard wing covers are shortened, leaving the abdomen exposed. Length ranges from $\frac{1}{25}$ to $\frac{1}{10}$ inch. Most rove beetles are insect pest predators. You'll find them under rocks, in moss or fungi, and in compost piles and organic mulches.

Squash slugs and snails. Both slugs and snails are soft-bodied and wormlike, measuring $\frac{1}{8}$ to 8 inches long. Snails have a spiral-shaped shell into which they withdraw when disturbed; slugs lack a shell. Both lay clear, jellylike egg masses under stones and other debris. They feed at night on most aboveground plant parts, leaving behind a shiny trail of mucous slime.

Building Soil Fertility

An easy way to boost soil organic matter content is to spread organic materials on the soil surface and let nature do the rest. One of the best organic materials to add is compost. You'll find custom composting advice in "Making and Using Compost," beginning on page 100.

You can also use living plants to add to soil fertility. Green manure crops are crops that you sow specifically to turn back into the soil to boost soil health. Living mulch is a cover crop sown among your garden crops to help suppress weeds and conserve soil moisture. We asked the experts how to get the best results from added organic material, green manures, and living mulch.

GIVE SOIL A BOOST, NOT A BLAST

Just because a little of something is good for your garden soil doesn't mean that a little *more* is better. Paul Sachs, the owner of North Country Organics, a Vermont wholesale supplier of natural soil amendments, likes to remind gardeners of the saying "Everything in moderation." According to Sachs, "Everything you add to soil, including organic fertilizers and compost, has a threshold where it's not helpful anymore and possibly begins doing harm." For example, if you add too much phosphorus-rich fertilizer to the soil, the phosphorus can combine chemically with other important micronutrients such as iron and manganese, making them unavailable to your plants.

Always determine the proper application rate for soil amendments. Excess fertilizer is just another name for pollution. "Even compost will leach nitrates [soluble nitrogen compounds] into groundwater if you're not careful," reminds Sachs.

Use compost as a general-purpose garden fertilizer, but don't overapply. On bare soil, avoid spreading it more than 2 inches thick. You can apply more compost later in the season, when garden plants are established and ready to soak up nitrogen released from the compost.

PLANT A GARDEN OF BUCKWHEAT

Buckwheat is a versatile cover crop that you can use all season long. Miriam Klein-Hansen, who taught homestead gardening at the National Center for Appropriate Technology in Montana, suggests using buckwheat as a living mulch around cabbage-family plants. In spring, sprinkle buckwheat seed between broccoli, cabbage, and cauliflower transplants, leaving about 8 inches of bare soil around each transplant stem.

Klein-Hansen uses a hoe to cut the buckwheat from its roots at the midpoint of its flowering period, when bottom seeds have set. These seeds give a second buckwheat "planting" that prevents late weeds from getting established. Klein-Hansen's husband, David, turns the buckwheat under in the fall before planting winter rye over the whole garden. As they decay, the buckwheat plants feed the soil, particularly with phosphorus, which the plants accumulate as they grow. Klein-Hansen says, "I only have to weed about twice a season. After a couple of years of buckwheat/buckwheat/rye, we find almost no witchgrass [quackgrass]."

COMPOST CALCULATIONS

You're ready with fork in hand to raid your compost pile and spread its bounty on your garden. But how much of that black gold should you shovel into your wheelbarrow or garden cart? In many cases, you won't have nearly as much as you want. But if you're lucky enough to have large reserves of compost or if you're getting compost from a municipal compost center or other outside source, these guidelines may be helpful for determining how much you need:

1. Measure the length and width (in feet) of the area you want to cover. Multiply the two dimensions to calculate the area.

2. Divide the area by 6. This will tell you the number of cubic feet of compost you need to spread a 2-inch-thick layer. (If you only want to spread a 1-inch-thick layer, divide by 12.)

3. Figure out a "measuring cup" for your compost. A 30-gallon garbage can holds about 4 cubic feet of compost. Most contractor's wheelbarrows have capacities of 4 to 5 cubic feet.

SET LIMITS WITH LIVING MULCH

Use caution with living mulch, or it can become a living nightmare. "The only good living mulch is one you've killed," says Robert F. Becker, a retired associate professor at Cornell University's New York Agricultural Experiment Station in Geneva. "Living mulches are hard to control. They can get away from you and begin competing with the crops." To avoid problems with having mulch that takes over the garden, Becker suggests waiting to seed the mulch after crops are already well-established.

Becker also recommends sowing oats as a cover crop in areas where you've harvested peas and other early crops. "The nice thing about oats is that they winter-kill," says Becker. "You don't have to deal with them in the spring. Unless, of course, it's a wet spring. The oat covering can impede drying of the soil, so I rake up the dead plants and remove them from the soil surface."

ADD NITROGEN NATURALLY

A great way to build soil fertility is to have your plants do it for you. Legumes like peas, beans, and alfalfa are plants that can transform nitrogen from the atmosphere into nitrogen compounds that can be absorbed by plant roots. Because of this, they don't need as much nitrogen added in the form of fertilizer. But to "fix" nitrogen, the legume roots must associate with certain kinds of soil-dwelling bacteria. You can add these bacteria to the soil—a technique known as inoculating soil. In mail-order catalogs and at some garden supply centers, you can find soil inoculants specifically formulated for various cover crops and leguminous vegetable crops. However, Marianne Sarrantonio, Ph.D., the legume project coordinator for the Rodale Institute Research Center in Pennsylvania, cautions gardeners not to rely solely on inoculants to supply nitrogen for their bean crops. "Beans are poor nitrogen fixers," she explains. "They'll only fix about 30 to 50 percent of what they need."

Follow these four guidelines to get the best results with inoculants:

1. Be sure you buy the right inoculant for the legume you plan to plant. It's a good idea to buy the inoculant from your seed supplier to be sure of getting the right match. Refer to "Inoculants for Legumes" on the opposite page for specifics on the proper inoculant for each type of legume.

2. Check for an expiration date. Store the inoculant in the refrigerator, and use it as soon as possible.

3. To use an inoculant, pour legume seeds in a bucket and mix them with enough water to moisten the surface. Add the inoculant and stir until the seeds are coated. You can refrigerate coated seed for short periods, but it is best to mix only enough to plant immediately. Plant as usual.

4. The bacteria can usually survive in garden soil for four years without a host. If you wait longer than that between plantings, re-inoculate.

Inoculants for Legumes

Using the right inoculant can improve the performance of your green manure crops and increase yields of peas and beans. Use the table below to determine which inoculant is best for the legume you want to grow. You can obtain the specific inoculant you need from your seed supplier.

Inoculant	Compatible Legumes
Alfalfa and medic rhizobium (*Rhizobium meliloti*)	Alfalfa, sweet clover, bur clover, and yellow trefoil
Bean rhizobium (*Rhizobium leguminosarum* biovar. *phaseoli*)	Bean group: common beans, pinto beans, and scarlet runner beans
Chick-pea rhizobium (*Rhizobium loti*)	Chick-peas and lupines
Clover rhizobium (*Rhizobium leguminosarum* biovar. *trifoli*)	Red clover, white clover, crimson clover, ladino clover, and other true clovers
Cowpea rhizobium (*Bradyrhizobium* spp.)	Cowpea group: cowpeas, peanuts, mung beans, lima beans, yard-long beans, black-eyed peas, pigeon peas, velvet beans, and jack beans
Pea rhizobium (*Rhizobium leguminosarum* biovar. *viceae*)	Pea and vetch group: garden peas, sweet peas, field peas, fava beans, hairy vetch, common vetch, and purple vetch
Soybean rhizobia (*Bradyrhizobium japonicum*, *Sinorhizobium fredii*, and *Rhizobium fredii*)	Soybeans

WHAT'S IN THE BAG?

While you're in the process of building up your soil, you may need to use fertilizers to help boost your plants. But how do you know if the fertilizer you're buying contains only organic products? Bill Wolf, the president of Necessary Trading Company, a Virginia company that manufactures and sells organic fertilizers, says one good way is to buy from a source you trust for good quality and service. Another good way is to look for the following clues on the fertilizer label:

The words "All-Natural Organic." Look at the fine print where the ingredients are listed. They should be natural ones such as blood meal, poultry litter, bonemeal, natural grains, seaweeds, and other organic products.

An analysis of readily available nitrogen (N), phosphorus (P), and potassium (K) that totals 15 or less. For example, the NPK ratios (listed as three numbers on the label) will be 5-5-5, 4-5-4, or 3-2-3 as a registered analysis. (Some organic lawn fertilizers contain as much as 10 percent nitrogen; the sum of their NPK ratios will be greater than 15.)

KEEPING WORMS HAPPY

Encouraging earthworm activity is a great natural way to improve your soil. Avoid the temptation to add purchased worms to your garden. The kind of worm most often available for sale only thrives in extremely nutrient-rich matter such as manure or compost, not garden soil. Matthew Werner, Ph.D., a soil ecologist with the University of California's Agroecology Program in Santa Cruz, recommends modifying habitat to attract earthworms by increasing the soil organic matter content and by keeping tilling to a minimum, especially during the seasons when earthworms are most active in your area.

You can also create an earthworm reservoir in your yard in order to supply your garden with earthworm-rich soil cubes. Pick an area to be your reservoir, and adjust the soil to bring it near a pH of 7.0. Then plant a cover crop there. Let the crop grow, and gently work it into the soil. Then periodically check the site. Once you find a thriving earthworm population, you can dig out cubic-foot blocks of soil from your garden and switch them with cubic-foot blocks of earthworm-rich soil. Be sure to supply the worms with organic matter in their new habitat. Also replant your reservoir area with a cover crop to maintain the organic matter supply there as well. Dr. Werner warns that this process requires patience, but in the long term, it can be effective for improving garden soil.

Working with Your Soil

Is your soil everything you want it to be? Unfortunately, most of us will answer no. The organic matter content may be low, or perhaps the topsoil layer is only 3 inches thick. Or maybe your soil is so high in clay content that it is full of rocklike clods. What can you do? There aren't always easy answers, but we asked our advisers for schemes for improving problem soils. We also collected their opinions on the best ways to cultivate the soil.

CLAY CAN STRENGTHEN SANDY SOIL

Sandy soil can benefit from added clay and organic matter. "I follow the adage that 'a load of clay is like a load of manure to a sandy soil,'" explains Eliot Coleman, an organic farmer and author of *The New Organic Grower*. "If clay isn't readily available, adding organic matter is the next best alternative." You'll have to have some idea of how much clay your soil already contains and how much heavier you want it to be. For example, a sandy loam soil—considered excellent for gardening—is composed of roughly 65 percent sand, 20 percent silt, and only 15 percent clay.

Coleman figures it this way: You can boost a sandy soil's clay content 25 percent by spreading a 1-inch layer of clay over the surface of your garden and tilling it into the top 4 inches of the soil. Add less clay for a lighter effect. To keep your soil in good shape, add clay the first year, and follow it with annual applications of organic matter. Contact a local landscape supplier, who can deliver clay by the truckload. Be sure to specify that you don't want wet clay.

OUTSMART CLAY SOIL

Soils with high clay content can be heavy and hard to work. Nino Ridgway, the owner of Squeaky Green Organic Produce, who raises organic vegetables on a heavy clay soil in Wisconsin, offers three time-tested rules for dealing with heavy soil:

1. "The best way to improve a clay soil is to add organic matter. And the best way to add organic matter is to grow it in the field," says Ridgway. She sows cover crops, such as buckwheat or rye, then tills them in when they're several inches tall. Ridgway advises, "A good rule of thumb for

gardeners is to keep 10 to 20 percent of their garden space in a cover crop each year."

2. Stay away when your soil is wet! See "Give Soil a Squeeze" at right for a simple test you can try to judge soil moisture. If your soil is wet, don't even enter your garden. Ridgway says, "You're shooting yourself in the foot if you go ahead and work it, because it turns to concrete and requires one or more years to mend."

3. Maintain a surface mulch—even a thin layer—to break the impact of raindrops. The mulch will help prevent the crust that forms after a rainstorm. Ridgway says, "Even a light mulch of fine grass clippings is enough to improve the germination rate of fine-seeded crops like carrots, which don't like a soil crust."

IT COULD BE A SAND TRAP

Can you improve the rate at which your soil drains by mixing in sand? "That could be the wrong thing to do," says Bonnie Lee Appleton, Ph.D., an associate professor and extension horticulturist at Virginia Polytechnic Institute and State University. "A little sand impairs drainage," she says. "If you want to improve drainage using sand, it takes huge amounts—60 to 80 percent of the soil needs to be sand." For example, in order to boost the sand component of the top 6 to 8 inches of your soil by 5 to 10 percent, you would need to add 3 to 5 tons of sand per 1,000 square feet of garden. So skip the sand, and stick with a regular plan for adding organic matter, suggests Dr. Appleton.

TRY SIMPLE "SINGLE DIGGING"

If your soil is too sandy or is heavy with clay, double digging is the classic way to improve it. This method of shoveling aside the top layer of soil and loosening the subsoil improves aeration, and you can work in plenty of compost or other organic materials as you dig. However, at the Rodale Institute and Research Center in Pennsylvania, Eileen Weinsteiger, the garden project manager, found that double digging soil "wasn't worth it, because our soil was already in such good condition after many years of organic gardening." Weinsteiger explains, "Double digging improves poor soil, but it's time-consuming, so I don't recommend it unless you're gardening at an unproductive or unimproved site."

You may want to try the same simple method that

GIVE SOIL A SQUEEZE

Always check soil moisture content before you work the soil. If the soil is too wet or too dry, cultivating can destroy soil structure. You can do a rough moisture test by picking up a handful of soil and squeezing it. If the soil crumbles apart when you open your fingers, it's too dry.

If the soil forms a solid ball, it's too wet.

If the soil holds together without packing densely, it's just right, and it's time to get out in the garden.

COARSENESS COUNTERACTS CLAY

The easiest and least-expensive way to improve heavy clay soils is by adding organic matter. Robert Parnes, a soil science consultant in Maine, advises working in plenty of coarse materials like straw, pine needles, or mature plant stalks. These materials help to open up the soil since they don't break down as quickly as fine, light materials. Pine needles are particularly resistant to decay because of the presence of resinous compounds. Straw is effective because of its tubelike shape. The bulkier the material, the better.

Weinsteiger follows to manage soil in garden beds at the research center: Each spring, turn the soil to a depth of 1 foot. That's the depth of most garden shovels. Use your foot to push the shovel in, then turn the clump of soil. You can dig in compost or green manures at the same time.

Beds *don't* require annual digging if they're free of weeds and other vegetation or if the soil is in the fluffy condition that's best for planting. *Do* dig annually to bury cover crops and old vegetation, to add fertilizers, or to reshape the beds (if they need it) after a long winter.

TAKE IT EASY WITH TILLING

Frequent tillage at the same soil depth can cause the development of a hardpan, a compacted layer of soil below the surface. Hardpans prevent root penetration, and they're difficult to remedy. Paul Sachs, the owner of North Country Organics, a Vermont wholesale supplier of natural soil amendments, says, "Rotary tillage is not necessarily the soil's best friend. Overtillage really depletes soil organic matter. When you till, don't till too deeply, and alter the depth of tillage to prevent the formation of a hardpan." Sachs adds that rotating garden crops with green manure crops also helps alleviate soil compaction and maintain soil organic matter content.

Overtillage is hardest on soils with high clay content. The more clay your soil contains, the less you should till. If you're starting a new garden area, till the first year to break up sod or to work in loads of organic materials or soil amendments. In following years, continue adding organic materials or growing green manures, and work them in by hand whenever possible.

When you have to till, shallow tillage is better than deep. For example, the first tilling in spring could be to a depth of 4 inches. If you put in a second crop during the season, till only 1 inch deep to make a seedbed, or just rake the surface. Over time, you may find that your soil becomes loose and open enough that you can retire your tiller for good.

THE GARDEN PROFESSIONALS

Bonnie Lee Appleton, Ph.D., is an associate professor of horticulture, researcher, and extension nursery specialist at Hampton Roads Agricultural Experiment Station, Virginia Polytechnic Institute and State University, in Virginia Beach. She is the author of *Landscape Rejuvenation*.

Robert F. Becker is a retired associate professor at Cornell University's New York State Agricultural Experiment Station in Geneva, New York. He now teaches, lectures, and writes about the history of fruit and vegetable production.

Eliot Coleman is an organic farmer and independent agricultural and gardening consultant in Harborside, Maine. He is the author of *The New Organic Grower* and *Four-Season Harvest.*

Linda Gilkeson, Ph.D., is the Integrated Pest Management Coordinator for the British Columbia Ministry of Environment, whose mission is to reduce the use of pesticides in the province and promote their alternatives.

Miriam Klein-Hansen is a commercial dried-flower grower and craftsperson in West Charleston, Vermont. She taught homestead gardening at the National Center for Appropriate Technology in Montana.

Vernon Meints, Ph.D., is a co-owner of Agri-Business Consultants, Inc., an independent crop consulting firm in Okemos, Michigan. He is also the former director of the Soil Testing Laboratory at Michigan State University.

Shepherd Ogden is the president and a co-owner of The Cook's Garden, a seed catalog and organic display garden in Londonderry, Vermont. He is the coauthor of *The Cook's Garden* and author of *Step by Step to Organic Vegetable Gardening.*

Robert Parnes is a part-time consultant in soil science in Mechanic Falls, Maine. He operated the soil testing department at Woods End Laboratory in Maine for ten years. He is the author of *Fertile Soil.*

Nino Ridgway is the assistant manager of Barthel Fruit Farm in Mequon, Wisconsin. Ridgway also owns Squeaky Green Organic Produce, selling vegetables and flowers for drying at Barthel Fruit Farm, farmers' markets, and natural food co-ops.

Paul Sachs is the owner and founder of North Country Organics, a wholesale supplier of natural soil amendments in Bradford, Vermont. He is a consultant on soil fertility and on the use of organic waste.

Marianne Sarrantonio, Ph.D., is the legume project coordinator for the Rodale Institute Research Center in Maxatawny, Pennsylvania.

Eileen Weinsteiger is the garden project manager at the Rodale Institute Research Center in Maxatawny, Pennsylvania.

Matthew Werner, Ph.D., is a soil ecologist with the University of California's Agroecology Program in Santa Cruz. He studies the interaction between agriculture and neighboring ecosystems and how the ecosystems are affected by farm management practices.

Jim Wilson is a cohost of public television's "The Victory Garden." He is the author of *Landscaping with Container Plants, Masters of the Victory Garden,* and *Landscaping with Wildflowers.*

Bill Wolf is the founder and president of Necessary Trading Company of New Castle, Virginia. The company manufactures Necessary Organics growing supplies and sells organic fertilizers and pest controls via mail order.

RAISED BEDS HAVE A LIMIT

Gardeners with problem soils frequently rely on making raised beds to get around the problem. But be careful not to overdo the raising, cautions Jim Wilson, a cohost of public television's "The Victory Garden." "We raised beds to 9 inches one year without timber around them, and the long sides of the beds were facing west. The plants on that side baked," Wilson recalls. "So now when I raise beds, I knock them down to 3 or 4 inches in height at the most." Gardeners in the arid West, the Midwest, and the South, where summer heat tends to be most extreme, might save their crops by learning from Wilson's experience.

Making and Using Compost

Compost is king in an organic garden. This mixture of decomposed plant materials supplies both organic matter to build your soil and a wide range of nutrients to feed your plants. When you layer and mix organic materials in a compost pile, you're essentially speeding up natural processes of decay and soil regeneration that occur in gardens as plants, grow, die, and return to the soil.

Composting makes the most of your garden efforts because it brings along the leftovers from last season to fertilize a new season's growth. In this chapter, you'll find expert strategies for making great compost and using it to best advantage in the garden.

Beyond the Basics

Most gardeners are familiar with the basics of making compost. A compost pile can be a simple heap of leaves left to slowly break down in a sheltered corner, or it can be a highly managed bin full of layered high-carbon and high-nitrogen organic materials. The following sections include tactics from veteran composters for easier, faster, and better compost making.

THE CLASSIC COMPOST PILE

At Ecology Action of the Midpeninsula in California, gardening students learn the finer points of making compost. Carol Cox, a garden research manager with Ecology Action, explains that she emphasizes the role of microorganisms, which power the composting process. "During the decomposition process," Cox explains, "microorganisms have three requirements: water, air, and food. Your goal is to provide them in the right amounts."

This is the composting method that Cox teaches:

1. Choose a site measuring about 3 × 3 feet, and use a garden spade or fork to loosen the top 1 foot of soil. Loosening the soil enhances aeration and drainage.

2. Make a base for the pile by laying down about 3 to 6 inches of rough debris, such as broken twigs. This layer also enhances pile aeration.

3. Using a 5-gallon bucket as your measuring tool, layer your pile as follows: 2 buckets full of high-carbon (dry and brown) materials, 2 buckets full of high-nitrogen (wet and green) materials, and ¼ bucket of garden soil. Adding soil helps cool the pile, preventing high temperatures that would kill decomposer organisms and burn off too much carbon. See "Common Compostables" at right for lists of common ingredients that are high in nitrogen or carbon.

4. Continue layering by repeating Step 3 until your pile is at least 3 feet high. Water the pile whenever you water your garden. How much water you should add will vary with the season. Your goal is for materials in the pile to have the moistness of a wrung-out sponge.

5. Turn the pile after three or four weeks, working to transpose outside materials and inside materials as you turn.

Cox says, "Your goal should be to turn the pile only once. That's possible when you get the right proportion of brown to green materials." In cool weather, you may have to turn the pile several times. Your compost should be ready in two to three months.

DOES YOUR COMPOST NEED A JUMP START?

If you're starting a new compost pile, try "seasoning" it with a million microorganisms. You can do so by adding a compost starter or activator—a commercial product that contains the bacteria and fungi that activate the composting process.

While these bacteria and fungi are present naturally on all plant and soil surfaces, there are certain circumstances when adding a compost starter can do your pile good, says Bill Wolf, the president of Necessary Trading Company, a Virginia company that manufactures and sells organic fertilizers. "But be sure to read the label and guarantee so you know that you're getting live microbes," Wolf cautions. He suggests using a compost starter if any of the following three situations apply to you.

COMMON COMPOSTABLES

You'll build your compost pile from a mixture of "green" (wet, high-nitrogen) materials and "brown" (dry, high-carbon) materials.

"Greens"

Coffee grounds
Cover crops
Eggs*
Eggshells
Feathers*
Fish and seafood scraps*
Fruit wastes
Grains
Grass clippings
Hair (pet or human)
Leaves
Manure
Milk
Seaweed
Vegetable scraps
Weeds

"Browns"

Corncobs
Cornstalks
Hay
Nutshells
Paper
Pine needles
Sawdust
Straw
Vegetable stalks and seeds

*Most animal scraps will attract animal pests and slow decomposition. Also, some communities have regulations restricting ingredients allowed in backyard piles.

MIX IT QUICK

If you stockpile grass clippings, weeds, and green fallen leaves for the compost pile, plan to mix them immediately with some other bulky material like sawdust, straw, or even soil. "Large masses of fresh and green compost ingredients like grass clippings form soggy, anaerobic clumps. Try mixing them with another material so they'll be easier to work with when it's time to build the pile," advises Carol Wentz, an Ohio gardening and design consultant.

DON'T DROP DROPPINGS IN COMPOST

Your compost pile is not the best place for the daily droppings from Fido and Kitty. Since our pets can transmit certain diseases to humans, it's best to minimize contact with their droppings. Don't put pet feces in the compost pile, and keep them away from the home food garden and your water well. It's safe to bury pet wastes near ornamentals. To bury pet wastes, dig a hole 12 inches deep, then place 3 to 4 inches of pet waste in the bottom of the hole. Use a shovel to chop and mix the droppings with the soil. Cover with at least 8 inches of soil to prevent rodents or other pets from digging them up.

1. You're making your very first pile, and you'd like to take every extra step to gain confidence that the pile will "cook."

2. You simply don't have the time or the best choice of materials to mix the right proportion of compost ingredients. (A starter will ensure quick decomposition.)

3. You're making a pile at a new, infertile site with a history of pesticide use. The soil at the site may not contain the microbial organisms that power decomposition. (If you can, get some soil from an active organic garden to add to the pile. Otherwise, using a commercial compost starter is a good alternative.)

Compost Troubleshooting

Is your compost heap just not cooking? The King County Solid Waste Division in Seattle, Washington, which runs one of the most successful municipal composting programs in the country, offers this guide to solving common composting problems.

Symptom	Problem	Solution
Compost has bad odor.	Not enough air	Turn the pile.
Center of pile is dry.	Not enough water	Moisten materials while you turn the pile.
Pile is damp and warm only in middle.	Pile too small	Build a larger pile; mix new materials with the old.
Pile is damp and sweet-smelling but remains cool.	Lack of nitrogen	Add a nitrogen source, such as fresh grass clippings, manure, or blood meal.

HEAT UP YOUR COMPOST

When your compost pile heats up, it does double-duty: It not only produces a great soil amendment but also helps break cycles of weed and disease problems in your garden.

The temperatures in a hot compost pile can kill weed seeds, bacteria, and fungal spores. "When making high-temperature compost, the backyard gardener's goal is to kill weed seeds and plant pathogens without killing the microbial organisms that perform decomposition," explains Harry Hoitink, Ph.D., the principal coordinator for the Ohio State University Composting Research and Education Program. When making high-temperature compost, keep in mind the following suggestions from Dr. Hoitink:

Be sure the pile is tall enough. Backyard piles should be 4 to 6 feet high. Build piles taller in cool weather. In summer, you can get away with a shorter pile.

Monitor temperatures. Compost-pile temperatures should range from 100° to 165°F. You can buy a special compost thermometer from garden supply stores or catalogs. Or use any small thermometer that reads within that temperature range by digging a hole in the side of the pile and burying the thermometer 1 foot deep for several minutes. (Tie a colorful string or ribbon around the thermometer first so it will be easier to find.)

At 100°F, weed seeds and pathogens survive for several weeks. At 130°F, they will last for only three days. Compost temperatures between 130° and 165°F will kill most pests in less than three days. Remember that temperatures greater than 165°F also kill beneficial microorganisms.

Turn your compost pile at approximately two-week intervals. That's about four times for the whole operation, from start to finish. Make sure that you exchange materials from the outside of the pile with materials from the center as you turn it so that all compost ingredients spend equal time in the hot interior of the pile.

FERTILIZE YOUR COMPOST

If your gardening plans include a springtime application of lime, phosphorus, or potassium, add them to your fall compost pile instead, suggests Harry Hoitink, Ph.D., the principal coordinator for the Ohio State University Composting Research and Education Program. He explains that this saves time during the busy spring season, because these soil amendments are then spread automatically and easily as you apply your compost.

BUILD A "BINLESS" COMPOST BIN

Make slow, cool compost with walls built of high-carbon materials that will decompose along with the wastes they contain. Veet Deha, an agricultural consultant and Master Composter, calls this "binless bin" composting. Build the sides and ends with materials like straw, old hay, or woody prunings. Bales of hay stacked in a U-shape work well. (This arrangement is shown in the illustration at right.) These materials will retain more water than a plastic or wood-sided bin, so the compost piles can hold their own when it comes to moisture, even during occasional droughts. "And during times of water rationing, you just don't have

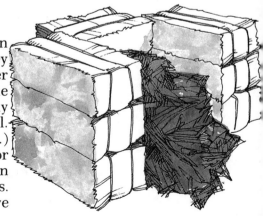

COVER CROPS FOR COMPOST

At Ecology Action of the Midpeninsula, staff gardeners sow and harvest cover crops especially for the compost pile. They sow either pure stands of a single crop or a mixed stand that includes some combination of wheat, rye, fava beans, and vetch. They plant and harvest such stands whenever it's convenient, because cover crop residues make excellent compost ingredients whether they're young and green or mature and brown.

Home gardeners traditionally rely on grass clippings to supply green material for the compost pile, but leaving the clippings on the lawn promotes lawn health. Cover crops are a great alternative. To use cover crops as compost ingredients, first chop the growth in the garden with a scythe or lawn mower. Sweep up the cuttings, then add them to your compost. This method helps minimize soil disturbance, since you won't have to dig the cover crop into your soil.

the luxury of watering a dry compost pile," says Deha. "Locate your pile in the shade to save even more water."

First, construct three walls for the pile—two sides and one end. They should be as high as three bales of straw. Then, start layering organic wastes inside. Deha explains, "That's where you'll put the high-nitrogen or 'green' things. Layer your organic wastes as usual, grabbing handfuls of high-carbon or 'brown' materials from the walls as you build." Build the pile up until it is level with the top of the bin. Then add the fourth wall.

Once the pile is built, let it stand for two years without turning. The outer layer will become a dry crust, but the compost will remain moist inside. Over time, the inner layers will settle, creating a depression on the top of the pile that captures rainwater. To reach the finished compost inside, just break through a wall.

SPEED COMPOST WITH SOAP

Spraying your compost with a simple soap spray can help speed the decomposition process. "Fall compost often isn't ready as soon as you'd like because there are so many dry leaves in the pile. They don't stay moist enough to break down quickly," says Jim Wilson, a cohost of public television's "The Victory Garden." Wilson sprays the layers of leaves with a soapy solution such as Murphy's Oil Soap or any other nondetergent soap. The soap acts as a surfactant to help hold moisture on the dry leaves. That way, Wilson has more finished compost by early spring when he needs it to work into his garden.

Wilson alternates an 8-inch layer of leaves with a ½-inch-thick sprinkling of cricket manure. (You can use other kinds of manure or any other high-nitrogen material.) He uses a hose-end sprayer to douse the leaf layers with the soapy solution as he builds the pile.

Advanced Composting

Once you've mastered the technique of building a backyard compost pile, you may want to try new and different ways of producing and using compost. Have fresh compost year-round by making it indoors with the help of composting worms. Or try screening your compost for an extra-fine soil amendment or making compost tea.

YOU CAN CAN COMPOST

A galvanized or plastic garbage can also serve as a compost bin. "It's my method for raccoon-free composting," quips Brenda Werner, a part-time compost technician with Cornell Cooperative Extension in New York. It also allows you to make compost in your basement or garage if you don't have room in your yard for a pile. A plastic can will last longer than metal because it won't rust. However, if you have rodent problems, use a metal can because rodents can chew through plastic.

Here's Werner's method for making garbage can compost:

1. In the bottom of a 30-gallon plastic or metal garbage can, drill several holes ¼ to ½ inch in diameter. Also drill holes 4 to 6 inches apart all around the sides of the can.

2. Place the can on bricks or cement blocks to ensure the best aeration. Place 2 to 3 inches of dry sawdust, wood chips, or chopped straw in the bottom of the can to absorb excess moisture.

3. Add food wastes in 2-inch-thick layers. Keep in mind that food wastes will compost more quickly and easily if you chop them into small pieces before adding. Top each food layer with 3 to 4 inches of shredded leaves, shredded newspaper, or straw, and a 1-inch layer of soil or sawdust.

4. Between additions, use a bungee cord to hold the lid securely closed to prevent animals from getting into your compost.

5. If you want to keep the compost active, mix weekly with a compost turner to add air and mix materials. Properly managed compost should be ready in six to eight months.

IS IT COMPOST YET?

You can't see the complex chemical reactions taking place over time as materials in a compost pile change, so it's difficult to tell when your compost is ready to use. Most experts advise that gardeners test their compost before using it since phytotoxins (chemicals that are toxic to plants) can form in immature compost piles. William F. Brinton, Jr., an agricultural chemist at Woods End Research Laboratory in Maine, says the best measure of compost quality is "the results you get in your garden." Vigorous, productive plants indicate that composting is working for

KITCHEN COMPOST COLLECTOR

Store kitchen wastes for the compost pile indoors without odor problems by layering the scraps with sawdust or soil in a bucket or other container. Each day, add kitchen scraps to the container and then top with a 1-inch layer of sawdust, soil, or coffee grounds to absorb and hold odors. Continue layering until you have enough materials to warrant a trip to the compost pile. Smaller households might get by with a single clay pot for a collector.

A new product that eliminates worries about odors is a biodegradable compost bag developed jointly by Wood's End Research Laboratory in Mount Vernon, Maine, and Stone Container Corporation of Louisville, Kentucky. The bag looks like a brown paper grocery bag. Inside, it's lined with natural cellulose, to hold liquids and prevent leaks. The surface allows air penetration to the wastes inside, which inhibits the development of odors. The bag stands upright on your kitchen counter; when it's full, just drop it in the compost bin. Within one week, bacteria and fungi will be eating holes through the bag's surface, turning everything into rich, dark compost. To find out how to obtain the compost bags, contact:

Stone Container Corporation
P.O. Box 37020
Louisville, KY 40233

you. Plants won't grow well if your compost lacks important nutrients, is high in phytotoxins, or is immature.

Brinton suggests these two ways of testing compost quality:

1. Put a handful of moist compost in a glass jar, seal the lid, then put the jar in a warm, sunny place. After three days, open the jar and sniff. Good-quality finished compost should have an odor similar to that of freshly turned soil. If the compost smells rotten or foul, your compost isn't mature. Retest at weekly intervals.

2. Mix together equal parts compost and potting soil, then plant lettuce or radish seeds in the mix. At the same time, plant the same kind and number of seeds in plain potting soil. If both groups of seeds germinate uniformly, the compost is safe to use. But if growth is slower in the compost mix, your compost isn't ready.

THE RIGHT WORM FOR THE JOB

Composting with worms, or vermicomposting, is the solution to many waste problems, big and small, but be sure to get the right kind of worm for the job. "Common garden worms aren't the best types to invite indoors," says Mary Appelhof, the author of *Worms Eat My Garbage.* The redworm (or manure worm) *Eisenia fetida* works best for indoor vermicomposting because it prefers an environment with more organic matter than soil. It reproduces quickly in culture and works in a wide temperature range—roughly 40° to 85°F. You're not likely to find *E. fetida* in large numbers outdoors, unless you're willing to dig through manure piles. Most people find it easier to buy them from local or mail-order worm dealers. See "Gardening Equipment" on page 331 for addresses of worm dealers.

To start your own vermicomposting system, you'll need a container, shredded newspaper and garden soil for bedding, worms, the right environment, and a regular supply of kitchen wastes.

1. To make the worm bin, drill several small holes in the sides and bottom of a wooden, metal, or plastic tub (20-gallon volume or larger).

2. In a garbage can or other container, make bedding by mixing together shredded newspaper and water (3 pounds

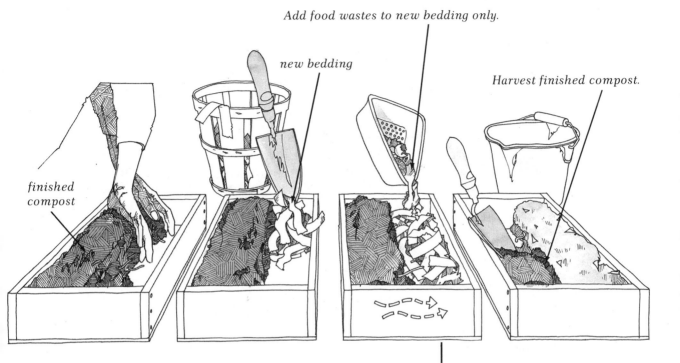

Add food wastes to new bedding only.

new bedding

Harvest finished compost.

finished compost

Worm compost is ready to harvest after two to three months. Push the finished compost to one side of the container, and fill the empty area with new bedding. Put food scraps only in the new bedding for a few weeks so worms will move into it. Then remove the old compost, and add more fresh bedding.

of water per 1 pound of newspaper) and a handful of garden soil.

3. Put the damp bedding into the worm bin. Add 1 pound of redworms. They'll disappear immediately into the bedding.

4. Bury kitchen wastes (in small, 1- to 2-pound batches, at first) in the bedding. After a week or so, the worms will adjust to their new environment and be ready to process larger quantities. In a tub measuring 24 × 24 × 8 inches, 1 pound of worms can process about 3½ pounds of organic waste per week. Each time you add new wastes, bury them in a different spot than the previous time; this will help avoid odors. Loosely cover the bin with a solid lid or a sheet of black plastic to maintain the proper humidity.

5. After two to three months, you can harvest the

WORM NUTRITION

Here are some suggestions for your worms' diet:

Do Feed Your Worms

Bread
Coffee filters
Coffee grounds
Eggshells
Fruit rinds and peels
Grains
Tea bags
Vegetable scraps

Don't Feed Your Worms

Animal products
Butter
Cheese
Fish
Food coated with oil
Meat

COMPOST SIFTER MATERIALS

Cutting List

10 pcs. 1½'' × 3½'' × 36'' (2 bases, 2 bottom crosspieces, 2 top rails, 2 top crosspieces, 2 sifter rails)

4 pcs. 1½'' × 3½'' × 6'' (outer base blocks)

4 pcs. 1½'' × 3½'' × 33'' (legs)

2 pcs. 1½'' × 3½'' × 14'' (middle base blocks)

2 pcs. 1½'' × 3½'' × 40'' (braces)

2 pcs. 1½'' × 3½'' × 25½'' (sifter crosspieces)

2 pcs. ¾'' × 1½'' × 12'' (handles)

Hardware

10d galvanized common nails, as needed

6d galvanized common nails, 4

32 ½'' × 40'' piece of ½'' wire mesh

⅜'' common staples, as needed

8 screw eyes

4 pieces of #3 double-link chain, 10'' long

4 double-ended snap hooks

worm castings (nutrient-rich worm droppings). Push the finished compost (the worm castings) to one side of the box, then add new bedding and kitchen wastes to the other side. For two to four weeks, add wastes to the fresh side only, to encourage your worms to vacate the finished compost. Then, remove the finished compost, and add fresh bedding.

BUILD A SWINGING COMPOST SIFTER

When you're ready for a new challenge in your composting, consider screening it before use. Nancy Ondra, an assistant editor of garden books at Rodale Press, uses a homemade sifter mounted on a wooden frame. "Sometimes compost still contains large chunks of undecomposed or woody matter, even when it's mostly finished," Ondra says. "If you sift the big stuff out, it's easier to mix compost into a potting mix, and it looks better as a surface mulch."

Ondra's compost sifter is made from materials that are available at any lumberyard. "Compost Sifter Materials" at left calls for nails, but if you have an electric drill to drive screws, consider using 2½-inch decking screws instead of the 10d nails and 1½-inch decking screws instead of the 6d nails. Screws cost a bit more, but they will make construction stronger and easier.

To make a compost sifter, gather the materials listed at left and assemble them, following the directions below. Use untreated pine to build the sifter. If desired, you can paint it with a preservative or flat black paint. Use 10d galvanized common nails throughout this project unless otherwise indicated, and follow the illustration at the bottom of the opposite page for positioning of pieces.

1. Cut the major frame parts. Cut the bases, bottom crosspieces, top rails, top crosspieces, and sifter rails to 36 inches long.

2. Assemble the bases and legs. Cut the outer base blocks to 6 inches long. Cut the legs to 33 inches long. Nail the outer base blocks to the bases. Nail the legs to the outer base blocks. Then nail through the bases into the legs. Put the bottom crosspieces in place against the legs, and nail them to the bases. Cut the middle base blocks to fit snugly between the bottom crosspieces. Nail the middle base blocks to the bases.

3. Cut and install the braces. Cut a 45-degree miter on one end of each 40-inch-long brace. Use a miter box if you have one; otherwise, lay out the angled cut and saw carefully to the line with a hand saw.

Check that the legs are square to the bases. Place a miter against the bottom of one leg and mark the other end of the brace for the other miter cut. Cut the miter as marked on the brace. Repeat with the other brace.

Nail through the legs into the mitered ends of the braces, making sure to position the nails far enough from the points of the miters so that they will not come through the braces.

4. Assemble the top of the frame. Nail the top rails to the legs. Position the top crosspieces square to the top rails and nail them in place.

5. Assemble the sifter. Cut the sifter crosspieces to 25½ inches long. Nail the sifter rails to the sifter crosspieces. Cut the wire mesh to the dimensions in the "Materials" list. Center the mesh over the bottom of the sifter, and staple it in place. Use metal snips to cut in from each corner of the mesh to the corresponding corner of the sifter. Fold the mesh up over the sides of the sifter, and staple it in place.

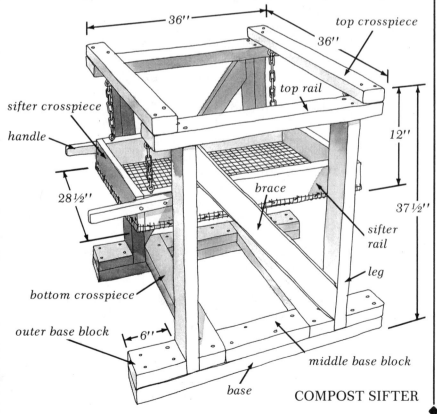

COMPOST SIFTER

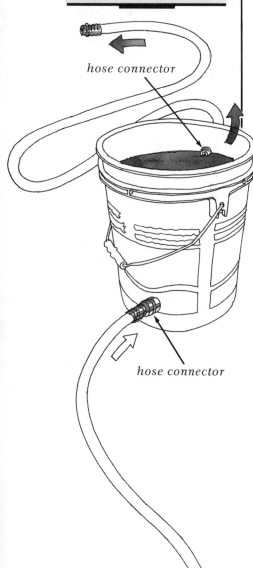

**COMPOST TEA
BREWER MATERIALS**

1 bucket with lid, 2 or 5 gallon
Electric drill and drill bit
2 garden hose replacement
   couplings
Epoxy
1 rubber band
1 piece of cheesecloth or light
   fabric, about 3'' × 3''

hose connector

hose connector

Cut the handles to ¾ × 1½ × 12 inches. Position the handles flush with the top of the sifter rails and overlapping the rails by 6 inches. Fasten the handles to the rails using 6d nails. Sand the edges of the handles to prevent splinters and to make them more comfortable to grasp.

6. Install the sifter. Thread a screw eye into each corner of the sifter. Center a screw eye across the top of each sifter rail ¾ inch from the end of the rail, and thread the eyes into the sifter. Now fasten screw eyes to the bottom of the top crosspieces of the frame, centering these eyes across the width of the crosspieces and locating them 4½ inches from the ends of the crosspieces.

Link a piece of chain to each of the screw eyes in the sifter. Attach a double-ended snap hook to the other end of each chain, and then attach the snap hooks to the screw eyes in the top crosspieces of the frame.

BREW COMPOST TEA ON THE SPOT

There's a simple system for making an instant supply of compost tea for sprinkling on your lawn, trees, flowers, and vegetables. Basically, all you need is your garden hose and a bucket. The 5-gallon plastic buckets in which paint primer or commercial food products are sold work well to make the device shown in the illustration at left. Or you may want to use a smaller bucket. "Ask for a pickle bucket at your local deli," says Fern Marshall Bradley, a garden book editor for Rodale Press. "I have a small garden, so I find a 2-gallon bucket holds enough compost for me, and it's easier to carry around." Here's how to make your compost tea brewer, using the materials listed at left:

1. Near the bottom of the bucket, drill a hole the size of a garden hose replacement coupling. Use epoxy to attach a coupling to the bucket, sealing the edges of the hole.

2. Drill a second hole near the top of the opposite side of the bucket, and use epoxy to attach a second hose coupling to the bucket.

3. Using the rubber band, secure the piece of cheesecloth or light fabric over the upper coupling on the inside of the bucket in order to prevent the solid compost from clogging the sprinkler head.

Fill the bucket with compost, and fasten the bucket lid securely in place. Then, attach your water source to the bottom hole and attach your sprinkler head or second hose to the top hole. As the water swirls around and flows out of the upper hole, you'll have instant compost tea. Carry the bucket around and serve your plants a nutrient-rich treat.

THE GARDEN PROFESSIONALS

Mary Appelhof is the owner of Flowerfield Enterprises, a mail-order business in Kalamazoo, Michigan, that develops and sells books and supplies for worm composting. She is the author of *Worms Eat My Garbage*.

Fern Marshall Bradley is a garden book editor for Rodale Press, Inc. She has a master's degree in horticulture from Rutgers University, and she has managed an organic market garden.

William F. Brinton, Jr., is an agricultural chemist at Woods End Research Laboratory, Inc., in Mount Vernon, Maine. He has written extensively on composting for farmers and industry.

Carol Cox is a garden research manager with Ecology Action of the Midpeninsula in Willits, California. Cox devises the yearly garden plan for Ecology Action, supervises day-to-day garden activities, and teaches apprentices and workshop participants the principles of sustainable biointensive mini-farming.

Veet Deha is an agricultural consultant with Crest Lane Designs in Ithaca, New York. As a Cooperative Extension Master Composter, she assists with informal adult education and provides home compost workshops.

Mary Frances Fenton is a coauthor of *Worms Eat Our Garbage* and is the illustrator for *Worms Eat My Garbage*. She is a certified organic grower in Michigan.

Harry Hoitink, Ph.D., is a professor and the program director for both the Department of Plant Pathology and the Plant Biotechnology Program at Ohio Agricultural Research and Development Center of Ohio State University in Wooster, Ohio.

Cathleen Lalicker is a co-owner and operator of Story House Herb Farm in Murray, Kentucky, which specializes in organic herb plants for the kitchen and garden.

Nancy Ondra is an associate editor of garden books at Rodale Press, Inc. She collects and propagates perennials and trees and maintains a large composting area on her home farm near Pennsburg, Pennsylvania.

Carol Wentz is a gardening and design consultant from Cincinnati, Ohio. She writes for several local publications and lectures widely on organic gardening methods.

Brenda Werner is a part-time compost technician with Cornell Cooperative Extension of Tompkins County, New York.

Jim Wilson is a cohost of public television's "The Victory Garden." He is the author of *Landscaping with Container Plants, Masters of the Victory Garden,* and *Landscaping with Wildflowers*.

Bill Wolf is the founder and president of Necessary Trading Company of New Castle, Virginia. The company manufactures Necessary Organics growing supplies and sells organic fertilizers and pest controls via mail order.

A SPOT OF COMPOST TEA

Compost tea isn't for drinking, of course. It is a great supplement for all of the plants in your yard and for houseplants and container plants, as well.

By the barrel. Fill a barrel or other large container one-quarter full of compost, then fill to the top with water. Stir several times during the next one or two days. Strain the resulting liquid and dilute it with water until it is a light amber color.

By the pot. Make a compost tea bag by placing a handful of finished compost in the center of a square of burlap or cheesecloth. Gather the edges to form a pouch, and tie the top together with string. Place the tea bag in a small bucket or watering can filled with water. Use immediately, or, for a stronger brew, allow it to steep.

Water garden plants with a weak solution of compost tea. At transplanting time, sprinkle the soil around each small plant with about 1 pint of the liquid. After plants are established, you can use 1 quart or more of compost tea per plant per week to maintain growth and production.

You can also make a liquid fertilizer by steeping manure in water. Follow the compost tea directions, substituting fresh or dried manure for the compost. Don't let undiluted manure tea come in contact with plant foliage—it will injure plant tissue.

We all know that water moves downward through soil. But how fast and how far it moves depends on the composition of the soil.

Soil particles collect a film of water, holding it against the pull of gravity. A clayey soil has many very fine particles with lots of surface area to hold water. A sandy soil, made up of fewer, larger particles, has less water-holding capacity. In a clay soil, if you apply 1 inch of water over a given area and allow it to soak in, it will wet the top 4 to 5 inches of soil, but in a sandy soil it will wet the top 12 inches of soil. Most plant roots are found in the top 6 inches of the soil, so applying an inch or more of water at a time to a clay soil makes sense. However, 1 inch of water would be excessive for a sandy soil, because some of it would quickly drain past the zone of most root growth and be wasted.

In heavier soils—those with a good percentage of clay—applying water to one spot, as with a drip emitter, can wet a 12-inch-diameter circle of soil.

Follow these guidelines for watering different types of soil:

Loamy soil. Water evenly and moderately for loam soils.

Sandy soil. Water less long but more often for sandy soils, which drain water quickly.

Clayey soil. Water longer for clay soils, allowing runoff to sink in before continuing.

For all soils, if the top 3 inches of soil are dry during the season of active growth, you probably need to water.

Maintaining the Home Landscape

If you'd rather spend your weekends puttering about with plants than with lawn mowers, you're not alone. We're all looking for ways to cut the time we spend on maintenance chores. Our experts have come up with some novel solutions for landscape maintenance.

Saving water is also a big concern for many of us. We'll show you new ways of looking at the situation, from choosing the right plants to knowing when to water. We also asked the experts for tips on the plants we love to hate: weeds. You'll find suggestions that will cut down on the time you spend fighting those unwanted plants, to leave you more time for enjoying the plants you love.

Save Time, Save Water

In a water-conscious era, we need to be as efficient as we can about water use. But most gardens need some supplemental water. Try these tips for reducing the amount of water you apply and the time you spend doing it.

DESIGN AROUND YOUR DOWNSPOUTS

Save a few spins on your water meter by taking advantage of downspouts to irrigate plants naturally. "Pay attention to where your downspouts are," advises Jim Borland, a Colorado garden writer and consultant on dryland gardening. If your downspouts lead directly to the gutter, reroute them to give your garden a boost.

Plan your design to make the most of rainwater, says Borland. Shape the soil into shallow basins to catch the runoff, or construct rills of slightly hilled soil to direct water to your plants. Place water-hungry plants closest to the extra moisture. In areas with frequent rainfall, some gardeners create a miniature marsh garden near downspouts, using plants such as cardinal flower (*Lobelia cardinalis*), lesser celandine (*Ranunculus ficaria*), marsh marigold (*Caltha palustris*), yellow flag (*Iris pseudacorus*), and water-loving sedges and rushes.

WAIT FOR SIGNS OF WATER STRESS

Instead of watering your entire landscape with an inch of the precious wet stuff every week, water only when the plants need it. Generally speaking, plants in pots may need water every day, lawns every three days, and established trees every ten days, says Tom Bressan, a California irrigation specialist. But watering needs vary widely depending on the species of the plant. Stretch the time between waterings until you see signs of distress, advises Bressan.

"Eyeball it!" he urges. Look at your plants to see which ones show stress first. Stay alert to the not-so-obvious signals of plant distress, such as foliage that seems dull or less glossy or shows curling edges. Watch for leaf drop, a signal that the plant is trying to conserve water. Serious wilting needs attention right away to save the plant.

WATER WISELY WITH A TIMER

Using a timer is one way to make sure your plants are getting the water they need. "Be sure your timer has separate zones for flowers, shrubs, lawn, or other areas," advises Susan A. Roth, the author of *The Weekend Garden Guide*, "so you can water them on different days for different lengths of time, according to their individual needs." Deep-rooted perennials, for instance, generally need less water than your lawn, and shaded areas stay moister than full-sun locations. You might keep lawn grass in one zone; drought-tolerant perennials, trees, and shrubs in another; and water lovers in a third.

A good timer is well worth the investment, Roth says. "Water infrequently but deeply," she urges. "Many timers can only deliver a quarter-inch of water each time they run. This is murder on your plants—and wasteful." It's also a good idea, adds Roth, to run that timer on the manual setting so you can provide water only when Mother Nature doesn't. If you set a timer on automatic, you are all too likely to end up watering your lawn during a rainstorm.

DEPEND ON DRIP

Drip irrigation is a tailor-made way of applying water just where you need it. Tom Bressan, a California irrigation specialist, recommends polyethylene tubing with emitters punched into it where you want them. Drip tapes with

MAKE A WATERING WAND

Generally, it's best to water plants at the base, around the soil and roots, rather than from the top, where moisture-loving fungal diseases can attack foliage. To make a watering wand that helps get the job done, use a sturdy tape, such as duct tape, to fasten a 4-foot length of broomstick or old mop handle along the end of your garden hose. Now you can direct the spray precisely around the bases of plants—without bending your back. Wheelchair gardeners, too, can use this trick to give them a longer reach.

THE CATCH CUP TEST

You can wiggle your finger into the soil to check watering depth in your garden beds, but how do you know how much water your lawn is getting? "Test your sprinkler system with catch cups," suggests Susan A. Roth, the author of *The Weekend Garden Guide*. "Then you can see how much water is being delivered with each watering." You can use empty coffee cans or other equal-size cups as your catch cups. Set them out at various spots in your sprinklered lawn or garden, making sure the catch cups are level. Then set your sprinkler as usual. Watch your sprinkler in action, too, to be sure you aren't wasting water by irrigating the driveway. When the cycle is done, use a ruler to measure the amount of water in each cup. (See "Water to Suit Soil Type" on the opposite page for guidance on how much water you should be applying.)

**UNCLOG YOUR
"LEAKY HOSE"**

Hard water can cause build-ups of minerals inside "leaky hose" irrigation tubing. Iron, calcium, and manganese collect inside tubing as it dries out. To prevent problems, bury your leaky hose under mulch, where the tubing stays damp. A water filter with a 150 or smaller mesh will help keep minerals out of your tubes.

To remove clogs that have formed due to minerals or soil, turn the water on and bend the tubing back and forth until you see water. Then open the end caps and flush the tubing by letting water run through for a few minutes.

---

holes, he says, are too thin-walled for permanent plantings.

It's easy to install drip irrigation in an existing bed. "Use the claw side of a hammer," Bressan advises. "Drag it along the ground to create a shallow trench for the tubing." Add extra emitters for plants that need more water. After your layout is complete, bury the tubing in mulch. (Avoid placing drip tubing on *top* of existing mulch, because the mulch will absorb the water intended for the soil.) Pull the mulch aside if the system needs maintenance.

In an annual bed or vegetable garden, Bressan uses the drip system without mulch. If the plantings are closely spaced, Bressan recommends using emitter lines with regularly spaced, pre-installed emitters. In an annual bed, the leaves screen the tubing, he says, and the impact of the flowers draws the eye away. And in a vegetable garden, no one objects to a visible irrigation system.

LET THIS HOSE LEAK

A leaky hose may be the best irrigation device for the vegetable garden. Arizona garden writer Lynn Tilton uses a lawn spray hose, which has holes punched all along its length, to irrigate his tomato and corn rows. The hose delivers a gentle spray of water every foot or so. Tilton mulches the beds with grass clippings and then lays out the hose. He turns on the water, and the hose sprays upward so the water falls on top of the mulch, binding it together. Then he flips the hose upside down so that the water is forced out directly through the mulch and into the soil. Tilton says, "Our sandy soil makes regular hose watering almost impossible. When I use the sprinkler hose, I get a better crop with one-third the water."

Wipe Out Weeding Woes

Weeds may be the organic gardener's worst problem. A healthy, organic soil can promote luxuriant growth of weeds along with the ornamentals and edibles. While we don't have the final solution for ending the weed war, here are some techniques to help you get the best of the battle. You'll also find suggestions for controlling weeds under "Mulch Better Solutions," beginning on page 118.

MAKE SEEDBEDS FOR SEEDS, NOT WEEDS

To avoid some of the worst spring weed problems, manage your seedbeds with sophistication. "The worst thing you can do," says Michael Maltas, the garden director of the organic showpiece garden for Fetzer Vineyards in California, "is to make a seedbed the way most people do—by tilling or digging it, raking it, and then throwing seeds into it. You just made a seedbed for weeds!"

Instead, make your seedbed like farmers around the world do, Maltas says. Dig and rake it, then wait for rain to bring the weeds. When the undesirables are about ½ inch tall, harrow or rake the bed to kill the weeds. If your new bed sprouted lots of weeds, wait a week or so and harrow or rake it again. Only then should you sow your seeds.

Even better, says Maltas, is to garden in permanent raised beds. People who move their beds around spread weeds around, too. In permanent beds, weeds are easier to pull and fewer in number. Maltas recommends a dock digger (also called a dandelion fork) to get out deep-rooted perennial weeds. A scuffle hoe keeps pathways neat. For directions on making a scuffle hoe out of a conventional hoe, see "Hack Your Hoe in Half" on page 157.

FIGHT THE SITE, NOT THE WEED

You spend hours pulling, cutting, and whacking weeds from a problem spot in your yard—only to have the same pestiferous plants pop up again and again. What to do?

Forget about killing the weeds, and change the growing conditions that favor them, says Matthew Cheever, the owner of Evergreen, a landscape design and maintenance company in Wisconsin. "Most weeds," says Cheever, "are very site-specific; they'll grow only under certain conditions. If you want to control them, you have to control the conditions."

A good example, says Cheever, is prostrate knotweed (*Polygonum aviculare*), a wiry, tenacious plant that grows between the cracks in sidewalks and in high-traffic areas in yards. "Knotweed grows only in compacted soil," says Cheever. "So to get rid of the knotweed, get rid of the compaction." Loosen or aerate the soil, work plenty of organic matter into it, and replant the spot with a desirable grass seed or groundcover. Or in places that get a lot of foot traffic and are subject to repeated compaction, simply put in mulched pathways.

HANDY HOSE GUIDES

A cheap hose kinks, cracks, and is generally a pain to use around the garden. But even a flexible, good-quality hose resists orderly behavior when you try to pull it around among garden rows and beds.

Protect your plants by installing guides at the corners and outward curves of beds. The guides hold the hose in place, preventing it from snapping the heads off of your favorite flowers or crushing your vegetable transplants when you give the hose a tug to reach a farther part of the bed. Just drive a 2-foot piece of galvanized pipe or steel rebar into the ground and slip a length of bamboo or PVC pipe over it. Be sure that the top edge of the bamboo or PVC pipe is sanded smooth and covers the sharp rebar.

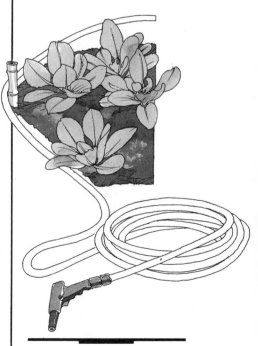

COVER THOSE BARE SPOTS

Expose soil to the elements, and you start a race with nature to cover the bald spot. But don't rush too fast to plant a bare spot. Have the soil tested first, says Matthew Cheever, the owner of Evergreen, a landscape design and maintenance company in Wisconsin. Once you know the soil's pH and overall fertility, you can amend the soil to suit your chosen plants. Or you can choose a plant or cultivar that will thrive in the existing conditions. For information on soil tests, see "Tracking Down a Test" on page 89. But remember, if you don't plant the area or cover it with natural mulch, nature will cover it for you — with weeds.

SKIMMING WEEDS
WITH A SPADE

Other weeds that favor compacted soil include Bermuda grass (*Cynodon dactylon*), puncture vine (*Tribulus terrestris*), goose grass (*Eleusine indica*), and stink grass (*Eragrostis cilianensis*).

Among weeds that prefer undernourished, infertile soil are smooth brome (*Bromus inermis*) and white clover (*Trifolium repens*). Fertilizer and compost will make the site less hospitable to them.

Likewise, trimming surrounding trees and bushes to let more sunlight in is sometimes all that's needed to chase away shade-loving weeds such as mouse-ear chickweed (*Cerastium vulgatum*) and common chickweed (*Stellaria media*).

FOR CLEARING WEEDS, A SPADE IS ACES

Most growers think of the classic rectangular-bladed garden spade as strictly a *digging* tool. But you can also use a spade to slice plant stems at or just below the soil surface, a technique called skimming (shown in the illustration at left). "I think of skimming as sort of giving the garden a haircut," says North Carolina garden writer Susan Sides. "It's a great way to give weedy pathways a quick trim. And I use it to cut back cover crops such as buckwheat and rye."

Sharpen your spade's blade using a mill file or sharpening stone before skimming. Sides prefers to create a cutting edge on the back side of her spade; others prefer the front. In either case, lay the spade down on something solid, and anchor it with your foot or knee. Run your sharpener several times over the blade edge at a moderate angle, moving the sharpener from left to right with each stroke. Once the lip is reasonably well-honed (it doesn't have to be knife-sharp) turn the blade over and give the opposite side a few quick strokes to "feather" the edge. You'll need to resharpen your spade from time to time. (You'll feel it when it needs it.) A single sharpening is generally sufficient for an hour or two of skimming.

Here's how to skim with a spade: Bend over so that you can insert the blade of the spade just below the soil surface with the blade almost parallel to the ground. Push the spade forward so that the blade cuts through the plants just below ground level. As you push the blade ahead, add a slight, circular sideways motion so that the sharpened edge slices the greenery. The spade should cut forward and across, rather than down into, the soil as you work. Lift the cut vegetation on the blade, tip it to one side or toss it into a wheelbarrow, skim off another section, and so on. You'll soon develop a working rhythm that will speed the whole process along.

"Sometimes, with really tall, thick vegetation, it's a good idea to cut the plants back with a scythe or sickle and then skim off the stubble," says Sides. "But in general, the spade alone will do the job."

WINTER'S FOR WEEDING, TOO

Cool-season annual weeds such as common chickweed (*Stellaria media*) and henbit (*Lamium amplexicaule*) germinate in the fall, grow slowly, and then set seed in early spring. By the time the weather's warm enough for you to plant, the weeds have already taken over.

Barbara W. Ellis, the managing editor of garden books for Rodale Press, has a method that not only avoids the problem but also gives gardeners with itching-to-get-going hands something to do during the off-season.

"Every January or February, there'll be an unusually warm day, say 50° or 55°F, when you're dying to get out," says Ellis. "It's still too early, and too cold, to dig or plant. But the top inch or so of soil is thawed. That's what makes it a perfect time to do some weeding."

In midwinter, most cool-season weeds are small and shallow-rooted, so they're easy to pull. Just be sure to bundle up before you go out—and take a kneeling pad with you to use as insulation between you and the cold ground.

"One session basically eliminates problems with cool-season annuals," says Ellis. "And pulling up tiny little weeds on a mild winter's day is a lot more pleasant than battling a bed full of weeds in the spring!"

COVERCROP YOUR QUACKGRASS AWAY

Among the toughest of all perennial weeds is quackgrass (*Agropyron repens*). Pull or till the plant, and new shoots spring up from fragments of stems or roots. Let it mature, and the wheatlike spikes cast seed that can remain viable in the soil for up to four years.

You *can* beat quackgrass and other stubborn weeds, though, by smothering them with cover crops.

"We had quackgrass throughout all our perennials," recalls Eileen Weinsteiger, the garden project manager at the Rodale Institute Research Center in Pennsylvania. "Finally, one summer, we just took everything out and sowed three succession plantings of buckwheat, and that really got rid of the quackgrass."

BE YOUR OWN WEED EATER

Many of the plants considered to be weeds make excellent eating and contain two to three times the nutritional value of greens such as spinach and chard. Of course, there are also poisonous weeds, so be sure you've identified plants correctly before you bite. See "Recommended Reading" on page 333 for titles of weed identification guides.

Mix a wild-greens salad. Use any combination of young leaves from dandelion (*Taraxacum officinale*), chicory (*Cichorium intybus*), lamb's quarters (*Chenopodium* spp.), shepherd's-purse (*Capsella bursa-pastoris*), and watercress (*Nasturtium officinale*). Serve with a simple oil-and-vinegar dressing.

Steam or sauté. Any of the above weeds, as well as curly dock (*Rumex crispus*), early winter cress (*Barbarea verna*), and sheep sorrel (*Rumex acetosella*), can be sautéed in olive oil and garlic or steamed. Drizzle the cooked greens with lemon juice.

Raise sprouts or bake seeds. Raise sprouts for salads and sandwiches by germinating the seeds of green amaranth (*Amaranthus hybridus*), plantains (*Plantago* spp.), or lamb's quarters (*Chenopodium* spp.). Or, for tasty muffins and breads, roast the seeds in a low-temperature oven for 1 hour, then grind them in a blender, and combine the resulting meal with unbleached or whole-wheat flour in proportions up to half-and-half. Use the mixture as you would regular flour.

GET THEM WHILE
THEY'RE YOUNG

We all recognize the familiar yellow flowers and fluffy white seed heads of dandelions. But do you know what a dandelion seedling looks like?

Small weed seedlings may seem like a low-priority concern, but small weeds are easy to pull or hoe, and you avoid the possibility of having them set seed and sow future weed problems. Become familiar with the seedling stage of the common weeds in your garden, and show them no mercy. The illustrations below and on the opposite page show the seedling stage of some of the most widespread weeds in North American gardens. You can also find illustrations of weed seedlings in good weed identification guides, such as those included in "Recommended Reading" on page 333.

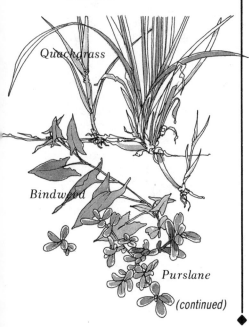

Quackgrass

Bindweed

Purslane

(continued)

Here's Weinsteiger's technique:

1. In early summer, remove any desirable plants from the problem spot. Till the soil, broadcast buckwheat seed (2 to 3 pounds per 1,000 square feet) over the entire area, and tamp it down with a hoe.

2. Just before the buckwheat flowers, till it under, and immediately reseed the area with buckwheat.

3. Repeat the till-and-reseed process when the second crop is about to bloom.

4. In the fall, till the third buckwheat stand under just before it blossoms. Then plant crimson clover (*Trifolium incarnatum*). Seed it heavily, up to 10 pounds per 1,000 square feet. The next year, allow the clover to flower, then turn it under. The area is now ready to be put back into production—with little or no quackgrass to worry over.

Mulch Better Solutions

Every organic gardener should be a mulch expert. Mulching is one of the best ways to fight weeds. It also improves the garden's appearance, reduces water loss, and protects soil from compaction and erosion. If you use an organic mulch, the icing on the cake is improved soil quality as the mulch decays.

CLEAR THE WAY WITH CARDBOARD

You can get a new site ready for planting without weeding the area and even without digging, says Susan Sides, a North Carolina garden writer. The key: cardboard.

Instead of hacking weeds away from a site and then digging or tilling, just put a layer of cardboard over the ground. Sides gets cardboard from her local recycling center. She says that chicken-feed or dog-food bags also fill the bill, as will newspaper.

Once you've covered the ground, wet the cardboard and spread a layer of organic mulch, such as grass clippings, on top. Allow at least two weeks for the grass and weeds underneath to decompose.

"I learned this trick from a woman who runs a plant nursery in Florida," says Sides. "Down there, grass and weeds are especially tough, and soil dries out quickly. But this technique takes care of both problems."

When you're ready to plant, just push a trowel through

the mulch and cardboard into the moist soil, and set your seedlings in place. "After that, you can throw more mulch on top whenever you want or need to," says Sides. "The cardboard breaks down pretty quickly; worms seem to love the stuff. It only takes a few months to a year, depending on your climate, for the cardboard to decompose completely. But because weeds haven't had any chance to grow during that time, the area stays pretty much weed-free as long as you keep adding mulch."

SOUR MULCH: BEAUTIFUL, BUT DEADLY

Wood chips and shredded bark make attractive mulch, but in some cases they can spell death to your plants. Improperly stored organic mulch materials can decompose anaerobically—without oxygen—and produce chemicals including methane and ammonia gas that are toxic to plants. "Soured" mulch also tends to lower soil pH, making nutrients less available. Symptoms of mulch toxicity include yellowing of leaf margins, loss of leaves, and even dead plants.

The key to avoiding the problem, says Donald Rakow, Ph.D., an associate professor of landscape horticulture at Cornell University, is to make sure mulch gets plenty of fresh air. Mulch stored in bins or in overly large piles can't "breathe." "Mulch piles should be turned and mixed at least once a month," says Dr. Rakow. "And the pile shouldn't be higher than 8 feet or wider than 10 to 12 feet." It's also important not to let moisture accumulate in the pile.

Keep Dr. Rakow's mulch-care principles in mind not only when storing the materials but also when shopping for them at garden centers. Ask yourself these questions: If it's sold in bulk, is the mulch kept in properly managed piles? And if it comes in bags, are those bags intact, or has rainwater seeped in through rips and tears?

One sure sign of soured mulch is its odor. According to Dr. Rakow, anaerobic decomposition results in mulch that has a pungent, astringent smell, instead of its usual pleasant, woodsy aroma.

It's also important, says Dr. Rakow, to limit the layer of mulch around landscape plants to just 3 or 4 inches. "A very deep mulch increases the chance of anaerobic decomposition," says Dr. Rakow. Instead of routinely adding several inches of new mulch around shrubs and flowers each year, fluff up the material that's already there. And when you do need to add a top layer of fresh mulch, limit it to just an inch or so.

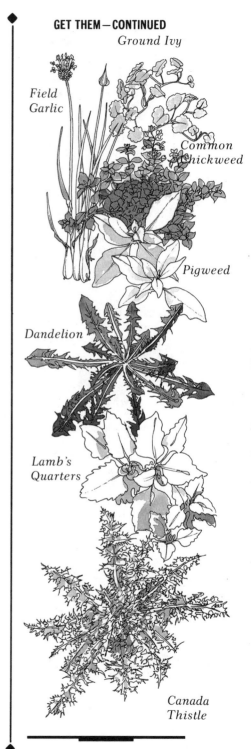

GET THEM—CONTINUED

Ground Ivy

Field Garlic

Common Chickweed

Pigweed

Dandelion

Lamb's Quarters

Canada Thistle

THE SUN AS WEED KILLER

Soil solarization is one of the most effective methods for ridding a site of weed seeds, as well as many insects and disease pathogens. The high heat and humidity produced by covering moist soil with clear plastic are lethal to most organisms. In order to be effective, however, the procedure *must* be done properly, during the hottest months of the summer.

Here's how to treat your soil with the sun's radiant energy, as shown in the illustration at right.

1. Clear the area or bed of all existing plants and debris. If previously uncultivated, till the soil to a depth of about 12 inches. Break up any clods of dirt, and rake the surface smooth.

2. Dig a trench 3 or 4 inches deep around the area.

3. Water the soil thoroughly, until it is literally soaking wet.

4. Before the soil has a chance to lose moisture, spread 1- to 4-mil clear (not black or colored) plastic film over the area and press it down so that it touches the soil.

5. Mound dirt over the plastic in the trench to seal off the edges.

6. Keep the soil covered for four to six weeks.

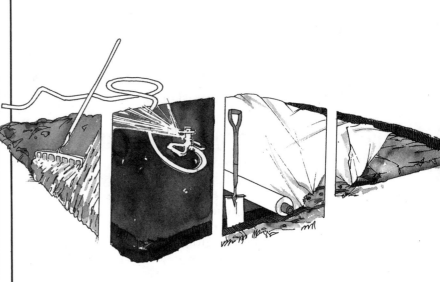

To kill weed seeds and some plant pathogens, solarize the soil by raking it smooth, wetting it thoroughly, and covering it tightly with plastic for several weeks. See "The Sun As Weed Killer" at left for step-by-step instructions for solarizing a garden plot.

CHUNKY MULCH FOR HEALTHIER SOIL

Choose mulches for permanent plantings with extra care. "The best mulch to use is a large-chunk bark," says Jim Borland, a Colorado garden writer and consultant. According to Borland, large-chunk bark is the optimum size for allowing air to reach the soil, while still retaining soil moisture. Air is essential for soil life, such as earthworms, soil bacteria, and many other too-small-to-see creatures. Plant roots, too, need oxygen.

A mulch with small pieces can prevent oxygen from moving down into the soil. And a mulch with much larger pieces allows for air spaces that are too big, drying out the soil faster. The thickness of each particle and the way they lay together in a chunk-size mulch provides optimum air spaces. A large-chunk pine bark mulch, says Borland, is just the right size for healthy soil, and it lasts at least two or three years.

MAKE AN ISLAND WITH MULCH

One great way to boost tree health and reduce yard maintenance in one step is to link groups of trees and shrubs with a groundcover of organic mulch. "A groundcover of mulch is ideal for trees because it doesn't disturb roots and doesn't compete for nutrients and water in the soil as planted groundcovers would," says Jack Siebenthaler, a registered landscape architect from Florida. The idea is to use spreads of mulch to create an "island" within a landscape, linking trees together visually the same way you would if you were planting the area with a groundcover. This is a popular solution on new building lots with a small grove of trees that were carved from existing woods.

The mulch also means no mowing or plant maintenance—just occasional weed control and remulching once or twice yearly. Bark is a handsome mulching material available throughout most of the country, while pine straw and other neat mulches are regional options. A layer about 3 inches deep is adequate for most sites. See "Mulch Shouldn't Touch Bark" on page 123 for more tips on how to lay mulch properly around the bases of trees.

THE LAWN AND SHORT OF GRASS MULCH

Generally, you should leave your grass clippings where they lay—they're an excellent source of nitrogen for your lawn, and (contrary to long-held belief) they *don't* contribute to excessive thatch buildup.

On the other hand, you may want to use some of those nutrient-rich clippings to mulch your vegetables and ornamentals. Eileen Weinsteiger, the garden project manager at the Rodale Institute Research Center in Pennsylvania, does just that to keep weeds down in the Research Center's growing beds. What's more, she uses a *living* grass mulch between the beds to smother weeds—and to provide a steady supply of clippings.

"Our growing beds are 5 × 12 feet," says Weinsteiger, "and they're separated by 2-foot-wide pathways planted in ordinary turfgrass." Nutrient runoff from compost applied to the beds in the spring helps the grass pathways thrive.

The grass pathways need weekly mowing. After the soil has warmed, in late May or June, Weinsteiger applies 4 inches of fresh, green grass clippings to the beds every six weeks. The mulch heats up as it decomposes, so she's careful not to put it too close to seedlings. "I like the idea of using something that's generated in the garden to mulch

WEEDS IN CRACKS BREAKING YOUR BACK?

Here's an easy trick for dealing with stubborn weeds that pop up between the cracks in sidewalks, patios, and paved pathways: Put ¼ cup of table salt in 1 quart of boiling water, and pour the hot liquid on the offending plants. You'll kill the weeds—and they won't come back.

HOW MUCH MULCH?

How thickly you lay mulch depends on the size of its particles. Thin, fine particles such as compost or finely shredded bark are best laid only 2 inches deep around most plants. If you apply a thicker layer, you risk reducing oxygen to the roots as well as burying the plant crown, which may invite rot. You can apply large chunks of bark or rock often used in tree and shrub areas to about 4 inches deep. The larger spaces between the chunks allow more air and light in, so you need a thicker layer for effective weed control.

GRANITE GROUNDCOVER

If you live in an arid climate, you may want to take the idea of a stone mulch one step farther, and use granite as a groundcover, says Paul Bessey, Ph.D., a retired horticulture extension specialist from Arizona. "Out here in Phoenix, what little rain we get usually comes in two blasts—one in January and one in July. Water is so expensive that most people limit its use to keeping alive a small flower garden, vegetable garden, or a little lawn," Dr. Bessey says. Dr. Bessey likes using decomposed granite because it keeps the dust down. "The best is a granite mix that comes in natural desert soil colors. I try to discourage the use of white gravel; in this bright light, it wears on the eyes," Dr. Bessey says.

the garden," says Weinsteiger, "and the grass does an excellent job of suppressing weeds."

Matthew Cheever, the owner of Evergreen, a landscape design and maintenance company in Wisconsin, recommends grass clippings as a weed-smothering mulch for ornamentals, too—but admits the material isn't especially attractive. His solution: Apply the clippings, then top them with a layer of decorative bark mulch.

STONE MULCH ANNUAL BEDS

Most gardeners find they never have enough organic mulch to go around—particularly after they've already generously mulched the perennial beds and vegetable patch. If you still want to put in some colorful annual flowers, but you're completely out of compost, leaves, pine straw, and wood chips, what do you do?

Use stones, as shown in the illustration below. Pat Williams, a copublisher of *HortIdeas* newsletter from Kentucky, says, "By the time I get around to planting annuals, there's never enough 'real' mulch left, so I use flat stones instead. I just arrange them around the plants, and lay them close together so there are only small cracks

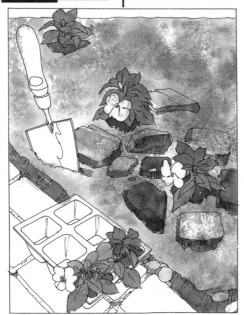

Lay flat stones around newly planted annuals as a mulch (*left*). The plants will cover the stones as they grow (*right*).

between them. The stones keep most of the weeds out and stabilize the soil temperature, too. As the flowers grow, they more or less cover up the mulch, and the stone that's still visible blends nicely with the foliage and blossoms. And when I go to plant annuals the following year, I just lift the stones up and dig."

Expert Solutions to Common Problems

We take pride in our gardens, and we want them to look their best. Here, we present great tips on small details that will give your yard that extra something. You'll also find ideas on how to deal with common problems in the home landscape, like a soggy low spot in the lawn and pesky lawn grass that won't stay out of your flower beds.

ADD INSTANT SHADE WITH AN ARBOR

A sunny yard is great for gardening, but it needs a shady corner where you can relax with a tall glass of iced tea after the digging and the planting. If you don't want to wait years for trees to grow tall enough to cast shade, consider a shady arbor. A shade structure is immediate, notes Michael Glassman, a California landscape designer. A structure attached to your house combines the feel of the outdoors with the cozy appeal of a room.

For best effect, Glassman recommends painting the arbor the color of the house or its trim so it becomes part of the house. "A natural redwood structure attached to a cream house with teal trim—right away you know it's an add-on," Glassman says. "But if you paint it cream or teal, it looks like it's been there forever." To further unify your outdoor room with the house, repeat materials used inside, such as unusual tiling, with those used outside. This continuity, says Glassman, makes the outdoor space look bigger.

Fast-growing vines such as sweet autumn clematis (*Clematis maximowicziana*), Virginia creeper (*Parthenocissus quinquefolia*), or wisterias (*Wisteria* spp.) keep a trellised shade structure cool and green in summer but let sunlight through in winter. When the trellis needs repainting, cut back the vines. They regrow quickly.

A FIELD OF FREE MULCH

Use your ingenuity when looking for local sources of free mulch. Lynn Tilton, an Arizona garden writer, suggests one possibility—your local high school's football field. Tilton spreads the grass clippings from the field on his vegetable beds a couple of inches thick.

Try checking with your local school to see whether you can collect grass clippings from the athletic fields. One caution: If you do, be sure to inquire whether the fields are ever sprayed with synthetic chemical pesticides. If they use chemicals, *don't* take their clippings.

MULCH SHOULDN'T TOUCH BARK

Mulching around your trees and shrubs can help reduce competition from weeds or grass and lessens the danger of sideswiping trunks with the lawn mower. However, a pile of mulch butting the base of trees or shrubs keeps the trunk and stems so moist that diseases such as canker can easily get started. Also, the bark can rot, and some types of boring insects like to make their home in the dark, moist area.

The correct way to apply mulch is to layer it about 3 inches deep at the drip line of the tree and taper it down to about a ½-inch-thick layer near the trunk, as shown on page 18. The mulch should not touch the bark.

MULCH CONSTRUCTION SITES

To reduce soil compaction from heavy vehicles during construction, spread a 6-inch layer of organic mulch such as bark or wood chips on the area to be driven over. The thick mulch cushions the soil and helps prevent deadly compaction of soil around tree roots or in open areas that will one day be planted in lawn, groundcover, or flower and shrub beds. A good source of large quantities of free chips and organic material is a municipal composting site or your local power company.

KEEP BEDS NEAT WITH MUSCLE POWER

Keeping grass from invading flower beds can be a trial. Garden edging strips are easy to install but not always easy to maintain. Virginia Blakelock, the past president of the Hobby Greenhouse Association, recommends edging beds by hand. "It's tiring work," she admits, "but it lasts for years with occasional touch-ups." To edge beds with muscle power, use a shovel or a half-moon edger with a very sharp edge. Cut straight down 3 to 4 inches into the sod near the edge of the bed. Then push the shovel handle and blade forward at a 45-degree angle into the bed to create a shallow V-shaped trench. Continue along the length of the entire bed. Then use the spade or edger to skim off and remove the sod.

TRY THE LAZY WAY TO BETTER DRAINAGE

"The easiest way to take care of a poorly drained area is to plant a willow," says Paul Solyn, the founding managing editor of *Trillium: The Journal of the Ohio Native Plant Society.* Fast-growing willows (*Salix* spp.) succeed in almost any soil. A smaller species such as the native pussy willow (*S. discolor*) is a good choice to help dry up a wet area because its smaller root system is much better behaved than that of large trees like the weeping willow (*S. babylonica*) or white willow (*S. alba*). A large willow will intrude on water and sewer lines many feet away, so it's only practical somewhat apart from civilization.

FLOWERS THAT LIKE IT WET AND WILD

Plant native American wildflowers to add color and attract butterflies to a drab, wet area. Robyn Fletcher, a co-owner of Gardens of the Blue Ridge in North Carolina, recommends ironweeds (*Vernonia* spp.), beautiful rich purple, 4- to 5-foot-tall plants that are uncomplaining about wet feet. "Joe-Pye weed [*Eupatorium purpureum*] is another good one for a wet spot," says Fletcher. Keep in mind that Joe-Pye weed can reach as much as 14 feet in height. Butterflies love its fuzzy, mauve puffs of flowers.

Striking red cardinal flower (*Lobelia cardinalis*) brightens the scene in late summer. Its growing popularity as a perennial for the border is evidence of its adaptability. In the wild, this water lover can be found along streams and lakes. Bee balm (*Monarda didyma*) is another native that thrives in wet spots. Both bee balm and cardinal flower are hummingbird favorites.

REMODEL THAT CLUMP OF GRASS

Building a bed may be the best solution for dealing with an out-of-place clump of ornamental grass. Grasses such as fast-growing pampas grass (*Cortaderia selloana*) or Japanese silver grass (*Miscanthus sinensis*) can quickly become permanently entrenched. It's hard, sometimes impossible, to dig and transplant a heavy, unwieldy clump of grass with its vigorous root system. Also, specimen clumps can stick out like sore thumbs sometimes, especially when you're redoing the rest of your home landscape in a less formal, more unified style.

If you're the proud owner of a healthy, established clump of grass—but you wish it were someplace else—don't call in the backhoe. "The best solution may be to build a bed around it," says Catherine Betz, the office manager at Kurt Bluemel, a Maryland nursery. Make the clump a focal point in a new bed, as shown in the illustration below, or back

RENOVATE ORNAMENTAL GRASSES

Some ornamental grasses begin to die out in the center after a few years of growth. There's no need to remove the clump, says Catherine Betz, the office manager at Kurt Bluemel, a Maryland nursery. Just dig a hole in the middle of it, says Betz, and put in a new, young plant of the same kind. The time for this operation is spring, when vigorous new growth is just beginning.

An overgrown clump of ornamental grass such as this one can look awkward and out-of-proportion (*left*). Change the scene for the better by making the grass the focal point of a mixed bed of perennials and other grasses (*right*).

SWEEP, DON'T RAKE

To keep your moss garden tidy, use your kitchen broom instead of your grass rake. A rake will rip up the moss in its tines, no matter how gentle you try to be. And handpicking twigs and leaves can be tedious work. As moss appreciators in Japan have known for centuries, a broom is just right for sweeping these sensitive greens. You can buy a loose, long-bristled Japanese broom at some oriental markets, or you can use an ordinary natural-bristle kitchen broom.

it with shrubs or trees. Or use a hatchet to sever divisions from the edge of the clump and make a massed planting of grass, adding shrubs and perennials for contrast and color.

LEARN MOSS APPRECIATION

For a rocky spot or an area that's shady and moist all the time, consider the quiet appeal of a velvety garden of moss. "We use it as a kind of pause—there's so much to look at in the rest of the garden," says Kipp McIntyre, who, with partner Lynne Randolph, co-owns Mostly Moss, a Georgia business that specializes in sculptured moss gardens. "A moss garden is restful, a good place to put a bench. It adds a different scale to the garden."

Choose a site that's the coolest and most comfortable spot to be on a hot summer day, advises McIntyre. Full summer sun can be devastating, though mosses will grow in heat as long as they have shade and moisture. Follow these steps and the illustrations on the opposite page to create the garden:

1. Remove all grass and weeds, and till to a depth of 6 inches. Remove the 6 inches of loosened soil, and set it aside.

2. In the excavated area, spread pea gravel to a depth of 3 inches. Then put back enough of the reserved soil to bring the area back to ground level.

3. Cover the area with nylon window screening. This will prevent weeds from growing up and into the moss.

4. Mix some of the remaining soil with rich compost, and spread a 1- to 2-inch layer on top of the screening.

5. Spread moss over the rich soil.

You can collect moss colonies from your own yard and carefully move them, or you can use dry, shredded moss. Moss is a wonder plant—it can stay dry for months at a time, then regrow into a lush carpet of green. McIntyre recalls visiting a bryologist at the University of Georgia: "He pulled out 50-year-old samples of mosses, sprayed them with a bit of water, and they began to open their leaves. Fifty years without water, and they're ready to grow again!"

Use a sprinkler with a fine-mist head to keep your moss garden evenly moist for three weeks. Water with a fine mist, as needed, to keep the plants green and thriving. And don't forget to add a bench!

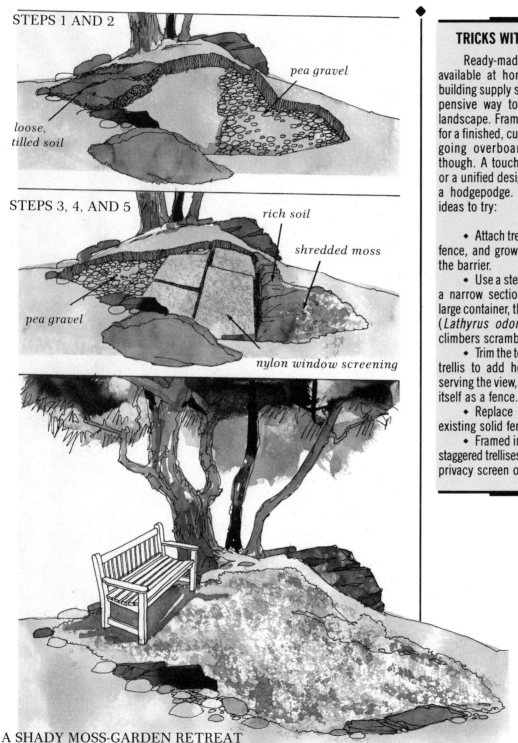

STEPS 1 AND 2

pea gravel

*loose,
tilled soil*

STEPS 3, 4, AND 5

rich soil

shredded moss

pea gravel

nylon window screening

A SHADY MOSS-GARDEN RETREAT

TRICKS WITH TRELLIS

Ready-made trellis, widely available at home centers and building supply stores, is an inexpensive way to decorate your landscape. Frame it with 1 × 4's for a finished, custom look. Avoid going overboard with trellis, though. A touch here and there or a unified design is better than a hodgepodge. Here are some ideas to try:

◆ Attach trellis to a stockade fence, and grow vines to soften the barrier.
◆ Use a steel pipe to anchor a narrow section of trellis in a large container, then let sweet pea (*Lathyrus odoratus*) or other climbers scramble up it.
◆ Trim the top of a fence with trellis to add height while preserving the view, or use the trellis itself as a fence.
◆ Replace a section of an existing solid fence with trellis.
◆ Framed in sturdy 2 × 4's, staggered trellises make an instant privacy screen or a windbreak.

SALT SOLUTIONS

If you live in the Upper Midwest or Northeast, your plants may suffer from damage due to use of de-icing salts on roadways. Here are some ways to reduce salt-damage problems:

- After roads are salted, water your plants thoroughly to wash off the salt.
- Remove salty snow from around plants before it melts.
- Dig runoff ditches so that salt doesn't accumulate in the soil near your plants.
- Plant salt-tolerant plants, including juniper, lilac, honey locust (*Gleditsia triacanthos*), smoke tree (*Cotinus coggygria*), and little-leaved linden (*Tilia cordata*).

◆ INVITE INVASIVES IN

Although the tenacity and vigor of invasive plants may be a bane in the garden, these hardy traits are welcome when you have a difficult spot to work with. Fast-moving spreaders like 'Silver King' artemisia (*Artemisia ludoviciana* 'Silver King'), bee balm (*Monarda didyma*), evening primroses (*Oenothera* spp.), hardy ageratum (*Eupatorium coelestinum*), and St.-John's-worts (*Hypericum* spp.) are right at home on a sunny roadside slope that's hard to mow. You'll find more information about planting and caring for fast-spreading groundcovers like these under "Groundcovers," beginning on page 319.

It's all a matter of right plant, right place. We appreciate groundcovers like ajugas (*Ajuga* spp.) and pachysandras for their takeover tendencies because we've learned how to use them. "Invasiveness depends on your conditions, too," says Anne Janisse, a Washington State garden designer. "Different microclimates or soil can cause a plant to go out of control—or can curb it." Janisse recommends keeping a watchful eye on any new planting of an invasive species. "With invasives, you can't turn your back for long!" Janisse warns. Her recommendation if a plant seems to be spreading out of control: Rip it out.

GIVE UP GRASS AND GO NATIVE

The front lawn is a firmly established aspect of most American homes, and your neighbors may look askance when you decide to eliminate that water guzzler and go natural. How do you get your neighbors to appreciate a mixed-grass prairie or a naturalized planting, when all they see is weeds? "The best way is by example," believes Jim Borland, a Colorado garden writer and consultant.

Two houses ago, Borland ripped out the bluegrass lawn and put in native grasses. "Our next-door neighbors looked at it totally aghast," he laughs. The first year was nothing to brag about; the plants were small, and it took a while for them to become established. But the following year, says Borland, "it bloomed its little head off!"

Design your alternative front yard just as you would any other garden. Add structure with rocks and shrubs, and plan for year-round interest. Neighbors will soon come to realize that your alternative front yard is a garden, especially when they see you walking and working in it.

Borland recommends focusing on American natives

to learn a new appreciation for our underutilized and underappreciated plants. As more gardeners plant natives, their appeal naturally increases. Ask your Cooperative Extension Service office what weeds are noxious in your area, and keep thistles and other unwelcome plants in check.

ADD GRASS TO WILDFLOWER MIXES

Planting a meadow is becoming a popular alternative to planting a standard lawn. It's low-maintenance, drought-tolerant, and beautiful in bloom. But when you plant a patch of meadow flowers, remember to think about what will happen when the blooming is over. A natural meadow, even on the vivid California hillsides, includes grasses among the flowers. When the burst of color is over, the grasses mature to a warm, golden tan, their seed heads adding texture and interest.

Those eye-catching sweeps of wildflowers in the photos are a fleeting glory. Most of the showy annuals bloom for about two weeks in their natural habitat and only a little longer in garden conditions. For a more interesting wildflower meadow, look for a seed mix with perennial grasses in it, says Steve Atwood, the president of Clyde Robin Seed Company in California. "You want a mix that looks like what nature has done," he says. Atwood's number one seller, Meadow in a Can, contains a blend of perennial bunch grasses along with the wildflowers. Use annuals as a nurse crop, he says, to give the planting a blast of color while perennials are getting established. By the third year, the perennials will take over. A planting on a hill shows the flowers off to best advantage and provides good drainage.

A RIVER OF STONE

If your yard is inundated every time there's a summer thunderstorm, consider building a river of stone to direct that extra water to a buried drainage line beneath the "river" or elsewhere. Smooth river rocks set in a natural-colored mix of portland cement and soil look like a stream even when there's no water flowing over them. You can weave these "rivers" between beds or below slopes, or follow the curve of your path. When rains deluge your garden with runoff, the rock-lined channel holds the water until it can drain, or it safely carries the water away.

THE GARDEN PROFESSIONALS

Steve Atwood is the president of Clyde Robin Seed Company, a primary grower of flower and wildflower seeds, located in Hayward, California. He is the author of *A Child's Garden.*

Paul Bessey, Ph.D., is a retired extension specialist in horticulture at the University of Arizona and a garden columnist for the *Arizona Daily Star.* He is president of the Tucson Botanical Gardens and the Men's Garden Club of Tucson.

Catherine Betz is the office manager at Kurt Bluemel, Inc., in Baldwin, Maryland—a wholesale and retail mail-order nursery specializing in ornamental grasses, sedges, rushes, bamboo, and perennials.

Virginia Blakelock is a free-lance garden writer from Yellow Springs, Ohio. She is the past president of the Hobby Greenhouse Association, Inc., a nonprofit organization of home greenhouse owners.

USING THE LEFTOVERS

Yard maintenance inevitably produces plant trimmings, weeds, and other plant leftovers that you'll want to get rid of. One great solution to yard waste problems is composting. See "Making and Using Compost" beginning on page 100 for a pileful of tips on that topic. Here are some suggestions for additional ways to use up yard waste:

Grass clippings. Use them as mulch around growing plants.

Leaves. Till them directly into the garden.

Pine straw. Use it as mulch for acid-loving plants.

Shrub prunings. Use evergreen boughs for winter protection of bulbs and perennials.

Twigs and limbs. Chip or shred them to use as mulch. Or gather them to use as fireplace kindling.

Vine prunings. Save selected pieces for wreaths and other decorations.

Jim Borland is a garden writer and consultant on dryland gardening in Denver. He has also worked as a propagator at the Denver Botanic Garden.

Tom Bressan is an irrigation specialist and partner at The Urban Farmer Store in San Francisco, California. He lectures on irrigation and is the author of *Drip Irrigation: The Basics,* an introductory text on drip irrigation used by municipal water departments and irrigation stores.

Matthew Cheever is a horticulturist and owner of Evergreen, a landscape design and maintenance company in Milton, Wisconsin.

Barbara W. Ellis is the managing editor of garden books at Rodale Press, Inc. She is a former publications director/editor for *American Horticulturist.*

Robyn Fletcher is a co-owner of Gardens of the Blue Ridge in Pineola, North Carolina. The 100-year-old family-run nursery and mail-order business specializes in native shrubs, trees, ferns, and wildflowers.

Michael Glassman is a landscape designer and owner of Environmental Creations, Inc., an award-winning landscape design and consulting firm in West Sacramento, California.

Anne Janisse is a garden designer for small urban residential gardens at the City People's Garden Store, a full-scale nursery and garden center in Seattle, Washington.

Kipp McIntyre and **Lynne Randolph** are co-owners of Mostly Moss, located in Brushy Knob, Georgia, a business specializing in the design and installation of sculptured moss gardens.

Michael Maltas is the garden director of the organic showpiece garden for Fetzer Vineyards in Hopland, California. Maltas grows acres of vegetables, flowers, and fruit at the Fetzer Valley Oaks Food and Wine Center.

Donald Rakow, Ph.D., is an associate professor of landscape horticulture at Cornell University in Ithaca, New York. He teaches landscape management and heads the landscape horticulture extension program.

Susan A. Roth is the president of Susan A. Roth and Company, which specializes in horticultural writing, editing, and photography. She is the author of *The Weekend Garden Guide* and *The Four-Season Landscape.*

Susan Sides is a garden writer from Fairview, North Carolina. She is the former head gardener at Mother Earth News Eco-Village.

Jack Siebenthaler is a registered landscape architect and a consulting arborist in Clearwater, Florida. He is also a former executive director of the American Society of Consulting Arborists.

Paul Solyn was the founding managing editor of *Trillium: The Journal of the Ohio Native Plant Society* and is a champion of native plants. He is currently the director of corporate and foundation relations at Connecticut College in New London.

Lynn Tilton is a writer and prize-winning gardener in Sierra Vista, Arizona. His prize-winning crops have been peanuts, tomatoes, cucumbers, and corn, but his favorite crop is melons.

Eileen Weinsteiger is the garden project manager at the Rodale Institute Research Center in Maxatawny, Pennsylvania.

Pat Williams and her husband, Greg, are the publishers of *HortIdeas* newsletter, a monthly digest of reports on horticultural research and techniques. They live and garden near Gravel Switch, Kentucky.

Controlling Insect and Disease Problems

What would gardening be without pesky insects, gluttonous slugs, and persistent leaf spots and fruit rots? *"Easier! And a whole lot more fun!"* you might say.

There's no denying that, at times, insect and disease pests can be vexing, if not downright defeating. It's equally true that most gardeners invest a great deal of time, energy, and money battling bugs and blights.

What organic gardeners learn from the struggle is that there are no real good guys and bad guys and there's no real battle to fight. The true key to pest control is knowledge—understanding the interconnections between the diverse life forms in your garden and how you can manage your garden to tip the scales in your favor without causing damaging side effects. In this chapter, you'll learn just these things from our experts' advice on creating habitat for beneficial insects and animals, on shielding crops and trapping pests, and on formulating safe but effective sprays and dusts.

Preventing Problems

One of the most important principles of organic gardening is problem prevention. The organic gardener's slogan isn't "The only good bug is a dead bug," it's "You don't have to fight a problem that never gets a foothold." Here, the experts offer tips on gardening practices that will help you avoid pest outbreaks.

EVICT PESTS BEFORE YOU PLANT

It's been a mild winter but a long one, and you're eager to start that spring garden. Or maybe it's midsummer, and you've cleared a new site for a fall crop. Either way, take

PICK FRUIT PROMPTLY

There's nothing quite like plucking a moist, plump, dead-ripe tomato from the vine — only to find some bug burrowing into its innards. "The trouble is, ripe fruit gives off fermentation products that attract pests," explains Matthew Cheever, the owner of Evergreen, a landscape design and maintenance company in Wisconsin. "For example, picnic beetles become a terrible pest on ripe black raspberries, and crickets will burrow into a dead-ripe tomato."

The answer is simple enough: Pick the fruit just before it's fully mature, while it still has some firmness, and let it ripen completely indoors. "You just have to watch your crop, and harvest a tiny bit early — not a week, more like a day or even just half a day," says Cheever. "That can make all the difference."

California garden writer Pam Peirce's advice: Don't plant anything just yet.

"If you have a site where pests have built up and you clear away the stuff they've been eating and immediately put in some tender little vegetable seedlings, oh boy, do those plants disappear fast," says Peirce, the author of *Environmentally Friendly Gardening: Controlling Vegetable Pests.* She advises taking care of the pests first and planting later.

Examine the site carefully, and evict all of the pests that you find. "Be sure to look for snails, earwigs, sow bugs, and pill bugs," suggests Peirce. "They're generally scavengers, but they'll eat tender plant parts if you take everything else away." Likely hiding places are under rocks, boards, and surface debris. "Just scoop the rascals up with a trowel, and get rid of them," she says.

Peirce also recommends being patient. "People are understandably eager to plant," she says. "But if you wait and don't plant anything for a couple of weeks, a lot of the pests will simply go somewhere else."

GIVE TRELLISES SOME SPACE

Trellises can be great space savers for growing climbing and vining crops such as cucumbers, tomatoes, peas, and beans. But the environment around closely spaced trellised crops can become warm and humid, fostering the growth of disease pathogens, says Andrew Schuerger, Ph.D., a senior plant pathologist at The Land Pavilion, an agricultural display at Epcot Center in Florida. "Botrytis stem rot is an example of a disease that often develops with close trellises," says Dr. Schuerger. "You can virtually eliminate Botrytis simply by allowing enough air movement to get through to the canopy."

Dr. Schuerger recommends leaving extra space between rows of trellised plants. "That'll get enough air circulating among the trellises to help the foliage dry out in the morning. Moisture promotes fungal growth, so it's important to dry the dew or other water from leaves fairly quickly," he says. Try planting two or three rows of low-growing crops such as cabbage or broccoli between trellis rows so the extra space will still be productive.

Also, he suggests trimming the foliage from the bases of trellised plants. "We prune off the lower 1½ to 2 feet of some of the trellised crops here in our greenhouses," says Dr. Schuerger. "On some crops, such as tomatoes, you can actually improve yield by trimming off 25 to 30 percent of the lower leaves, because you reduce fungal disease and cut off corridors for crawling insects. And wounding a plant slightly by pruning often stimulates it to grow faster and more vigorously."

TOUGH PLANTS SURVIVE IN A CEMETERY

The secret to establishing a trouble-free landscape is to choose trouble-free trees and shrubs—plants that are naturally and strongly resistant to the diseases, insects, and weather extremes in your area. But how do you find such plants? How do you determine which cultivars will survive and thrive not just over the next dozen years or so, but over the long haul?

"If you're really interested in figuring out which landscape plants are low-maintenance and durable, take a look around the old cemeteries in your community," says Matthew Cheever, the owner of Evergreen, a landscape design and maintenance company in Wisconsin. "Natives don't necessarily perform well outside a wild environment," says Cheever. "But the plants in old cemeteries have lived their entire lives in a landscape setting. You can pretty much be sure the same varieties will do nicely under similar conditions around your home. You'll find interesting old trees and shrubs that have been there for half a century or more. In most cases, nobody has taken care of them; they've simply survived on their own."

DRESS FOR NO-PEST SUCCESS

Bright, colorful clothing can do a lot for your disposition, but you may be picking up more than just your spirits when you wear such fashions into the garden. "Some insect pests are attracted to bright colors," says Larry Hollar, a horticultural instructor at Blue Ridge Technical College in North Carolina. "That's why commercial growers use sticky yellow-colored boards to trap or monitor whiteflies and blue boards for thrips." If you wear bright yellow or blue clothes while gardening, you may actually attract those pests and spread them around.

In fact, because of concern over color as an insect attractant, some commercial greenhouse managers now require their employees to wear only subdued clothing to work. Bright might be right in haute couture, but, among gardeners, dull is definitely the latest word in fashion.

LOOK BEFORE YOU SQUISH

Despite all of the insect sprays, traps, and repellents that are available to gardeners, hand-picking pests—and destroying them—remains one of the best ways to reduce populations fast.

But don't be *too* quick to kill, says garden writer Libby Goldstein, a Pennsylvania food and garden writer. "Don't assume that every odd bug you see is bad," cautions Goldstein. She recalls the first time she saw a tomato hornworm with clusters of little white "eggs" poking up all over its back. "I thought, 'Aha, here you are, and you've got your family with you, too,' and I squished everybody," she recalls. "Later I found out those eggs were actually the cocoons of braconid wasps. I'd murdered a whole generation of future hornworm predators!"

You'll find more information about soil-dwelling beneficial insects in "Should You Squash or Save?" on page 91. Other beneficials that are often mistaken for harmful pests include rove beetles (which resemble earwigs without pincers), soldier beetles, minute pirate bugs, firefly larvae, and ground beetles. Goldstein's advice: "Get a good insect manual," she says, "and the next time you see a creature that you're not absolutely, positively sure about, look it up!"

Bringing In the Good Bugs

One easy, effective way to reduce insect problems is to make your garden a comfortable home for beneficial insects. Lady beetles, ground beetles, and tiny predatory and parasitic wasps can be great allies in fighting pests.

OFFER GOOD BUGS A DRINK

Hot, dry, summer weather can be hard on beneficial insects. "You can see them out there in the morning struggling to get some dew," says Linda Gilkeson, Ph.D., the Integrated Pest Management coordinator for the British Columbia Ministry of Environment. "But if it has been a cool night and they can't fly yet, the dew is gone before they're able to move around and get a drink. So I like to put out a water source to help them out."

To make a "bug bath" for your garden, partially fill an old birdbath or some other container with rocks or gravel, and then add just enough water to keep the stones moist. The insects can drown in standing water, so the idea is to create wet surfaces with lots of dry islands.

Of course, insects don't actually *bathe* in a bug bath. But the water helps them survive summer drought—and it gives you a better chance of keeping a healthy population of good bugs in your garden.

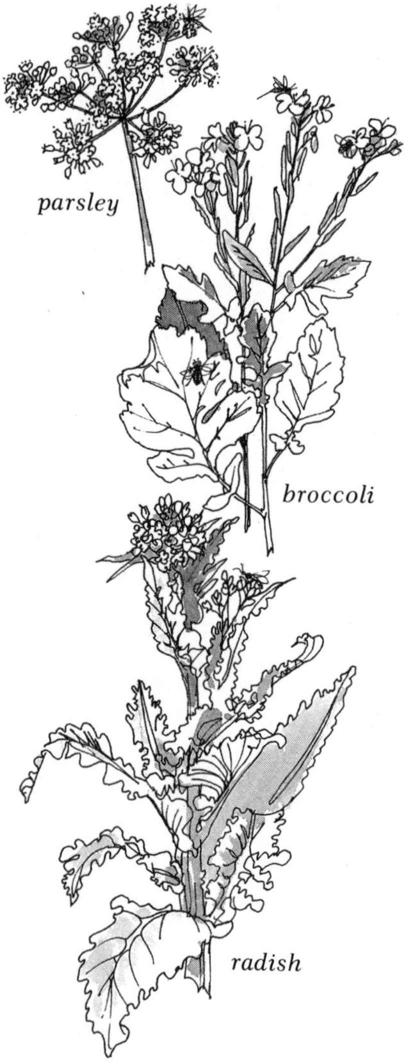

BOLTING FOR BENEFICIALS

One way to draw beneficial bees, wasps, and flies to your garden is to grow some of the small, flowering plants they prefer. Members of the mint, carrot, and daisy families seem to be especially attractive to beneficials.

"Actually, though, there's an even easier way," says Linda Gilkeson, Ph.D., the Integrated Pest Management coordinator for the British Columbia Ministry of Environment. "Just let some of your vegetables bolt and flower." Dr. Gilkeson says that radishes, Chinese cabbage, mustard, and broccoli all produce blossoms that entice beneficials. Some of these plants are shown in the illustration at left.

Dr. Gilkeson's favorite "bug crop" is parsley, a biennial that produces clusters of small, attractive white or yellow flowers in its second year. "A lot of parasitic wasps and predatory flies, including syrphid flies, are attracted to parsley," says Dr. Gilkeson.

To keep a rotation of parsley going for both you and the

parsley

broccoli

radish

CROPS THAT ATTRACT
BENEFICIALS

beneficial insects, plant at least two patches each year, using one for the table and leaving the other to flower the following season. "Parsley tends to be self-seeding," says Dr. Gilkeson, "so pretty soon you get little patches of plants all over the place."

USE "SPIDER MULCH"

Mulching your crops with hay or dried grass when you plant in the spring will attract spiders—a formidable natural "pesticide" that can drastically reduce insect damage in vegetable gardens, says Susan Riechert, Ph.D., a professor of zoology at the University of Tennessee at Knoxville. Dr. Riechert conducted a two-year study comparing the insect damage in hay-mulched and bare-ground vegetable plots. She found 60 to 80 percent less damage—and natural spider populations 10 to 30 times higher—in the hay-mulched gardens. Then when Dr. Riechert regularly removed the arachnids from the mulched plots, insect damage immediately climbed to levels comparable to those in the bare-ground gardens.

Spiders need high humidity, moderate temperature, and some type of structure to hide in. Peak spider migration occurs in April and May, when most gardens are still fairly bare. A garden mulched early in the growing season will provide a better habitat and end up with more resident spiders, Dr. Riechert explains.

Any bulky mulch that keeps the ground moist and cool offers an attractive habitat. Hay mulch, shredded newspaper, and leaf litter are examples.

Dr. Riechert adds, "You can't use any chemicals, or you'll wipe out the spiders along with the pests. But that shouldn't be a problem. In my opinion, backyard gardeners can virtually eliminate the need for chemicals by using spiders."

GIVE A TOAD A HOME

Few natural pest controls are as effective as the lowly "hoptoad." Biologists have found that during the summer just one toad consumes as many as 110 slugs, cutworms, caterpillars, and other flying and crawling creatures every day. And although a portion of a toad's diet does include beneficial species such as earthworms and honeybees, most of its menu is composed of pests.

Fortunately, in most areas all you have to do to lure toads is provide a cool, sheltered place. "My mother taught me that years ago," says Bill Bricker, a co-owner of Bricker's Organic Farm in Georgia. "She'd never throw a broken

BENEFICIAL BORDERS

At the Rodale Institute Research Center, researchers have studied beneficial insect habitats. They recommend planting the following plants in and around your garden beds and borders to attract and nurture beneficial insects:

Anethum graveolens (dill)
Anthemis tinctoria 'Kelwayi' (hardy marguerite)
Carum carvi (caraway)
Cosmos bipinnatus 'White Sensation' ('White Sensation' cosmos)
Fagopyrum esculentum (buckwheat)
Foeniculum vulgare (fennel)
Mentha spicata (spearmint)
Tagetes tenuifolia 'Lemon Gem' ('Lemon Gem' marigold)
Tanacetum vulgare (common tansy)
Trifolium incarnatum (crimson clover)
Trifolium repens (white clover)

TOAD
HOUSES

VACUUM THE VARMINTS!

You can use a hand-held rechargeable vacuum cleaner to suck whiteflies, Japanese beetles, Colorado potato beetles, and cucumber beetles off your plants. Hold your portable vacuum in one hand and move it lightly over the tops of the plants. Support the foliage with your other hand to lessen the chance of damage to tender leaves and shoots. Limit vacuuming to the upper leaves of plants to avoid sucking up fragile beneficial wasps, which tend to stay near lower parts of plants.

The vacuumed insects will be stunned by their forced evacuation but probably not killed. So be prepared to open the vacuum (away from your plants) afterward, and dump the pests into soapy water.

ceramic pot away. Instead, she'd put it upside down in the garden for the toads." Bricker has discovered another way to attract toads. "We put 5-gallon plastic buckets with the bottoms cut out over our irrigation valves to keep soil away. Well, it didn't take long for toads to find those buckets. Momma toads crawl in there and lay their eggs, and every year we have a real good crop of toads," he says.

To make a toad house out of a plastic bucket, turn it upside down, and cut a toad-size archway at the base, as shown in the illustration at left. Put the shelter in a moist place out of the sun, and throw a little soil up around the side to keep it anchored.

Barriers and Traps

There's no limit to the ingenious devices you can buy or make that will protect your plants from pests or lure them away, frequently to an unexpected demise. Barriers and traps are great organic controls. They are simple to use and quite effective, and they generally pose no hazard to you or the environment. You'll enjoy baffling pests with barriers and tricking them with traps.

TUCK IN YOUR BED COVERS

There's good reason why floating row covers made of super-light spunbonded polypropylene are so popular among gardeners: These inexpensive, gauzy barriers keep pests off plants while allowing light and moisture to pass through. And they're easy to use: You just drape the fabric over your crops and perhaps weight it down with rocks.

"But that's not good enough," says Pam Peirce, the author of *Environmentally Friendly Gardening: Controlling Vegetable Pests.* "Insects are struggling for survival. Getting to a food supply is a matter of life and death for them. If you leave an opening between the soil and the row cover, they'll probably find it."

Peirce literally seals off the row cover's edges by tucking them firmly into the soil. "Lay the fabric over the raised bed, and make a 'bubble' in the middle to give plants room to grow. Push the edges of the fabric into the soil, and pat the dirt down," she says. (It's like tucking in a sheet on a bed.) Gardeners with conventional rather than raised-bed gardens can mound 1 or 2 inches of soil onto the fabric's edges.

The soil in the bed to be covered should be somewhat moist, but Peirce recommends watering plants in the bed *after* the cover is installed, not just before. "If you water everything first, the soil will be soggy, and you'll have a mess putting the fabric in place," she cautions.

FABULOUS FRAMED FLOATING ROW COVERS

If you use floating row covers for long periods to keep pests away from your plants, you'll want to try a simple "row cover box," developed by Pam Peirce, the author of *Environmentally Friendly Gardening: Controlling Vegetable Pests.* This simple covered frame lets you avoid the hassle of untucking and then retucking row covers every time you weed or harvest.

Begin by building a wooden frame out of 1 × 2's, as shown in the illustration below. Use nonrusting galvanized roofing nails to hold the frame together. Make the base of the frame out of 1 × 3's or 1 × 4's so you can push the box

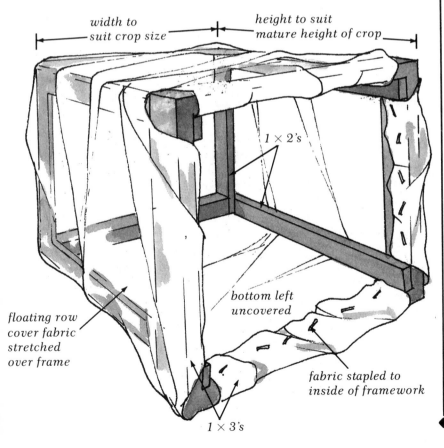

width to suit crop size

height to suit mature height of crop

1 × 2's

bottom left uncovered

floating row cover fabric stretched over frame

fabric stapled to inside of framework

1 × 3's

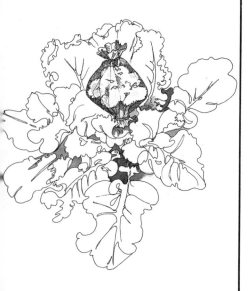

PANTY HOSE
PLANT PROTECTOR

well into the soil. The dimensions of the box will vary depending on the crop. Make the box a little taller than the mature height of the crop you're growing and as long and wide as necessary to straddle the crop. "You could build one 6 inches wide and fairly long, and set it over a row of peas," says Peirce. "Or you could make one a few feet square and about a foot high to protect a planting of lettuce."

Cover the frame with floating row cover. "Wrap it like a present," says Peirce. Bring the row cover material down over the outside of the frame and back up the inside, and staple it in place. "Package wrap" the ends, making sure there's enough excess fabric to allow you to bring the folded fabric up under the wood and staple it to the inside bottom. You can also use a needle and thread to "tack" the end folds together here and there, just to make doubly sure that insects won't get through.

Set your finished box in place over the crop, and push the box well into the soil. When you need to tend the plants, just lift off the box and do your work. Put the covered frame back when you're finished, and rest easy. Although *you* have easy access to your crops, flying and crawling insects will have to look elsewhere for a meal.

PANTY HOSE: IT'S NOT JUST FOR MELONS

Wrapping cantaloupes and other melons in "socks" made of old panty hose is an old and reliable pest-protection trick. But if you're willing to take the time and trouble, says Susan Sides, a North Carolina garden writer, you can use panty hose to keep bugs off almost any vegetable crop, as shown in the illustration at left.

"If you have a small corn patch and an hour or two to spare, you can cover up each and every ear," says Sides. "And panty hose work great on crops such as cabbages because, as the heads grow, the material expands right along with them." Cauliflower, cucumbers, and squash are among the other crops Sides successfully shields with panty hose. And if you have a prize tomato, there's no better way to keep pests off the flesh.

To make a plant protector, cut a section from the leg of old panty hose and sew or tie off one end. Then slip the nylon "sock" over the vegetable or fruit, pull it tight, and tie the other end shut.

Sprays and Dusts

Organic gardeners save insecticidal and fungicidal sprays and dusts for the last resort. They know the possible hazards to the environment, to beneficial insects and animals, and to their own safety. Their motto: "Why take the risk?" But, on rare occasions, pest problems *do* require intervention with dusts and sprays. Here are some tips on the best ways to use them and on some low-toxicity common substances that do surprisingly effective double-duty in the garden.

WHEN DUSTING PLANTS, SOCK IT TO 'EM

Applying insecticides such as *Bacillus thuringiensis* (BT) or rotenone can be a messy, frustrating task. Sprays just drip off the leaves, and shaking powders from a canister seems to put more of the stuff on your shoes and on the ground than on your plants. Plus, the instructions always urge you to be sure to cover the *undersides* of leaves as well—a mission that seems just about impossible.

"I've discovered the absolute best way to get the job done," says Susan Sides, a North Carolina garden writer. "Put rotenone or BT powder—or whatever you're applying—in an old cotton sock," she suggests. "Then go out in the early morning, and just shake the sock over and between the plants you want to cover. At that time of day, there's something about the dew—every leaf is covered, top and bottom, with perfect, tiny droplets. The powder that comes through the sock is very fine and slowly floats down and all around the plant and sticks to the drops, even underneath the leaves." Sides usually shakes the sock over the tops of the plants first and then comes back along the rows and dusts between the plants.

GIVE PLANTS A BICARB

Sodium bicarbonate—plain old baking soda—may be one of the most effective broad-spectrum, environmentally safe fungicides known. "It's effective against a wide range of fungi," says Thomas A. Zitter, Ph.D., a plant pathology professor at Cornell University in New York. Dr. Zitter has successfully tested bicarbonate spray on a variety of vege-

MAKE YOUR OWN BT

Most organic gardeners know that the bacterium *Bacillus thuringiensis* (BT) is an effective biological control against larval pests such as cabbage loopers and tomato hornworms. It's widely sold in nurseries and garden centers under such brand names as Dipel or Thuricide, but you can also make your own.

Just gather up a handful of caterpillars that have been sprayed with BT and are dead or dying. Mash the pests up a bit, and add them to 2 cups of milk. Cover and label the container, and put it out of reach of pets and small children. Let the mixture stand at room temperature for three days. Then strain it, add enough water to make a gallon, and apply it as you would a commercial product.

BT RULE OF THUMB

When is the best time to apply *Bacillus thuringiensis* (BT) to pest-infested plants? "Wait until the caterpillars are just big enough to eat a hole through a leaf," says Linda Gilkeson, Ph.D., the Integrated Pest Management coordinator for the British Columbia Ministry of Environment. "If you spray when they're teeny, they probably won't eat enough BT to kill themselves. But if they're able to bite through the leaf, they're more likely to ingest enough to kill them. Also, you won't have to be super careful to spray the underside of every single leaf, because the pests will be chewing both sides anyway."

tables, including squash, cucumbers, melons, pumpkins, and tomatoes. His tests indicate that the mixture — a simple solution of baking soda, water, and horticultural oil — controls powdery mildew, leaf blight, gummy stem, anthracnose, leaf spot, and even early blight on tomatoes. "It really is almost unbelievable," says Ken Horst, Ph.D., a professor in the Department of Plant Pathology at Cornell University in New York. Dr. Horst found the simple spray to be an effective protectant and eradicant for both blackspot and powdery mildew on roses.

To make your own "plant bicarb," mix 2 to 3 teaspoons of baking soda in 1 gallon of water along with 2 or 3 tablespoons of SunSpray Ultrafine Oil (available from garden centers and mail-order suppliers). Dr. Zitter explains that while baking soda alone is effective, adding oil improves results. The oil not only helps the spray stick to the leaves but also cleanses pathogens from the feeding parts of aphids that might feed on the infected leaves and then transmit the disease to other plants.

Use the spray as soon as you see any signs of fungal infection on a plant. Apply it once every five to seven days, making sure to cover the undersides of leaves. Continue the treatment as long as any signs of infection persist.

RUBBING ALCOHOL RUBS OUT PESTS

Plain old isopropyl alcohol, or rubbing alcohol, is one the most effective and most overlooked insect sprays around. "Most sprays are water-based," says Matthew Cheever, the owner of Evergreen, a landscape design and maintenance company in Wisconsin, "and they just roll off the backs of most insects. But alcohol penetrates the bugs' waxy cuticles and leaves them susceptible to all sorts of things. If nothing else, they lose body moisture and die."

Rubbing alcohol is effective against mealybugs, whiteflies, red spider mites, aphids, fungus gnats, and scales. You can use a cotton ball soaked in 70 percent rubbing alcohol solution to wipe scales off plants. For a whole-plant spray, combine 1 to 2 cups of rubbing alcohol with 1 quart of water. Test-spray a small area on one plant first. Then wait a day, and check the plants for spray damage.

Rubbing alcohol also increases the effectiveness of insecticidal soaps and horticultural oils. Add ½ to 1 cup of rubbing alcohol to 1 quart of spray.

INSECTS DON'T LIKE DUSTING

There's a new use for lime in the garden: pest control. "A hundred years ago, a long section of the minutes of the Pennsylvania Fruit Growers Society was devoted to using dust as a pest control," says Ward Sinclair, an organic vegetable farmer from Pennsylvania. "They used coal dust, road dust, ashes—any dusty product. So we decided to try it with hydrated lime." Sinclair's partner, Cass Peterson, made a tool that delivers a fine dusting very quickly. It's shown in the illustration at right. Peterson punched about a dozen holes in the bottom of a 3-pound coffee can. She used duct tape to attach the can to a tomato stake about 1½ feet from the bottom.

Peterson fills the can with lime, covers it with the plastic top, and tamps the stake next to plants as she walks down the row. Sinclair says, "The lime comes out in a cloud of dust. Apply it when the plants are wet, morning usually, so that the lime sticks to the leaves." Sinclair and Peterson have had success controlling flea beetles, cucumber beetles, squash bugs, and Colorado potato beetles with the lime. Sinclair cautions, "Be careful on summer squash. The lime can burn it. But it works beautifully on eggplants, potatoes, cabbage-family crops, and peppers. The dust also protects sweet potato vines from marauding deer."

Pennsylvania organic grower Frank Pollock also uses hydrated lime to prevent disease problems on his fruit trees. "I think the caustic lime fries the disease spores when they land on the leaves," speculates Pollock. "I just dust the trees once a week through the spring and into the early summer. Once the new growth starts to toughen, I taper off." Pollock finds that the trees he dusts weekly have less disease damage than those he doesn't dust as regularly.

Because hydrated lime is caustic to eyes and skin, be sure to wear appropriate protective gear as suggested in "A Word of Warning" on page 138 whenever you apply it.

REMEMBER THE "RULE OF 140"

If you're thinking of spraying your plants with horticultural oil or some other oil-based spray, do a little math first. Add the outdoor temperature (in degrees Fahrenheit) to the relative humidity (expressed as a percentage). If the total is 140 or more, wait for a cooler or less humid day to spray, says Larry Hollar, a horticultural instructor at Blue

HOMEMADE LIME DUSTER

MAKE YOUR OWN "FIREWATER"

Here's a recipe for an irritant spray that's effective against aphids, thrips, and grasshoppers. Rabbits, too, seldom take more than a single taste of plants treated with this fiery concoction.

2-4 'Jalapeño', 'Serrano', or 'Habanero' peppers
3 cloves garlic
1 quart water

Mix all of the ingredients in a blender, or chop the garlic and peppers and let them steep in a quart jar of water set in the sun for several days. Strain through cheesecloth. Spray as needed; repeat after a rain.

SLUG-STOPPING STRATEGIES

Here are some suggestions for coping with one of gardening's most difficult pests:

Put sandpaper collars around your plants. Cut "doughnuts" from sheets of sandpaper, or simply recycle used sandpaper discs from orbital sanders. Cut a slit to the center of each circle, and slip the collars around the stems, laying them on the ground.

Build a slug fence. Edge beds or individual plants with 8-inch-wide strips of wire screening. Push the bottom 2 to 3 inches of the screening into the soil. Unravel the top three horizontal strands of the screening, and bend the exposed vertical strands outward. Be sure to handpick slugs from the fenced-in area just before and just after you erect the barrier.

Use chopsticks for more palatable handpicking. Picking slugs off plants leaves a disgusting, hard-to-remove layer of slime on your fingers. Gloves make the job cumbersome, but chopsticks (or tweezers) allow you to keep both your manual dexterity *and* your stomach.

Ridge Technical College in North Carolina.

Why? "Because high temperature and high humidity have a big determining effect on whether plants will suffer phytotoxic burn after they've been sprayed," Hollar explains. Phytotoxic burn occurs when plant tissues react adversely to a spray. Leaves become discolored, and in extreme cases the whole plant can die. The problem is a concern mostly to those who use synthetic chemical pesticides. But some oil-based sprays, increasingly popular among organic growers, can also cause burn.

"If you just remember the 'Rule of 140,' though,"says Hollar, "you don't have to worry much."

It may seem like combined temperature and humidity always exceed 140 during the summer in hot, humid parts of the country. If you live in such an area, try checking the temperature and humidity in the early morning or in the evening—you may find conditions will be suitable for spraying then.

Foiling the Peskiest Pests

We all have our particular insect nemesis, but some pests have a troublesome reputation throughout most of North America. Here is advice from our experts on how to deal with some of these obnoxious insect foes.

KILL SLUGS WITH . . . QUACKGRASS?

As if to prove that there really is a silver lining in every cloud, researchers have found that quackgrass (*Agropyron repens*), that perennial weedy headache, can be toxic to slugs. "And the effect is specific to slugs," says Roger D. Hagin, a USDA Agricultural Research Service agronomist in New York. "The molluscicide in quackgrass is apparently harmless to earthworms and snails."

Hagin emphasizes that his research is ongoing and therefore should be applied somewhat tentatively. But he believes homeowners can successfully use quackgrass as a slug-killing mulch on such plants as roses and tomatoes.

To do so, cut quackgrass, and allow it to dry completely in the sun. Fresh quackgrass *won't* work; the molluscicidal compound is present only after the plant is dry. Chop the leaves and stems into small pieces, either by hand or by running them through a shredder or chipper, and apply the chopped mulch in a thin layer around plants.

Hagin cautions that quackgrass, particularly if it's not completely dried, may have some herbicidal properties. He suggests that backyard experimenters test out the mulch on one or two plants of each species that they want to protect before they mulch around the whole crop.

BEAT BEETLES WITH BEETLE BATTLE PADDLES

Flea beetles are among the toughest of all pests to control. Cleaning the garden of debris in the fall helps by eliminating their winter homes. And giving infested leaves a dusting of wood ashes or lime can keep the tiny jumping insects off for a few days—or until the next rain washes the protective powder from the foliage. But in chronic cases, you may be tempted to give up altogether on some susceptible crops, such as potatoes.

Before you do, though, try using agriculture writer Miranda Smith's flea beetle paddles, which are shown in the illustration below. "Just take a stick," says Smith, "and staple or nail a big, wide piece of cardboard [about 10×12 inches] to it at one end. Make a second paddle just like the

stake

cardboard
coated with
sticky surface

JAPANESE BEETLES PREFER . . .

Japanese beetles are a persistent pest everywhere east of the Mississippi River. When choosing landscape plants, keep in mind that some are especially susceptible to damage from the beetles, while others are notably resistant.

Susceptible Plants

Acer palmatum (Japanese maple)
Acer platanoides (Norway maple)
Aesculus hippocastanum
   (common horse chestnut)
Alcea rosea (hollyhock)
Betula populifolia (gray birch)
Hibiscus syriacus (rose-of-
   Sharon)
Juglans nigra (black walnut)
Malus spp. (crab apples)
Rosa spp. (roses)
Sorbus americana (American
   mountain ash)
Ulmus procera (English elm)
Vitis spp. (grapes)

Resistant Plants

Abies spp. (firs)
Acer negundo (box elder)
Acer rubrum (red maple)
Diospyros virginiana (common
   persimmon)
Fraxinus americana (white ash)
Ilex spp. (hollies)
Juglans cinerea (butternut)
Liriodendron tulipifera (tulip tree)
Picea spp. (spruces)
Pinus spp. (pines)
Populus alba (white poplar)
Pyrus communis (common pear)
Quercus coccinea (scarlet oak)
Rhododendron spp.
   (rhododendrons)
Syringa vulgaris (common lilac)
Taxus spp. (yews)
Tsuga spp. (hemlocks)

◆

first. Put Tangle-Trap or some other sticky substance on both pieces of cardboard so they're really gooey. Then simply walk down the row, holding a paddle on each side of the plants, and jostle the plants with your foot. As the flea beetles hop off the plants, they get stuck on the paddles."

COVERED CAGES KEEP OUT FLEA BEETLES

Flea beetles seem more attracted to eggplant than just about any other crop in the vegetable garden. You can shield your eggplants from flea beetles and encourage plant growth by surrounding them with tomato cages covered with floating row cover fabric, suggests Charles Kauffman, the director of Agricultural and Environmental Programs at the Accokeek Foundation in Maryland. Kauffman, who likes to experiment in his backyard garden, found that eggplant leaves were often damaged by friction of the row cover fabric he draped over plants to control flea beetles. But when plants were protected inside cages, they responded with vigorous growth and more pest-free fruit. "Keeping the beetles off at the beginning is most important," says Kauffman. Just wrap the cages with row cover fabric, fold over the seams at the top and sides, then staple them closed. Remove the staples, and open the tops for pollination when plants begin to blossom. Don't remove the cages, though, because you could damage the plant if you did. Also, you'll find that your eggplants are so big and vigorous, they'll need the support!

SET UP A STICKY SITUATION

Sticky barrier bands wrapped around tree trunks keep gypsy moth caterpillars from crawling up and devouring foliage. Ralph E. Webb, Ph.D., a USDA research entomologist from Maryland, suggests making your own barrier bands using duct tape and Tanglefoot, a substance made of natural gums and resins.

"Actually, the Tanglefoot all by itself repels caterpillars," says Dr. Webb. "But the downside is that you can't get it off, and it leaves a black band around the tree." Tape coated with Tanglefoot is easy to remove at the end of caterpillar season. The trick is to apply it in such a way that the caterpillars can't evade the trap. "You don't want to leave any gaps between the tape and the tree for caterpillars to crawl under," says Dr. Webb. "And since some trees have very shaggy bark, getting the band on so that it's completely

◆

GIVE BEETLES THE BRUSH OFF

Colorado potato beetles can devastate your potato or tomato crops. But these beetles are vulnerable because they drop like stones when the plants they're feeding on are disturbed. Stewart Hoyt, a Vermont market gardener, takes advantage of this by holding a big bucket under the plants and jostling them as he moves down the row. Hoyt explains that he was inspired by a European grower's example. He says, "A grower in Europe has designed a tractor-driven rig that has dangling chains that disturb the plants. The bugs drop into long plastic 'boats' that hang below the plants." Once you've got a bucket full of Colorado potato beetles, you can fill it with soapy water to finish them off.

sealed can be a real art." Here are Dr. Webb's suggestions for a caterpillar-proof barrier:

1. Put up the bands before gypsy moth eggs hatch. The farther north you live, the longer you can wait to do this. In Virginia, the deadline is April 1. In New York, it's May 1.

2. Choose an area on the trunk with relatively few bumps and cracks; chest height is ideal, since the band will be out of the reach of pets and children.

3. Remove any loose bark, dirt, or moss.

4. Wrap 2-inch-wide duct tape horizontally around the trunk. Take care to push it into bark crevices and over and around vines, as shown in the illustration below. If necessary, use a staple gun to staple the tape to stubborn areas. Overlap the ends of the tape to form a complete circle.

5. Using a stick, spread the Tanglefoot on the duct tape. Leave a ¼-inch margin at the top and the bottom of the band. If you notice any small gaps at the band's bottom edge, however, smear a little Tanglefoot on the band and tree to fill them in.

APPLYING A STICKY
BARRIER BAND

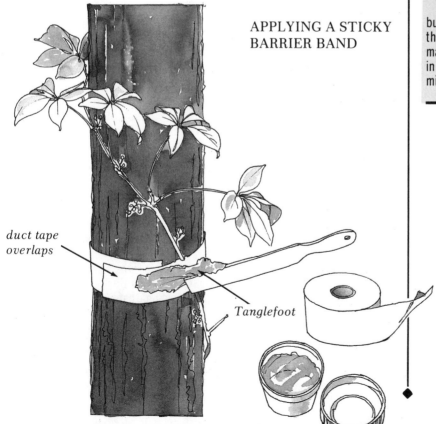

duct tape overlaps

Tanglefoot

BLEND A BATCH OF BUG JUICE

Here's the gardener's version of the old adage about fighting fire with fire! Collect about ½ cup of whichever insect pest is bothering your plants, mash up the insects, mix them with 2 cups of water, and pour it through cheesecloth, straining out the solid matter to keep your sprayer from getting clogged.

Mix ¼ cup of the strained bug juice with 2 cups of water and a few drops of liquid dishwashing detergent (such as Dawn, Dove, Ivory, Joy, or Palmolive), and spray. (It's advisable to wear rubber gloves and to use nonfood containers and utensils when making bug juice.)

Theories vary regarding why bug juice works, but it's likely that diseases carried by the mashed-up bugs are contained in the spray and are then transmitted to other insects.

WHICH CONTROL WORKS?

You had aphids all over your broccoli last season, and you're determined not to let it happen again, so you launch an all-out effort. You dump hundreds of mail-order lady beetles on your plants. You mulch the seedlings with reflective foil. Every three days, you turn a hose on the leaves to knock off any pests. You spray the plants weekly with horticultural oil. And sure enough, your broccoli thrives, 100 percent aphid-free.

Trouble is, you have no way of knowing which of those techniques worked and which didn't. "If you want to know whether a pest control technique is effective, you have to try one method at a time," says Pam Peirce, the author of *Environmentally Friendly Gardening: Controlling Vegetable Pests*. "It's a matter of good science."

The best way to test a method is to try it on one part of a crop and to leave the rest of that crop entirely alone. In scientific terms, the untreated part serves as a control. "That can be hard to do, because you don't want to risk any plants," admits Peirce. "But it's the only way to tell whether a given technique is better than doing nothing at all."

Libby Goldstein, a Pennsylvania food and garden writer, offers another example of the need to evaluate pest control techniques scientifically, one at a time. "One year," she says jokingly, "I had this pair of tiny dragon earrings that I wore to the garden all the time, and you know what? I didn't get *any* bean beetles or potato bugs . . ."

6. Leave the bands in place until late July or August, after the moths have pupated. When you remove the barriers, wear gloves, roll the tape backward onto itself, and place in a trash bag for disposal.

GOD DIDN'T MAKE THESE LITTLE GREEN APPLES

If you live in the East and have even one apple or plum tree, chances are you're acquainted with the homely little snout-nosed weevils called plum curculios. The pests lay their eggs under the skin of developing fruits, causing the fruit to drop or at least be left with a telltale half-moon scar. Organically acceptable pesticides don't do more than give curculios a slight headache, so these insects are an organic grower's nightmare. Helen Atthowe, an organic farmer in Montana, has had good luck controlling them in New Jersey with homemade apple-green sticky ball traps. "The curculio is looking for a green fruit to lay its egg in, and it stands to reason it will go for a large, green sphere," says Michael Maltas, the garden director of the organic showpiece garden for Fetzer Vineyards in California.

To make the traps, just buy some green enamel paint (the closest color you can get to a green 'Granny Smith' apple) and paint commercial red sphere traps with it. Then coat the traps with a sticky coating, such as Tangle-Trap, and hang them in your trees at blossom time. Some growers think that a squirt of apple-scented perfume adds to the trap's attractiveness to curculios.

THE GARDEN PROFESSIONALS

Helen Atthowe is a plant production manager for Bitterroot Native Growers, a wholesale nursery specializing in native plants, located in Corvallis, Montana. She also manages her own organic farm, raising tomatoes, strawberries, raspberries, and apples.

Bill Bricker is a co-owner of Bricker's Organic Farm, a producer of organic topsoil, mulches, and compost, in Augusta, Georgia. He is also a co-owner of Avrett Hardware Farm and Garden Supply, an old-time hardware store in Augusta.

Matthew Cheever is a horticulturist and owner of Evergreen, a landscape design and maintenance company in Milton, Wisconsin.

Linda Gilkeson, Ph.D., is the Integrated Pest Management coordinator for the British Columbia Ministry of Environment, whose mission is to reduce the use of pesticides in the province and promote their alternatives.

Libby Goldstein is a food and garden writer and is the president of the

Philadelphia Food and Agriculture Task Force, a coalition of organizations involved in food and agricultural policy. As a former Philadelphia county extension director, she was a prime force in establishing community gardens in downtown Philadelphia.

Roger D. Hagin is an agronomist for the USDA Agricultural Research Service at Cornell University in Ithaca, New York.

Larry Hollar is a horticultural instructor at Blue Ridge Technical College in Flat Rock, North Carolina. He is also an editor of *Landscape IPM Updates,* a newsletter on integrated pest management for landscape professionals and turf managers.

Ken Horst, Ph.D., is a professor in the Department of Plant Pathology at Cornell University in Ithaca, New York. He has written *The Compendium of Rose Diseases* and the revisions for the fourth and fifth editions of *Westcott's Plant Disease Handbook.*

Stewart Hoyt is a market gardener and operates a Community Supported Agriculture (CSA) operation in Barnet, Vermont.

Charles Kauffman is the director of Agricultural and Environmental Programs, including the Ecosystem Farm, at the Accokeek Foundation in Accokeek, Maryland, a land trust that manages the 4,700-acre Piscataway National Park.

Michael Maltas is the garden director of the organic showpiece garden for Fetzer Vineyards in Hopland, California. Maltas grows acres of vegetables, flowers, and fruit at the Fetzer Valley Oaks Food and Wine Center.

Pam Peirce is a garden writer, horticultural photographer, and photo editor from San Francisco, California. She is the author of *Golden Gate Gardening* and *Environmentally Friendly Gardening: Controlling Vegetable Pests.*

Cass Peterson and **Ward Sinclair** are the owners of Flickerville Mountain Farm and Groundhog Ranch, an organic vegetable farm in Dott, Pennsylvania. They raise more than 70 different kinds of vegetables, flowers, and herbs on the farm.

Frank Pollock is an organic grower. He raises garlic and specialty potatoes on his Rolling Hills Farm in Saylorsburg, Pennsylvania, and sells them via mail order across the United States.

Susan Riechert, Ph.D., is a professor of zoology and a U.T.K. distinguished professor of zoology at the University of Tennessee at Knoxville. She is an international authority on spider behavior and ecology.

Andrew Schuerger, Ph.D., is a senior plant pathologist at The Land Pavilion, Epcot Center, in Orlando, Florida. The Land Pavilion is an agricultural display that includes 1½ acres of greenhouses that showcase world food crops.

Susan Sides is a garden writer from Fairview, North Carolina. She is the former head gardener at Mother Earth News Eco-Village.

Miranda Smith is an agriculture writer and organic market gardener from Belchertown, Massachusetts. She is the editor and writer of *The Farmer Speaks: Organic and Low-Input Farming in the Northeast* for the federal Low-Input Sustainable Agriculture (LISA) program.

Ralph E. Webb, Ph.D., is a research entomologist in the insect biocontrol laboratory of the USDA Agricultural Research Service at Beltsville Agricultural Research Center in Beltsville, Maryland.

Thomas A. Zitter, Ph.D., is a professor of plant pathology at Cornell University in Ithaca, New York. He is currently researching fungal and viral diseases on tomatoes, peppers, and cucurbits.

FEED YOUR SLUGS DOG CHOW

Slugs can be creatures of broad appetites, and believe it or not, they love dog chow. The classic technique for luring slugs to an untimely demise is to set out shallow saucers of beer. The pests literally drown themselves in the brew. "But the old beer trick doesn't work nearly as well as feeding your slugs dog chow," says Miranda Smith, an agriculture writer and organic market gardener from Massachusetts. Smith soaks ordinary dry dog food in water just enough to make the chow slightly squishy. Then she puts small piles of the bait directly on the ground in the paths between her beds. "When you come back later that night, the slugs will be clustered around the dog chow, and you can just scoop them up and do what you want with them," says Smith.

Foiling Animal Pests

Is there a sure and simple way to keep marauding bird and animal pests out of the garden? Unfortunately, the answer is no. Our growing human population and expanding urbanization are depriving more and more animals of their natural habitat and food. As a result, they're becoming serious pests for more and more gardeners. And sadly, there are no sure cures — except, perhaps, trapping and killing the offenders or building a formidable (and expensive) fence.

There are, however, a number of less drastic measures that will help you cope with four-legged or winged garden raiders. Some, such as using soap to repel deer, have the ring of gardening folklore, but contemporary research proves their effectiveness. Others, such as using spices to repel rabbits, have little or no basis in science but have been used successfully enough to be recommended here.

Just remember: There are no guaranteed solutions when it comes to animal and bird pest control. In many cases, the best you can do is follow the example of the self-same persistent pests you're trying to foil: If at first you don't succeed, try, try again.

Repel or Scare Pests

One line of defense against animal pests is to make your plants smell or taste so bad that the animals won't eat them. Another tactic is to make animals think their enemies are on patrol in your garden.

PUT UP A "SPRAY-ON" DEER FENCE

Wettable sulfur — an organically acceptable fungicide — can also serve as a deer repellent. "One of the traditional methods for repelling deer is to spray beaten eggs around your garden," says Sylvia Ehrhardt, a co-owner of an organic farm in Maryland. "When the egg turns rotten, it smells bad. It keeps the animals away." Lacking enough eggs to do the job, Ehrhardt tried spraying wettable sulfur. "When you spray it, the sulfur exudes a distinct rotten-egg odor," says Ehrhardt. She finds that it keeps deer away from potato plants and fruit trees.

Wettable sulfur is sold inexpensively at farm and orchard supply centers. Mix it according to label instructions. Or you can concoct the more traditional rotten-egg treatment: In a blender, combine 2 or 3 eggs and 1 quart of water. Then pour the mixture into a container with enough additional water to make 1 gallon. Sprayed on plants, the eggs in the solution turn rotten and give off an aroma that's mercifully subtle to humans but repulsive enough to deer to make them look elsewhere for a meal.

BAR DEER WITH SOAP TREE ORNAMENTS

Studies have consistently shown that soap repels deer. In fact, it's more effective than many commercial chemical repellents. Field studies in two New England apple orchards show that soap bars hung with their wrappers intact provide better protection from deer than the soap or the wrappers alone. And given normal weather conditions, a single bar lasts an entire season.

"The longevity of a bar of soap is greatly increased if you leave it in the wrapper," says James A. Parkhurst, Ph.D., an extension specialist in wildlife damage management at the University of Massachusetts at Amherst. "And apparently the wrapper adds a visual cue that, combined with the soap odor, reinforces the repellent effect."

"Hotel-size bars that measure about $3 \times 1\frac{1}{2}$ inches are what we recommend to growers who need to buy and use large quantities," says Dr. Parkhurst. Here's how to make a soap tree ornament, which is shown in the illustration at right:

1. Drill a small hole centered about ½ inch down from the top of a regular or medium-size bar of soap.

2. Slip a piece of wire through the hole, and wrap as shown in the illustration.

3. Bend the top end of the wire to form a hook.

For best protection, hang one bar ornament in each small (sapling-size) tree. In large trees, hang several bars within a deer's reach (about 6 feet from the ground), leaving no more than 3 feet between bars.

A BETTER USE FOR SOAP BITS

You can make a deer repellent by recycling those soap-bar remnants from the sink and shower: Make a pouch by cutting small lengths of panty hose or cheesecloth and tying off one end. Fill the pouch with soap bits, tie off the open end, and hang the bag in the tree or shrub you want to protect.

SOAP BAR ORNAMENT

SCARY STUFF YOU CAN MAKE

You can buy owl decoys or inflatable scare-eye balloons to frighten animal pests. However, here are some ways to scare away pests with highly effective (and inexpensive) devices that you make yourself:

Scare them with snakes. Cut old green garden hose into snake-like lengths 4 or 5 feet long. Wrap yellow, red, black, or brown plastic tape around the hose at intervals to simulate stripes. Hang the snakes in fruit trees or place them in plain view among garden rows.

Menace them with Mylar. Tie helium-filled Mylar party balloons to tomato stakes and fence posts around the garden. The reflective inflatables are often left for the taking after special occasions. Most businesses that sell them will refill deflated balloons for little or no charge.

Terrorize them with tape. Stretch a length of audio-cassette tape tightly between stakes placed at either end of a row of plants. The humming noise created by the tape vibrating in the wind can scare off birds.

What's the best *kind* of soap to use? In one Connecticut study, researchers compared the repellent effects of Ivory, Shield, Coast, Safeguard, Dial, Irish Spring, and Cashmere Bouquet and found only negligible differences. "Basically, any kind seems to perform as well as any other," Dr. Parkhurst says. Dr. Parkhurst also adds a note of realism: "Repellents can be effective in areas with low to somewhat moderate deer populations," he says, "but in an area where food is limited and the number of deer is phenomenal, repellents won't make a hill of beans of difference. People with a serious deer problem are better off investing in a good fence."

HANG HAIR TO SCARE DEER

Deer don't like people, so human hair can serve as a deer repellent. Robert Lester, the owner of a Pennsylvania nursery that specializes in bamboo, relies on this inexpensive solution to protect his acres of rare and unusual plants. Each winter, he fills small cheesecloth bags with hair that he gets from a barbershop and ties one bag to the trunk of each tree at deer-nose height (about 6 feet off the ground). "My nursery is surrounded by woods, and I have high deer pressure, but these bags really work," Lester says.

DON'T FORGET MAN'S BEST FRIENDS

Barriers, repellents, and scare devices can keep some animal pests away some of the time—but few critter-control techniques are as sure and reliable as keeping a domestic cat or dog around. "Other than a fence," says Matthew Cheever, the owner of Evergreen, a landscape design and maintenance company in Wisconsin, "cats and dogs work better than anything I know of." Eileen Weinsteiger, the garden project manager at the Rodale Institute Research Center in Pennsylvania, agrees. "Cats and dogs are absolutely the best for controlling rodents. Having a dog or one or two cats near the garden is great for pest control."

DRIVE CROWS AWAY WITH "SCARE BAGS"

Crows and other birds with a taste for tender, just-sprouted corn, peas, beans, and other vegetable tidbits aren't easily frightened. But believe it or not, the answer to controlling them can be as simple as blowing up a balloon.

Sylvia Ehrhardt, who, with her husband, Walter, grows organic produce under contract for 60 families, explains: "A neighbor who's lived here in the Appalachians all of her life told me about 'scare bags,'" she says. "They do an excellent job of keeping crows away." To make a scare bag, blow into an ordinary plastic grocery bag (almost any size will work), and fill it with air, just as you'd inflate a balloon. Then, give the end a twist or two, close it off with a rubber band, and tie the bag securely to the top of a 3- or 4-foot wooden stake.

"I usually just put a few scare bags on the poles I've used to stake my tomatoes," says Sylvia, "and then I'll use extra stakes to stagger more bags throughout the garden. And I try to use different colors of bags—brown, white, green, or whatever."

The bags move and rustle in the wind. Sylvia theorizes that from a distance they resemble a person leaning over working. She says, "Sometimes I'll look out my window at the garden and one of the bags will catch my eye, and for a moment I'll think there's someone out there. I guess that's why they keep birds away. All I know is, they're very effective, and that's why we use them."

BEFUDDLE THOSE FEATHERED FILCHERS

Variety is the spice of life, and it may also be the solution to your problem with birds who have an uncanny way of beating you to harvesting your ripe fruit.

Scare devices like mirrors, plastic owls, and Mylar balloons all work, but none for more than a day or two, say animal damage control experts Kristin E. Brugger, Ph.D., a former wildlife research biologist for the USDA, and David Hayes, the assistant state director of animal damage control for Montana. For maximum effect, they suggest using a selection of devices that incorporate light, movement, bright colors (birds see in color), sound, and predator resemblance. Change the locations of the devices daily, and hide some of them in a shed periodically to help keep birds from getting used to them.

Hayes says, "The most feeding damage occurs in the early morning, so you need 2 to 3 hours of high activity in the garden during that time." Try relocating devices in the evening so that the scene is new in the morning. Unfortunately, both experts also agree that the only sure-fire protection against birds is good-quality netting.

SPINNING SCARE-BOTTLE

Try this easy-to-make whirling bird-and-rabbit scarer:

1. In the middle of the bottom of a 2-liter plastic soda bottle, drill a 3/16-inch hole.

2. Draw or scribe seven vertical lines spaced equally around the container. Make each line 4½ inches long, extending up from the bottle's base section.

3. Cut along the lines using a utilty knife or single-edged razor blade. Make a 1-inch cut at a right angle to each end of each slit. Fold the resulting "fins" outward at a 65- or 70-degree angle.

4. Center a 3/32-inch hole in one end of a 3- or 4-foot-long, ½- or ¾-inch-diameter dowel. Whittle the other end to a point.

5. Slip the bottle neck-side-down over the dowel's drilled end and screw the wind catcher to the rod using a #5 × ¾-inch wood screw. Don't tighten it completely; leave enough play to allow the vessel to spin freely. (Adding metal washers will help.)

6. Poke the dowel's pointed end into the ground between rows or beds.

EASY MOVABLE FENCING

Here's an easy way to make a temporary, portable fence to protect individual beds or crops from animal pests:

1. Cut several 4- or 5-foot lengths of 1-inch-mesh chicken wire (available at hardware stores).

2. Attach a metal or fiberglass post to each end of each chicken-wire panel. Allow an extra foot or so of the post to extend past the bottom of the fencing, so that the posts can be pushed into the ground.

3. Use the panels to surround susceptible crops such as young broccoli or lettuce plants. When they're no longer needed, take the panels down, and store them flat.

A Fence for Defense

Our experts agree that a strong fence is the only sure way to keep animals from reaching your treasured plants. They're not as quick, simple, or cheap to use as repellents and scare devices, but if none of those tactics have served you well, try these expert tips on fencing out animals.

BURY YOUR GARDEN FENCE

If it's rabbits that are munching away your lettuce and broccoli, a simple 3-foot-high fence made of chicken wire should take care of the problem. Not so with woodchucks and other burrowing critters, though. For these garden raiders, you'll need a fence like the one that surrounds the Kentucky garden of Greg and Pat Williams, copublishers of *HortIdeas* newsletter. "We live in the middle of the woods," says Pat, "so we had to come up with a fence that would keep out all sorts of animals."

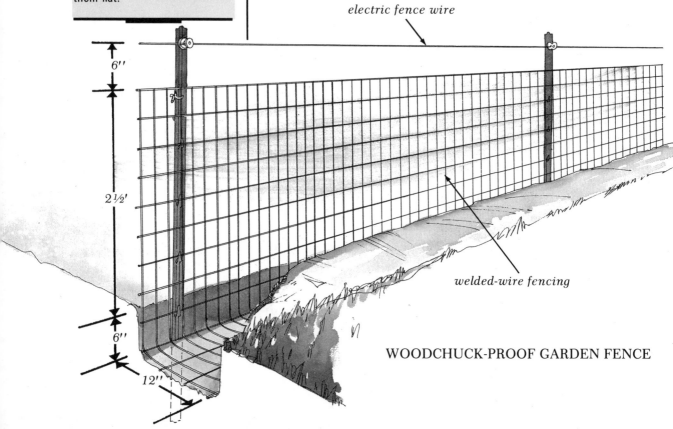

electric fence wire

welded-wire fencing

6''

2½'

6''

12''

WOODCHUCK-PROOF GARDEN FENCE

The Williamses' fence keeps critters from climbing over *and* from tunneling under. It's shown in the illustration on the opposite page. To put a similar barrier around your garden, follow these steps:

1. Dig a trench about 6 inches deep and 12 inches wide around the outside of your garden.

2. Set metal or fiberglass fence posts on the garden side of the trench. You'll need one post for each corner and additional posts for long stretches of fence.

3. Attach 4-foot welded-wire fencing to the posts—but before you clip or staple it in place, bend the lower 1 foot of the fence outward at a right angle so that it lines the trench bottom.

4. Fill in the trench with dirt, and, using safety procedures recommended by the manufacturer, add a single strand of electric fence wire a few inches above the top of the welded-wire fence.

MAKE A FABRIC FENCE

Floating row covers, which are widely used as season extenders and insect barriers, also serve as an effective "fence" against animal pests. Simply laying the lightweight polypropylene material, such as Reemay, over crops seems to keep four-legged pests from finding the munchies underneath.

"The only way I can win the battle against groundhogs [woodchucks] is to cover my crops with Reemay," says Maryland grower Sylvia Ehrhardt. According to Ehrhardt, the woodchucks make no effort to dig under the fabric or to push it aside.

Eileen Weinsteiger, the garden project manager at the Rodale Institute Research Center in Pennsylvania, also relies on the wispy barriers. "Floating row cover is all I need to keep rabbits and woodchucks away," she says.

Reemay and products like it come in a variety of widths and are sold in rolls (usually 25 feet or more) at garden centers. To install the cover, just lay the fabric directly on top of a row or bed of plants, and anchor the edges with boards or soil. You can also make a floating row cover box that's easy to put on and lift off a bed of plants. See "Fabulous Framed Floating Row Covers" on page 137 for directions.

WINNING THE WOODCHUCK WAR

Woodchucks can devastate a whole crop of beans and frustrate you to tears by taking one or two nibbles out of each and every butternut squash on the vine. Here are some hints for discouraging them:

Blow their cover. "Landscape" the areas directly around woodchuck burrows by removing all brush, tall weeds and grasses, and other forms of protective cover. Replace the plants with onions and garlic, which repel woodchucks.

Put out the "unwelcome mat." If you have a dog, give your pet a small scrap of carpet remnant (sold inexpensively at carpet stores) to sleep on for a week or two. Then place the canine-scented unwelcome mat among plants favored by woodchucks and give your pet a new carpet bed, also destined for the garden. Swap the beds every few weeks, keeping the rotation going for the whole season.

Make them hot under the collar. Sprinkle cayenne pepper in and around woodchuck burrows and among the crops they like best.

TRY THIS HARE TONIC

Here are some tricks for ridding your garden of rabbit pests:

Fill 1-gallon glass jugs with water, and set them near the rabbits' favorite vegetables. The jars reflect light, which startles the animals.

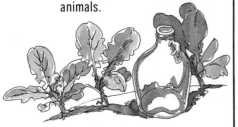

Put milk jugs with their bottoms cut out over seedlings in the spring. (Be sure to remove them during the hottest part of the day.)

Set old shoes or sneakers among rows and beds to give your garden a human aroma.

Special Strategies

Depending on where you live, you may have no problems with deer but a constant battle with woodchucks. Or perhaps you're frustrated by pesky crows in your corn patch. Here are some specific strategies for coping with particular animal pests.

PLANT A "RABBIT LAWN"

Rabbits aren't particularly fussy eaters and are often as happy to munch on weeds as on lettuce and beet tops. But if you do have a problem with rabbits raiding your garden, consider offering them a diversionary menu.

"At home, I use a lawn mix that has a lot of clover in it," says Eileen Weinsteiger, the garden project manager at the Rodale Institute Research Center in Pennsylvania. "The rabbits are more attracted to the clover than to the vegetables I grow, so they don't come into the garden."

Other animal pests also are distracted by "buffer crops." Some rural growers plant patches of soybeans or alfalfa and clover well away from their plots to divert woodchucks. Orchardists have used perimeter plantings of alfalfa to ease the appetites of hungry deer. And placing small patches of field corn outside the garden can keep raccoons from raiding the sweet corn inside. (It's important, though, to choose cultivars of field corn that will mature at the same time as your sweet corn.)

If you have a small yard, you may not have room to plant meals for local wildlife. If so, try repelling those rabbits instead of feeding them. Plant onions, garlic, or African marigolds around the garden's perimeter or among your crops. Or sprinkle chili powder, garlic powder, blood meal, or dried mint leaves on rabbit-preferred plants.

SPUDS KEEP CROWS FROM CORN

Crows will yank up corn seedlings to get the sprouted kernel beneath. A half-dozen of the raucous birds can wipe out a garden corn patch in short order. An ingenious way to stop crows from pulling up young corn plants is to plant potatoes in the corn patch.

"I used to have a tremendous problem with crows," says Clark Tibbits, a homestead gardener from North

Carolina. "I tried scarecrows and stretching string over the rows and all sorts of things. Then an old gentleman in Lesotho, a little country in southern Africa, showed me the technique of interplanting corn with potatoes."

Tibbits plants his potato rows about 3¼ feet apart. When the potatoes are about 1 foot tall, he plants corn between the rows.

"The crows can see the young corn from the air, but they won't come down in among the potatoes," says Tibbits, who hasn't lost corn to crows since he started using the technique. "Apparently they're afraid something might be lurking in all that foliage, so they stay away."

A straw mulch can also hide a fledgling corn crop from crows. "I sprinkle straw on top after I've planted, before the corn even emerges," says Sylvia Ehrhardt, a co-owner of an organic farm in Maryland. Ehrhardt warns gardeners to apply only a thin layer of straw, to avoid cooling the soil. "You just want to put enough down to keep crows from seeing the seedlings when they come up," she says.

Another way to apply the same principle: Start your corn plants indoors and set them out as full-fledged seedlings, after they've grown beyond the sprouted-seed stage.

MANAGE MULCH TO KEEP MICE AWAY

Applying organic mulch such as pine bark around landscape trees and shrubs conserves soil moisture, moderates soil temperature, and helps keep weeds down. It also keeps mowers and weed trimmers at a safe distance. But piling bark mulch directly up against the trunks invites rodent damage, says Bonnie Lee Appleton, Ph.D., an associate professor and extension horticulturist at Virginia Polytechnic Institute and State University.

"If you put too much mulch up against ornamentals, rodents get in there and nest and feed on the bark, and soon you have serious damage," says Dr. Appleton.

To avoid the problem, apply mulch no more than 2 or 3 inches deep—a layer too shallow for mice and voles to take up residence—and leave several inches of ground around the trunks unmulched.

Also, if winter-hungry rabbits or rodents nibble at the bark of trees and shrubs, wrap the trunks with a circle of hardware cloth or ordinary window screening. Make sure each barrier covers its trunk from the ground to 1 foot above the typical amount of snow cover in your area.

RACCOON CURES

You'll probably never see a raccoon in your garden, as they're shyer than woodchucks and more strictly nocturnal. But you may find their footprints! (For an illustration of raccoon footprints, see page 148.) If you do, try the following:

Make a moat. Encircle your corn or melon patch with a 3-foot-wide "moat" made by laying black plastic or mesh fencing on the ground. A raccoon's feet are hairless, sensitive, and plantigrade, which means that the entire bottom of the foot touches the ground when it walks. The animal doesn't like to tread on unusual surfaces.

Make a raccoon night-light. Put a blinking or rotating light in the garden at night. Like other nocturnal animals, raccoons have an extra set of light-gathering cells in their eyes. Flashing light is unsettling to them.

Irritate them. Plant a scratchy vine crop such as winter squash or pumpkins around and among your corn to irritate and discourage the masked raiders.

Surround your crops. Sprinkle hydrated lime in a 4- or 5-inch-wide band around your corn crop when it ripens.

Cover your ears. Wrap individual corn ears in paper bags, foil, or plastic, and secure the covering with a rubber band.

Let your fence top flop. If you use a chicken-wire fence, don't attach the top 1 foot of wire to the posts. When a coon tries to climb up, the loose portion will bend backward and keep the animal from making it over the top.

DEER-RESISTANT LANDSCAPE PLANTS

No plant is entirely safe from a determined deer with a healthy appetite. But some plants *are* notably distasteful to deer. Others can withstand occasional nibbling and still grow well. Here's a list of some of the ornamentals cited by researchers at the universities of California and Georgia as being (more or less) deer-resistant:

Buddleia davidii (orange-eye butterfly bush)
Buxus spp. (boxwoods)
Calendula officinalis (pot marigold)
Chrysanthemum spp. (chrysanthemums)
Cotinus coggygria (smoke tree)
Cytisus scoparius (Scotch broom)
Helleborus orientalis (lenten rose)
Juniperus spp. (junipers)
Kerria japonica (kerria)
Mahonia spp. (mahonias)
Nandina domestica (heavenly bamboo)
Narcissus spp. (daffodils)
Nerium oleander (oleanders)
Rhododendron spp. (rhododendrons only, not azaleas)
Tulipa spp. (tulips)

THE GARDEN PROFESSIONALS

Bonnie Lee Appleton, Ph.D., is an associate professor of horticulture, researcher, and extension nursery specialist at Hampton Roads Agricultural Experiment Station, Virginia Polytechnic Institute and State University, in Virginia Beach. She is the author of *Landscape Rejuvenation*.

Kristin E. Brugger, Ph.D., is a research biologist for Dupont Agricultural Products in Delaware. She is a former wildlife research biologist for the USDA's Denver Wildlife Research Center field station in Gainesville, Florida.

Matthew Cheever is a horticulturist and owner of Evergreen, a landscape design and maintenance company in Milton, Wisconsin.

Sylvia Ehrhardt and her husband, Walter, are owners of Ehrhardt Organic Farm in Knoxville, Maryland. They sell produce to area restaurants and co-ops and operate a Community Supported Agriculture (CSA) program for 60 families. They also conduct organic agriculture workshops at the farm.

David Hayes is the assistant state director of animal damage control for Montana. He has worked previously at the USDA's Denver Wildlife Research Center and for the U.S. Fish and Wildlife Service in Colorado.

Robert Lester is the owner of Robert Lester Associates "Springhill," a nursery in Easton, Pennsylvania, that specializes in bamboo, ornamental grasses, maples, and rare, exotic plants.

James A. Parkhurst, Ph.D, is an extension specialist in wildlife damage management and vertebrate integrated pest management at the University of Massachusetts at Amherst.

Clark Tibbits is a homestead gardener living in Celo Community near Burnsville, North Carolina. He is also a part-time management consultant for universities and has trained Peace Corps volunteers in bio-intensive agriculture in Lesotho, South Africa.

Eileen Weinsteiger is the garden project manager at the Rodale Institute Research Center in Maxatawny, Pennsylvania.

Pat Williams and her husband, Greg, are the publishers of *HortIdeas* newsletter, a monthly digest of reports on horticultural research and techniques. They live and garden near Gravel Switch, Kentucky.

Getting the Best from Your Tools

The notion that a tool is nothing more than a device for doing work stops at the garden gate. Anyone who has worked soil with a well-balanced fork or rake or sliced weeds effortlessly with a skillfully sharpened hoe knows that a high-quality tool not only gets the job done but also adds pleasure to the doing. Little wonder that gardeners come to think of their most effective tools as friends.

In this chapter, several of our experts describe the tools that they have found to be most efficient and explain why. In addition, there are tips to help you in your own search for the "perfect" tool repertoire. You'll learn how to choose and use tools, how to take care of them, and even how to improve them. You may even be inspired to come up with a new garden use for a common household item. The possibilities are endless!

Improving Tools

The tool that's sold in the local hardware store isn't always just what you need to do your best work. There's immense satisfaction in learning how to modify a tool to do its job more efficiently. Try the following expert tips for improving on standard tools, and see if they don't help lighten those gardening chores.

HACK YOUR HOE IN HALF

There's a whole slew of new, lightweight, efficient hoes on the market these days. "I'm a big fan of the Dutch scuffle hoe," says Phil Colson, the garden center manager at Highland Hardware in Georgia. "It's light and has a long handle, and the blade lays flat to the ground, so you just push and pull it back and forth through the soil to cultivate or cut weeds. Ergonomically, anything that works by pushing and pulling has a distinct advantage over the old design."

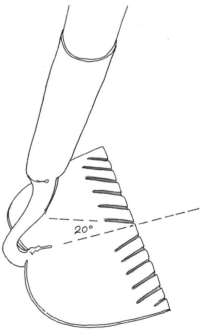

20°

TWO TIPS FOR HANDY HOES

The traditional American pattern hoe is a basic tool that easily lends itself to customization by enterprising gardeners. Here are two ideas for getting more from your standard hoe:

1. Use a hacksaw to cut the hoe blade from its two top corners to the center of its bottom edge, forming an inverted triangle. Sharpen the sides, and bend the blade inward a bit, and you'll have a good weed-slicer/furrow-maker for tight spots and close plantings.

2. Use a hacksaw to cut a V-shaped notch into one side of your hoe, with the point of the V facing inward. Sharpen the notch's inside edges, and use it to snag and slice tough weeds that have grown too big for ordinary cultivation.

Too bad the new hoes are so expensive—and in most areas, difficult to find at the local hardware store. If you can't find (or afford) these new hoes, you can always modify a conventional hoe to act like a scuffle hoe. The conversion couldn't be simpler; it's shown in the illustration below. Using a hacksaw, cut the hoe's blade in half from left to right. Then file the cut edge to restore the bevel at the outside bottom edge. (For directions on filing tool edges, see "Sharp Tools Save Time and Energy" on the opposite page.) Use a hammer to bend the blade inward slightly to give it a better angle for chopping weeds. "That's all there is to it," says Colson. "You'll have a hoe that's easier to use and that does a much better job of cultivating and weeding."

MODIFYING A HOE

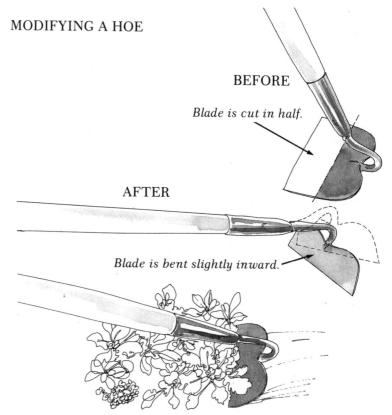

BEFORE

Blade is cut in half.

AFTER

Blade is bent slightly inward.

COLORFUL TOOLS ARE HARD TO LOSE

You know how it is. You could swear you put that darn tool down *right there*, but somehow it walked off on its own, and you can't find it anywhere. Then, after three days of rain, you find your favorite hoe on the ground, soaking wet and sporting little orange circles of rust-to-be. Susan Sides, a North Carolina garden writer, offers this sensible solution: Paint your tool handles bright red or some other attention-getting color. "It's almost impossible to lose a tool that's painted some loud color," says Sides. It is also a not-so-subtle reminder to friends who tend to borrow tools and forget to bring them back—they'll think twice about hanging onto your hot-pink hoe or glowing yellow shovel!

TAKE TIME TO HANDLE THE HANDLES

It pays to take a few minutes to work out with a new wooden-handled tool, says Phil Colson, the garden center manager at Highland Hardware in Georgia. "The first thing I do when I bring a new tool home is sand the handle smooth," says Colson. "Then I close my eyes and start feeling the surface. Instead of looking at it with my eyes, I look at it with my hands, because they're the ones that'll be grabbing it."

Use a rasp to round off any sharp edges, corners, or other places that don't feel comfortable, says Colson. Then give your hands another "look" at the handle. When the feel is just right, give the entire handle a final sanding with fine-grit sandpaper.

Then, instead of using boiled linseed oil (the usual recommendation), Colson advises that you rub tung oil into the wood. "The trouble with boiled linseed oil is that it takes forever to dry, and it's always evaporating," says Colson. And you have to keep putting more on. Tung oil, though, penetrates and sets up overnight, and it seals the wood to keep out moisture. "To my mind," claims Colson, "it's a better way to go."

Maintaining Your Tools

Tool maintenance just isn't as much fun as using the tools in the garden. But with the size of the investment they represent, it's time well-spent. Here is advice from the experts on how to keep your tools in tip-top shape.

SHARP TOOLS SAVE TIME AND ENERGY

To give yourself an edge in the garden, grab a file and put an edge on your garden tools. "You won't believe how

PADDED HANDLES PROTECT HANDS

No matter whether it's a trowel or a tiller—the longer you use it, the harder and more unforgiving its handle seems to get. Even gloved hands become sore and cramped.

The solution? "I use pipe insulation to make the handles on my tools softer and easier to grab," says Matthew Cheever, the owner of Evergreen, a landscape design and maintenance company in Wisconsin. Cheever says the foam cushions help him avoid blisters when using trowels, shovels, and rakes, and they allow him to use a tiller for hours at a time "without getting white-finger disease from all the vibration."

Plastic-foam pipe insulation is sold in 3-foot lengths and in most common pipe diameters at hardware and discount stores. The cushioned sleeves are slit along one side. To pad a tool handle, just cut the insulation to length, slip the insulation over the handle, and wrap duct tape or electrical tape around each end to hold it in place.

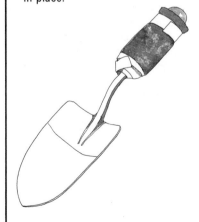

FIND THE CUTTING EDGE

To determine the right sharpening angle for a garden hoe, hold the tool just as though you were weeding with it, and scrape the blade across a hard surface. The resulting scratch marks will show you where to sharpen an edge that's beveled to suit your height and stance.

FALL CARE FOR HAND TOOLS

Assembling a collection of good-quality gardening tools is not an inexpensive endeavor. Protect your investment by taking care of your tools and storing them properly for winter. Come spring, you'll be glad you did!

Check handles for cracks and chips. Sand chipped handles and rub tung oil into the wood to make it smooth again. If a handle is cracked or broken, replace it.

Clean off the mud. This is something you should *always* do before putting any tool away; it will prevent rust spots. Clean the metal with a piece of burlap, steel wool, or a wire brush, or dip it a few times in a bucket of sand to scour the metal clean.

Sharpen your tools. If you put a tool away with a dull blade, it will still be dull and hard-to-use when you go to use it in the spring. Take the time to learn how to sharpen your own tools, or take them to a professional before storing them for the season.

Oil your tools. Coat metal parts of tools with a light coat of oil, and hang the tools in a dry place to protect them from rust.

much easier a sharpened spade or shovel cuts through dirt," says Susan Sides, a North Carolina garden writer. "And the same holds true for almost any other garden tool with a blade. You'll save yourself a ton of work if you sharpen your digging and weeding tools and touch them up occasionally when you're out working with them in the garden."

Here are three tips for quick and easy sharpening:

1. Sharpen single-beveled tools such as spades, shovels, and traditional hoes on the beveled side only. Never sharpen the flat side.

2. Use a file that matches the contour of the surface—for instance, a flat file for a flat-faced garden spade and a half-round file for a curved shovel.

3. Sharpen the blade at whatever angle will serve you best. Generally, that means following the same angle as the original bevel. But remember that sharpening at a shallow angle gives you a sharper edge—a good choice for weed-slicing tools. Sharpening at a steeper angle produces a longer-lasting edge that's good for digging.

To sharpen, push the file forward and across the tool's blade, pressing down hard and using the file's full length on each stroke. Lift the file up off the blade on the back stroke. Keep filing until you can feel a slight burr—a barely detectable buildup of metal—along the full width of the blade's opposite side. Finish the edge by running your file lightly across the burr to remove it.

How often should you *resharpen* a tool? As often as it takes to keep the tool useful and efficient. "When I feel that the work has slowed down," says Sides, "I'll try scraping any mud buildup off the blade. Sometimes that cleaning makes the difference. If not, I'll clean the blade with an oily rag and give it a few swipes with the file to take the dullness off."

STRAIGHTEN THOSE TINES

If you use a standard triangular-tined digging fork, known in most regions as a potato fork, you know that the tines tend to bend occasionally—or more than occasionally, depending on how hard the ground is (and how old the fork is). Straightening the tines can be a real bother. "But a piece of pipe makes the job really easy," says Phil Colson, the garden center manager at Highland Hardware in Georgia.

To make a tine straightener, just drive a 3-foot length of 1-inch-diameter galvanized pipe into the ground near the place where you store your tools, leaving about 1 foot of the pipe above ground. "When you're finished using your fork and you notice a tine is bent, just stick it down into the pipe and bend it back the way it's supposed to be," says Colson. This technique is shown in the illustration at right.

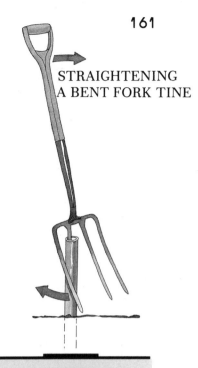

STRAIGHTENING A BENT FORK TINE

AN "A-MAIZING" TOOL CLEANER

Garden tools have a way of repeatedly caking up with dirt and mud, and your work really slows if you don't take time to clean the stuff off. What to use? "A dry corncob makes a great in-the-garden tool cleaner," says Susan Sides, a North Carolina garden writer. "The rough surface gets all of the soil off fast, and when you're done with the corncob, you can just throw it in the compost pile."

QUICK TIPS FOR SPRING STARTUPS

Ah, spring at last, and there's work to do. You get out the old mower or tiller, yank on the starter rope—nothing. A few more useless yanks later, and you're ready to call it quits. But first, try these tips from Mike Ferrara, a senior editor for *Organic Gardening* magazine:

1. Replace any old fuel in the tank with new, fresh gas.
2. Buy and install a new spark plug.
3. Change the oil—old oil can gum up the works. Also, if it's a cool day, set the machine in the sun to warm and "thin" the oil.
4. Disconnect the spark plug and check the machine's working parts—such as tiller tines and mower blades—for tangled vegetation, twine, or the like. Clear away any obstructions, and reconnect the spark plug.

"Nine times out of ten, doing just those four things will get a sluggish engine up and going," says Ferrara.

PREVENT SPRAYER CLOGS WITH PANTY HOSE

Spraying is enough of a chore without being stalled by a clogged nozzle. Especially if you're spraying compost or manure tea, particles clogging the nozzle can be a real problem. Michael Maltas, the garden director of the organic

---

EASY MACHINE MAINTENANCE

Here are some things you should keep in mind as you winterize your machinery:

1. Clean off all dust, dirt, matted grass, and excess grease.

2. Look for loose or missing screws, bolts, or nuts; replace if necessary.

3. Disconnect the spark plug wire, and check the blades or tines of your machine. If necessary, sharpen and oil the blades or tines before replacing them.

4. If your machine has a 4-cycle engine, change the oil.

5. Clean and oil the air filter, following the manufacturer's directions.

6. To clean out the fuel line, drain out all gasoline, and then run the engine until it stops.

7. Remove, clean, and replace the spark plug.

BUYING USED EQUIPMENT

Buying a used tiller, mower, or chipper/shredder can save you big money — or cost you big money. The first step to getting good equipment at a good price is to let dealers know that you're looking. Most name-brand power equipment dealers sell reconditioned models, but the bargains go fast. Talk to local dealers, tell them you're looking, and leave your name and phone number. Once you find a machine you are interested in, use this checklist to make sure you are getting a good deal:

Start the engine. Check to see that the engine starts easily.

Examine the spark plugs. Dark carbon deposits mean only that a tune-up is overdue. Oil-fouled plugs spell trouble.

Look at the crankcase oil. Dirty oil or a nearly empty crankcase suggests poor maintenance and serves as a warning of future repairs.

Watch for other signs of neglect. A dirty air cleaner, clogged cooling fins, or a rusty or oil-gummed throttle linkage are all signs that a machine has not been properly cared for.

If you're buying a tiller, watch out for oil leaks, low transmission oil level, unusual grinding noises, or bent or worn tines.

On chipper/shredders, look for loose welds, stress cracks, low oil, and excessive vibration when the engine is running.

For walk-behind mowers, check for rust, excessive vibrations, and faulty oil seals. Avoid mowers lacking an automatic no-operator shutoff control.

showpiece garden for Fetzer Vineyards in California, suggests this cheap and effective spray strainer: "Take a pair of discarded panty hose and turn one leg inside the other to form one double-thick leg. Let the toe dangle into the spray tank, and stretch the top of the hose over the opening of your sprayer tank, securing it with a rubber band. When you pour your spray into the [panty hose] strainer, the nozzle-clogging particles will be trapped." Before spraying, remove and discard the used strainer — particles and all — or rinse it out for future use.

Clues for Saving Cash

Gardeners tend to be an ingenious group, especially when it comes to saving time and money. And they're always on the lookout for ways to ease the strain on those aching backs. We asked the experts for some of their favorite tips and techniques for stretching a dollar (and not stretching a muscle!).

TIPS FOR TROUBLE-FREE RENTALS

Renting can be the best option for tools and power equipment that you need only once or twice a year, suggests Mike Ferrara, a senior editor for *Organic Gardening* magazine. "Chipper/shredders, heavy-duty tillers, lawn aerators, dethatchers, sod cutters, lawn rollers, stump grinders, fertilizer spreaders, and chain saws are all examples of equipment that many people don't need full-time but that are awfully useful when you do need them," says Ferrara. Some tips to keep in mind:

Most tools are rented by the day or half-day. If you think you'll need it for only a couple of hours, ask friends or neighbors if they're interested in using the tool and sharing the rental fee with you.

Try out the tool before you take it home. In the case of power equipment, start the engine, and run the machine just as if you were using it. And be sure you know how to *stop* it, too.

Consider hiring instead. Before you rent, check around to see if someone can do the job *for* you for less money. Sometimes it's actually cheaper to hire a professional with his or her own equipment than it is to do it yourself with a rental.

Shop around. The price, terms, and condition of tools

can vary widely among rental stores.

Return the equipment on time. Some rental yards charge stiff penalty fees for late returns; others just call the sheriff.

PAD YOUR KNEES TO SAVE YOUR BACK

Slip-on knee pads and cushioned mats are sold at garden centers as "ground softeners" for gardener's knees. "But what knee pads really do is save your back," says Phil Colson, the garden center manager at Highland Hardware in Georgia. "Most people," he observes, "hate to get down on their knees because it's uncomfortable and often the ground is wet or muddy. So they end up bending over the whole time they're weeding or whatever, and pretty soon they've got back problems."

Can't find the special cushions at your hardware or garden store? Look for slip-on knee pads at sporting goods stores. Or make your own garden kneeling mat by filling an old hot water bottle with sand or sawdust.

KITCHEN KNIVES CUT GARDEN CHORES

Want a handy, inexpensive, multipurpose, nearly indestructible garden tool? Then shop around for old kitchen knives at flea markets, suggests Susan Sides, a North Carolina garden writer. "I have several old knives that I keep out in the garden all the time," says Sides. "I just stick them on fence posts where I can find them and where the kids can't get them. The knives don't rust because they're stainless steel—and they don't get lost as soon as you put them down, the way a pocketknife does."

Sides uses different knives for different chores, including weeding, harvesting, cutting off seed heads, and snipping twine. "I have one knife with a blade that's 2 inches wide and about 7 inches long that I use as a sort of mini-machete," she says. Smaller-bladed types, like a little butter knife, are great for pricking out seedlings for transplanting.

PICK UP A PICKLE BUCKET

"I couldn't garden without a 5-gallon bucket!" declares Virginia Blakelock, the past president of the Hobby Greenhouse Association. Blakelock loads her garden cart with buckets full of mulch, then pulls the cart to where she's

COFFEE-CAN TOOL CADDY

Long-handled rakes, shovels, hoes, and such have a way of "sinking" into the soil as soon as you need them. Here's a simple way to keep them organized and upright while you're working.

Cut the top and bottom from a large metal can, and nail the can to a fence post, about 3 feet up the post. Now when you're done with a tool, just slip the long handle through the metal can ring to hold it in place. A single 5-pound coffee can is big enough to hold two or three long-handled implements.

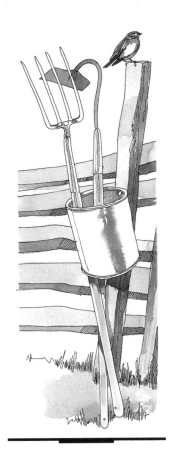

START KIDS OUT RIGHT

Beginning gardeners need encouragement, not frustration. Plastic hoes and rakes from the toy store don't do the job, and adult-size tools are hard to handle. Equip your children with a sturdy set of tools just their size. A hoe, shovel, and rake are the basics. A just-my-size wheelbarrow or wagon encourages willing helpers, too. For suppliers of such tools, see "Gardening Equipment" on page 331.

USE SLED POWER

Rescue that plastic sledding disc from the garage, attach a long rope to one side, and use it to slide loads of mulch or compost to where you want them. A plastic sled is also good for hauling plants that you're transplanting from one part of the garden to another.

working. She finds it's easy to carry a bucket of mulch into the perennial bed and spread the mulch just where she wants it. She also uses the buckets to mix up 5-gallon batches of liquid fertilizer such as fish emulsion. (See "Brew Compost Tea on the Spot" on page 110 for another tip on using plastic buckets in the garden.)

Driveway sealer and other home-maintenance products are often packed in 5-gallon plastic buckets. You can also find the buckets at restaurants or luncheonettes—wherever pickles are served—often free for the asking. Clean your buckets thoroughly before relegating them to the garden.

Favorite Tools

What tools are the best? Everyone has their own special favorites. We asked our experts for their top picks in tools: Here are their answers.

WHEEL HOES FOR REAL POWER

The classic wheel hoe (a tool with long handles, a single front wheel, and a tool bar attachment behind) is generally considered strictly a weeding tool. But modern updates of the traditional high-wheel design have created a much more efficient, versatile tool, says Stewart Hoyt, a Vermont market gardener. "The wheel is smaller, and there are stirrup-style oscillating-hoe attachments in varying widths that cut just below the surface," says Hoyt.

"I'm interested in ways of working the soil as shallowly as possible," Hoyt says. "I don't see any point in destroying the good work of the worms and the frost and such. I just want to be able to incorporate a cover crop and compost into the top 1½ inches of soil. A wheel hoe does a good job of that and cuts up weeds nicely, too."

SUSAN SIDES'S FAVORITE TOOLS

During her many years as head gardener at the Mother Earth News Eco-Village, Susan Sides, a North Carolina garden writer, refined her choices of tools. Her list of favorites is sheer simplicity: a Smith & Hawken garden spade, digging fork, and trowel, and a good-quality stirrup hoe.

Sides uses the first three "because they're really well-made." As for a good stirrup hoe, she advises that you get one that pivots from the end of the handle, with a stirrup blade that bows downward toward the soil. "And that's really all I need," says Sides. "Give me a spade, a fork, a stirrup hoe, and a trowel, and I can do almost anything."

SUSAN SIDES'S FAVORITES

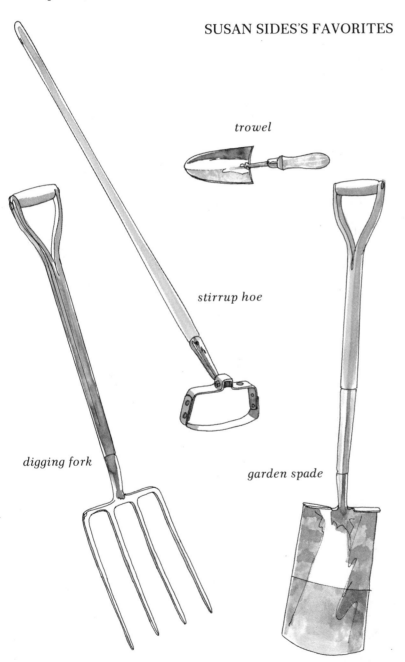

trowel

stirrup hoe

digging fork

garden spade

GARDEN BEDSPREADS

Linda Askey Weathers, the garden editor for *Southern Accents* magazine, brings new life to tattered old bedspreads by using them as garden tarps. An old bedspread spread on the ground is perfect for collecting leaves or refuse. Lay the spread open on the ground and rake or drop the leaves or refuse in a pile in the middle. When you're ready to carry it away, turn up the corners of the spread and carry it in gunny-sack fashion to the compost pile. Or, if it's too heavy, just drag it.

CLEAN YOUR SHOES

Here's an old-fashioned idea that's still worthwhile today. Mount a shoe and boot scraper by the back door to keep soil and mud outside where it belongs. A pair of stiff scrub brushes nailed to a frame of scrap wood will do the trick.

◆ PHIL COLSON'S FAVORITE TOOLS

Few people are as knowledgeable — or as opinionated — about garden tools as Phil Colson, the garden center manager at Highland Hardware in Georgia.

"I'm basically lazy," says Colson, "so my whole focus on tools is to find the most efficient implement for the job." Here are a few of his favorites:

English square-tined digging fork. "Nothing's better for separating and breaking up soil," he claims.

Floral shovel. "Most of my tools hang in the shed, but my floral shovel never gets hung because I'm always using it," says Colson. "It's about two-thirds the size of a regular shovel, with a blade about 8 inches across. You can't beat it for planting bulbs, digging, and transplanting."

Italian grape hoe. "An incredible digging tool for jobs like planting a tree," says Colson. "You use it like a pickax; just throw it in the ground, and rock it back. You can lift soil up with its wide blade, push dirt around, and trench with it."

Dutch scuffle hoe. "I like this one because you just push the blade over the soil to weed and cultivate. And it

PHIL COLSON'S FAVORITES

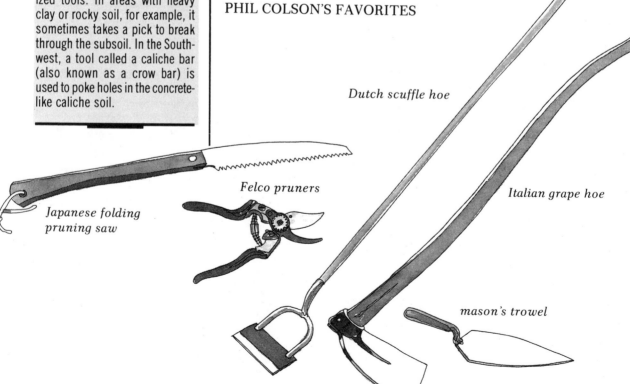

Dutch scuffle hoe

Felco pruners

Japanese folding pruning saw

Italian grape hoe

mason's trowel

has a long handle that lets you reach without having to take a step," says Colson.

Conventional wheelbarrow. Unlike a garden cart, a wheelbarrow doesn't require a wide path or a lot of clearance; it dumps right, left, and forward; and it's a great leverage tool for picking up heavy objects. Just lean it on its side and work the bottom edge under whatever you're trying to lift, then use your body weight to rock the wheelbarrow back up. "I've lifted 300-pound boulders that way—by myself," says Colson.

Japanese folding pruning saw. "You can carry this little 8-inch saw around in your pocket and just flip it out like a jackknife when you need it," says Colson. "It cuts on the pull stroke, and it's really sharp. It'll go through a ¾-inch branch with one pull. I hardly ever use loppers any more."

Japanese grubbing knife. "Nothing's better for getting out tenacious weeds like crabgrass and slicing off dandelions, particularly in rocky soil," says Colson.

Mason's trowel. Colson suggests this as an alternative to a high-quality garden trowel, which can be expensive. A mason's trowel is "made for lifting cement, so it's really strong, but it doesn't cost much," he says.

Felco pruners. "They give you a good, clean cut, particularly on woody material," says Colson.

THE GARDEN PROFESSIONALS

Virginia Blakelock is a free-lance garden writer from Yellow Springs, Ohio. She is the past president of the Hobby Greenhouse Association, Inc., a nonprofit organization of home greenhouse owners.

Matthew Cheever is a horticulturist and owner of Evergreen, a landscape design and maintenance company in Milton, Wisconsin.

Phil Colson is the garden center manager at Highland Hardware, a fine-tools shop in Atlanta, Georgia.

Mike Ferrara is a senior editor for *Organic Gardening* magazine in charge of outdoor power equipment coverage.

Stewart Hoyt is a market gardener and operates a Community Supported Agriculture (CSA) operation in Barnet, Vermont.

Michael Maltas is the garden director of the organic showpiece garden for Fetzer Vineyards in Hopland, California. Maltas grows acres of vegetables, flowers, and fruit at the Fetzer Valley Oaks Food and Wine Center.

Susan Sides is a garden writer from Fairview, North Carolina. She is the former head gardener at Mother Earth News Eco-Village.

Linda Askey Weathers is the garden editor for *Southern Accents* magazine and the associate garden editor of *Southern Living* magazine.

MAILBOX TOOLSHED

As all growers know, the closer you can keep your garden tools to the garden, the better. But not everyone's vegetable patch is within a few feet of the garage— and not everyone can build a separate toolshed.

Create a sort of on-the-spot shed for small hand tools with a conventional mailbox. Mailboxes are sturdy, weatherproof, and just the right size for a trowel, some seed packets, string, and other small items. It's a simple matter to set a mailbox on a post by the entrance to your garden. And you can always dress it up with a coat of paint or by planting flowers around it.

PART 3

GET THE BEST FROM YOUR YARD AND GARDEN

Some gardeners lavish most of their garden hours on beds of succulent vegetable crops, while others are happiest trimming, transplanting, and staking flowers. And then there are gardeners who want to grow all kinds of plants, and more of them, every year. It's always exciting to learn secrets that will help you reap a greater harvest, be it getting the earliest tomato, the best-tasting berries, or the most aromatic herbs. It's also a thrill to find new ways to combine color and form in flower beds and borders and to use shrubs and trees to highlight your yard.

Remember these pointers for a better bean harvest:

• Soaking or presprouting seeds may cause them to rot.

• Unless planting where beans were before, dust seeds with a bacterial inoculant, to boost nitrogen fixation.

• Wait until soil temperatures reach 60°F to plant.

• Most beans, except fava beans, are sensitive to frost. They prefer air temperatures of 70° to 80°F.

• Keep plants evenly watered during germination and flowering, or harvest may be poor.

• Beans yield about 50 quarts per 100 feet of row.

• Pick snap beans when pencil-size and tender, and before pods are bumpy.

• Harvest bush beans almost daily to encourage production. Pinch off bush beans with your thumbnail and fingers.

• Use scissors to harvest pole and runner beans.

• For eating fresh, pick shell beans when pods are plump but tender. To eat dry, pick when seeds rattle in the brown pods.

Vegetables

What could we possibly write about growing vegetables that hasn't been written before? There may be no other subject in gardening that has been so thoroughly discussed as how to plant and care for a backyard vegetable garden.

If you're a beginning vegetable gardener, you may not find all of the answers to your basic questions here. Refer to the list of books in "Recommended Reading" on page 333 for several good references for new gardeners. Also, keep in mind that you'll find excellent tips on growing vegetables throughout this book. One easy way to find these tips is to refer to the index; look under the "Vegetable Gardening" heading or under the name of the particular crop that interests you.

In this chapter, we skip past the preliminaries. Read on to discover the best new ideas that our experts have derived from their many years of experimentation and experience growing vegetables.

Bountiful Beans

There's an endless list of beans you can plant. Bush or pole beans, for fresh eating or drying, are a crop you won't want to be without.

BUILD A BEAN TUNNEL

If you grow pole beans, you've probably tried different trellises and teepees for supporting them. William and Brenda Reid, who have an award-winning design for their home landscape and garden, built a bean tunnel for their children. On hot afternoons, the dappled shade beneath the tunnel is a cool retreat.

The Reids made the tunnel from three cattle panels, which are lengths of fencing made of flexible steel rods spaced 6 inches apart. Each panel is 4×16 feet. The cattle panels are galvanized steel, and they don't rust. To make a tunnel, bend a panel to form an arch, drive in a stake at each corner, and tie the panels to the stakes. The Reids use a series of three panels to form a 12-foot-long tunnel. Be careful when bending the cattle panels into arches. The panels can spring up suddenly—a dangerous occurrence if you're not on your guard for it.

Once you've set up your tunnel, plant pole beans along the outside of both tunnel walls. The beans will grow up the walls and meet in the middle. "Beans are easy to pick from this structure since they hang down," William explains. The tunnels also make good trellises for other climbing plants, particularly cucumbers, since the wide spaces between the rods allow fruits to expand without getting pinched.

ADD A BEAN ARBOR

A variation on bean trellising is a bean arbor. Nancy Farrell, an innovative organic gardener from Vermont, made a low-cost arbor from old lath strips that her neighbor was throwing away. You can copy her design, which is shown in the illustration below. Here's how:

1. Nail the lath together in a widely spaced cross-hatch pattern to make the arbor roof.
2. Measure the dimensions of the roof.

lath   *nails*

COVER FALL BEANS

In the South, you can plant a fall crop of beans in early August. Covering the seeds with a layer of vermiculite will help get the crop started, suggests H. S. Stevens, a Texas garden writer. Very few beans will germinate if the soil temperature is over 90°F, as it sometimes is near the surface in late summer. But covering the beans with a layer of moist vermiculite will reflect some heat and aid germination.

COOK IN THE PODS

Soybeans and many other kinds of dry beans take well to being cooked in the pod. Harvest when the beans are full-size but before the pods begin to dry. Drop pods in boiling water and cook for 10 to 15 minutes, until the beans are tender. Drain and put a bowl of pods on the table along with bowls for spent pods. People can squish out their own beans. Children are particularly fond of this cooking style. A word of caution: You may want to serve these beans only when children are eating outside. It doesn't take long for them to discover that a good squishing action can send a bean as far as most peashooters can.

3. Pound two rows of stakes (each about 6 to 8 feet long) into place at the site where you plan to erect the arbor. The two rows should be the same distance apart as the width of the roof piece. Make each row as long as the length of the roof piece, spacing the stakes about 6 inches apart.

4. Use twine or nails to attach the roof to the supporting stakes.

5. Plant pole beans at the base of the stakes.

The beans will twine up the stakes as usual but crawl along the roof when they hit it. Farrell says, "It's easy to pick beans that hang down from the lath."

CROSS YOUR TEEPEES

Here's a variation on the traditional bean teepee that makes the crop more accessible and less likely to have disease problems. Charlie Nardozzi, a horticultural specialist for the National Gardening Association in Vermont, has adapted his bean teepees so that the poles cross one another at waist level rather than at the top, as shown in the illustration below. Choose wooden stakes or poles about 8

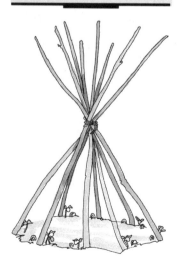

A MODIFIED BEAN TEEPEE

feet long, and use twine to tie them together at a central point. Plants growing up these supports have greater air circulation, giving them added disease resistance. "But mainly," Nardozzi says, "having the pods spread out that much makes picking faster and more efficient."

BEANS CAN TAKE SHADE

We think of beans as a sun-loving crop, but Nancy Farrell, an innovative organic gardener from Vermont, finds that beans can tolerate some shade. Farrell's garden receives filtered shade for most of the day. As a result, she's learned what can take shade and what can't. Farrell says, "With good soil, even my pole beans set good crops as long as they get an hour of morning sun. They yield later, but they still yield, and I can rotate in that area with kale, chard, root crops, broccoli, and lettuce."

Cole Crops

Cabbage, broccoli, and their less-common cousins like kale and brussels sprouts all belong to the same family of plants—Cruciferae. They're cool-weather crops that are good for planting in spring and fall.

KEEP THE CABBAGE COMING

If you don't want all of your cabbages to be ready for harvest at once, try this simple technique for prolonging the harvest: "An old-timer taught me this trick," says Bill McDorman, the founder of High Altitude Gardens, an Idaho mail-order seed company. "If your cabbage is maturing all at once and you're worried that some of the heads will split or get tougher than you want, give some heads a half-twist, breaking part of the stem. This will slow the maturation process."

WATCH YOUR BROCCOLI MIGRATE

Harvesting sideshoots after cutting the main head from broccoli plants gives you greater yields per plant. But did you know that you can push your broccoli plants to keep

CULTURE CLUES: CABBAGE

Heat and improper watering are two factors that can foil your cabbages. Here are some other growing tips:

• Cool weather brings out the flavor in maturing cabbages.

• Wide spacings produce bigger heads, but young, small cabbages are tastier. To get both, space plants 6 inches apart and harvest every other one before maturity. Stagger plantings at two-week intervals for a longer harvest.

• Water evenly to prevent cracking of heads. Don't get foliage wet during cool weather or periods of high humidity. Cut back on water as cabbages mature.

• Carefully weed by hand around roots; apply a thick mulch to keep soil moist and cool.

• If leaves start to yellow, provide a mid-season nitrogen boost with manure tea.

• Harvest firm heads with a sharp knife. Leave stalks and roots in place to produce small cabbages.

MODIFY SIDESHOOT SIZE

If you want a bonus harvest of broccoli sideshoots, choose cultivars carefully: Some produce more sideshoots than others. For maximum sideshoot yield, space plants about 18 inches apart. To increase the number of sideshoots, take as little of the stem as possible when cutting the central head. For fewer but larger sideshoots, cut 6 to 8 inches of the stem when you cut the central head.

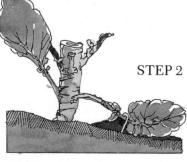

STEP 1

STEP 2

STEP 3

STEP 4

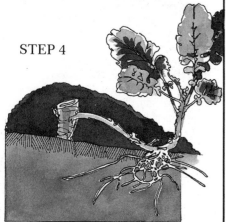

REGENERATING BROCCOLI

producing for several growing seasons? Tim Peters, the research director for Territorial Seed Company in Oregon, suggests the following method for regenerating broccoli for continuous harvest:

1. Harvest your broccoli as usual. When a plant becomes unproductive, cut it back and allow suckers to grow from the stump.

2. When suckers are 4 to 5 inches long, select one to be the next "generation" of the plant. The one closest to the base of the plant is usually the best to choose. Anchor the sucker to the ground with a wire hook or a small rock so that approximately 4 inches of stem is oriented horizontally, touching the soil, as shown in the illustration at left. Remove the other suckers from the stump, and discard them.

3. When the anchored sucker grows to 6 or 7 inches, cut the stump back to just above the point where the sucker emerges from it. At this point, you can either leave the anchoring hook in place or remove it.

4. Mound soil over the old stump and over the anchored part of the sucker. This may decrease disease at the wound and encourage roots to form for the new plant.

5. Allow time for the stump wound to heal before cold, damp weather arrives. Remove flower shoots that form when the plant overwinters and begins to go to seed. The following spring, about the time when late tulips bloom, prune back the plant hard, and begin the process again.

Peters cautions that this technique is somewhat of an art, and gardeners shouldn't expect 100 percent success. The plants will require good air circulation and an area free of debris, which could rot and encourage disease in the vulnerable wounded area. Discard leaves and suckers that you remove from the plant.

The secret of the technique is the "crook" created in the plant's stem by anchoring the sucker. The crook stimulates growth of new suckers along the horizontal stem and seems to slow the passage of disease organisms through the stem into the root system. "You can let the stem grow straight up out of the ground, and it'll regenerate itself from that stump," Peters says. "But you're going to lose more plants." Gardeners in areas with harsh winters may have more cold-damaged plants than gardeners in areas with mild winters. You can also try this technique with collards, late cabbages, brussels sprouts, kale, and kohlrabi.

PLANT SUMMER BROCCOLI UNDER BOARDS

In most parts of the country, mid- to late summer is the time to sow broccoli for a fall harvest. But dry soil and hot, dog-day weather can seriously slow and reduce—or even prevent—germination.

"I used to have a hard time starting summer broccoli," says Pat Stone, the garden editor for *BackHome* magazine, "but then I discovered the lumber method. The first time I tried it, the plants came up so fast I thought they must be weeds." Here's how Stone does it:

1. Dig a shallow (1- to 2-inch-deep) trench, and line it with well-aged compost or good garden soil.
2. Scatter broccoli seeds in the trench, cover the seeds shallowly with more soil or compost, and water the trench thoroughly. Then lay boards across the trench.
3. Check under the boards every day, and remove them as soon as you see small, pale yellow seedlings come up.

"You can plant the seeds thickly, and then thin and transplant them after you take the boards off," says Stone. "Or you can just space them out when you first plant and leave them in place to mature."

You can also try Stone's technique for starting fall crops of cabbage, cauliflower, and Chinese cabbage.

PLANT A CLOVER COVER

Planting white clover (*Trifolium repens*) as a living mulch under broccoli and other cole crops will keep them weed-free and will improve the soil at the same time. "I learned the trick of undersowing broccoli with white clover from garden writer Eliot Coleman," says Pat Stone, the garden editor for *BackHome* magazine. One month after Stone transplants broccoli to his garden, he scratches up the soil, broadcasts white clover seed at the rate of 4 to 8 ounces per 1,000 square feet, and then covers the seed. "Pretty soon the clover comes up an inch or three. As the broccoli matures to harvest, the bed looks like a little grassy meadow under a stand of miniature trees," Stone quips. Remove the broccoli plants after they have finished producing, and you'll have a well-established leguminous cover crop for the winter or summer. When it's time to replant, turn the clover under. For more tips on using living mulches, see "Building Soil Fertility," beginning on page 92.

CULTURE CLUES: BROCCOLI

Try these growing hints for better broccoli:

• Unexpected warm spells will cause heads to open too soon. However, a prolonged period of nights around 30°F and days in the 50° to 60°F range can produce tiny, immature heads called buttons. Use row covers or cloches during cool weather.

• Top-dress with manure tea or side-dress with blood meal or fish emulsion two to three weeks after transplanting and water deeply. Repeat monthly until a week before harvest.

• When daytime temperatures exceed 75°F, put down a thick layer of organic mulch.

• Be sure to provide more than 1½ inches of water a week, or your spring crops will have tough stems. Fall crops need steady (but slightly less) water.

• Harvest before the florets start to open and turn yellow. Cut just below the point where the stems begin to separate. Once the main head is harvested, pick the sideshoots that form in the leaf axils and along the lower stalk.

BEAUTIFUL BROCCOLI

'Premium Crop' is the favorite cultivar of most of the experts. 'Emperor' is well-liked by northeast growers. Fred Hoover, an organic market gardener, likes 'Packman' and 'Pirate', a mid-season cultivar that doesn't make sideshoots but has very tight buds.

Root disturbance and lack of nutrients can both hamper your corn crop. Keep these points in mind as well:

• If planting directly, wait until all danger of frost is past and the soil warms up to 60°F. If the weather stays cool, spread black plastic on the planting area to speed ground warming.

• If you start corn indoors, use peat pots to avoid disturbing the roots at transplanting time.

• For early plantings, sow seeds 1 inch deep; in the hot weather of midsummer, sow 4 inches deep.

• Remove unwanted seedlings by cutting them off at soil level.

• Cultivate thoroughly around the stalks for the first month of growth. After that, control weeds by applying mulch (to avoid damaging the shallow roots).

• To avoid cross-pollination, keep different corn cultivars 400 or more yards apart, or plant so they tassel two weeks apart.

• To promote pollination, plant the same cultivar in blocks or hand-pollinate.

• Corn is a heavy feeder, especially on nitrogen. It thrives where earth-enriching crops like beans or clover grew the previous year.

• Three weeks after corn silks appear, pull back part of the husk and pierce a kernel with your thumbnail. If "milk" spurts out, the sweet corn is ripe. A completely dry silk or a yellow or faded green sheath means the ear is past its prime.

STAKE SNOWBOUND SPROUTS

Brussels sprouts can stay in the garden through the winter for harvest whenever you want them. But in northern areas, the plants may be buried under a blanket of snow. "It's easy to lose the brussels sprouts in the snow," says Bill McDorman, the founder of High Altitude Gardens, an Idaho mail-order seed company. "But if you stick 4- to 5-foot-high stakes or poles on either side of the plants in the fall, you can wade out into the garden to find them after the first few snows."

Homegrown Corn

Growing sweet corn in the home garden requires a considerable amount of space, and you may suffer the disappointment of poorly filled or worm-ridden ears. And then there are the local wild animals, who also love the taste of ripe corn. (You'll find some great tips on keeping crows and others away from your corn in "Repel or Scare Pests," beginning on page 148.) But despite the crop's finicky nature, that wonderful homegrown flavor is well worth all of the effort.

PRACTICE PROPER CORN CARE

"Corn needs tender loving care all through its growth," says William E. Watson, the president of Liberty Seed Company in Ohio. "The cells that become an ear of corn form when the plant is just a few inches high, and any stress alters the end product." Here are Watson's principles for proper corn care:

Give corn plenty of space. Rows should be at least 32 inches apart, but "36 inches is better," says Watson. Plant spacing in the row should be 9 inches at minimum.

Keep it fertilized. At planting, Watson recommends putting down a balanced fertilizer that provides the equivalent of 50 pounds of nitrogen per acre. Many commercial organic fertilizers, such as soybean meal, cottonseed meal, and blood meal, contain about 6 percent nitrogen, so you'd need to apply slightly less than 2 pounds of fertilizer per 100 square feet. Watson also suggests side-dressing when the corn is 6 inches tall by sprinkling nitrogen fertilizer in a shallow trench about 6 inches to one side of each row. Follow up with a second side-dressing on the other side of the rows when you see tassels forming on the plants.

Water when necessary. Corn needs at least 1 inch of water per week. If rainfall is inadequate, give the soil a good soaking. Don't water from above. (Watering from above can wash pollen off of the tassels.)

SAVE THOSE EXTRA TASSELS

If your corn plants produce sideshoots, which are called suckers, should you pull them off to concentrate the plant's production on the main stalk? David Cavagnaro, a garden manager at Heritage Farm for Seed Savers Exchange in Iowa, never removes corn suckers. "In hot, dry summers, the main tassels can burn, leaving you with no pollen. But suckers produce tassels, too—generally a bit later. Since the silks stay viable for a while, the pollen from the tassels on the suckers can save a crop. I know they've saved mine many times." Cavagnaro also points out that the extra foliage means extra photosynthesis, which translates into more food to bolster developing ears.

RAISE YOUR MAIZE

If you've had problems getting corn to grow due to wet soil conditions, consider planting it in raised beds. A study by the USDA's Soil Drainage Research Unit in Columbus, Ohio, shows that growing corn in raised beds can increase yields over corn grown in a flat field.

"The advantage here," says Norman R. Fausey, Ph.D., a USDA soil scientist, "is that you get some surface drainage." This helps ensure that the germinating seed and seedling always get enough oxygen, which is necessary for growth. In a heavy, wet soil, all the soil pores can fill with water, blocking oxygen from the young plant.

If you decide to plant corn in a raised bed, don't forget that it's a wind-pollinated crop. If you plant it in a traditional long, narrow raised bed, pollination may be poor, resulting in poor ear development. You may want to try a few raised blocks, with three or four short rows per block. Otherwise, plan to hand-pollinate.

DON'T LET BEETLES HIT THE SILK

Corn borers, corn earworms, and cutworms—those are the pests that come to mind most often when you think of threats to your corn crop. But when the silk on your corn

CLASSY CORN

Here are a few experts' favorites from the sweet corn patch:

Cold-resistant corn. Bill McDorman, the founder of High Altitude Gardens, an Idaho mail-order seed company, likes open-pollinated corn cultivars, particularly 'Fisher's Earliest', a variety bred at 5,000 feet in Montana. He says that he's seen it survive temperatures as low as 23°F and watched it stand up again after being beaten down by hailstones.

A hot-climate hero. Fred Hoover, an organic market gardener in Arizona, likes 'Breeders Choice' for flavor and performance in his hot climate.

A dried cornmeal cultivar. Ken Ryan, an organic farmer and farm manager from New England, likes 'Bloody Butcher' for a dried cornmeal cultivar. He says, "It's red, and it grows about 15 feet tall, even in Massachusetts."

WIPE SILKS AWAY

After husking corn and removing most of the silks, capture the stubborn ones with a damp cloth. Rub the cloth down the ear, from tip to base, and it will pick up the leftover silks.

Avoiding high heat and root disturbance will help deliver a good lettuce crop. Here are some other good tips to remember:

• As the weather warms, plant heat-resistant cultivars. Planting in shady areas and watering frequently will help prevent bolting. If the soil is very warm, try pre-sprouting the seeds to get better germination.

• Keep the soil surface moist but not soggy. Make sure the crop gets at least 1 inch of water a week.

• To help prevent disease, water on sunny mornings so the leaves will dry by evening.

• After a good watering, apply a thick layer of mulch to conserve moisture, suffocate weeds around the easily damaged roots, and keep lettuce leaves clean.

• Lettuce needs plenty of nitrogen. To promote quick growth, side-dress with manure tea or fish emulsion once or twice during the growing season.

• Just before bolting, lettuce plants start to elongate and form a bitter sap. To keep this from happening, pinch off the top center of the plant.

• Lettuce is crispest if picked in the morning. Watch your crop closely, as mature plants decline quickly. To test the firmness of heading types, press down gently on lettuce hearts with the back of your hand; don't pinch them, as this can bruise the hearts. Use a sharp knife to cut heads below the lowest leaves, or pull plants out by the roots.

first emerges, you'd best watch out for yet another menace: beetles. "If you're not careful," says William E. Watson, the president of Liberty Seed Company in Ohio, "you can wind up with zip for corn. Spotted cucumber beetles and Japanese beetles will settle on the silk and eat it right down to the husk. No silk, no pollination. No pollination, no corn kernels."

Fortunately, the beetles are relatively easy to control—if you get to them quickly. Severe infestations may require dusting the silk with rotenone, but in most cases handpicking will do the job. "You have to do it every day or at least every other day, as soon as the silk shows," says Watson. "Corn silk grows fast, and it's very tender and succulent. Beetles go straight for it."

Leafy Crops

There's a lot more to leaf crops than lettuce. You can enjoy a variety of leaf crops from early spring through late fall—and right through the winter in many areas.

TUCK IN A SALAD BED

Mesclun—a mixture of young, tender salad greens—is touted as a gourmet treat. But it's easy to grow your own mesclun mix, says Miriam Klein-Hansen, who taught homestead gardening at the National Center for Appropriate Technology in Montana. She plants mixed salad beds, much like a giant mesclun mix, four times during the season: early spring, late spring, early summer, and late summer. She combines seven or eight different types of lettuce as well as bok choy, mizuna (*Brassica juncea* var. *japonica*), peppergrass (*Lepidium sativum*), and other short-season oriental greens, and spreads them thickly—two seeds per inch in rows about 8 inches apart. Klein-Hansen says, "I harvest outer leaves rather than whole plants. Because I always have a new bed going, I can turn the old plants under when they begin to get tired and bitter. I interplant sunflowers with the early-summer bed for the shade, and I put the last bed of the year under a plastic tunnel."

Richard de Wilde, a Wisconsin organic farmer, also prefers making up his own mesclun mixes, rather than buying commercially packaged seed mixes. "Plants in commercial mixes do not mature at the same time, making them very difficult to harvest efficiently," says de Wilde. "I also like to use a broader selection of plants than you can find in a commercial mix." Rather than plant all of the cultivars in a mixed bed, de Wilde grows the components of his mix separately so that he can harvest and replant selectively. De Wilde says, "The secret to good mesclun mixes is to cut them while they're young. Many greens get bitter after the first cutting, and it's wise to till them in rather than extend their season. I plant mesclun greens every week during the season."

COAXING COOL-LOVERS IN HOT CLIMATES

Most greens prefer cool conditions and don't do well during southern summers. But Barbara Pleasant, the author of *Warm-Climate Gardening*, gives several tips for growing cool-lovers in the South:

Don't wait too long to plant. "First of all, plant spring crops really early," says Pleasant. "Most southern gardeners plant too late in the year. They miss some of the best growing weather we have." For greens, you can plant six weeks or so before the last frost date.

Thin those greens. Keep greens thinned so that none of their leaves touch, even in a fertile soil. Crowding slows growth, and southern gardeners can't afford to lose the time during their short cool seasons.

Choose cultivars carefully. "Some lettuces are more heat-resistant than others. Iceburg types almost never work well," says Pleasant. She reminds people that fall-planted greens such as Chinese cabbage and other oriental leaf crops do as well as or better than spring crops.

Try some heat-tolerant greens. Collards, basella (also called Malabar spinach), New Zealand spinach, and Swiss chard can take the heat better than regular spinach and lettuce can.

HARVEST EXTRA-EARLY SPINACH

If you want your spinach greens as soon as possible, make a hospitable microclimate in the snow. Charlie Nardozzi, a horticultural specialist for the National Gardening Association in Vermont, says that his method gives him at least a two-week jump on the spinach harvest. "Extra-early greens are very important to me," says Nardozzi. Two or three weeks before he plans to plant, Nardozzi sets up a

HEAT-TOLERANT GREENS

There are some greens that can take the heat and still produce a good crop. Collards are a traditional southern vegetable that can resist cold and grow well in cooler climates. Basella, also called Malabar spinach, is a vine that grows best when trellised. New Zealand spinach is not a true spinach but has a similar flavor. Swiss chard produces huge, mild-flavored leaves.

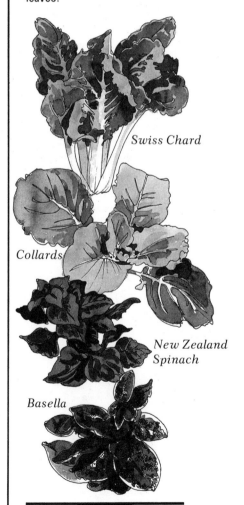

Swiss Chard

Collards

New Zealand Spinach

Basella

CULTURE CLUES: SPINACH

Spinach needs cool conditions and moist soil for best growth. Here are several pointers for better spinach:

• In warm climates, plant spinach in the shade of tall crops to help prevent bolting.
• In warm weather, freeze the seeds for a few days, then moisten and refrigerate them for a few more days before sowing.
• In many areas, spinach will grow in cold frames all winter.
• Fertilize with manure tea or fish emulsion when plants have four true leaves.
• Cover with shade cloth if the temperature goes above 80°F.
• Start harvesting when plants have at least six leaves that are 3 to 4 inches long. Carefully cutting the outside leaves will extend harvests, particularly with fall crops.

movable cold frame in a sunny spot. He lays black plastic over the snow-covered ground under the cold frame. The snow melts, and the soil slowly thaws. In a few weeks, the microclimate is warm enough for spinach. Nardozzi removes the black plastic before he plants the spinach, but he leaves the cold frame in place as long as it's needed to keep plants from freezing.

LOOK FOR LETTUCE NOOKS

Lettuce is a great crop to plant in the leftover bits of open space in the garden. Because it matures so quickly, you can often plant it in and around other crops while they're young. You'll be able to pick the lettuce before the other crops reach full size. "I transplant lettuces between my broccoli plants and under the pole bean trellis," says Charlie Nardozzi, a horticultural specialist for the National Gardening Association in Vermont. "It matures and is harvested before the beans or broccoli leaves shade the bed."

California grower Guinness McFadden finds that he needs shade for summer lettuce. "The only way we can get really good midsummer lettuce is to hide it under the tomato plants," says McFadden. "We seed it when we transplant the tomatoes. They give it the shade it needs, and, in turn, the lettuce keeps the soil under the tomatoes from overheating."

REPEATED LETTUCE HARVESTS

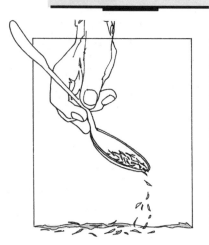 

Make several lettuce harvests from one bed by cutting plants when they are small and letting them regrow. Mix together seed of several loose-leaved cultivars. Broadcast the seed from a spoon onto a prepared seedbed. When the lettuces are about 6 inches tall, snip off the plants about 1 inch above ground level. After harvest, water and fertilize if needed, and let the plants regrow. In about three weeks, you should be able to harvest again.

WET LETTUCE KEEPS COOL

While nothing beats drip irrigation for watering efficiency, sprinkling may have other benefits for your lettuce crop. Pennsylvania organic market gardener Ward Sinclair uses drip irrigation for many of his crops but says, "It's not for lettuce. Overhead sprinkling is much better for its cooling effect." Sinclair uses Rainbird sprinklers, and he recommends plastic sprayhead attachments over metal ones. The plastic sprayheads work just as well as metal ones, cost much less, and last if you take care of them, says Sinclair. He also decided that the commercially available towers designed for the sprinklers were an unnecessary expense. Instead, he uses 1-inch-diameter PVC pipes driven into the ground and drops the Rainbird sprinklers into the pipes.

EASY EARLY LETTUCE

For a constant supply of fresh lettuce, it's best to make frequent small sowings. But you can forget about early-spring sowings if you remember a fall trick recommended by Oregon farming consultant Lynn Coody. She says of her family: "We eat a lot of salads, so I make new plantings every seven to ten days. But I don't spend time sowing my earliest spring plantings anymore." Instead, Coody lets a few lettuce plants set seed in the fall. When she finally pulls up the plants, she shakes the seed clusters over the bed where she's planning to grow lettuce the following year and leaves the bed alone until early March. By then, it's time to weed and thin the patch of mixed "self-sown" lettuces. Coody's family is eating fresh salads by mid-April. (If you live in a climate harsher than Zone 8, try covering the seeded area with a portable cold frame after seeding.)

Onions and Garlic

The pungent flavor and aroma of onions and garlic add life to our cooking. They're also well-known, at least in garden folklore, as great companion plants that will keep pests from plaguing your more mellow-flavored vegetables.

PLANT BULB CROPS IN DRY BEDS

During growth periods, onions, garlic, and shallots need as much water as most other plants. But after the

---

GIVE LETTUCE A SOYBEAN MEAL

Between one lettuce planting and the next, Rick Estes, a New Hampshire organic farmer, supplements his field fertility with soybean meal as a nitrogen source. The soybean meal drops from a spreader mounted on the front of the tractor and is mixed with the soil by a tiller mounted on the rear. In a home garden, you can adapt this trick by sprinkling a light covering of soybean or alfalfa meal along the row as you harvest early crops. Dig the meal into the top 2 inches of the soil before planting your late crop.

HARVEST WITH A HOE

If you grow spinach in quantity for processing, harvesting can be difficult and time consuming. Seth Jacobs and Martha Johnson, organic farmers in New York State, have developed a time-saving harvesting method. Rather than crawling along the row and pulling and trimming individual plants, they harvest a row at a time with a push hoe. (A push hoe has an open triangular blade, which you push through the soil to sever plants from their roots.) Jacobs says, "You have to keep the hoe sharp to make this system work." They move the hoe along just under the soil surface. The sharp edge cuts the plant's crown from the roots, leaving the plants easy to pick up and trim.

EASY MULCH FOR ONIONS

Onions hate weeds and gardeners often hate weeding. Make your life easier by laying down a newspaper mulch on onion beds. Water the mulch thoroughly and weight it with rocks or scrap lumber to prevent it from blowing. Plant onion sets in holes punched in the mulch.

bulbs form and the tops start to die back, water should be withheld to help the crop cure properly. Too much water can greatly shorten the bulbs' storage life.

"That's why it's a good idea to grow those crops in beds close together, away from other plants," says garden writer Susan Sides. "A lot of books tell you to stick onions here and there among other vegetables to save space, but then you have a hard time watering the plants that need it while keeping the curing crops dry." Sides finds it easier to set aside a "dry area" for growing onions and related plants, as well as other crops, like strawflowers, that need a period of restricted water. You can still plant onions and garlic as companion plants in other parts of your garden, but you won't be dependent on them for your main crop.

PLANT A BLOCK OF ONIONS

If you grow onions from seed, try growing several seedlings together in a soil block, as shown in the illustration below. Rather than planting only one onion seed in a soil block, Eliot Coleman, an organic farmer and the author of *The New Organic Grower,* plants four seeds per block. "This trick comes from some Dutch growers I know," says Coleman. "It saves time and makes weeding more efficient. I set out the soil blocks at a 1-foot spacing in each direction.

—— 12" ——

As the onions grow, they push away from each other. As long as their roots have enough room, it doesn't hurt to crowd them this way. It makes weeding much easier, too. I can cross-cultivate and don't have to worry about in-row weeds." Coleman also uses this technique for broccoli and dill. He plants three broccoli seeds to a block and six dill seeds to a block. "The broccoli heads are smaller with this system," he says. "But this planting trick is good for a home garden because the heads mature at different times. You just have to remember to leave adequate space between the blocks." Space blocks of multi-seeded dill 12 inches apart in each direction and broccoli 30 to 36 inches apart.

COUNT YOUR GARLIC SKINS

Timing the harvest and proper curing are crucial to good garlic production, says market gardener Stewart Hoyt. "If you let garlic sit too long, the heads are apt to start separating," says Hoyt. According to Hoyt, garlic is ready when it has formed seven layers of skin. "You have to dig it up every week or so, starting in early July here [in Vermont], to check on maturity," he asserts.

GROW GOOD GARLIC

New York State market gardeners Seth Jacobs and Martha Johnson specialize in growing garlic. They have several tips for producing good garlic in the Northeast:

Start with the soil. "Garlic likes a rich, weed-free soil. We've also discovered that it really responds to trace elements," says Jacobs. He coats his cloves with a mixture of elemental sulfur and wood ash before planting, and he sprinkles a band of kelp meal along the rows.

Save the biggest cloves for replanting. "The size of the clove you plant affects the size you'll harvest. Garlic always tends to downsize, too," Jacobs explains.

Make sure to mulch. Plant in fall, and then mulch for winter protection. Jacobs and Johnson plant garlic around October 15, mulch it with spoiled haylage (compost or straw would also work) for the winter months, and harvest in July.

Take care when you cure. Cure garlic where air circulation is high. Jacobs and Johnson cure their garlic on shelves in their barn.

CULTURE CLUES: ONIONS

Onions don't like too much heat early in their growth or too much nitrogen. For better onion bulbs, also keep these hints in mind:

◆ Sets are easier to plant than seeds or transplants. They mature earlier and are less susceptible to disease. Unfortunately, cultivar selection is limited for sets.

◆ Look for ½-inch-diameter sets. Larger ones often go to seed before producing decent-size bulbs, and anything smaller may not grow well.

◆ Keep planted beds well-weeded, using a sharp hoe to cut off weeds at soil level. Pulling weeds can damage onions' shallow roots.

◆ Once soil has warmed, put down a mulch around plants to discourage weeds and conserve soil moisture.

◆ Dry conditions cause bulbs to split. Water when necessary to provide at least 1 inch of water each week. Keep in mind that transplants require more water than sets do.

◆ New growth from the center will stop when bulbs start forming.

◆ To harvest, use the back of a rake to horizontally bend over yellowed onion tops. A day or so later, when the tops turn brown, pull or dig the bulbs on a sunny day, and leave them to dry in the sun. When the outer skins are dry, wipe off any soil, and remove the tops. Store in a cool, dry place; hang them in mesh bags or braids in an airy area.

OLD CARPET AS A MULCH

◆ STRAW MULCH YOUR ONIONS AND GARLIC

Onions and garlic need plenty of moisture during most of their growth, and they are difficult to weed without damaging the plants. So mulching the crop makes a lot of sense—especially if you use clean straw, says former Mother Earth News head gardener Susan Sides.

"Just spread 4 or 5 inches of straw on and around the plants when they're coming up," says Sides, "and the tops push their way through it." At that point, Sides adds 2 inches of small or shredded leaves to compensate for the straw's tendency to compact.

Perfect Peas

Fresh peas are one of the garden's sweetest, crispiest treats. If you're a pea lover, half of your harvest probably ends up eaten before you're even out of the garden. But the pods that make it to the house make a wonderful addition to your cooking and salads.

CARPET THE PEA PATCH

If you grow bush peas, harvesting can get hard on the knees. Miriam Klein-Hansen, who taught homestead gardening at the National Center for Appropriate Technology in Montana, uses old carpet strips to make a softer aisle between her double rows of peas, as shown in the illustration at left. As a bonus, the carpeting also keeps down weeds in the paths. She says, "With this many peas, you can get really tired of picking them, especially when you're shelling them straight into plastic bags for the freezer. I don't blanch shell peas; I just move them from the garden to the freezer as fast as I can. The carpet really makes a difference; it's a lot more comfortable to kneel and walk on than bare soil would be, and I never have to weed it." Klein-Hansen recommends removing the carpeting from the garden each fall. Otherwise, she says, it will deteriorate quickly.

PLANT PEAS FOR FALL

Unpredictable frosts and weather conditions can make it harder to successfully grow a fall crop of peas. George DeVault, who runs an organic market garden in Pennsylvania, has been growing a fall crop of peas for the past eight years and has mastered the nuances. "More people should try fall peas. We get high yields, and it's nice to have fresh peas at that time of year," says DeVault. He recommends 'Sugar Ann', a bush-type sugar snap cultivar.

DeVault tills strips in sod to create a planting area for the crop. Each strip is about 1½ times the width of the tiller tines. Of course, you can also plant the crop in one of your regular garden beds, where space is open after harvest of one of your early-season crops. He sows seeds 1 inch apart in rows 24 inches apart, planting in later July or very early August. (Your timing will depend on the length of your growing season.) He thins the plants to 2 to 3 inches apart. If the weather begins to get too cool, DeVault covers the peas with floating row covers.

PUT A COAT ON YOUR PEA SEEDS

Peas are legumes, and they can make some of their own nitrogen fertilizer through a process called nitrogen fixation. You can help ensure that your pea plants fix nitrogen by coating the seeds with a bacterial inoculant before you plant. (For information on nitrogen fixation and inoculants, see "Add Nitrogen Naturally" on page 94.) "Using fresh inoculant every year is the secret to growing good peas," says Richard de Wilde, a Wisconsin organic farmer. He has a simple method for coating the seeds with the inoculant. First, he puts some inoculant into an open container. He then mists the seeds with a heavy solution of liquid seaweed and pours the wet seeds into the container. To make sure the seeds are evenly coated, he dumps the seeds back and forth between an empty container and the inoculant container several times.

Pepper Pointers

Whether you like them sweet or hot, for stuffing or frying, there's a pepper for you—and for your garden. You'll also find some special hints for growing heat-loving peppers in cold climates in "Season Extension," beginning on page 202.

PREVENT PEPPER ROTS

Bringing a good crop of bell peppers all the way to harvest is an art that Cass Peterson and Ward Sinclair,

---

CULTURE CLUES: PEPPERS

Peppers can be finicky. They may not yield well if moisture levels or temperatures fluctuate too much. Here are some other strategies for better peppers:

• To avoid root rot, plant in well-drained soil.

• When buying transplants, look for strong stems and dark green leaves. Pass up ones with blossoms or fruit because such plants won't produce well.

• Spread a thick but light mulch, such as straw or grass clippings, around plants. Water deeply during dry spells to encourage deep root development. Lack of water can produce bitter-tasting peppers.

• To avoid damaging roots, gently hand-pull weeds.

• Temperatures over 90°F often cause blossoms to drop and plants to wilt. To avoid this, plant so that taller plants will shade peppers during the hottest hours. Peppers grow best when soil is at least 60°F.

• Pale leaves and slow growth may indicate a need for liquid fertilizer, such as manure tea.

• Most sweet and hot peppers are at their best when mature. Early in the season, however, harvest before peppers ripen to encourage the plant to keep bearing.

• Always cut (don't pull) peppers from the plant.

• When frost is predicted, pick all fruit, or pull up plants by the roots and hang them in a dry, cool place indoors until fruits ripen.

PERKY PEPPERS

Our experts had lots of favorite peppers to tell us about:

An Italian beauty. Ken Ryan, an organic farmer and farm manager from New England, and other growers like 'Corno di Toro', originally from Italy. Ryan says, "Fruits are 10 to 12 inches long and a couple of inches in diameter. When you roast and skin them, the flesh is shiny, smooth, and thick; they've got a good cavity for stuffing; and they have wonderful flavor and texture, cooked or raw."

Favorites for frying and roasting. Ward Sinclair, an organic vegetable farmer from Pennsylvania, says that 'LaParie' is his favorite frying pepper. He says, "It's 1 foot long, red, and sweet." He also favors 'Orobelle' because it's a deep green when it's young, sizes quickly, and ripens to a rich gold. Sinclair adds, "Red 'Pimento' is a good roaster because it's meaty, and 'Oriole' is a nice orange and has been a good performer. 'Blue Jay' is a good-looking lavender-blue and does well."

Choice cultivars. Eileen Weinsteiger of the Rodale Institute Research Center says 'Vidi' is one of her favorites. She also likes 'Ace' for an early green and red cultivar.

organic vegetable farmers from Pennsylvania, have worked hard to master. "We've discovered that magnesium prevents rot problems on peppers," says Sinclair. "We fertilize them with a tablespoon or so of blood meal around the base of each plant at the three- to four-week stage." They find that the early dose of nitrogen in the blood meal gives the peppers a jump-start. "After a month, we water-in an Epsom salt dilution for magnesium. We've discovered that the peppers keep longer when they're picked when they're about half-colored, too," says Sinclair. To make the Epsom salt dilution, mix 1 ounce of Epsom salts in 1 cup of boiling water, and stir thoroughly. If the Epsom salts are not all dissolved, add another cup of boiling water, and stir again. Add this mixture to enough water to make 1 gallon.

Peterson and Sinclair store newly harvested peppers in a building that maintains temperatures in the 60°F range, about the temperature of many basements in the summer. It takes the peppers three or four days to turn fully red, gold, or orange, even in the dark. Sinclair says, "Peppers keep anywhere from ten days to two weeks in this environment."

WAIT OUT THE MID-SEASON SLUMP

Although peppers are warm-season crops, bell peppers can slow down in the intense heat of southern summers. "Hot peppers will bear all summer, and some of the small-fruited types such as 'Sweet Banana' will, too," says Barbara Pleasant, the author of *Warm-Climate Gardening*. "The bells just sit there till the second part of August. But don't give up on them. A single plant can put on a dozen fruits between August 15 and October 15."

DELAY FRUIT SET FOR PEPPIER PEPPERS

In colder climates, peppers don't always yield well. Eliot Coleman, an organic farmer and the author of *The New Organic Grower*, relies on a trick he learned from a researcher in Maine. He picks off all of the blossoms that form on his pepper plants in early summer. The Fourth of July is his easy-to-remember date for beginning to let flowers form fruits. "You're allowing the plant to grow a nice strong root system and really get established before it turns to fruit production. Plants not only yield more, they are also more resistant to diseases," says Coleman. He often prunes tomato flowers for the same reason: "It strengthens the plant to remove all but four flowers on the first couple of trusses [flower clusters]."

SQUEEZE SPACING TO STOP SUNSCALD

Direct sun can cause ugly, brown, scalded areas to appear on pepper fruits. The scalded areas decay quickly. "Protecting peppers from sunscald is important in Arkansas," says Janet Bachmann, a co-owner of a small organic farm in Arkansas. "We space them as closely as possible for the shade that a crowded bed gives." According to Bachmann, if your soil has good fertility, you can space some cultivars as closely as 12 to 18 inches.

Impressive Potatoes

Potatoes for the home garden come in a wide range of sizes, colors, and flavors. You'll enjoy getting to know the exciting potential of potatoes if you grow your own.

SPROUTED SPUDS

Pre-sprouting potatoes can speed their growth after planting and help sidestep the problems of seed pieces rotting in cold spring soils before sprouting. Robert F. Becker, a retired associate professor at Cornell University's New York Agricultural Experiment Station in Geneva, cuts his seed potatoes into pieces that have a couple of eyes apiece and spreads them out in his basement for a day to air-heal. Then he pre-sprouts them. "I put a layer of sawdust or cedar bark mulch in wooden flats. I set healed potato pieces on it and add another layer to cover the potatoes," says Becker. "Then I put these flats outside in the sunshine for a week or more." It's a good idea to monitor the progress of the pieces as they sprout. Becker also suggests bringing in the flats on nights when frost threatens. "I plant the potatoes when sprouts are anywhere from ¼ to ¾ inch long. They take right off once they're in the ground, and I don't lose any to rot," Becker says.

POSTHOLES FOR POTATOES

If you prefer a one-time effort to a season-long one, try planting potatoes in deep holes. "Hilling potatoes is lots of work," says John Dromgoole, the host of PBS television's "The New Garden." "I've got a simpler method that gives

---

CULTURE CLUES: POTATOES

Potatoes can develop disease problems in heavy or waterlogged soils. They're also sensitive to weather conditions. For healthier potatoes, try the following tips:

• Potatoes need fertile, airy, well-drained soil.

• Acid soil is ideal (not essential) and reduces chance of scab.

• Only plant certified disease-free seed potatoes. Cure cut pieces by spreading them out in a bright, airy place for 24 hours, or until they are slightly dry and the cut areas have hardened.

• In wet climates, dust seed potatoes with sulfur to help prevent rot.

• Keep the developing tubers covered; when exposed to sunlight, tubers turn green and contain a mildly toxic substance called solanine.

• Once plants flower, stop hilling up soil. Apply thick mulch to save water and fight weeds.

• Keep the area evenly moist but not soggy. Take special care to keep plants well-watered from six to ten weeks after planting, as tubers are starting to develop.

• When flowers open, harvest "new" potatoes. Pull aside earth around the base of the plants, and gently pick tubers. Once foliage starts to wither and die back, tubers are full-grown. If the weather is not too warm or wet, tubers will keep in the ground for several weeks. Dig them up with a spading fork before the first frost. Nicked or bruised potatoes won't store well, so eat them first.

ALL POTATOES AREN'T THE SAME

Have you ever wondered why catalog descriptions of potatoes recommend certain cultivars for baking, others for mashed potatoes, and still others for frying? It's because the texture of a cooked potato depends on its starch content. Higher starch content yields a drier, flakier texture. New potatoes of most cultivars are 90 percent water and only 7 percent starch. At maturity, most bakers contain 15 to 18 percent starch. However, cultivars used for potato chips and french fries contain as much as 22 percent starch. So be sure to consider the end use of your potato crop when you select cultivars for planting.

NATURAL POTASSIUM FOR POTATOES

Potatoes love potassium. Rather than adding it with a rock powder or nutrient solution, old-fashioned gardeners lay slightly wilted, chopped green alfalfa or comfrey leaves in the planting trenches. Both of these crops return significant amounts of potassium to the soil as they decompose.

DEEP PLANTING POTATOES

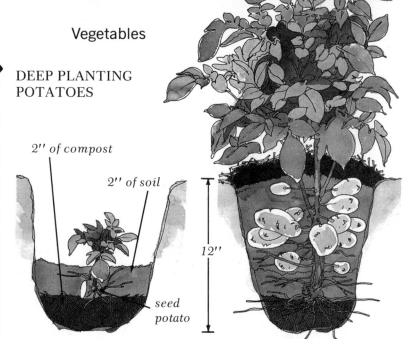

2'' of compost

2'' of soil

12''

seed potato

me really high yields." In his vegetable garden, Dromgoole digs holes at least 12 inches deep with his posthole digger, as shown in the illustration above. He digs in 2 inches of good compost and a handful of rock phosphate in the bottom of each hole and lays down a potato seed piece. Then he adds another couple of inches of soil. As the plants grow, he just pushes the soil back into the holes. Dromgoole says, "By the time the plant gets to the soil surface, it's already been dirted 1 foot deep." So there's no need to worry about hilling up soil around the stems. Keep in mind that this method is not for damp, cool climates, where the poor air circulation in the holes could lead to fungal diseases.

POTATOES IN THE BIN

If you're not willing to give up precious bed space for potatoes, try growing them intensively above ground. Lynn Coody, an organic farming consultant in Oregon, has refined a system that yields 60 pounds of potatoes in a 3 × 3-foot area. Coody uses inexpensive circular plastic compost bins that have 2½-inch holes punched out of their sides. She positions the bin in the garden, puts a layer of straw over the soil that the bin rests on, and then adds a layer of compost or rotted manure. She places her seed pieces in the compost near the bottom holes of the bin. The vines grow right out of the holes as well as toward the top, as shown in the illustration on the opposite page. Coody adds soil and compost or rotted manure as the plants grow. The

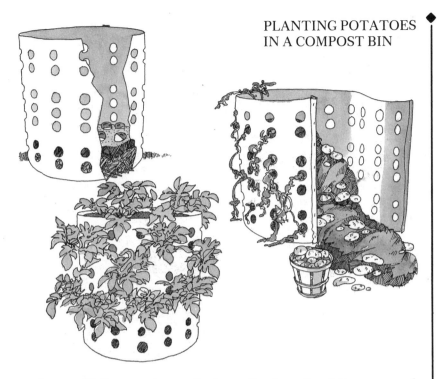

PLANTING POTATOES
IN A COMPOST BIN

plant will form tubers all along the length of the covered stems.

"The bin is just beautiful. Potato vines crawl out all of the holes and, eventually, over the top, too," says Coody. "I can pick new potatoes by just sticking my hand through a hole in the side of the bin. And best of all, because you can undo these bins along one side, fully mature potatoes just fall out. No digging, no splitting the tubers with a fork."

Vine Crops

The mellow flavors of summer and winter squash, the crispness of a fresh cucumber, and the sweet taste of melons are the joys of vine crops in the vegetable garden. The two biggest problems in raising squash-family crops, also called cucurbits, can be finding the space for the sprawling vines and protecting the vines from diseases.

RE-ROOT THE SQUASH

Bacterial wilt, squash bugs, and squash vine borers can significantly reduce squash yields. David Cavagnaro, a

CULTURE CLUES: SQUASH

Squash and other cucurbits love warm growing conditions and rich soil. Grow your best squash ever by following these guidelines:

• Plant when soil is at least 60°F. Use cloches to protect cold-sensitive seedlings.

• Water seedlings thoroughly. Keep soil moist throughout the season. To avoid transmitting diseases to the plants, water the soil, not the foliage, and don't handle plants when they're wet.

• Pull weeds until squash vines begin to lengthen, then apply a thick mulch of hay, straw, or leaves.

• Apply compost tea or manure tea when the first fruits set.

• When vines grow to 5 feet, pinch off the growing tips to encourage fruit-bearing sideshoots.

• By midsummer, remove remaining flowers of winter squash to focus the plant's energy on the ripening crop.

• To avoid rot, put a board or thick mulch under fruit.

• During dry weather, harvest by using a sharp knife to cut fruit off the vine, leaving 3 to 4 inches of stem on the fruit. For summer squash, pick each fruit before the blossom drops off the tip, or the plant will quit producing. Before expected frost, pick ripe winter squash, and cover any unripe squash with heavy mulch. Don't store bruised or washed winter squash. Dry winter types (except acorn squash) in the sun until stems shrivel and turn gray. Store winter squash in a cool, dry area with temperatures of 45° to 50°F and with 65 to 70 percent humidity.

It's easy to grow cucumbers vertically, and it's a great way to save space in the garden. Try these cucumber trellising methods:

Single stakes. Tie the main stem to a 4- to 6-foot-long stake at 1-foot intervals as the stem grows. This works best with traditional American cultivars.

(continued)

garden manager at Heritage Farm for Seed Savers Exchange in Iowa, has devised several methods to keep his running squash in production all season long. "Squash plants send out two roots at each node of the plant. The bottom one will grow into the soil in a wet spring. But I encourage this by burying both roots, being careful not to bury the flowerstalks that also emerge at these nodes. The extra roots make the plant more vigorous and help with borers, too—they generally strike at the base of the central stem. I wrap the base of the plants with nylon stockings or row cover material and police for the borers' bright red eggs. I also bury the base of the plant. But adding to the root system gives me great insurance against disaster," says Cavagnaro.

TURN THUMBS DOWN ON SQUASH ROT

Most gardeners know too well that squash fruit can sometimes develop a mushy, rotting spot at its broad end, where the flower has withered. "There are two reasons why that happens," says Pam Peirce, the author of *Environmentally Friendly Gardening: Controlling Vegetable Pests.* "One is that the fruit develops a disease similar to tomato blossom end rot, which has to do with a calcium deficiency brought on by an uneven water supply." You can prevent this by mulching to keep the soil moist and by watering the plants when necessary.

"The second reason," says Peirce, "is that the blossoms themselves get a fungus, and rot right back into the fruit." This problem is especially prevalent in areas with high relative humidity, as well as in gardens where the plants are watered from above or otherwise kept wet for extended periods.

In any case, the solution is simple: Remove the blossoms once the young fruits begin to swell, Peirce instructs. "And if there's any decay starting, take your thumbnail and gently scrape the end of the fruit," says Peirce. "In a short time, a scar will form there, the decay will stop, and you'll get a good, mature squash."

TAKE STEPS TO STOP MILDEW

Good air circulation and good nutrition will help prevent mildew problems on cucurbits in hot, humid climates, says John Dromgoole, the host of PBS television's "The New Garden." He counts trellising and foliar feeding as his defenses. "Trellising keeps the air circulation high, and that's a must in this climate [humid South]. I also foliar-feed with liquid seaweed about every eight days or so, all through the season. It really makes a difference," he says.

DETECT SIGNS OF RIPENESS

Melon grower and Arizona garden writer Lynn Tilton has a good method of determining ripeness in watermelons. He says, "First, the tendril by the stem has to be brown and dry. If so, I turn the melon over and look at the underside. They're ready when the white spot turns a light yellow color." But just to be sure, Tilton gives the watermelon the fingernail test. "If a melon is ripe, the skin will come off easily under a nail drawn across it. If my nail skids, the melon's not ripe," he says.

PLANT MELONS IN A WELL

A special "water well" planting technique can help ensure that your melons get all of the water they need, especially if your soil is sandy or low in organic matter. Arizona garden writer Lynn Tilton devised this method to retain moisture for his cantaloupes and watermelons:

1. Mark a grid planting pattern so that the planting hills will be 5 feet apart in all directions.

2. Dig a hole 3 to 4 inches deep and 18 inches wide at each spot where you'll plant a hill.

3. Fill the holes with compost to make the planting hills, water it well, and let it sit for seven to ten days.

4. In each hill, plant six to eight seeds in the compost, and apply a surface mulch after the seedlings emerge. Thin seedlings to three plants per hill.

The compost-rich area around the melon roots retains moisture much better than plain garden soil. Tilton also makes sure that he waters each well deeply at least every six days during his dry June days. "Both July and August are rainy here, so I don't usually have to irrigate then. But if they weren't, I'd make certain to keep the soil moisture high," says Tilton.

CLOSE QUARTERS FOR MELONS

If you've worked to develop a high-fertility, high organic matter soil, experiment with closely spaced melons. "In a

CUKES—CONTINUED

Double arch. Plant four cucumbers in a 2 × 5-foot plot. Mulch well. Use wire mesh to make an arch about 2 feet high over the plot. Insert stakes to lead the vines up to the arch. You can put a second arch of PVC pipe hoops over the wire arch to support a floating row cover.

Tall trellis. Erect a 5-foot-tall wire trellis down the center of a 4- to 5-foot-wide row. Plant cucumbers on either side of the trellis. Train the stems up the wires.

good soil, melons can go on 12-inch centers," says Fred Hoover, an organic market gardener in Arizona. (Note: This is for single plants, not for hills of plants.) With his dense planting scheme, the vines cover the bed more quickly, reducing the need to weed and preventing the sun from baking the soil around the plants. Hoover sets up his drip irrigation to account for this spacing, placing an emitter every 12 inches along the line.

Top Tomatoes

What would summer be without tomatoes? Real tomatoes, that is: bright red, juicy, full of tangy sweetness. Of course, you'll also want to plant some yellow tomatoes and some cherry tomatoes for salads and snacking—and don't forget plum tomatoes for sauces.

BIG ROOT BALLS FOR EARLY CROPS

Try planting some tomatoes extra early this year. "I set out 'Glacier' tomatoes anytime from late April to early May, which is very early for my New Hampshire climate," says Rick Estes, a New Hampshire organic farmer. "But they not only survive, they also give me a big crop of fine-flavored fruit." Estes finds that one secret to success with early tomatoes is to be sure they have big root balls. He finds that the larger root mass not only strengthens the plant, it also promotes higher yields. Estes uses 2-inch soil blocks for most of his tomato transplants but uses 4-inch soil blocks for these extra-early ones. If you don't use soil blocks for your transplants, try potting up some seedlings into 6-inch plastic pots instead. Estes protects each of his early plants with a Wallo'Water, covering the top with plastic, if necessary.

PUT YOUR TOMATOES ON THE WAGON

An old-fashioned wagon makes an easy-to-move base for off-season tomato plants, as shown on the opposite page. "A friend of mine has fresh, red tomatoes until Christmas," says Bill McDorman, the founder of High Altitude Gardens, an Idaho mail-order seed company. "He has a patio door

that opens onto a south-facing and protected deck. As he can move plants in and out very easily through this door, he came up with a wonderful system. He puts two 10-gallon pots in a little red wagon. He transplants young tomatoes into these pots in August. They grow outside as long as it's warm, but as soon as temperatures begin to fall, he wheels the wagon in at night. It doesn't take more than a minute or two, and it's well worth the trouble."

WRAP UP YOUR TOMATO CAGES

Insect pests such as thrips can transmit viral diseases to tomato plants. There's no cure for these diseases, so the only control is to prevent insect feeding. John Dromgoole, the host of PBS television's "The New Garden," wraps his tomato cages with row cover material. "That protects them in the early stages. By the time you have to take the cover off of the cage, the plants are big enough to be more resistant," Dromgoole says. He adds that grow-bags—clear plastic, vented sleeves that fit over cages—also work. "Using this

TREASURE THAT TOMATO TASTE

Once the tomato harvest gains momentum, those big, juicy tomatoes are practically rolling off the vines and into your kitchen. What's the best way to enjoy their vine-ripened flavor? A USDA scientist cautions against cutting open a tomato until right before you plan to eat it. Three minutes after slicing, the wonderful tomato aroma and flavor start to fade. And don't store extra tomatoes in the refrigerator: They lose their aroma and flavor that way, too.

SOUTHERN SELF-SOWERS

"Tomatoes can get to be weeds in Alabama," says Barbara Pleasant, the author of *Warm-Climate Gardening.* "But I like that. I just thin them out or move them around." She adds that basil and dill can also seed themselves three or four times over the summer.

SUN-DRY YOUR OWN TOMATOES

In a dry, hot climate, you can sun-dry tomatoes outside. Slice them in half, and spread them on screening. Tent cheesecloth over the tomatoes to protect them from insect and dust contamination. On cool nights, you may want to bring them inside. They'll dry in a day or two.

system, I've more than doubled my tomato production," says Dromgoole. "I use the same trick with peppers, but that's more for temperature protection than insect control. Once a pepper plant lignifies, which it does if exposed to cool winds, it has a hard time coming out of it. That really cuts production."

SUPPORT TOMATOES WITH STURDY WIRE

If you have problems with soilborne fungal diseases like early blight, try trellising your tomatoes. They'll have less contact with the soil and better air circulation. David Cavagnaro, a garden manager who grows over 3,000 kinds of tomatoes at Heritage Farm for Seed Savers Exchange in Iowa, makes a trellis by stretching a double course of concrete-reinforcing wire between sturdy posts. The wire mesh extends about 5 feet above ground, giving the tomatoes plenty of room. He plants on one side of this structure and weaves binder twine through the wire as the plants grow to tie up the stems. While Cavagnaro doesn't prune his huge collection of trellised tomatoes, he does recommend pruning for a few vines in a small garden. He says, "You may get fewer tomatoes that way, but they're much nicer. The extra work of trellising is always worth it because it decreases incidence of splash-borne blight so much."

STAKE YOUR CAGES

If your tomato plants are so vigorous that they overgrow their cages, add stakes to anchor the cages in place. Charlie Nardozzi, a horticultural specialist for the National Gardening Association in Vermont, says he came up with this solution because he got tired of watching heavy tomato plants pull down their cages. "I secure the cages by weaving two stakes through the cages and driving them into the ground. The stakes give me the added benefit of extra height. I can tie plants to them if they overgrow the cages," Nardozzi says.

CONVERT CAGES TO ARCHES

Try an unusual way to use tomato cages suggested by Barbara Pleasant, the author of *Warm-Climate Gardening*. Rather than setting them upright around her tomato plants, she opens them up along the side where they're attached to themselves. She says, "I set them up like arches over the plants and use fabric strips to tie the plants to the wires." Pleasant says she can use one cage to support three plants. The cage-to-plant ratio will depend on the size of your cages and your plants; be sure not to crowd your plants too much. This system works well for determinate tomato cultivars, which grow about 1 to 3 feet tall and set their fruit all at once. The arches probably won't provide enough support for indeterminate cultivars, which continue growing taller and producing fruit until they are stopped by frost or pest problems.

CORRALLING THE TOMATOES

You can cut back on staking and supporting time by corralling your tomatoes like Ken Ryan, an organic farmer and farm manager from New England. Ryan, who grows 5 to 6 acres of tomatoes every year, says, "That's a lot of tomatoes to stake. This system makes it faster, though." Ryan begins by setting stakes every 10 feet along the row where he plans to plant tomatoes. He then sets out his plants 2 feet apart down the row. Rather than tying them to the stakes, Ryan "ropes them in," using rolls of seam binding that he buys from a sewing supply house. Baler twine and old sheets torn into strips also work well for roping in the plants. Here's how to rope tomatoes, as shown in the illustration on page 196:

1. Tie the "rope" onto the first stake in the row.
2. Extend it down the row on one side of the plants to the next stake.
3. Wrap the rope around the stake, leading it out on the opposite side of the plants.
4. Continue extending the rope down the row on this side of the plants to the next stake.
5. Wrap the rope around this stake, leading it out on the opposite side. Continue in this serpentine pattern to the end of the row.
6. Make the return trip back up the row, working on the opposing sides so that the plants are enclosed with rope on both sides.

As the season progresses, Ryan adds layers of binding higher up on the stakes to keep the plants erect as they grow taller.

HAIRY VETCH HELPS TOMATOES

Fertilize, add organic matter, and control weeds in one pass! Sow hairy vetch (1 to 2 pounds per 1,000 square feet) in late summer or early fall wherever you plan to grow tomatoes next year. Hairy vetch is a biennial cover crop that fixes nitrogen. (For more information on nitrogen fixation, see "Add Nitrogen Naturally" on page 94.)

The following spring, mow the vetch to a height of 1 inch. In a small plot, you can just clip it by hand and lay down the clippings as a surface mulch. You'll be left with a thick mat of dead vegetation, but don't plow. Instead, plant your tomatoes at the usual spacing, through the dead cover crop. The decaying mulch slowly releases nutrients, adds organic matter, and controls weeds. USDA researchers found that tomato yield and number of fruits per plant were greatly increased using this regimen.

CARE FOR CARDOON?

Once-popular cardoon (*Cynara cardunculus*) has gone out of fashion these days. But Cass Peterson and Ward Sinclair, organic vegetable farmers from Pennsylvania, are bringing it back on their truck farm. They wrap it with newspapers to blanch the stems. "It's pretty impressive," says Sinclair. "It'll grow 6 feet high, and it's a perennial to boot." Cardoon is a relative of the artichoke but looks more like a cross between burdock and celery. Peterson and Sinclair start plants indoors in early spring and then transplant them after the last frost to a well-drained soil with high fertility and good moisture levels. They blanch the stalks when they are about 3 feet tall.

Harvest cardoon early for finest flavor. Cut stalks when they are 1 to 2 feet tall, and remove and discard the bitter leaves. Remove the fibrous outside skin and strings from the stalks and preblanch the stalks in lemon to get rid of the acrid flavor. Then, boil or steam them until they're tender. Eat "as is," or do as your grandmother did — dip them in an egg-and-flour batter, and fry them until the batter's crisp.

Save time on staking by using seam binding, strips of old sheets, or baling twine to corral tomato plants between stakes set about 10 feet apart along a row of plants.

PROLONG PICKING YOUR TOMATOES

Careful cultivar selection leads to maximum enjoyment of fresh-picked garden tomatoes. Lynn Coody, an organic farming consultant in Oregon, plants several types of tomatoes each year, planning in advance for a prolonged picking season. She says, "By using varieties [cultivars] with different maturity dates, we enjoy big tomato crops from early in the season until late fall without having to do succession plantings."

TRY SOME SOUTHERN SHADE FOR TOMATOES

While northern growers want every bit of sunshine they can get to ripen their tomatoes, southern growers may want to provide a little shade for their plants. Barbara Pleasant, the author of *Warm-Climate Gardening*, says,

"Morning sun is magic, but afternoon sun can be too hot here." Pleasant says she regularly plants tomatoes and cucumbers in areas where they will get afternoon shade.

Harvest Basket Hints

There's seemingly no end to the types of crops for today's vegetable garden. From artichokes to radicchio and beyond, try a wide sampling of crops for fun and variety.

CONFUSE THE ARTICHOKES

The globe artichoke plant requires moderate climates because it frost-kills easily and doesn't begin bearing until its second year. It simply isn't adapted for a northern climate, so most gardeners in cold regions are content to buy artichokes at the grocery store. However, Eliot Coleman, an organic farmer and the author of *The New Organic Grower*, has devised a way to grow a nice yield of medium-size artichokes in the North.

BALED CARROTS WON'T FREEZE

Storing carrots and other root crops in the ground can be an efficient and convenient method. But in northern areas, these crops need extra protection to prevent freezing. "Thinly mulched carrots freeze during our long, cold winters," says Miriam Klein-Hansen, who taught homestead gardening at the National Center for Appropriate Technology in Montana. "But with advance planning, we can prevent this. Plant the carrot seeds in double rows that are slightly more narrow than a hay bale. In the fall, cover the double rows with whole bales, and cover the bales with plastic. This never freezes!"

The trick is to simulate summer planting followed by an overwintering period. To do this, you start plants indoors early and then expose them to a cool period in a cold frame before planting them in the garden. Coleman suggests starting seeds inside about six weeks before the date when temperatures in your area hold at 26°F or higher. In Coleman's area of Vermont, that's usually around February 15.

Coleman moves the artichoke plants to the cold frame around April 1 and "runs the cold frame backwards, more to cool than warm." He props the frames open as long temperatures are 26°F or above, trying to achieve temperatures in the frame between 39° and 43°F. After six weeks, the artichokes are ready to be transplanted. Coleman says, "During the first six weeks, while they're still inside, they think it's summer. And then, during the following six weeks, they think it's winter. When you put them out, they think that they're two years old and it's time to make flowers."

Coleman spaces plants 24 inches apart in 30-inch rows and mulches immediately. The plants prefer uniformly moist soil with high organic matter content. About 5 percent of the plants don't bear at all. The others yield from six to eight small to medium artichokes each. Coleman says, "Because they're going to be small in a northern climate, you don't wait for them to size up to grocery-store proportions. You cut them as soon as the bottom leaves start to open." 'Grand Beurre' from Thompson and Morgan is Coleman's favorite cultivar. (He notes that this cultivar is available only at garden supply stores, not through mail-order catalogs.)

Coleman adds that an alternative method is to seed flats, leave them for a day or two, and then move them to the refrigerator for a month as a substitute for the cold frame system.

CELERY TASTE IN A ROOT

If you have trouble growing celery, try a root crop with a celery-like flavor. "Celery is a hard crop to grow well in this climate," says Stewart Hoyt, a Vermont market gardener. "Instead, we grow celeriac." This large, gnarly root requires the same rich soils as celery, is also a moisture lover, and must be transplanted in most areas because it needs about 120 frost-free days to size up. However, it's more tolerant than celery to temperature fluctuations when it's small, so it doesn't bolt as easily. Harvest celeriac just before frost, dry without washing, and store in a cool room or root cellar where it keeps like beets. Enormously patient people pare it with a vegetable peeler, but using a knife is faster.

LET LEEKS GO GREEN

Many gardeners don't grow leeks because of the time it takes to hill the stems to blanch them. They also don't like the trouble of washing out the bits of soil that get trapped in the layers of leaves. An alternative? Don't blanch. "We don't blanch leeks anymore," says Stewart Hoyt, a Vermont market gardener. "It's too much work for the return. With good, rich soils and steady moisture, they grow well, and the green part of the stem is just as tender as the white. The only difference I notice is the color."

OKRA ON ICE

If you have a hard time getting okra to sprout, Texas garden writer H. S. Stevens has a solution: Freeze the seeds in ice cubes, and plant the cubes. "The USDA sets minimum germination standards for vegetable seeds shipped in interstate commerce," he says, "and okra has the lowest at 50 percent. The ice cube method has raised that percentage to 75 to 80 percent for me." The procedure is simple: You drop a seed into each compartment of the tray, fill the tray half-full with hot water, and freeze for a couple of days. Then you plant the ice cubes, as shown at right. "I always tell my classes to do this at night," says Stevens, who teaches classes for the local extension service. "You don't want your neighbors to see you planting ice cubes."

BE PRACTICAL: PLANT PARSNIPS

Parsnips suffer from a bad reputation. "My children gobble up parsnips without any added sauce or camouflage. Too many gardeners ignore this tender and sweet, very practical crop," says Richard de Wilde, a Wisconsin organic farmer. Because de Wilde grows parsnips as a cash crop on his farm, he's developed good techniques with this root. De Wilde plants in early spring, spacing seeds 1¼ inches apart in the row. Germination rates are low, generally somewhere around 50 percent. Even so, de Wilde thins if necessary, leaving 2½ to 3 inches between plants. He says, "Parsnips shouldn't be planted on high-fertility areas. I

REVIVE OLD OKRA

If your okra plants get scraggly toward the end of the season, try the method developed by Barbara Pleasant, the author of *Warm-Climate Gardening,* for bringing them back into production. "When the plants begin to flag in mid-season, I lop off the top one-third," she says. "The sideshoots grow vigorously and give me a whole new crop."

AN OLD-FASHIONED ROOT

Skirret (*Sium sisarum*) was once popular in the United States and Europe but is rarely eaten outside of the Orient these days. It's worth a try. The 2-foot-tall, airy foliage is decorative enough to plant in a flower bed. The bloom is not lavish but attracts beneficial parasitic wasps. Plant skirret in the spring, on 12-inch centers. You can use seeds or root cuttings. Dig the roots after the first frost, and store them in a root cellar or in the refrigerator. You can boil, bake, stew, or batter-fry skirret, or you can mash skirret with potatoes.

plant them on a piece of ground that was composted the year before, and I never add supplementary fertilizer. Too high a fertility content in the soil, and they produce too many root hairs." He mulches the roots over winter and harvests them in the spring.

THE GARDEN PROFESSIONALS

Janet Bachmann is the coordinator for the Mid-South Farmers Network for the Rodale Institute. She and Jim Lukens are joint owners of a home-scale farm near Fayetteville, Arkansas.

Robert F. Becker is a retired associate professor at Cornell University's New York State Agricultural Experiment Station in Geneva, New York. He now teaches, lectures, and writes about the history of fruit and vegetable production.

David Cavagnaro is a garden manager in charge of preservation gardens at Heritage Farm for Seed Savers Exchange in Decorah, Iowa. In addition, he is a nature and horticultural photographer.

Eliot Coleman is an organic farmer and independent agricultural and gardening consultant in Harborside, Maine. He is the author of *The New Organic Grower* and *Four-Season Harvest*.

Lynn Coody is a farming consultant for Organic Agsystems Consulting in Cottage Grove, Oregon. She won second place in the 1984 Gardener of the Year contest, sponsored by *Organic Gardening* magazine.

George DeVault is the U.S. editor of *Novii Fermer*, a Russian-language farming magazine, and the former editor of *The New Farm*. He also runs an organic market garden near Emmaus, Pennsylvania.

Richard de Wilde is the owner and operator of Harmony Valley Farm, a 200-acre farm in Chaseburg, Wisconsin. He grows 30 acres of certified organic, fresh market vegetables, specializing in salad greens and root crops.

Mark Dornstreich and his wife, Judy, co-own and operate Branch Creek Farm in Perkasie, Pennsylvania. They manage 8 acres of organically grown vegetables and a greenhouse of herbs and small salad greens.

John Dromgoole is a manager and part owner of Garden-Ville of Austin, a catalog and supply company located in Austin, Texas. He hosts a national television show dedicated to organic gardening on PBS called "The New Garden."

Rick Estes and Geri Veroneau grow certified organic vegetables and small fruit on 5 acres in Salisbury, New Hampshire. They run a Community Supported Agriculture (CSA) operation and sell to restaurants and grocery stores.

Nancy Farrell is an organic gardener in Burlington, Vermont, who enjoys experimenting with innovative methods.

Norman R. Fausey, Ph.D., is a soil scientist with the USDA Soil Drainage Research Unit in Columbus, Ohio.

Fred Hoover and his wife, Barbara, own Fre-Bar, Inc., a 3½-acre organic market operation in Phoenix, Arizona, selling primarily to health food stores, restaurants, and grocery stores in Arizona.

Stewart Hoyt is a market gardener and operates a Community Supported Agriculture (CSA) operation in Barnet, Vermont.

Seth Jacobs and **Martha Johnson** are co-owners of Slack Hollow Farm in Argyle, New York. They specialize in growing root and leafy crops. They sell their produce through food co-ops, a Community Supported Agriculture (CSA) operation, and farmers' markets.

Miriam Klein-Hansen is a commercial dried-flower grower and craftsperson in West Charleston, Vermont. She taught homestead gardening at the National Center for Appropriate Technology in Montana.

Bill McDorman is the founder and president of High Altitude Gardens in Ketchum, Idaho. The mail-order seed company tests and sells seeds for high altitudes, cold climates, and short seasons.

Guinness McFadden runs a commercial certified organic farm in Potter Valley, California. He grows 140 acres of grapes, raises cattle, and produces wild rice, herbs, tomatoes for sun-dried tomatoes, potatoes, beans, and hay.

Charlie Nardozzi is a horticultural specialist for the National Gardening Association in Burlington, Vermont. He also hosts a weekly call-in radio show called "The Gardening Hotline," which airs in Burlington.

Pam Peirce is a garden writer, horticultural photographer, and photo editor from San Francisco, California. She is the author of *Golden Gate Gardening* and *Environmentally Friendly Gardening: Controlling Vegetable Pests*.

Tim Peters is the research director for Territorial Seed Company, a mail-order company, located in Cottage Grove, Oregon, that specializes in vegetables for the maritime northwest.

Cass Peterson and **Ward Sinclair** are the owners of Flickerville Mountain Farm and Groundhog Ranch, an organic vegetable farm in Dott, Pennsylvania. They raise more than 70 different kinds of vegetables, flowers, and herbs on the farm.

Barbara Pleasant is a garden writer who lives in Huntsville, Alabama. She is the author of *Warm-Climate Gardening* and a contributing editor to *Organic Gardening* magazine.

William Reid is the director of the pecan experiment field at Kansas State University in Manhattan. **Brenda Reid,** his wife, is a research assistant in fruit breeding at the University of Arkansas in Fayetteville. The Reids live in Chetopa, Kansas; the design of their home landscape and garden has been recognized in the *National Gardening* competition.

Ken Ryan is the farm manager at Lookout Farm, which grows specialty vegetables, herbs, and edible flowers in South Natik, Massachusetts. He is the former owner of Herban Gardens, a certified organic farm in Litchfield, New Hampshire.

Susan Sides is a garden writer from Fairview, North Carolina. She is the former head gardener at Mother Earth News Eco-Village.

H. S. Stevens is a garden writer in Texas. He developed an urban gardening program in Dallas, through the Texas Agricultural Extension Service, for use in schools, handicapped groups, prisons, and drug rehabilitation programs.

Pat Stone is the garden editor for *BackHome* magazine and the editor of *GreenPrints: The Weeder's Digest,* a quarterly publication that shares the human side of gardening.

Lynn Tilton is a writer and prize-winning gardener in Sierra Vista, Arizona. His prize-winning crops have been peanuts, tomatoes, cucumbers, and corn, but his favorite crop is melons.

William E. Watson is the president of Liberty Seed Company, New Philadelphia, Ohio, an independent seed company that specializes in sweet corn and heritage cultivars, selling primarily to commercial growers.

PUT RADICCHIO UNDER A POT

Radicchio is a gourmet treat that you can easily grow in your home garden. Ken Ryan, an organic farmer and farm manager from New England, has developed a nifty way to blanch radicchio. He sets 1-foot-deep white plastic flowerpots over the plants. He says, "The white pots don't cook the plants. Black ones do; the plants just bake inside them." Ryan points out that this system could work for other crops such as celery, too.

SUCCESS FOR THE SOUTH

In warm climates, success with cool-loving crops like lettuce and spinach can be simple. The key is timing your plantings so they mature in either early spring or in fall, during the most favorable conditions. Avoid plantings that will mature during hot weather—they will tend to be bitter and often go to seed quickly. For more tips on how to raise cool-loving crops in the South, see "Coaxing Cool-Lovers in Hot Climates" on page 179.

A CORNY TIP

Over the years of gardening in the tough climate of Zaokski, Russia, Jacob R. Mittleider, Ph.D., who teaches beginning farmers there, has worked out some sure-fire tips for sweet corn in a short-summer area. First, he starts with a fast-maturing cultivar. He plants the seeds indoors and then transplants them out into raised beds covered with black plastic. (The plastic comes off once the plants are established.) After the ears are formed, he cuts the tassels off of the plants to allow more sunlight to reach the leaves. The extra light promotes photosynthesis and encourages faster ripening.

Season Extension

Gardeners are never satisfied with the weather. It's either too wet or too dry, too hot or too cool. Northern gardeners struggle to grow heat-loving crops like melons, tomatoes, and peppers; southern gardeners strive for sweet, succulent lettuce, crispy radishes, and tender peas. While you can't change your climate (unless you're prepared to move and face a new set of challenges!), there are things you can do to create more-favorable microclimates within your garden.

In cold-climate areas, cold frames and row covers are standard weapons in the battle against late-spring and early-fall frosts. You may also want to choose cold-tolerant or fast-maturing cultivars of your favorite crops. In hot-summer areas, gardeners use shade cloth and heat-tolerant cultivars to extend the growing season for choice cool-season crops. In this chapter, you'll find helpful tips from expert growers across the country on how they stretch their growing seasons.

Simple Tricks for Extending the Season

Your efforts at season extension don't have to be fancy or complicated to work. Tools as simple as a piece of plastic or a few rocks can help you get an earlier start on the season.

WARM YOUR BEDS WITH PLASTIC SHEETS

Get a head start on planting your garden by prewarming the soil. Alton Eliason, who was named Farmer of the Year in 1991 by the Natural Organic Farming Association, plants two to three weeks earlier than his neighbors. Eliason says, "In mid-February, about six weeks before my first planting date, I cover the garden with a sheet of clear plastic, right on top of the snow. Clear plastic raises the temperature by 10° to 15°F, whereas black plastic only raises it by 5° or so. The snow melts right off, and the soil's always ready a few weeks earlier than normal." Eliason gets his big plastic sheets from area greenhouse growers who replace their glazing every two or three years.

NEW WAVE PLANTING TECHNIQUES

The lay of the land in your garden beds can affect how and when soil warms. Bill McDorman, the founder of High Altitude Gardens, an Idaho mail-order seed company, finds that one of the most effective techniques for combatting cold soils is shaping the garden surface before planting.

"This is similar to making raised beds, except that you shape the beds like waves in the ocean. I make the beds 3 to 4 feet wide, and slope them to the south," explains McDorman. He plants warm-weather crop seeds, such as squash, on the south face of his waves, just below the ridge, as shown in the illustration below. The soil drains well there, just as it does in a raised bed. The southern exposure warms the soil, and cold air is directed by the soil configuration to fall into the "valley" beyond the wave. Other heat lovers like basil and corn also benefit from this planting technique.

DOWN IN THE TRENCHES

To get an early start on the season, Miranda Smith, an agriculture writer and organic market gardener from Massachusetts, plants sweet corn in trenches 4 inches deep. First, she digs a trench in the soil and covers it with clear plastic for one week or so. After the soil has warmed, she plants in the trench and re-covers the furrow with plastic. "By the time the corn hits the plastic, it's time to take it off," she says.

Cold air runs down the slope.

SOUTH

GROW THEM FAST UP NORTH

Extending the growing season is an absolute necessity in places like Glover, Vermont, home of Lewis Hill, a nursery owner and the author of *Cold-Climate Gardening*. Hill's growing season is only 90 to 110 days, with occasional frosts in July. "This is the icebox of New England," says Hill.

How does Hill successfully produce corn, tomatoes, peppers, eggplant, pumpkins, and squash in such a harsh environment? "My favorite technique is to get intensive growth as fast as possible during the early part of summer when the days are long," explains Hill. To promote vigorous plant growth, he waters frequently and makes liberal use of liquid fertilizers, such as manure tea and fish emulsion. Standard season-extension tricks like covering seed beds and young plants with floating row covers or plastic jugs are a necessity for keeping the chilly spring and fall air from the plants. To stack the odds in favor of a good harvest, it's also smart to start with cold-tolerant and fast-maturing cultivars of normally slow-ripening crops like melons and winter squash.

TRANSPLANT TO HASTEN HARVESTS

Looking for a way to get your heat-loving crops off to a fast start? Take a tip from Jacob R. Mittleider, Ph.D., who teaches beginning farmers in Zaokski, Russia, a town about 100 miles south of Moscow (at about the same latitude as Edmonton, Alberta, in Canada). In the summer of 1991, he and his students produced more than 220 tons of food on 23 acres.

What is his secret? "I transplant everything: beans, corn, beets," says Dr. Mittleider. "I would do it with carrots, but if I do, they will never get larger than 4 inches. Transplanting gives an even harvest, not a mix of big plants and little plants."

Dr. Mittleider plants his transplants outdoors with special care so they won't lose ground during the transition. He plants in shallow trenches in raised beds and protects the young plants until they are well-established by covering them with heavy plastic supported by wire hoops.

PUTTING ROCKS INTO THE GARDEN?

Gardeners are always trying to get rid of rocks in their garden soil, but here's one tip that calls for using rocks. "I plant on the south side of rock or concrete walls wherever I can. This generally speeds plants up by as much as one month. But I don't have as much wall space as I'd like, so I import rocks into the garden," says Bill McDorman, the founder of High Altitude Gardens, an Idaho mail-order seed company.

To use McDorman's method, cover the soil around the base of each plant with a circle of whatever rocks you can find. Place the rocks close to but not touching the plants to avoid damaging the tender stems, as shown in the illustration at right. The rocks gather and store heat during the day. At night, the rocks release the heat, helping to protect the young plants from frost. The rocks also help to moderate changes in soil temperature, encouraging better root growth. You can leave the rocks in place all season, and they'll serve as a mulch to keep moisture in the soil and prevent weed growth around your plants.

Cold Frames and Other Covers

The greenhouse effect is a phenomenon that northern gardeners can take advantage of to help extend their growing season. No, not on a global scale, but by using enclosures like plastic or glass covers that trap the sun's heat and create tiny oases of warm air around growing plants.

MAKE A MINI-GREENHOUSE

A simple but effective plastic tunnel can house fresh cold-hardy crops all winter long. Pat Stone, the garden editor for *BackHome* magazine, makes these tunnels using 1½-foot lengths of ½-inch-diameter metal stakes, flexible ¾-inch-diameter PVC pipe, clear plastic, and boards or bricks. Here's how to do it:

1. Pound the stakes about halfway into the soil on both sides of a growing bed. Position the stakes in pairs opposite one another, spaced 3 feet apart along the bed length.

2. Arch a piece of PVC pipe over the bed, sliding one pipe over the ends of each pair of metal stakes. The length of the PVC pipe you use will depend on how wide and high you want the tunnel to be. Gardeners generally make the center of the arch 5 to 7 feet high. Making a taller house will require somewhat more pipe and plastic, but the added

PROTECT COLD FRAMES

To keep cold frames warm in the fall and early spring, surround them with bales of hay or bags of autumn leaves. On very cold nights, throw old blankets over the glass or plastic to keep in the warmth. Place cold frames to the south side of a fence or building, too; they will get the sunshine but will be protected from cold northern winds.

DOUBLE YOUR COVERS

In a hurry for the first tender, juicy lettuce of the season? Ward Sinclair and Cass Peterson, organic vegetable farmers from Pennsylvania, suggest putting a double layer of floating row cover over your freshly planted bed of lettuce. You'll have a harvestable crop much more quickly than if you use the standard single layer. "We just stumbled on that inadvertently," says Sinclair. "We had some row cover we had to overlap. Later, we found that the lettuce under the double layer was ready weeks before the other stuff."

ROW COVERS ON A STICK

At the Rodale Institute Research Center in Pennsylvania, garden project manager Eileen Weinsteiger uses a floating row cover to extend her growing season. "We also use it as an insect barrier. It works really well for raised beds," she says.

But although the light weight of this material keeps it from holding down your plants, it also makes the covers fair game for the lightest breeze. To keep the wind from ripping the covers off of her beds, Weinsteiger weights each side with a 12-foot-long 2×4. "We wrap the edge of the cover around each board one time so it is secure. Then after the weather warms up, we can take off the cover and wrap it up around a board." The wrapped-up row cover is easy to store, and it's all ready to use if you need it in a hurry.

expense may be worth it to you for the luxury of being able to stand upright inside it.

3. Cover the arches with the sheet of clear plastic, allowing some of the plastic to hang over on both sides, and use the boards or bricks to weight down the edges.

Stone leaves the ends (or one side) open for ventilation or picking but closes them when the weather is cold. Besides kale, other fairly compact, cold-tolerant greens like spinach and oriental greens will thrive in a mini-greenhouse like this one.

Where to find the fixings for your own tunnel? If you live near a company that sells greenhouse supplies, that's a good place to start looking. Otherwise, ask local greenhouse or nursery owners where they get their supplies.

SLITTED TUNNELS FOR SUPER TOMATOES

Plastic covers suspended over rows of plants are a great way to protect tender crops from spring chills. But they do require regular ventilation to prevent heat from building up inside on sunny days. If you don't have the time or inclination to keep raising and lowering the sides of a solid plastic cover, try a slitted row cover instead.

A slitted row cover is "a tunnel with 6-inch openings punched through at regular intervals to ventilate the tunnel. It has been a great season extender for us," says Ward Sinclair, an organic vegetable farmer from Pennsylvania.

One year, he and his partner, Cass Peterson, planted 'Siberia' tomatoes in the field in early April and covered them with slitted row covers. "The tomatoes were flowering like crazy on Memorial Day," recalls Sinclair. "They were bursting out of the tunnels, just lifting the plastic off of the ground."

But the plants are not the only thing that tries to lift row covers at their Flickerville Mountain Farm and Groundhog Ranch. "Our main problem is wind," adds Sinclair. "You have to cover the edges of the plastic with soil along the whole length of the tunnel. You can't just put a handful of soil here and there and expect it to hold." Long metal pipes or boards also make good anchors for row covers. They are easy to move and reposition when you need to temporarily uncover the plants for maintenance or harvesting.

PROTECT PLANTS WITH PORTABLE FRAMES

If you want to protect a lot of plants with plastic row covers, try framing the row covers to make them easier to set up and take down. Robert F. Becker, a retired associate professor at Cornell University's New York Agricultural Experiment Station in Geneva, has created a design for sturdy framed covers that are easy to move around the garden. Here's how to make them:

1. Using 2×4's and nails or screws, make a square wooden frame, 18 inches on each side.

2. Drill four holes halfway through the frame from the top, one in each corner.

3. Make two arches of rigid wire (9- or 10-gauge works well). Position each arch diagonally over the frame, inserting the ends of the wires into the holes. This creates a dome shape as shown in the illustration below.

4. Cover the frame with a piece of clear plastic, stapling it to the wooden frame.

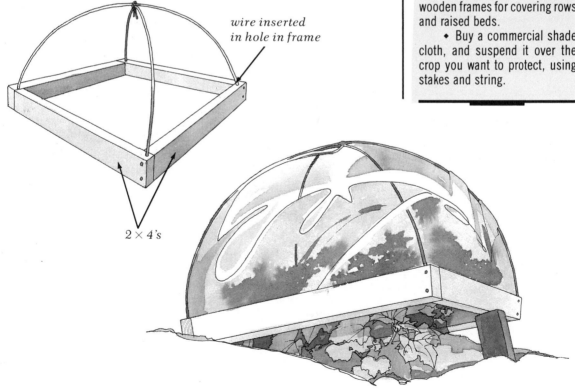

wire inserted in hole in frame

2×4's

SHADE BEATS THE HEAT

No matter what climate you live in, shade can be your best weapon in the battle against summer heat. Here are some tips for making the most out of shade in your garden:

• Arrange your garden so taller plants like corn and tomatoes will provide some shade for maturing spring crops or late-summer transplants.

• Set light lawn chairs over your tender young transplants to provide temporary shade.

• Make screens of lath or snow fencing to create portable shade structures.

• Staple burlap or muslin to wooden frames for covering rows and raised beds.

• Buy a commercial shade cloth, and suspend it over the crop you want to protect, using stakes and string.

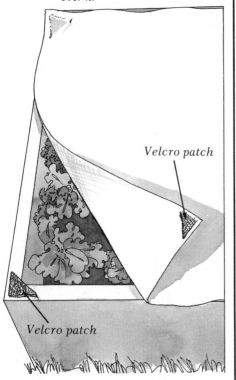
The wire domes sit about 1 foot above the soil surface, giving enclosed plants plenty of head room. Becker cuts a ventilation hole in the side facing south after positioning the frames. When plants need additional ventilation, Becker props up one side of the frame with a brick or rock. This extra ventilation helps harden off the plants before he removes the cap. "The only trouble with these frames is storage," admits Becker. "You need a place to keep them during the winter. I like them, though, because they're portable and inexpensive. The plastic needs to be replaced every two to three years, but the frames last for years."

KEEP PLANTS WARM WITH WATER

Wallo'Waters surround individual plants with water-filled plastic tubes, which store heat during the day and radiate it out at night to keep plants warm and toasty. Ward Sinclair, an organic vegetable farmer from Pennsylvania, thinks they are one of the best season extenders around.

"It's a fantastic device," Sinclair declares. "It keeps peppers perfectly at 9°F." Sinclair has used Wallo'Waters to produce early tomatoes and muskmelons that blossom on Memorial Day. Once the danger of frost is past, he plants basil between the tomatoes. "I lift the Wallo'Waters off the tomatoes and set them over the basil," he says. The result? Basil a month early, to complement your early tomatoes!

One way to save some money when buying Wallo'Waters is to buy a full case of 36 and split it with your gardening neighbors, friends, and relatives. Or if you're extremely thrifty, you can follow the example of Miranda Smith, an agriculture writer and organic market gardener from Massachusetts, and build your own. Just fill 2-liter plastic soda bottles with water, set them around peppers or eggplants, and encircle the ring of bottles with a sheet of plastic.

THE WORLD'S LARGEST ROW COVER

Ever wonder what you could grow if you put your entire garden under cover? It's not as farfetched as it sounds, according to Otho Wells, Ph.D., a New Hampshire Cooperative Extension vegetable specialist. Dr. Wells calls garden-size covers "high tunnels" because they are about 6½ feet tall at the center. "Make a Mini-Greenhouse" on page 205 gives instructions for making a basic high tunnel.

"I would recommend a 14 × 36-foot tunnel for a garden," Dr. Wells suggests. "You can put an awful lot of stuff in a

14 × 36, especially when you consider companion planting." You can grow just about anything from sweet potatoes to cut flowers inside of a high tunnel. Only a few crops such as sweet corn or winter squash take up too much room.

High tunnels "give you two to four weeks head start in the spring, depending on the conditions, then take you into the fall, to Thanksgiving, and even to Christmas," says Dr. Wells. "They're like small greenhouses, but they're not greenhouses because they have roll-up sides. They give you tremendous protection against the environment: wind, rain, insects, and diseases."

THE GARDEN PROFESSIONALS

Robert F. Becker is a retired associate professor at Cornell University's New York State Agricultural Experiment Station in Geneva, New York. He now teaches, lectures, and writes about the history of fruit and vegetable production.

Alton Eliason is an organic gardener in North Branford, Connecticut. He was named the Natural Organic Farming Association (NOFA) Farmer of the Year in 1991 and is a former president of the Connecticut chapter of NOFA.

Lewis Hill is a co-owner and operator of Vermont Day Lilies in Greensboro, Vermont. He is the author of *Cold-Climate Gardening* and *Fruits and Berries for the Home Garden*.

Bill McDorman is the founder and president of High Altitude Gardens in Ketchum, Idaho. The mail-order seed company tests and sells seeds for high altitudes, cold climates, and short seasons.

Jacob R. Mittleider, Ph.D., teaches a course for beginning farmers in Russia. He has been teaching intensive vegetable production for over 30 years. He is the author of *Grow-Bed Gardening* and *More Food from Your Garden.*

Cass Peterson and **Ward Sinclair** are the owners of Flickerville Mountain Farm and Groundhog Ranch, an organic vegetable farm in Dott, Pennsylvania. They raise more than 70 different kinds of vegetables, flowers, and herbs on the farm.

Barbara Pleasant is a garden writer who lives in Huntsville, Alabama. She is the author of *Warm-Climate Gardening* and a contributing editor to *Organic Gardening* magazine.

Miranda Smith is an agriculture writer and organic market gardener from Belchertown, Massachusetts. She is the editor and writer of *The Farmer Speaks: Organic and Low-Input Farming in the Northeast* for the federal Low-Input Sustainable Agriculture (LISA) program.

Pat Stone is the garden editor for *BackHome* magazine and the editor of *GreenPrints: The Weeder's Digest,* a quarterly publication that shares the human side of gardening.

Eileen Weinsteiger is the garden project manager at the Rodale Institute Research Center in Maxatawny, Pennsylvania.

Otho Wells, Ph.D., is a professor of plant biology at the University of New Hampshire at Durham. He is also a vegetable specialist for Cooperative Extension.

MILK JUG COVERS

You can protect young plants easily and economically with 1-gallon plastic milk jugs, says Eileen Weinsteiger, the garden project manager at the Rodale Institute Research Center in Pennsylvania. Just use a pocketknife to cut the bottom out of a jug, and set the jug over a tender young seedling to form a mini-greenhouse. During warm weather, take the cap off of the jug for ventilation during the day.

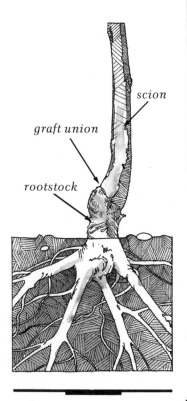

scion

graft union

rootstock

Fruits and Nuts

The best tip for the home gardener who has never tried raising fruit crops in the backyard is: Just do it! With new disease-resistant and dwarf cultivars, it's possible to raise good fruit organically in a small space. You'll be delighted by the wonderful variety of backyard fruits from the first summer raspberries to succulent summer peaches and the autumn bounty of apples. More-adventurous gardeners may also want to try the longer-term project of planting and raising their own nut trees.

In this chapter, you'll find great tips from nursery owners and commercial fruit growers on pruning and caring for tree fruits, trellising and harvesting great berries, and more. We couldn't offer all of the basic information on fruit culture here. If you're a novice fruit grower, you'll probably also want to consult some of the references on fruit growing that are listed in "Recommended Reading" on page 333.

Tree Fruits

Apples, cherries, peaches, pears, and plums are the most popular tree fruit crops in American gardens. For information about planting trees, see "Planting and Transplanting," beginning on page 13. In the following section, you'll find tips about selecting, fertilizing, and pruning and training fruit trees. It may help to review the instructions on making basic pruning cuts in "Pruning and Training," beginning on page 35, before trying the pruning tips from our experts.

A SNIP IN TIME SAVES NINE

No amount of pruning five years down the road can produce the tree that you can craft with a few snips while it's young. "Pruning is the most important part of caring for a tree for the first two or three years, and planting time is the time to start," advises Roger Joy, the manager of Canyon View Nursery in Montana. "A strong set of side branches and a good trunk make all the difference in how a tree will perform in years to come."

Bruce Barritt, Ph.D., a horticulturist at the Washington State University Tree Fruit Research and Extension Center, gives the following three pieces of advice for pruning young trees:

1. Don't prune the roots at all; the tree needs every one it has left.

2. Cut the main stem off 30 to 36 inches above the soil. This will cause side branches to form 20 to 36 inches above the ground. Make your cut just above a healthy-looking bud.

3. If the tree already has good side branches, cut the main stem off about 12 inches above the top branch. Select five or six branches, cut each back by one-quarter to one-third of its length, and remove any extras.

Joy prefers to shorten selected side branches even more. He leaves only two or three buds, cutting each branch just above an outward-facing bud. Joy also advises rubbing off the bud just below the end one on the pruned branches. This bud tends to throw a narrow crotch angle and compete with the end shoot, Joy explains, so it's better to get rid of it before it sprouts.

GIVE BUDS THE BRUSH-OFF

Stroking your new tree will help it concentrate on developing a strong trunk and branches. "Rub off all of the buds and sideshoots on the bottom 2 feet of the main trunk so the tree won't waste time and energy on them," advises Roger Joy, the manager of Canyon View Nursery in Montana. "When the tree starts to leaf out, put on a leather glove and run it down the trunk. The buds will all break off cleanly." If you delay, you'll have to clip each shoot off with hand pruners instead.

PRUNING POINTERS

Understanding how your fruit trees grow and following some simple rules can make good pruning much easier. "With these five rules and an understanding of the theory of apical dominance, anyone can be a good pruner," says Roger Joy, the manager of Canyon View Nursery in Montana. Apical dominance sounds like a fancy theory, but it's simple in practice. "The top or end [apical] bud will outgrow

GOOD GROWTH

You can judge whether your trees are getting enough nutrients by how much new growth they put out in a year. Refer to the following table to see if your trees are properly fed. If you see obvious deficiency symptoms, be sure to take action to correct them.

Tree	New Growth (inches)
Apple	6-18
Apricot	10-18
Cherry	18-24
Peach	6-24
Pear	12-24
Plum	12-18

If your trees are putting out much more growth than this in one growing season, don't fertilize them until they slow down. Too much nitrogen especially results in too much tender new growth, which is susceptible to insect and disease problems and increases your pruning chores. You may be able to reduce the nutrient supply under a tree by allowing grass or weeds to grow and removing the mowings periodically.

ROOTSTOCK ROULETTE

Choosing a suitable root-stock for your grafted trees is very important. Different root-stocks are suited to different soil conditions, and many dwarf the tree to varying extents. Below are some tips on rootstocks, along with their dwarfing tendencies (given in parentheses). Consult your supplier or extension agent for more details. (For details on the actual size ranges of dwarf, semidwarf, and standard trees, see "Sizing Up Fruit Trees" on page 87.)

Apples

'**M.7**' (50 to 60 percent of standard). This is a good all-around rootstock, does poorly in wet or very sandy soil, and may be slow to bear.

'**Mark**' (35 to 45 percent of standard). This prefers heavy, wet soil and bears very early. Remove all flowers the first year or two so it won't stunt itself.

'**M.9**' (25 to 30 percent of standard). This is a good dwarf that tolerates heavy soils and needs staking.

'**M.27**' (15 to 20 percent of standard). This is a good container tree that needs excellent drainage and loose soil.

Pears

'**Quince EMLA A**' (some-what dwarfing). This tolerates wet soil and doesn't graft well to some pear cultivars.

'**OH × F**' **series** (quite dwarf-ing). This is compatible with all pears.

(continued)

any other bud on the tree or branch. If you cut off the highest bud, the bud just below the cut will outgrow any bud on the tree or branch," explains Joy. His pruning rules are:

♦ Remove dead wood any time of the year.
♦ Rub off water sprouts and suckers as they develop.
♦ If two branches rub or cross, remove the less desir-able branch.
♦ Prune to promote strong (wide) crotch angles.
♦ Always prune to a distinct point — an outward-facing bud, an outward-facing branch, or the trunk — to reduce rebranching. Don't leave stubs.

Bruce Barritt, Ph.D., a horticulturist at the Washington State University Tree Fruit Research and Extension Center, concurs. "The point of pruning is to let light in to all parts of the tree," reminds Dr. Barritt. "In some cases, you may take all of the new growth off and even cut back into older wood to get a tree under control and prevent regrowth."

BANISH FROZEN FINGERS

Pruning in the dead of winter can be chilly, uncomfortable business. "But there's a better alternative," says Robert Kourik, an edible-landscaping consultant in California. "Try summer pruning. People are brainwashed that you can only prune in the winter. They are afraid their trees will 'bleed' to death if they summer-prune, but it's not true. Summer pruning is the best shot you have at controlling rank growth. I prune my plum trees only in the summer."

If you plan to summer-prune, wait as long as possible past peak growth in summer to reduce regrowth. Just be sure to prune at least two to five weeks before frost. Otherwise, the wood just below the pruning cuts and any succulent regrowth will not have time to harden off properly and will be prone to cold injury.

CLIP CLOTHESPINS ON YOUR TREES

Lessen your pruning chores by weighting down the branch tips of your fruit trees with clip-on clothespins. Robert Kourik, an edible-landscaping consultant in California, explains: "Wait until each shoot is 1 to 1½ feet long, and then weight down the tip with one or two clothespins. Once

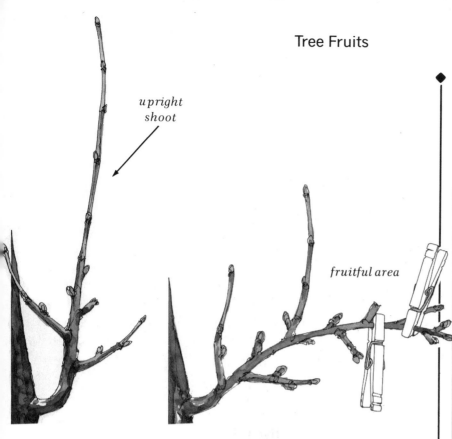

upright shoot

fruitful area

Bending an upright shoot slows its growth and causes fruit buds to form along the shoot. You can use this trick to manipulate the growth of your fruit trees.

the tip is lower than the shoot, its growth slows, and the outer buds become fruitful." Remove the clothespins during the winter; by then the branches will hold their shape. The following spring, weight down the tips of the next season's growth.

This technique can even work to turn suckers and water sprouts into productive branches, says Kourik. "Suckers and water sprouts are only useless if they are allowed to grow straight up. If you bend any shoot over, it will slow down, and you can make it into a useful, fruitful branch," says Kourik. You should remove suckers that sprout below the graft union of a grafted tree since they are part of the rootstock, not the scion cultivar.

BE YOUR TREE'S ORTHODONTIST

Like children's teeth, some tree branches grow at odd angles or too close together. Help your trees develop strong, spreading branches by gently bending down any skyward-

---

ROOTSTOCK—CONTINUED
Cherries

'Mahaleb' (not dwarfing). This is very cold-hardy, compatible with tart cherries, and needs good drainage.
'Mazzard' (not dwarfing). This is compatible with tart and sweet cherries and tolerates heavy soil.

Peaches

'Siberian C' (85 percent of standard). This works for peaches and some apricot cultivars. It is drought-resistant and cold-hardy.
'Citation' (70 to 75 percent of standard). This is dwarfing. It doesn't work for some peach cultivars and isn't very cold-hardy.

For smaller peach trees, try a genetic dwarf cultivar, or contain standard trees by pruning and training.

TREES FOR WET SITES

Not everyone is graced with perfect, well-drained-but-not-too-dry soil. While very few fruits will grow in boggy soil, quince trees (*Cydonia oblonga*) and pears on quince rootstocks are tolerant of clay and less-than-ideal drainage conditions. Elderberries (*Sambucus* spp.) often grow in moist areas in the wild. You can also deal with a poorly drained site by building and planting a large raised bed.

toothpick spreader

wood-and-nail spreader

reaching branches and bracing them at a desirable angle until they harden.

"During the first half of the season, I use round hardwood toothpicks to spread branches," says Robert Kourik, an edible-landscaping consultant in California. Toothpicks have many advantages: They are cheap, a whole orchard's-worth will fit in your pocket, and they just fall out and decompose on their own. To spread a new branch with a toothpick, gently press one end into the shoot 2 to 4 inches away from the crotch. Spread the shoot a little farther than you want it to set, and press the other end of the toothpick into the main stem, as shown in the illustration at left. "I tell visitors I'm making instant hors d'oeuvres," laughs Kourik.

If you miss spreading a branch the first year and it has hardened in an undesirable position, you'll need to use a more substantial spreader. Kourik recommends the following method of making your own sturdy spreaders:

1. Cut lengths of 1×1 lumber. (A variety of 6- to 36-inch lengths works well.)

2. Pound a 2-inch finishing nail a little more than halfway into the cut face of both ends of each length of lumber.

3. Use a large pair of wire cutters to snip off the heads of the finishing nails at an angle. This will give you a sharp point on each end of your homemade spreader.

Insert your wood-and-nail spreaders as you would toothpicks, but farther from the crotch.

FLOOR COVERINGS FOR YOUR ORCHARD

Caring for the surface of the soil under your fruit trees is important for the ultimate success of the trees themselves. Any vegetation growing under the trees or in their root zones competes for water and nutrients. Michael Maltas, the garden director of the organic showpiece garden for Fetzer Vineyards in California, gives the following advice: "Keep the soil clear of vegetation all the way out to the drip line for the first three to four years so the trees get a good start. Then let grass grow under the trees to help control the growth of the tree."

Robert Kourik, an edible-landscaping consultant in California, prefers to keep the ground under his trees clear of vegetation permanently. "I use old carpet, spread upside down and covered with 2 inches of wood chips, to mulch under my pear trees. Not only does this prevent competition from grass and weeds and make a clean walking surface, but it has effectively suppressed the once-rampant blackberries and poison oak."

WEANING TREES FROM WATERING

You can manage your fruit trees to reduce the amount of water they'll need over their lifetime. Robert Kourik, an edible-landscaping consultant in California, recommends watering fruit trees heavily the first two or three years then weaning them off to no irrigation. "Trees watered this way get off to a good start and are quite drought-resistant in the long run," explains Kourik. "I like to water daily to keep the soil moist [but not waterlogged] at all times. I have also found that, in my soil, most plants benefit from more water, often two to three times more than is generally recommended for them." Since a common recommendation for most fruit trees is 1 to 2 inches of water per week, Kourik's recommendation would be at least twice that amount.

PROTECT TRUNKS WITH POWER PAINT

Painting tree trunks at planting and each fall with diluted white latex paint is a common recommendation for good tree care. Make the paint do double-duty by using a half-and-half mixture of lime-sulfur (diluted according to the label instructions) and white latex paint. Apply the mixture from the soil level up to the first main branches. "The paint helps keep the sunny side of the trunk from heating up too rapidly and possibly cracking, while the lime-sulfur helps protect the tree from pests and diseases," explains Helen Atthowe, an organic farmer in Montana.

Atthowe uses the same mixture to paint wounds in trees, especially peach trees during the growing season. "If you dig borers out of the trunk, paint the wound with this mix. If you see cankers, prune back to healthy, normal-colored wood (usually about 2 inches below the canker), and paint the cut end with the mix." Be sure to burn or deeply bury the cankered prunings.

MIX A PROTECTIVE MUD PIE

If you sometimes feel that childish urge to make mud pies, here's a way to indulge yourself and protect your trees

SUPER-HARDY APPLES

It's worth your while to check the offerings of catalogs that specialize in super-hardy fruits. Bill MacKentley, a co-owner of St. Lawrence Nurseries, a New York mail-order company that specializes in hardy fruits and nuts, is an expert on plants that will thrive in northern zones. His number one favorite apple is 'Honeycrisp', a crisp-textured apple that thrives through Zone 4; stores well, and is wonderful for eating out of hand. MacKentley points out that many of the best super-hardy apples have been named in the last 20 to 30 years and that more are being released every year.

Roger Joy, the manager of Canyon View Nursery in Montana, gives 'Liberty' as his first choice for a fresh eating apple. He is fond of 'Earligold', a green-skinned apple, and 'Goodland', which is considered to be the Canadian standard of apple excellence. 'Carroll', 'Spartan', and 'McIntosh' are also favored by Joy. All six are also exceptionally winter-hardy.

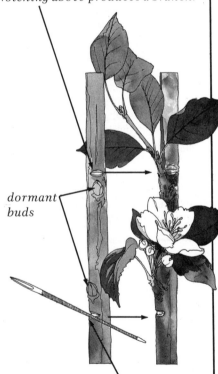

Notching above produces a branch.

dormant
buds

*Notching below produces
fruit buds.*

NOTCHING BRANCHES

from sunscald at the same time. Michael Maltas, the garden director of the organic showpiece garden for Fetzer Vineyards in California, uses a mixture of 3 parts light-colored bentonite clay and 1 part cow manure (fresh, if possible) or compost to protect his trees' trunks. (Bentonite clay is available from farm stores for pond sealing.)

Maltas soaks the clay overnight, then drains off any excess water and mixes the clay with the manure to get a thick, spreadable paste. "Spread it on the trunks on a nice, dry day so it will dry good and hard," recommends Maltas. "Add a raw egg and a handful of blood meal to each gallon of the mixture to help repel nibbling mice and rabbits. Of course, a good, tall hardware-cloth collar around each tree is a more surefire way to prevent rodent damage."

Maltas prefers to use fresh manure in the mixture because it makes it stick onto the trunks best. He hypothesizes that some of the nutrients from the manure or compost are absorbed through the bark. It is also possible that it helps protect the trunk from disease.

JUST FIDDLE FOR FRUIT

There's an easy way to speed up a tree that's slow to bear fruit. Robert Kourik, an edible-landscaping consultant in California, gives reluctant trees a gentle nudge by selectively notching branches near buds, as shown at left. "In late winter through early summer, stroke a coarse ⅜-inch rat-tail file like a violin bow around half of the diameter of a one-year-old branch just below a dormant bud," Kourik explains. "Go deep enough to just see the white of the wood through the green underbark. This will often induce a dormant bud to develop into a fat fruit bud." Under-notching works by interrupting the downward flow of carbohydrates. The extra carbohydrates (food) then collect around the bud and stimulate it to become a flower bud.

"A notch just above a dormant bud will often induce a new branch to develop, which can be a useful thing to know if you need a branch in a specific place," Kourik adds. Over-notching works by blocking the downward flow of growth-regulating compounds that keep the side buds dormant. If less of the compounds reach the bud, it can break dormancy and grow into a shoot.

CRAFT A FIVE-FLAVOR TREE

Grafted trees usually consist of one rootstock and one fruiting cultivar, but you can graft two or more cultivars onto the same tree. These multicultivar trees are useful for small families and small gardens, and they're fun for any adventurous gardener to try. Select cultivars that ripen at different times or that are good for different uses. Match cultivars that require cross-pollination to appropriate pollinators.

Hunter Carleton, a co-owner of Bear Creek Nursery in Washington State, which specializes in fruits and nuts, outlines this procedure (illustrated on page 218) for crafting your own five-way apple tree:

1. Select the five cultivars you want to grow. Order one upright-growing cultivar on a semidwarf rootstock and plant in early spring. Cut the scion back to about 20 inches to encourage new shoots to grow. In early summer, select the strongest, most upright shoot, and carefully remove the others. Order bud wood for your other four cultivars now. Schedule it to arrive in late summer. When it arrives, store it in the refrigerator until you need it. If you want to collect your own bud wood, see "Gathering Bud Sticks" at right for directions.

2. Watch your tree carefully to catch the right time to bud. See "Is It Time to Bud?" on page 218 for clues on timing. Water it deeply twice within the five days prior to budding. Carleton gives his trees the equivalent of 1½ inches at each watering. "The more sap you can get running in that tree, the better," he says.

3. On budding day, strip leaves off of the lower part of the current year's growth. Make a shallow 1- to 1½-inch-long vertical cut in the bark near the base of the shoot. At the top of the first cut, make a horizontal cut to finish the T. This cut should be just long enough to slip the bud chip into. (See Step 4 for information on how to cut a bud chip from your bud stick.) Cut only through the bark and not into the actual wood. Carleton cautions not to touch knife blades or freshly cut surfaces with your fingers. "Use alcohol, not saliva, to clean your knife periodically. Oil from your skin or saliva will prevent any callous formation, and your graft will fail," he notes.

4. Select a firm bud on the first cultivar bud stick. Make a shallow horizontal cut just above the bud. Then position the knife blade about ¾ inch below the bud. Pare off the bud and surrounding bark up to the horizontal cut, and lift the resulting bud chip by its handle.

5. Loosen the flaps of the T with the knife tip, and slide the bud chip down behind them. (Make sure you keep the

GATHERING BUD STICKS

If you have several apple trees or access to someone else's trees, you can collect your own bud sticks for budding. The buds you choose need to be mature and dormant. They should look plump and not bright green and should feel firm rather than soft. If they aren't plump and firm, they will wither and die after you insert them. If you don't think the buds are ready, wait another week and check them again, if the weather will allow it.

Harvest bud wood early in the morning while the buds are cool and at their plumpest. Select the center section of the current year's growth. If you have 2 feet of new growth, you can harvest up to a 1-foot section out of the middle. If you have only 1 foot of new growth, then only three or four buds in the middle are good prospects for budding. Avoid collecting buds from near the base of the current year's growth, and discard the skinny shoot tip.

Snip the leaves off, leaving ½-inch "handles." Firmly twist on a label with the cultivar's name. Place the bud sticks in a plastic bag with a wet paper towel, and keep them cool until ready to use.

IS IT TIME TO BUD?

Apple trees are easy to graft by a technique called budding. Late summer is the time to bud, but knowing exactly the right time is more than a matter of looking at the calender. "Most books just say late summer, and then dwell on the mechanical techniques of grafting," says Hunter Carleton, a co-owner of Bear Creek Nursery in Washington State, which specializes in fruits and nuts. "But in my experience, 80 to 90 percent of success lies in the grafter's timing, not the technique. The condition of the rootstock, the condition of the bud wood, and the weather are far more important than the date."

Keep an eye on both your to-be-grafted tree and the weather as summer starts winding down. When the new growth on the tree has slowed and is starting to harden, it is ready to prepare for budding. If you try to bud before growth slows, the shoot will be too succulent and the graft won't take. If you wait too long, the shoot will be going dormant. Buds won't take on dormant shoots either. This is primarily a problem for northerners working with cold-hardy cultivars that may go dormant early in the fall.

You need two to three weeks of good weather after you bud for a successful graft. In this case, good weather means nights that are above 50°F and warmer days. Carleton has found that if the weather is too cold in August, he can gamble (and often win) by waiting and budding in September when the weather warms again.

right side up, or it won't take.) Wrap the union with a grafting rubber or with masking tape. Then wrap the budded section with a 3- to 4-inch-wide strip of plastic wrap. Secure the edges with tape to keep the bud from drying out. Attach a label with the bud's cultivar name. Be sure the label is attached loosely enough so that it won't girdle and kill your tree.

6. Make another T-cut 2 to 3 inches above the first and a quarter of the way around the trunk. Prepare a bud chip from another cultivar. Insert, wrap, and label as before. Repeat this procedure for the remaining two cultivars.

7. Splint the budded section. Each budding site is a potential weak spot, which may snap in a strong wind or ice storm. Place a thin, strong stake along the shoot, and tie it securely above and below the grafts at several places. Twist ties work fine, but remember not to tie so tightly that you girdle the tree.

8. Water your tree generously every few days for the first week or so. "The buds need to callous firmly to the

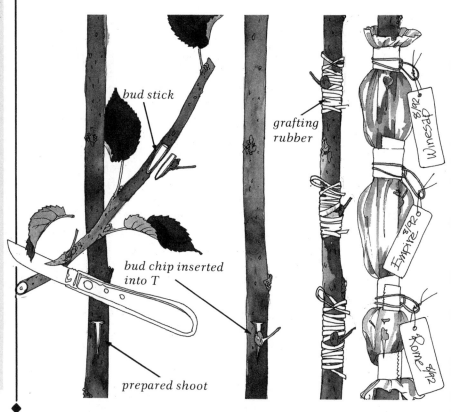

bud stick

grafting rubber

bud chip inserted into T

prepared shoot

shoot if the graft is to be successful, and this healing process takes lots of juice. The more juice, the better," says Carleton.

9. Check the buds three to four weeks later. If they are plump and green, you did it! If a bud is brown and shriveled, it didn't make it. Try rebudding that cultivar farther up the shoot, or enjoy your four-flavor tree. Successful buds won't sprout the same fall. Don't despair—they're dormant. Look for them to pop in the spring.

10. In late winter, cut the center shoot back to leave three or four buds above the highest grafted bud. If you don't, the central cultivar will outgrow the other cultivar buds and may even prevent them from sprouting.

For pruning and training information for a multicultivar tree, see "Training a Multiflavor Tree" below.

TRAINING A MULTIFLAVOR TREE

Whether you craft your own five-way apple tree or buy one ready-made, you'll want to be sure to train and prune it properly. According to Hunter Carleton, a co-owner of Bear Creek Nursery in Washington State, which specializes in fruits and nuts, the training and pruning is similar to that of any other apple tree, with one exception: "You must keep the five cultivars in balance," says Carleton.

If you budded your own tree, as described in "Craft a Five-Flavor Tree" on page 216, you'll have to train it during the first growing season. When the shoots from the grafted buds are about 6 inches long, gently spread each to a 45- to 60-degree angle. Move the identifying labels onto the new branches. Be sure to keep the labels loose so they won't girdle the rapidly growing branches. Rub off any buds that start to grow from the rootstock or from the main shoot near the grafted buds. Select the strongest, most upright shoot from the main stem cultivar, and remove the others. Remove any flowers.

In late winter, prune your tree by removing the top one-third of each branch. If any of the branches have greatly outgrown the others, cut them back farther to the same finished length as the others.

If you buy a ready-made tree, plant it in the early spring. Examine it carefully, and identify each cultivar. Loosen any existing labels, and put on permanent labels if there are none. If the tree hasn't been pruned, prune it by cutting back the branches as described above.

APPLES FOR THE SOUTH

Many apples will thrive in areas with warm winters, says Eunice Messner, a fruit specialist coordinator for the California Rare Fruit Growers. "And they are very, very tasty, just like any other apples," says Messner. 'Fuji' and 'Mutsu' are two good cultivars which originated in Japan. 'Gala' and 'Jonagold' are both superb. 'Anna' fruits very early (at the end of June). 'Dorsett Golden' is a good pollinator for 'Anna' and tasty in its own right. Crisp, refreshing 'Granny Smith' does well in long seasons.

MAKE A LIVING BRACE

There's a simple technique that can strengthen your tree's branch framework by causing it to grow its own branch supports. Twist two young shoots together and see where the two will touch. Unwind them and use a flat file or rasp to remove the outer bark from a 2- to 3-inch-long strip in the area where they made contact. Twist them together again, and tie the filed areas together with twine, masking tape, or strips of panty hose. Callus tissue will form where the bark was filed off, and the two shoots will grow as one in a few weeks. Once the union is complete, snip off the ends of the shoots. Suckers may sprout from the brace; just nip these off in late summer.

For home- or nursery-grafted trees, spread new branches and remove any strongly vertical shoots during the growing season. Rub off any buds that start to grow from the rootstock or from the main shoot near the grafted buds. As the main branches develop side branches, spread them to 60- to 75-degree angles from the main branches. In the following years, try to keep each section of the tree about the same size as each of the other sections. Some will need more pruning than others.

RUSSET APPLES: BEAUTY MORE THAN SKIN DEEP

The catch-22 of disease-resistant apples is that they are just as attractive to insects as non-disease-resistant cultivars. Bill MacKentley, a co-owner of St. Lawrence Nurseries, a New York mail-order company that specializes in hardy fruits and nuts, suggests an alternative to modern disease-resistant cultivars: Plant antique russet cultivars. "The russets tend to be somewhat more insect-resistant because of their sturdy skins," says MacKentley, "and their wonderful flavor makes them a very good choice for homeowners."

Frank Pollock, an organic grower from Pennsylvania, also grows and recommends russets. "The flavors are just *so* good," says Pollock. "Once you get past the unfamiliar look of the skin and bite into it, you'll never be satisfied by a run-of-the-mill apple again for eating or baking." Pollock finds he has fewer disease and insect problems on his russet fruits than on his smooth-skinned apples. Russets are renowned for cider making and tend to keep well, often getting sweeter in storage. What more could you ask for in an apple? Two russets to try are 'Golden Russet' and 'Ashmead's Kernel'.

ZIP YOUR TREES INTO DORMANCY

Southern gardeners may find that their apple trees hold onto their leaves and pretend they are evergreen, then fail to flower in the spring. Eunice Messner, a fruit specialist coordinator for the California Rare Fruit Growers, says it's quite easy to help apple trees get their needed leafless, dormant period. "In the fall, I just take my hand and run it down the length of the branch like a zipper to remove all of the leaves," she says. Messner recommends doing this when other plants are naturally losing their leaves. Other temperate fruits such as pears will also benefit from having their leaves stripped. Peaches and other stone fruits normally drop their leaves without intervention.

USE HONEY TO CLARIFY FRUIT JUICE

Ever wondered why your homemade fruit juice is never as clear as commercial juice? Most commercial juices are treated with an enzyme called pectinase to remove the cloudiness. Unfortunately, pectinase removes the pectin, a source of soluble fiber, and the requisite heating (pectinase doesn't work in the cold) destroys some of the juice's flavor.

Robert Kime, a research scientist at Cornell University's Agricultural Experiment Station in New York, suggests a simple alternative: honey. Added to cold juice, honey clarifies without removing valuable pectin. Also, the flavor of the clarified juice is much closer to that of fresh juice. Kime explains that the protein in the honey slowly precipitates out the tannins that contribute to the cloudiness.

To clarify apple juice, mix 4 tablespoons of honey into each quart of raw juice, and leave it in the refrigerator overnight. The next day, draw the clear juice off of the settled solids. Drink it fresh, or freeze it for future use. You can bottle the clarified juice by heating it rapidly to 190°F and holding it at that temperature for 3 minutes. Pour the juice into warm, sterilized jars, and seal according to the manufacturers' directions. Lay the jars on their sides for 3 minutes, then place them in a sink full of warm water, and start adding cold water to cool the juice as rapidly as possible. "The faster you heat and cool the juice, the better the flavor and the vitamin retention will be," says Kime.

GET THE BEST OF TWO FRUITS

"Apple-pears," otherwise known as Asian pears, combine the superb flavor of a perfectly ripe pear with the crisp flesh of an apple. Plus, Asian pears ripen to perfection on the tree, so determining when to pick is easy.

Asian pears are easy to grow, says Jim Gilbert, the owner of Northwoods Wholesale Nursery in Oregon, which specializes in unusual fruiting plants. "Asian pears tend to be healthier in general than standard pears," says Gilbert, "and you take care of them just the same way as standard pears. Besides, the range of flavors is phenomenal."

Gilbert likes 'Shinseiki', an early pear with tender, yellow skin and delicious, crisp, juicy flesh, and 'Chojuro', which has a beautiful brown-russet skin and a pronounced winy flavor.

BEST PICKS: PEARS

Pear trees are great for the home garden. They generally suffer from fewer pest problems than apples do in most areas, and homegrown pears are a luscious treat.

There are several super-hardy cultivars. " 'Flemish Beauty' is my favorite," says Bill MacKentley, a co-owner of St. Lawrence Nurseries, a New York mail-order company that specializes in hardy fruits and nuts. It's hardy through Zone 2 but is susceptible to fire blight. MacKentley also likes 'Nova', which is large and round with melt-in-your-mouth, juicy fruit. 'Nova' trees bear when young, and they are somewhat resistant to fire blight. 'Golden Spice', 'Luscious', 'Sauvignac', and 'Summer Crisp' are also good pears for northern areas.

Roger Joy, the manager of Canyon View Nursery in Montana, has less of a problem with super-cold winters and more of a problem with fire blight. "If fire blight is a problem in your area," advises Joy, "avoid 'Bartlett' or any pear with 'Bartlett' in its pedigree." Joy likes 'Seckel', a small pear with excellent flavor. He also favors 'Flemish Beauty' and 'Golden Spice'. For regions with extreme fire blight problems, he recommends Siberian pear (*Pyrus ussuriensis*) hybrids such as 'John' and 'Ure'. While these hybrids may not have the best fruit quality, they are resistant to fire blight and are super-hardy.

STARVE PEAR PSYLLAS

Pear psyllas are tiny sucking insects. When they feed, they secrete a sticky honeydew. A sooty black mold inevitably forms on the honeydew, marring fruit appearance and reducing growth. Since psylla are most attracted to soft, rapidly growing tissue, you can reduce problems by denying them their food source. Avoid high-nitrogen soil amendments, which encourage succulent growth, and remove water sprouts and suckers during the growing season.

PEST-FREE CHERRIES

Cherry growers agree that two of the major pests they compete with are cherry fruit flies and birds. Lon J. Rombough, an independent consultant and breeder of unusual fruits in Oregon, suggests outwitting both pests by growing 'Jan' and 'Joy'. These 4-foot bushes bear red, tart-type cherries that ripen in the late summer to fall, when cherry fruit flies are not a problem and birds feed less on fruit. They are hardy to −30°F but also thrive in the South and West. Both resist powdery mildew and Japanese beetles and need little pruning. And to top that off, the little bushes resemble flowering almonds and make great landscape plants, says Michael McConkey, the owner of Edible Landscaping, a Virginia mail-order company that specializes in edible plants.

SPRAY SEAWEED TO SEE MORE FRUIT

To help your fruit trees set a good crop even if a cold snap coincides with bloom, try spraying them with seaweed spray as frost insurance. Helen Atthowe, an organic farmer in Montana, found that spraying apples and peaches with seaweed prevented loss of fruit set when a cold snap occurred during flowering. Atthowe recalls, "It was really amazing. We harvested a full crop while our neighbors only had about a third of their normal crop." Atthowe speculates that the natural growth regulators in the seaweed helped some of the fruit buds recover from the shock of the cold and develop into a good crop.

If your spring is warm and there is no frost during bloom, seaweed treatment won't increase your final harvest. (You'll be thinning out the extra fruit in the early summer.) Even so, the seaweed sprays will give your trees a healthy spring boost.

It takes just a few applications of seaweed each spring to give your trees frost insurance. Spray peaches with a mixture of seaweed and fish emulsion when you can just see pink at the ends of the flower buds. Repeat just after the petals fall off. Apples and pears get three sprays: the first when about ½ inch of green leaf is showing at the tips of the buds on your earliest flowering trees, the second when you can just see pink at the ends of the flower buds, and the third when the petals fall off. Seaweed and fish emulsion are available separately or pre-blended. Mix with water to make a spray according to the foliar-feeding instructions on the label.

TRY THIS HONEY OF A SOLUTION

Preserve the wonderful taste and color of fresh-sliced fruit with a touch of honey. Robert Kime, a research scientist at Cornell University's Agricultural Experiment Station in New York, has found that a honey solution will keep fresh or dried fruit slices from browning without adding a taste of its own. "The honey-treated dried fruit has more of its original fruity flavor," says Kime.

Prepare your honey solution by mixing 1 cup of any mild or fruity honey with 4 cups of water. Cut fruit into the solution, and let the fruit soak in it for 15 to 20 minutes in the refrigerator. Then drain the fruit, and refrigerate or dry it.

GROW TART CHERRIES FOR TARTS AND MORE

Do you love fresh cherries but have put off planting a tree because you've heard they're a lot of trouble? Or maybe you have a huge old sweet-cherry tree, and all you get is a fabulous flower display and the heartache of watching the birds harvest all of the fruit. Take heart: Frank Pollock, an organic grower from Pennsylvania, recommends growing tart cherries for fresh eating as well as cooking. "They are generally much easier to grow without synthetic poisons than sweet cherries," says Pollock. Tart cherries are smaller trees by nature, though they still require yearly pruning. To enjoy your own tart cherries fresh, let them hang on the tree a bit longer than you would for cooking so that they can soften and sweeten.

Great Grapes

Grapes have been cultivated for fresh eating and making raisins, juice, and wine in many cultures from time immemorial. The vigorous vines can also provide cool shade under a trellis or transform an unattractive fence into a green and fruitful screen.

GROW GORGEOUS GRAPES

Growing grapes in your backyard is much easier than you may have supposed. Lon J. Rombough, an independent consultant and breeder of unusual fruits in Oregon, offers these four simple tips to get you started with grapes:

1. Choose the most disease-resistant cultivars that will thrive in your area. Disease problems in grapes can be one of the biggest headaches for backyard gardeners.
2. Weed control is very important, especially for the first few years. Keep the soil under your vines bare or mulched.
3. Go easy on fertilizer. "A thin layer of compost each spring is plenty," Rombough explains. "If you give grapes too much fertilizer, they will go all to vines and set no fruit."
4. Go easy on the water, too. New vines will need watering until they get established. Try watering once a day for a week, once a week for a month, and then once a month for the rest of the growing season (when it's dry). After the

MAKE A SIMPLE FRUIT PRESS

You can make an inexpensive press that does a good job of extracting juice from small quantities of berries or other fruit that's been crushed or ground. Cut two paddle-shaped pieces of wood, and drill two holes in the paddle end of each piece, as shown in the illustration below. Tie the paddles together with rope for a hinged effect, tightly enough so they don't flop about but loosely enough so the paddles will open and close.

Remove large pits from stone fruits and grind large fruits such as apples in a food processor or with a meat grinder to allow the juice to flow. Soft fruits such as berries can go in whole. Grapes should be "popped" by stomping on them in a bucket to break the skins. Place your prepared fruit pulp in an old pillowcase or bag made of strong cloth such as muslin. Tie the pillowcase or bag tightly above the pulp, and hang the bag over a bucket or bowl. Pinch the bag between the paddles, and squeeze.

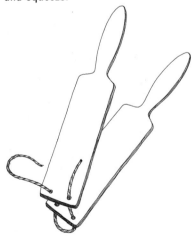

DISEASE-RESISTANT GRAPES

Grapes have been cultivated since before recorded history. Today we can pick from cultivars that thrive from the frigid North ('Valiant' has taken −50°F and still fruited) to the Deep South. Improved rootstocks make it possible to grow European wine grapes in many parts of the country, and disease-resistant cultivars can reduce problems in hot, humid areas.

Grapes for the North

Lon J. Rombough, an independent consultant and breeder of unusual fruits in Oregon, recommends three disease-resistant cultivars for the North: 'Edelweiss' is a white table grape that can be made into an acceptable wine. 'Espirit' is a white table grape and makes a good neutral-flavored wine. 'Swenson Red' is a red to purple table grape, which makes an acceptable wine.

Rombough's personal favorite for flavor is 'Swenson Red'. Coming in as a close second flavor-wise is 'New York Muscat', which has an "intense flowery flavor like nothing else you have ever tasted," says Rombough. 'New York Muscat' is hardy to at least 0°F and is reasonably disease-resistant.

(continued)

first season, hold the water. "Most places will get more water than grapes need," says Rombough. "I grow grass in the paths to help use up excess moisture."

Once your vines are growing, you get to the most confusing part (if you believe all of the books on the subject): pruning. True, there are a great many specific methods, but relax. All share the same goals: to control the lush growth of the vine and help it ripen a few clusters of large, sweet, flavorful berries. All of the methods are variations of just two systems: cane pruning and spur pruning. You can learn the details of grape pruning by referring to references on growing fruit listed in "Recommended Reading" on page 333.

"Most cultivars will bear with any pruning system," says Rombough, "but a few are more sensitive." Some only bear on one-year-old wood and need to be cane-pruned. "The biggest problem people have with pruning these grapes is that they cut off all of the new wood," says Rombough. "If you cut it all off, you get no crop." Other cultivars will kill themselves by over-bearing if cane-pruned so they need to be spur-pruned instead. Check with your supplier to see if your chosen cultivar has specific pruning requirements.

FEED VINES WITH WOOD

Looking at how nature does things can often lead us to good gardening ideas. "On Cape Cod, wild grapes grow on trees and are nourished by the decomposing bark and twigs. Since they are rarely bothered by pests and diseases, I decided to try growing my grapes the same way," explains Robert T. Olsen, Ph.D., who raises grapes in his ¼-acre research vineyard on Cape Cod. "More than ten years of growing have told me I'm on the right track." Dr. Olsen uses well-rotted wood in the planting holes and mulches the vines with wood and bark scraps, and his grapes are nearly free of pests and diseases even though they are unsprayed. Years ago, his worst problem was crown gall, so he devised a method of encasing the base of the trunk with sand to keep the soil and mulch from touching it. He credits his method with all but eliminating crown gall from his vineyard. Here is his method, which is shown in the illustration on the opposite page:

1. Dig a hole 18 inches deep and 18 inches across, placing the topsoil on a tarp as you go. Mix compost into the topsoil, using about 1 part compost for each 6 parts soil.

2. Make a cone-shaped pile of the amended topsoil in the bottom of the hole.

3. Spread the vine's roots over the cone. The top roots of the vine should be about 3 inches below the surface level of the original soil.

4. Add amended topsoil and water until the resulting slurry just covers the roots.

5. Cover the slurry with 1 gallon of the richest, oldest rotten wood you can find (or, failing that, good compost).

6. Cover the rotten wood with coarse washed sand up to the soil surface, and water it well.

7. Roll a 2½-foot-long strip of 8- to 10-inch-wide plastic or metal into a shape like a bottomless bucket. (Dr. Olsen makes his out of the thick rubber strips that are used between the inner tubes and the rims of tractor-trailer tires, but any material will do the job as long as it is rot- and sun-resistant.)

8. Stand the collar around the vine, and fill it with 7 to 9 inches of coarse washed sand. If your vine isn't taller than

GRAPES—CONTINUED

Grapes for the South

For southern areas, Rombough recommends these three disease-resistant cultivars: 'Champanel' is dark blue and makes great juice and jelly. It's also a good table grape if you let it hang on the vine for two weeks after it turns blue. 'Xlanta' and 'America' also grow well in hot, humid areas without fungicidal sprays.

All three cultivars also will grow in the North, but their fruit may be rather acidic in short, cooler summers.

Southerners can try muscadine cultivars such as 'Fry', 'Jumbo', and 'Magnolia'. Muscadines are resistant to most diseases and require very little spraying. They are only hardy to about 0°F.

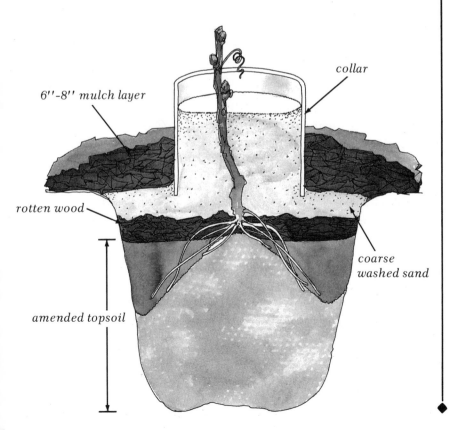

6''-8'' mulch layer

collar

rotten wood

coarse washed sand

amended topsoil

BLUEBERRIES FOR THE NORTH

Wild lowbush blueberries thrive north of the Arctic Circle, so no matter where you live, you can grow them. Try some of the new lowbush cultivars that have been selected for large fruit and crops. If you prefer a taller bush, choose some of the new half-high cultivars, such as 'Northblue' and 'Northland'. These moderate-size hybrids do well in areas with snow cover through the winter because they will be covered by the snow and escape injury. Half-highs are also great foundation plants: You can combine your blueberry patch with your foundation plantings and still see out your windows.

the collar, put in a few inches of sand now, and add more when the vine has grown a bit.

9. Mulch outside the collar with 6 or 8 inches of coarse wood and bark bits.

10. Water the vine every day for a week, then every week for a month, and it is off and growing.

You can also renovate existing vines with Dr. Olsen's method. Dig away the surface soil down to the main roots and add rotten wood, sand, and a sand collar as described for a new vine.

DON'T LET MUMMIES BECOME MOMMIES

Here's how to combat black rot—one of the most destructive grape diseases in humid areas—without using fungicidal sprays. Bill Nash, the owner of Owens Nursery, a Georgia firm that specializes in hostas and muscadines, has this advice: "The best place to break the cycle is the overwintering stage—the dried-up berries." The fungus in these dried-up berries, called mummies, comes to life in the spring and produces large quantities of spores. The spores are ejected during spring rains and land on the new foliage, starting the cycle anew.

To break the cycle when you prune, pick up and destroy all of the clippings, or put them in sealed containers for disposal with your household trash. At the same time, pick off and remove any mummified fruit hanging on the remaining canes. If your vines have a severe black rot problem, also remove any fallen fruit you find on the ground. For added protection, Nash grows crimson clover (*Trifolium incarnatum*) between and under the vines and never cuts the clover lower than 4 or 5 inches. The clover blocks the spores that are released from any mummies remaining on the ground.

Bountiful Berries

No home garden should be without berries. They are easy to grow and take up very little room. Try a blueberry bush, a strawberry patch, and some raspberry or blackberry canes, as well.

SPRINKLE SULFUR AROUND YOUR BLUES

Experts agree that the most important key to growing blueberries is to keep the soil pH in the 3.5 to 4.5 range. Bill MacKentley, a co-owner of St. Lawrence Nurseries, a New York mail-order company that specializes in hardy fruits and nuts, suggests using elemental sulfur to lower pH. He also uses a good, thick layer of acidic organic mulch such as pine needles and oak leaves. "I like to top-dress everything because that's the way nature adds things to the soil, so I put a light sprinkling of sulfur on the surface of the mulch once a year and let it work its way down," MacKentley says. MacKentley also warns against cultivating close to your blueberry bushes because they have lots of fine roots near the surface.

STIRRING STOPS MUMMY BERRY

You can use your bare hands to control mummy berry, one of the most bothersome diseases of blueberries. "Mummy berry is easy to control if you know the life cycle," says Bill MacKentley, a co-owner of St. Lawrence Nurseries, a New York mail-order company that specializes in hardy fruits and nuts. Dried-up fruits infected by the fungus drop to the ground in the fall. They overwinter there, and in the spring, they produce fruiting bodies up to 1 inch tall, which release spores that perpetuate the disease in the new season. These fruiting bodies are fragile, "so a little disturbance will completely interrupt the disease cycle. If you have a nice organic mulch, all you have to do is stir up the surface of it with your hands in early spring," says MacKentley. The stirring will break the fruiting bodies into bits and prevent them from producing and distributing spores to infect the new berries. Be sure to do this before new growth starts.

BLUEBERRIES BIRDS IGNORE

There's a simple way to keep birds from gobbling your blueberries. "Hard to believe, but it's true," says Frank Pollock, an organic grower from Pennsylvania. Most blueberries ripen in July, and commercial growers and backyard gardeners must fight to keep any of the berries for themselves. "I grow 'Elliott', which doesn't ripen until around Labor Day," says Pollock. "By then, the birds are done raising their families and just aren't much of a problem." 'Burlington' is another cultivar that ripens almost as late as 'Elliott'.

PICK HANDS-FREE

It's faster and easier to pick blueberries with two hands. You can make a simple hands-free picking container from an empty number-ten can or a small plastic bucket. Use a can opener to make two triangular holes just under the can rim and tie a short loop of string through each hole. (On a bucket, thread string through the handle holes.) Then tie a 3 × 36-inch strip of cloth to each string loop. Tie the strips around your waist like apron strings, or tie them into a loop and hang the loop over your neck.

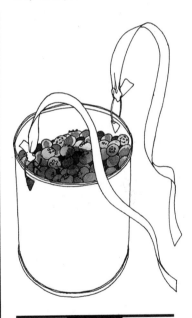

Brambles (raspberries and blackberries) are one of the most popular small fruits for backyard gardeners. Here is a sampling of the experts' favorite cultivars:

Red Fall Raspberries

Randolph E. McCoy, Ph. D., the owner of Champlain Isle Agro Associates, a Vermont company specializing in disease-tested planting stock, and Barbara Goulart, Ph.D., an associate professor of pomology at the Pennsylvania State University, both recommend 'Heritage'. Dr. Goulart also recommends 'Ruby'.

Red Summer Raspberries

Roger Joy, the manager of Canyon View Nursery in Montana, grows only summer-bearing red raspberries. He likes 'Boyne' for its dependable yields and good flavor.

'Latham' is disease-resistant and cold-hardy, but the flavor is only "pretty okay," says Dr. Goulart. Her first pick for flavor is 'Reveille'. 'Sentry' and 'Amos' are also good berries. 'Titan' resists raspberry aphid and bears enormous, mild-flavored berries.

Other Raspberries

'Royalty' is a purple cultivar that makes superb preserves, and it has some aphid resistance, which reduces the chance of a virus being introduced. 'Jewel' and 'Allen' are black raspberry cultivars that have good size and vigor. The best yellow berry is 'Honey Queen', a very productive summer bearer.

(continued)

GROW THE BEST BRAMBLES

Sun-warm raspberries and blackberries evoke memories of lazy summer days and country roads. It's easy to grow your own, and they taste even better than you remember. Here are a few tips from the experts on starting out right with bramble fruits:

Choose the best possible site. Cultivated raspberries and blackberries need full sun, good drainage, and good air flow, stresses Barbara Goulart, Ph.D., an associate professor of pomology at the Pennsylvania State University. "Most failures I see are due to poor sites," says Dr. Goulart.

Choose the best plants. "Get good, clean, virus-free plants. Tissue-culture plants are best; certified [disease-free] canes are the least you should consider. Getting sprouts from friends can bring on virus problems sooner, so you should avoid them at all costs. They're just not worth it," warns Randolph E. McCoy, Ph.D., the owner of Champlain Isle Agro Associates, a Vermont company specializing in disease-tested planting stock. Tissue-culture plants are started in test tubes from virus-free plant material. They are small, but "after you see tissue-culture plants grow out, compared to transplanted canes, you'll never plant anything else," says Dr. McCoy. Be sure to keep the small plants well-weeded, and mulch right after planting with an organic mulch such as straw.

Keep the plants well-watered until they are established. Tissue-culture plants are especially sensitive to water stress. As an additional measure of protection, Paul Otten, the general manager of North Star Gardens, a Minnesota nursery that specializes in bramble fruits, treats all of the tissue-culture plants shipped from the nursery with an antitranspirant. He recommends that gardeners treat tissue-culture plants from other sources with an antitranspirant, such as Wilt-Pruf, when they are unpacked. "It's simple, and there's a big, big difference between treated and non-treated plants after two to four weeks," says Otten.

Cut back canes. If you choose to plant canes, "be sure and cut the handles [canes] right down to 1 inch above the ground," warns Roger Joy, the manager of Canyon View Nursery in Montana. "The problem with leaving more of the old cane is that every bud will try to grow and produce fruit. That will prevent the plants from getting established and developing a good root system. You can see a difference in productivity even years later."

TERRIFIC BRAMBLE TRELLISES

Giving brambles the support of a trellis makes it easier to care for the canes and to harvest the fruit. Fall-bearing raspberries only need a light-duty trellis. A few metal fence posts with heavy twine strung along them will suffice, or try the Econotrellis illustrated on page 230. Both systems have the advantage of being easy to move when the time comes to mow down the canes in late winter.

Summer-bearing raspberries are more of a challenge because you must contend with the older canes bearing the present season's crop, as well as young canes that must overwinter and fruit the following season. Barbara Goulart, Ph.D., an associate professor of pomology at the Pennsylvania State University, suggests using a T-shaped trellis. "It spreads the fruit-bearing canes out where you can easily find and pick the fruit without getting scratched," says Dr. Goulart. The uprights of a T-shaped trellis are positioned in the center of the bed of canes. Each upright has a 6-foot-long cross arm mounted 2½ to 3 feet above ground level. These cross arms support wires, which, in turn, support the canes. To erect a T-trellis, sink wooden fence posts down the center of your bramble bed, with 25 to 35 feet between posts within the row. Mount the cross arms 2½ to 3 feet above ground level to form a T. String three courses of galvanized wires on each side of the cross arms, as shown in the illustration on page 230.

Train the vegetative canes (next year's fruiting canes) to the wires as soon as they are long enough to be tied, usually about early August. You can attach the canes to the trellis by sandwiching the canes between cords and the trellis wire, tying the cord to the wires every 3 feet or so. Or you can tie each individual cane to the trellis with twine or twist ties.

There are two ways to manage training the canes:

♦ Train all of the canes to one side of the T so that the following year's vegetative canes can be tied to the other side.
♦ Train the canes to both sides of the T. The following year's vegetative canes will then be held in the center of the trellis until after the trained canes fruit.

If you choose to tie canes to both sides, string two lengths of cord or wire along each side of the top section of

BRAMBLES—CONTINUED
Blackberries

Dr. Goulart recommends 'Chester' and 'Hull', both thornless, semi-erect cultivars. Dr. Goulart says that 'Navaho' is a thornless, upright cultivar that doesn't need to be trellised but adds that its cold-hardiness has not been tested in her region. She also likes the thorny 'Shawnee', one of the sweetest blackberries she has tasted; however, its cold-hardiness is also not known.

Timothy Nourse, owner of Nourse Farms, wholesale producers of strawberry and raspberry plants in Massachusetts, also recommends 'Chester'. Nourse says 'Illini Hardy' is the hardiest cultivar he has tried. It is erect and has thorns.

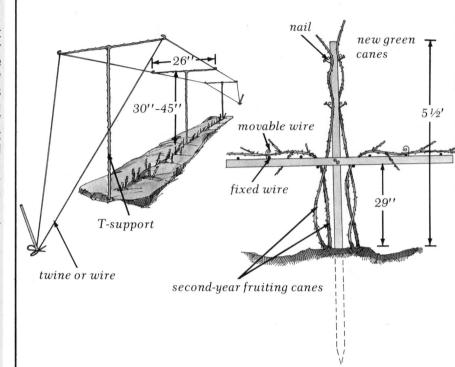

ECONOTRELLIS   T-TRELLIS

the uprights, as shown in the illustration above. As the new crop of vegetative canes grows, hold the canes upright in the center of the row by sandwiching them between these movable wires or cords. After harvest, remove the spent fruiting canes. Remove the wires or cords holding the new canes, and let them spread out for the rest of the growing season.

Blackberries are more robust plants than raspberries. Upright cultivars need no trellising. Thornless cultivars tend to be less self-supporting and benefit from some support. A split rail fence or a row of sturdy posts with permanent wires strung 3 and 6 feet above ground level will support them. Weeping blackberries need to be trained on a sturdy trellis.

TURN PLANT TIPS INTO NEW PLANTS

Canes of blackberries and black raspberries sometimes bend to the ground naturally, and the tip takes root. You can make use of this propensity to gain more plants for your garden.

Jean M. A. Nick, a garden book editor for Rodale Press,

has a diverse collection of brambles in her home garden. She explains how to help your plants multiply themselves, as shown in the illustration at right. "Choose healthy plants that bear good fruit to be your mother plants. When the new canes are about 3 feet tall, cut them back to 30 inches to encourage them to make lots of sideshoots. As the sideshoots grow, they will naturally begin to droop toward the ground. When the growing ends of the shoots start to look stretched and the newest leaves are very small, it's time to give nature a hand. Use a trowel and dig a hole with slanted sides in the soil under the trailing tip. Insert about 3 inches of the tip of the shoot into the ground, and firm the soil over it. And that's all there is to it," says Nick.

Your new plants will be ready to move in the fall. Clip the original cane between the mother plant and the new plant to leave a 6-inch "handle" above the roots of the new plant, and carefully move the rooted tip to its new home.

rooted tip ready to plant

TIP LAYERING
A BRAMBLE CANE

START RIGHT WITH STRAWBERRIES

Lavish some extra effort on preparing your new strawberry bed, and you will be richly repaid by extra years of bountiful harvest. Sonia Schloemann, the strawberry Integrated Pest Management coordinator at the University of Massachusetts at Amherst, recommends the following preparation for your new strawberry patch:

1. Till or dig the prospective patch, especially if it's in sod, one year before you plan to plant your new strawberry plants.

2. Plant buckwheat (*Fagopyrum esculentum*) as a summer-season cover crop. Turn it under just as it starts flowering, and replant with more buckwheat seed. Repeat until late summer. Then plant a winter cover crop of hairy vetch (*Vicia villosa*) and winter rye (*Secale cereale*). Seed ½ cup of hairy vetch and 1 cup of winter rye per 100 square feet.

3. Order strawberry plants to arrive the following spring. Turn under the vetch-and-rye mix a few weeks before planting time.

This preparation will help suppress pests and weeds and build organic matter in the soil. An alternative is to convert part of your vegetable garden into your new strawberry bed. "I like to use a section where I've grown carrots, but any well-fertilized and weed-free area will do," says

Joey Klein, a certified organic market gardener in Vermont. Both experts agree on one thing: Make sure you remove *all* of the perennial weeds before you plant. Weeds are the number one problem when growing strawberries.

PICK FLOWERS NOW FOR FRUIT LATER

Sonia Schloemann, the strawberry Integrated Pest Management coordinator at the University of Massachusetts at Amherst, firmly recommends picking off all flowers from your newly planted strawberry plants so the plants can get established. "It's hard to make yourself do it, because of course you won't get any fruit. But the plants will produce far more fruit the following years than they would if you didn't pick off the flowers that first season," Schloemann explains.

RENOVATE FOR RELIABLE RETURNS

Once you finish the season's strawberry harvest, it's time to give next year's crop a boost. Sonia Schloemann, the strawberry Integrated Pest Management coordinator at the University of Massachusetts at Amherst, explains how:

1. Mow off the tops leaving an inch or so of leafstalk to protect the crowns. (It's important not to injure the crowns because that can kill or at least stunt the plants.) Catch the leaves in the grass bag of the lawn mower, or rake them up and remove them from the bed to remove any diseased material or insects that may be present. Compost the trimmings well away from the patch.

2. Remove the runners that have rooted on either side of the rows until the remaining rows are no wider than 2 feet. This will give you better fruit because it gives more row edges, which is where the best fruit is borne. It also encourages good air circulation, which helps prevent disease problems, and it makes the fruit easier to reach at harvest time.

3. *Weed.* "Your diligence — or lack of it — in weeding is the most important determining factor of the length of your bed's useful life. With good care, you can get six, seven, or even more good years out of a bed," says Schloemann. If you thin out the strawberry plants, keep the big, robust plants and remove the smaller plants. The original mother plants are the best producers.

4. Spread 1 inch of compost over the plants. Not only does this feed the plants, it keeps the crowns in proper position. Strawberries have a tendency to grow themselves right out of the ground since they add a new crown on top of the old one each year. If you don't have compost, spread 1 inch of good soil instead.

Joey Klein, a certified organic market gardener in Vermont, adds two more recommendations: Spread a thin layer of a high-nitrogen fertilizer such as soybean or alfalfa meal over the bed after renovation, and water the bed regularly if the weather is dry.

BUGS WITH A TARNISHED REPUTATION

Mention tarnished plant bugs to a strawberry grower, especially an organic grower, and you'll hear grinding teeth and unkind words. Tarnished plant bugs inject toxin into buds and young fruit as they feed on them, which results in small, deformed fruit. Here's what the experts recommend to combat them:

Keep your beds clean and covered. If you've had tarnished plant bug problems in the past, renovate beds after harvest by removing all leaves and garden refuse. Cover plants with floating row covers as soon as you remove the winter mulch in the early spring. (Be careful, row covers may collect too much heat in midsummer. Use other controls during summer heat.)

Set up traps. Hang white sticky traps at the same level as the leaves as soon as the first flower buds appear (or even earlier). "Traps can't control them alone. They will help and do provide a good indicator for applying other controls," says Craig Harmer, an entomologist for Gardens Alive!, a mail-order organic gardening supply company in Indiana. Two or three traps per patch provides a monitor; one trap every 3 feet provides some control.

Give your plants a checkup. It's the young tarnished plant bugs (nymphs) that really do the damage, says Joey Klein, a certified organic market gardener in Vermont. Once you have adults, the nymphs will be along in a week or so. "Check for the nymphs themselves with a stiff sheet of white paper. Hold it under the flower clusters, and shake them. See if any little green things fall off onto the paper and start dashing away," explains Klein. If you see them, you are having problems *now*.

Attract beneficial bugs. Harmer says that natural tarnished plant bug parasites do exist and recommends plant-

BEDDY-BYE FOR STRAWBERRIES

Strawberries are called that for a reason. Straw is a good material for mulching paths in the strawberry bed during the summer. And in winter, covering the plants with 4 to 6 inches of straw mulch is very important. (Other organic mulches such as pine needles or sawdust also work well.)

Sonia Schloemann, the strawberry Integrated Pest Management coordinator at the University of Massachusetts at Amherst, recommends putting down mulch around Thanksgiving in Massachusetts or whenever the plants have become dormant for the winter in your area. "They need to be snuggled in to prevent cold damage and frost heaving, but as soon as they begin to grow in the spring, the mulch needs to come off the plants and into the rows," cautions Schloemann.

INSTALLING BIRD TAPE

ing fennel, which may help attract and overwinter them. Releases of minute pirate bugs may also help provide control.

Apply sabadilla as a last resort. "Sabadilla provides fairly effective control," says Sonia Schloemann, the strawberry Integrated Pest Management coordinator at the University of Massachusetts at Amherst. "Protect the flowers during bloom and early fruit set because that's when the tarnished plant bugs will do the most damage." Schloemann recommends using sabadilla about once a week.

BYE-BYE BIRDIE

Try bird tape to keep birds from nabbing your strawberries. Leonard R. Askham, Ph.D., an associate professor of vertebrate pest management at Washington State University at Pullman, has discovered that this narrow reflective tape is an inexpensive and effective way to scare birds. "But you've got to install it properly. Just laying it on the plants or along the top of a fence will have little or no effect after the first day or so," says Dr. Askham.

To install an effective bird foil, you'll need to suspend two parallel strips of tape along the length of each row, as shown in the illustration at left. The tape needs to be close to but not touching the plants and just at fruit level. Here's the method that Dr. Askham recommends:

1. Collect a roll of ½-inch-wide Mylar bird tape, some sturdy 1- to 1½-foot wooden stakes, a ball of strong string, a roll of fiberglass-reinforced strapping tape, a hand sledge, and a pair of scissors.

2. Draw an imaginary line along each side of the first row of plants about 4 inches away from the tips of the leaves. Pound in a stake on either side of the row at each end of your imaginary line. Pound in two more stakes at the other end of the row, for a total of four stakes. (If your rows are more than 30 feet long, add additional stakes on each side to break the row into shorter segments.)

3. Repeat Step 2 for each of your rows. If your walkways are very narrow (1 foot or less from leaf to leaf), use just one set of stakes between each two rows.

4. Tie a 2-foot-long piece of string around each stake 3 to 5 inches above the ground or mulch. Leave the ends hanging. (Tie two strings to stakes in the middles of the rows.)

5. Stick the end of a 6-inch-long strip of strapping tape to the end of the Mylar tape. Fold the strapping tape around and stick the loose end onto the other side of the Mylar tape to form a loop. Pinch the center of the strapping tape to itself lengthwise to keep the loop open.

6. Tie the loop to the string on an end stake. Unroll the Mylar tape to the next stake along the row. (The Mylar tape will be parallel to the row.) Cut the Mylar tape about 6 inches short of the next stake.

7. Following the instructions in Step 5, make a strapping tape loop on the end you just cut.

8. Give the Mylar tape 3 to 4 twists. "It's the twists that really make it work," stresses Dr. Askham. "They make the tape flash in all directions when the sun hits it." Slip the loop you just made onto the string on the current stake. Tighten the string until the tape is between 3 and 5 inches off the ground but still sagging slightly. Tie the string to keep the tape at that level.

9. Repeat Steps 4 through 8 until each row has Mylar tape along its length.

10. Walk along each row and make sure that nothing is touching the Mylar tape. It needs to move freely so that it flashes with the slightest breath of air. Remove any leaves and press down any mulch that may be touching the tape. It's a good idea to recheck the tape every few days during the season, too.

Nifty Fruits Indoors and Out

No matter where you live, there is a wide variety of interesting and tasty unusual fruits you can grow. There are hardy North American natives that thrive outdoors even in northern areas. If you have a small yard, there are plenty of delicious and even exotic fruits you can grow in containers. Try dwarf versions of conventional tree fruits like apples, or strike out in a more tropical vein.

GROW BLUEBERRY TASTE-ALIKES

Juneberries (*Amelanchier* spp.), also known as serviceberries and saskatoons, may be the most care-free berry you can plant. Michael McConkey, the owner of Edible Landscaping, a Virginia mail-order company that specializes in edible plants, thinks that everyone should have a bush or two. "They grow in just about any soil, unlike blueberries," says McConkey. "They're great to eat out of hand and taste a lot like blueberries. The small seeds are

Jujube

Pawpaw

Juneberry

softer than blueberry seeds and have a mild almond flavor. Cooked, the taste is indistinguishable from blueberries." McConkey's favorite is 'Jennybelle'.

Bill MacKentley, a co-owner of St. Lawrence Nurseries, a New York mail-order company that specializes in hardy fruits and nuts, is also a big fan of juneberries. "They are quite disease-resistant, and I've never seen any insect problems," he says. They're also a pretty ornamental, sporting showy white flowers in the spring and red leaves in the fall. MacKentley says that birds like juneberries, too, and so suggests planting a cultivar, such as 'Smokey' and 'Thiessen', that develops as a small tree. Each tree will bear huge quantities of fruit. You can leave the upper fruits for the birds and harvest your own from the lower branches.

PLANT PUCKER-FREE PERSIMMONS

Ripe persimmons have a rich, honeylike flavor and a jellylike texture. (Unripe persimmons can be puckery, to say the least.) American or native persimmons (*Diospyros virginiana*) are hardy to −25°F. Jim Gilbert, the owner of Northwoods Wholesale Nursery in Oregon, which specializes in unusual fruiting plants, recommends them as a low-maintenance tree. "They don't seem to be fussy about soil, don't suffer from pests or diseases or drought, and leaf out and bloom late, so they tend to avoid frost problems. They are also very attractive trees in the landscape," he says. 'Meader' is a very hardy and productive cultivar. It has delicious medium-size orange fruit, which is seedless, provided there are no male trees around to pollinate it. 'Garretson' is also good. It is very productive and ripens very early. The fruit is larger than that of 'Meader', and it is also often seedless.

Asian persimmons (*D. kaki*) are larger than their American cousins and do well where winters don't drop below 0°F. Gardeners in Zone 7 and south can try 'Jiro' (also known as 'Fuyu'), a non-astringent Asian cultivar with delicious fruit that can be eaten firm or soft.

JUJUBES: DATES FOR THE NORTH

Jujubes (*Ziziphus jujuba*), also called red or Chinese dates, are small trees with glossy leaves and attractive gnarled branches; they are hardy to −20°F. They bear loads of very sweet, reddish brown fruits that taste like apples when fresh. If they are allowed to hang on the tree after they ripen, they get shriveled and resemble dates in flavor and appearance. Michael McConkey, the owner of Edible Landscaping, a Virginia mail-order company that specializes in edible plants, says the trees require "no care, bear good fruit from an early age, and are very pretty." McConkey recommends against cultivating around jujubes since most are grafted on a thorny rootstock that will sucker freely if the roots are disturbed.

GET YOUR PAWS ON A PAWPAW

Plant a pawpaw (*Asimina triloba*) and you'll be planting an attractive, hardy, native American tree. Chances are you've never seen or tasted a pawpaw, but "pawpaw fruit is delicious," says Jim Gilbert, the owner of Northwoods Wholesale Nursery in Oregon, which specializes in unusual fruiting plants. "It has a custardy texture and a fruity banana-like taste. It's outrageous—very, very tasty. And the trees don't have any disease or pest problems." Gilbert gives this advice to would-be pawpaw planters:

◆ Get a plant that has been grown in and is sold in a deep pot. Don't buy a bareroot tree because they are very hard to transplant successfully.

◆ Named cultivars (grafted trees) are a better bet than seedlings for reliable fruit quality.

◆ Plant at least two trees for good fruit set. "Our trees set plenty of fruit every year, but some homeowners hand-pollinate the flowers to get more fruit," says Gilbert.

KEEP YOUR ORCHARD SHORT AND SWEET

Dwarf apples and peaches make delightful additions to your patio or yard. Robert Kourik, an edible-landscaping consultant in California, gives this advice for orcharding in containers: Choose the biggest container possible, and fill it with a coarse, lightweight potting mix. Consider setting your container on a sturdy, wheeled platform before filling and planting so that you can move it when you need to. Water your trees daily with a dilute seaweed/fish fertilizer solution to keep the soil moisture constant; if the mix dries out, it is almost impossible to re-wet. Kourik recommends 'Honey Babe' and 'Nectar Babe' as the best-flavored of the genetic dwarf peaches. Another genetic dwarf peach, 'Gar-

---

TRY TROPICAL FRUITS

If your tastes run to tropical and subtropical fruits, you can learn more about how to grow your own by joining the California Rare Fruit Growers (CRFG). Members share information about growing subtropicals via a quarterly magazine called *The Fruit Gardener* and a network of expert specialists. Despite the name, the organization isn't limited to California. For more information, write to:

CRFG
c/o Fullerton Arboretum
California State University
Fullerton, CA 92634

BURYING A FIG TREE

For northern gardeners, burying a fig tree in a 2-foot-deep trench lined with wooden boards is the surest way to avoid frost damage to the buds. In late fall, prune back the tree, and tie the branches with rope or twine. Dig out soil from the roots opposite the trench, and tip the tree into the trench as shown in the illustration below. Fill around the tree with straw or leaves. Cover the trench with a board, and shovel the excavated soil on top. Uncover the tree in spring after danger of hard frost is past.

den Delight', is a spectacularly beautiful tree in the spring when it is covered with double, dark pink blossoms. "I grow it even though it doesn't set much fruit in my climate," says Kourik. Almost any apple cultivar on 'M.27' rootstock makes a fine container tree.

FILL UP ON FIGS

Figs (*Ficus carica*) are a delightful fruit that you can grow outdoors or in containers. "The best fig for container growing is 'Petite Negri'," says Michael McConkey, the owner of Edible Landscaping, a Virginia mail-order company that specializes in edible plants. "It is a naturally dwarf plant and bears two crops of large, black fruit with a red, jamlike interior every year. One of our container plants was only about 3 feet high, and it bore 65 full-size figs at the same time." McConkey says figs are not as fussy as citrus about soil, but you should still use a coarse, well-draining mix. (See "Peel and Eat Appealing Citrus" on the opposite page for more information on container fruit growing.)

The aboveground parts of a fig tree are hardy to about 10°F, and the roots are much hardier. Some northern fig lovers successfully wrap the trees to protect them during the winter. Still others bury the entire tree for the winter, as explained in "Burying a Fig Tree" at left.

BURYING A FIG TREE

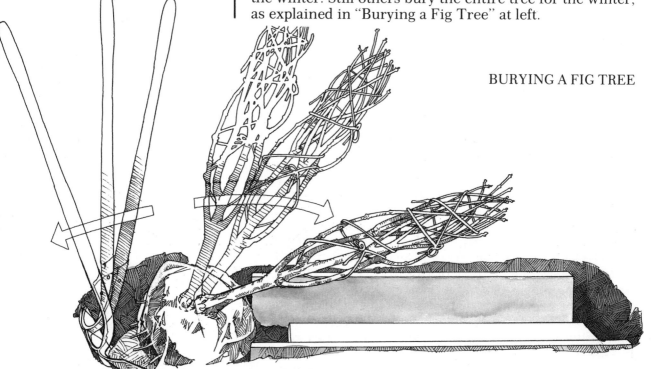

KISS A KIWI FOR DOWN-UNDER TASTE

Chances are you're familiar with the sprightly green flesh of the fuzzy kiwi (*Actinidia deliciosa*), the "grocery-store" kiwi. But did you know that you can grow these fruits in pots at home? "Fuzzy kiwis will bear fruit in a pot faster than they will in the ground. In fact, our plants often fruit in the nursery," says Jim Gilbert, the owner of Northwoods Wholesale Nursery in Oregon, which specializes in unusual fruiting plants. 'Blake' is a good choice for pot culture. It is a little less vigorous than some of the other fuzzy cultivars, and you only need one since it's self-fertile. Fuzzy kiwis are hardy to 0°F.

Hardy kiwis (*A. kolomikta* and *A. arguta*) taste like their larger cousins. They have smaller, fuzzless fruits so you can pop them into your mouth whole. Hardy kiwis are also good container subjects. In pots or in the ground, "the only way to grow kiwi is summer spur pruning," says Michael McConkey, owner of Edible Landscaping, a Virginia mail-order company that specializes in edible plants. "In the wild, a young kiwi wants to grow straight up. But when you are growing them for fruit, you want to rechannel that vigor into fruit production." McConkey recommends allowing the plant to grow without pruning until the main trunk is as high as you want it to reach. Then, pinch the growing tip so the plant won't get any taller. Each year when side-shoots get to be 8 inches long, pinch each shoot back to 4 inches with your fingers. McConkey recommends *A. arguta* 'Issai' for container growing. *A. kolomikta* cultivars (also known as super-hardy kiwi) are hardy to −40°F. *A. arguta* cultivars are hardy to −25°F.

PEEL AND EAT APPEALING CITRUS

With some special care, lemon, lime, and even grape-fruit trees will thrive and bear fruit in containers. "The most important thing in succeeding with citrus trees in containers is the soil you use. If it doesn't drain well enough, the tree will drown," says Michael McConkey, the owner of Edible Landscaping, a Virginia mail-order company that specializes in edible plants. "You need a loose mix that won't bog down. Use a mix of two-thirds peat, one-third perlite. Or try to copy the soil that the plant is growing in when you buy it." Water your citrus tree with dilute fish emulsion to feed it. 'Spanish Pink' lemon is one of the most beautiful of the citrus, with variegated green-and-white leaves and green-and-yellow-striped, pink-fleshed fruit.

SEXING KIWI

Most kiwi cultivars bear only male or female flowers so you need at least one male and one female to get fruit. If you buy a pair of kiwi plants and one dies, you'll need to plant another of the missing sex. If the plants are labeled, you can order a replacement right away. If not, just wait until the remaining vine flowers and see what sex those flowers are. Female flowers have a visible mini-kiwifruit in the center, while males have only anthers.

male flower

female flower

McConkey also recommends 'Persian' lime, 'Satsuma' mandarin, 'Moro' blood orange, and 'Oro Blanco' grapefruit as well-suited to pot culture.

Jim Gilbert, the owner of Northwoods Wholesale Nursery in Oregon, which specializes in unusual fruiting plants, says that a citrus tree in a container will do fine with half a day of sunshine. He warns that rapid climate changes such as moving a plant in or out of the house can cause plants to go into shock and lose leaves. "Make the change gradually," suggests Gilbert. "Put the container on wheels, and put it out for a few hours, then bring it back in. Each subsequent day, put it out a little longer. By the end of two weeks, it can stay out for the season." Reverse the procedure to bring the tree in at the end of the season. Gilbert also says that potted citrus trees are self-fertile and generally set fruit without being hand-pollinated. However, if your blossoms drop and no fruit forms, try using an artist's paintbrush to pollinate the next batch. To keep your citrus tree healthy, take it out of its pot every few years and root-prune it.

Nutty over Nuts

Nuts are perhaps the most overlooked type of plant in the home landscape. Nut trees have a great deal to offer, and they demand very little care in return. If you have sufficient space in your yard, you may want to try some of these tips from the experts and learn the pleasures of raising your own nut crops.

SEEDLING NUT TREES MAKE THE GRADE

When you shop for a nut tree, you will need to choose between grafted trees of named cultivars and seedling trees. Both types of trees have advantages. Seedlings often bear enough good nuts for a home planting. They are less expensive—a plus for tight budgets or for planting in quantity. A grafted tree will produce a known quantity of quality nuts but is more costly and may be a bit more delicate in the first few years.

If you want a few nuts to enjoy and have space for a few trees, it may make sense to plant seedling trees. "Since nuts haven't been bred and selected as much as many fruits have been, seedling nut trees are more likely to closely resemble their parents," explains Bill MacKentley, a co-owner of St. Lawrence Nurseries, a New York mail-order company that specializes in hardy fruits and nuts.

If you decide to get a grafted tree, be aware that some nurseries do not make a clear distinction between a grafted tree of a known cultivar and seedlings of that cultivar (which are *not* that cultivar anymore). If a tree's label doesn't say it's grafted, it's probably a seedling.

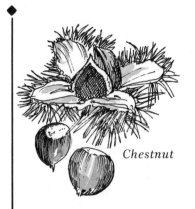
Chestnut

CULTIVATE USER-FRIENDLY PERSIANS

English walnuts (*Juglans regia*) have nothing to do with England and are more correctly referred to as Persian or Carpathian walnuts. Mostly, of course, they are just called walnuts. Walnuts have a reputation of being very tender trees, but "they can be grown anywhere peaches are grown. They share the same liability: Both have a low chilling requirement. They will break dormancy and start to open their buds in a January warm spell and then freeze," explains Bill MacKentley, a co-owner of St. Lawrence Nurseries, a New York mail-order company that specializes in hardy fruits and nuts.

Walnuts are easy to grow. They like rich, deep, well-drained soil and full sun. They grow slowly for the first few years, so be sure to keep the weeds away from them. Also, stake the trees so you won't mow them by mistake.

Black Walnut

CRACK INTO AN ELUSIVE BLACK WALNUT

Anyone who has ever tried to get the meat of a black walnut (*Juglans nigra*) out of its shell knows that it doesn't come out easily. Bill MacKentley, a co-owner of St. Lawrence Nurseries, a New York mail-order company that specializes in hardy fruits and nuts, explains the best way to get the meat out using a hammer: "Set the nut on its flatter side, with the suture line parallel to the surface it's setting on, and whack it with the hammer. [Not too hard, you don't want to pulverize the nut.] Then pick out the meat." For larger quantities of nuts, there are a number of crackers designed for efficient black walnut meat liberation.

Pine Nut

Black walnuts are great nuts for fresh eating, and their flavor stands up well to baking. They are higher in protein and lower in oil than English walnuts (*J. regia*). Black walnuts are also very productive trees. A full-grown tree produces 1,000 pounds of nuts or about 300 pounds of nut meats. "Now multiply *that* by the per-pound cost of black walnut meats at the supermarket," enthuses MacKentley, "and you'll really appreciate your tree's value."

There is one drawback to black walnuts. The trees put a substance into the soil around them that suppresses the growth of some other plants. Tomatoes, for example, will not grow under or near a black walnut. There are lots of plants which will, though, so don't let this prevent you from planting a tree or two. "Black walnuts have gotten a bad rap," says MacKentley. "Some things actually grow better under them. I find that raspberries and blackberries like growing under black walnuts."

GROW YOUR OWN PINE NUTS

Along with basil, cheese, garlic, and olive oil, pine nuts (*Pinus* spp.) are an essential ingredient of pesto. You may grow your own basil, but have you ever thought of growing the pine nuts yourself, too? Michael McConkey, the owner of Edible Landscaping, a Virginia mail-order company that specializes in edible plants, says "Anyone with a bit of patience can grow them. I recommend planting a Swiss stone pine [*P. cembra*]. It's a care-free tree with an extremely tight pyramidal form and makes a good substitute for spruce or fir in the landscape. It likes full sun and needs good air circulation but is tolerant of salt. A single tree will set a crop, and you'll be able to start making pesto in about ten years."

EMPTY NUT SYNDROME

No, this isn't a yuppy preoccupation of thirty-something-year-old nut trees, but it is a frustrating problem for would-be nut eaters. You crack open a plump nut, only to find a shriveled bit of brown skin instead of a fat nut meat. Bill MacKentley, a co-owner of St. Lawrence Nurseries, a New York mail-order company that specializes in hardy fruits and nuts, suggests a few reasons why this may happen:

Some nuts need cross-pollination to make nut meats. Butternuts (*Juglans cinerea*) need cross-pollination to make nut meats; black walnuts (*J. nigra*) don't Check with your supplier before you plant, and get two trees if they need cross-pollination. If you already have a tree that needs cross-pollination, plant another tree near it. Once the new tree starts to bloom, you should get filled nuts.

Winter injury can cause empty shells. Check with your

supplier and make sure that any tree you plant is hardy in your area. If you have a bearing tree that isn't hardy, you may want to replace it with a hardier tree that will fill nuts every year.

Climate can affect nut production. "If your nuts are partially filled, pollination isn't your problem," says McKentley. Partially filled nuts may mean the tree needs a longer growing season than you have. Again, check with your supplier before you plant, and consider replacing an existing tree with a more suitable tree.

THE GARDEN PROFESSIONALS

Leonard R. Askham, Ph.D., is an associate professor of vertebrate pest management in the Department of Horticulture and Landscape Architecture at Washington State University at Pullman.

Helen Atthowe is a plant production manager for Bitterroot Native Growers, a wholesale nursery specializing in native plants, located in Corvallis, Montana. She also manages her own organic farm, raising tomatoes, strawberries, raspberries, and apples.

Bruce Barritt, Ph.D., is a horticulturist at the Washington State University Tree Fruit Research and Extension Center in Wenatchee, Washington. His area of research is orchard systems, especially tree pruning and training, tree density, and rootstock support systems.

Sam Benowitz is the owner of Raintree Nursery in Morton, Washington. The nursery specializes in edible plants for the home gardener, primarily fruit trees, nut trees, and berries.

Hunter Carleton is co-owner of Bear Creek Nursery, a mail-order nursery near Northport, Washington, that specializes in antique and cold-hardy apple cultivars, as well as other fruits and nuts.

Jim Gilbert is the owner of Northwoods Wholesale Nursery in Molalla, Oregon. He specializes in unusual fruiting plants such as kiwis, persimmons, figs, Asian pears, passionflowers, and passion fruits.

Barbara Goulart, Ph.D., is an associate professor of pomology at the Pennsylvania State University in University Park, Pennsylvania. She conducts research and extension programs focusing on strawberries, raspberries, and blueberries.

Craig Harmer is an entomologist for Gardens Alive!, a mail-order company in Lawrenceburg, Indiana, that sells organic gardening and farming products. Harmer manages the biocontrol laboratory, where insects are produced and shipped.

Roger Joy is the founder and manager of Canyon View Nursery in Corvallis, Montana, and is a horticultural consultant. He has more than 20 years of experience in the nursery business; his specialty is grafted nursery stock.

Robert Kime is a research scientist at Cornell University's Agricultural Experiment Station in Geneva, New York. His research work concerns clarification and haze problems of fruit juices and wine. He also keeps bees and

---

CULTIVARS GALORE

If you are looking for a specific cultivar or trying to locate mail-order sources that specialize in a certain type of fruit, you will find your answer in a book called *Fruit, Berry, and Nut Inventory*. This extensive listing of cultivar names is compiled by the Seed Savers Exchange. Check it out at your local library, or to buy a copy, contact:

Seed Saver Publications
R. R. 3, Box 239
Decorah, IA 52101

THE NEWEST OF THE NEW

You can be the first on the block to plant that new and superior cultivar, sometimes even before it has a name. The New York State Fruit Testing Cooperative Association (NYSFTA) gives you the chance to plant the newest apples, strawberries, plums, peaches, and many other fruits. Members receive an extensive catalog and can purchase nursery stock available nowhere else. For more information, write to:

NYSFTA
P.O. Box 462
Geneva, NY 14456

produces Kime Farms honey, a beeswax moisturizing cream, and honey wine.

Joey Klein is the owner of Littlewood Farm in Plainfield, Vermont. He is a certified organic market gardener, specializing in strawberries, broccoli, carrots, and kale. He sells directly from his farm and through nearby food co-ops.

Robert Kourik is a free-lance writer, publisher, consultant, and landscape designer in Occidental, California. He is the author of *Designing and Maintaining Your Edible Landscape Naturally*.

Michael McConkey is the owner of Edible Landscaping, a retail mail-order company in Afton, Virginia. He specializes in less-care edibles such as persimmons, mulberries, figs, and blueberries.

Randolph E. McCoy, Ph.D., is the owner of Champlain Isle Agro Associates in Isle LaMotte, Vermont, a company specializing in tissue culture production of disease-tested planting stock, especially bramble fruits.

Bill and Diana MacKentley are co-owners of St. Lawrence Nurseries in Potsdam, New York, a mail-order company specializing in northern hardy fruit and nut trees.

Michael Maltas is the garden director of the organic showpiece garden for Fetzer Vineyards in Hopland, California. Maltas grows acres of vegetables, flowers, and fruit at the Fetzer Valley Oaks Food and Wine Center.

Eunice Messner is a fruit specialist coordinator for the California Rare Fruit Growers, Inc. She grows many kinds of fruits and vegetables on an intensively planted, terraced slope in her backyard in Anaheim Hills, California.

Bill Nash is the owner of Owens Nursery in Gay, Georgia. Owens Nursery is a retail and wholesale mail-order company, specializing in hostas and muscadines.

Jean M. A. Nick is an associate editor of garden books for Rodale Press, Inc. She has extensive experience in the commercial greenhouse industry and currently raises vegetables and small fruits on 1 acre in her home garden.

Timothy Nourse is the president and owner of Nourse Farms, Inc., in South Deerfield, Massachusetts. Nourse Farms produces strawberry and raspberry plants, selling primarily to commercial growers.

Robert T. Olsen, Ph.D., is a retired chemist who has grown over 50 different cultivars of grapes in his ¼-acre research vineyard on Cape Cod.

Paul Otten is the general manager of North Star Gardens in St. Paul, Minnesota. The nursery specializes in bramble fruits, selling primarily to commercial berry producers and garden centers but also to small-scale growers.

Frank Pollock is an organic grower. He raises garlic and specialty potatoes on his Rolling Hills Farm in Saylorsburg, Pennsylvania, and sells them via mail order across the United States.

Lon J. Rombough is an independent consultant and breeder of unusual fruits in Aurora, Oregon. He is also the coordinator of fruit interest groups of the North American Fruit Explorers (NAFEX) and the consultant for NAFEX's grape test group.

Sonia Schloemann is the strawberry Integrated Pest Management coordinator in the Department of Plant Pathology at the University of Massachusetts at Amherst. She does research on crop rotation schemes, cover crop rotations, and selected compost applications for strawberry production, and she leads on-farm visits and workshops for growers.

Herbs

Growing herbs is a pleasure for all of your senses. You can enjoy their beauty in the garden and in arrangements, their marvelous flavors in cooking, and their pungent scents in potpourri and cosmetics. In this chapter, you'll find lots of tips from the experts on how to make growing and using herbs fun and easy.

Herb-Growing Basics

Herbs are great for the novice gardener. They grow quickly, and most can tolerate a range of soil conditions. Plus, many are naturally pest-resistant. Whether you grow them indoors or out, in the garden or in containers, there's an exciting variety of herbs and herb-growing methods to choose from.

GETTING OFF TO A GOOD START

There's no mystery to growing great herbs—just meet their basic needs, and they'll reward you with bountiful harvests. At Well-Sweep Herb Farm in New Jersey, Louise Hyde, a co-owner of the farm, teaches workshops to guide beginning growers through their first herb garden. Here are the tips she stresses:

Choose the right site. Most herbs need lots of sun and well-drained, fertile soil.

Have your soil tested. If you have any doubts as to your soil's fertility, it's best to have it tested and then make adjustments to balance fertility levels. "It's a myth that herbs don't need nutrients," says Hyde. "What you put in is what you get out." At Well-Sweep, plenty of compost is added to the soil each year.

Start with plants, not seeds. With most herbs, buying plants is easier than starting your own from seed. "The exceptions are easy annuals like dill and borage, which can be sown directly outdoors," says Hyde. She adds that you can start basil seeds indoors in pots and then transplant the seedlings outdoors.

COLLARS KEEP HERBS CLEAN

Keep your culinary herbs free of grit by surrounding them with an easy-to-make collar. Simply take a plastic flowerpot, cut out the bottom, and set the pot over the plant, bottom-end-up. The collar supports the stems of herbs like parsley, chives, and oregano that tend to get floppy. This keeps the leaves from resting on the soil, so they stay clean. All you need to do is snip them off and give them a quick rinse before using.

Make a plan before you plant. First decide on a focal point, like a birdbath or sundial, then add paths for easy access and to define planting areas. Give your garden a permanent spot, but leave room for expansion.

Plant at the proper spacing. For perennials, 18 to 24 inches between plants is a good rule of thumb. Some herbs such as thyme and parsley tolerate closer planting (about 6 to 8 inches apart).

Water immediately after transplanting, then check the soil and water only as needed. "Herbs don't like to be wet," says Hyde. "Wait until the top inch of the soil is dry before watering again. This will help prevent problems with fungal diseases."

Don't forget to mulch. After you plant, spread a fine mulch to conserve moisture and control weeds. Be sure to continue to pull weeds that grow through the mulch.

KEEP CREEPING HERBS UNDER CONTROL

Some herbs—mints, costmary, and bee balm, for example—can grow *too* well and will readily spread far beyond the site in which they were planted. How can you keep them from taking over garden space needed for other plants?

"Just put mints and other spreaders someplace where it doesn't matter if they spread," says Marjie Fortier, a co-owner of Meadowbrook Herb Garden in Rhode Island. "Plant them beside the garage or along an edge of the lawn, and simply mow over the ones that creep out too far."

Fairman Jayne, who along with Kate Jayne co-owns Sandy Mush Herb Nursery in North Carolina, offers the same advice, adding that the aromatic plants scent the air when mown, making yard work a little more pleasant. Fairman also suggests another technique for controlling invasives: "Cut the bottom out of a plastic bucket, sink all but the top inch or two in the ground, fill it with soil, and plant your mint or whatever in there," he says.

Another control tip: "Never till under an herb that spreads by creeping stems [root stolons]," says Kate. "If you do, every little piece will root and grow. Before you know it, you'll have an entire garden full of that one herb." Comfrey, mint, and horseradish are examples of herbs best left untilled. Give them their own beds well away from plants that need cultivation.

Growing herbs in containers can serve several purposes in the garden. Bottomless containers are a great way to control the outward creep of spreading herbs like mint. Or if you are growing frost-tender herbs like lemon verbena and rosemary, sink their pots into the garden soil during the growing season. Come fall, it's easy to lift the plant, pot and all, and bring it indoors.

PUT THE LIGHT ON HERBS

When choosing a location for herbs, remember that most types prefer at least 5 hours of full sun a day. Some, however, will do just fine in shadier spots. Here's a useful rule of thumb from Fairman Jayne, a co-owner of Sandy Mush Herb Nursery in North Carolina. "In general," says Jayne, "plants with narrow, thick leaves—such as rosemary or lavender—need lots of sun and relatively little moisture. Plants with broad, thinner leaves—basil, for instance—will tolerate some shade and need more moisture."

Jayne encourages growers with less-than-ideal sites to try growing the herbs they want anyway. "You might end up with leggy plants," he says, "but you'll still get good, fresh herbs."

KELP SPRAYS HELP BUILD HEALTHY HERBS

"Kelp is the best-kept horticultural secret," says Bertha Reppert, the owner of The Rosemary House and Gardens in Pennsylvania. Besides supplying plant nutrients, liquid kelp also helps control insect pests and prepares perennial herbs for winters spent indoors or outdoors.

A LITTLE OFF THE TOP

Stimulate new growth and keep your plants in good shape by pruning your herbs regularly. Herbs such as pineapple sage (*Salvia elegans*), basil, scented geraniums, and thymes quickly become spindly without pruning or harvesting. So if your herb plants are strictly ornamental, plan to prune and shape them at least once each month when they're actively growing during warm summer months. If you have culinary herbs, harvest from them as needed or trim them on the same schedule as your ornamentals.

ALWAYS BE PREPARED

On each trip to the garden, no matter the purpose, carry your shears or clippers and make sure to stop by the herb patch. You may not have planned on harvesting today, but there's almost sure to be something (a snip of this, a blossom of that) you can trim and bring indoors to add to the next meal.

THESE HERBS SOW THEMSELVES

Many herbs are so easy to grow that they'll practically plant themselves. You need to sow or transplant them into the garden the first year and then let a few of each kind go to seed. The seeds will fall and germinate the following spring. Some seedlings may pop up in the most unexpected places. Enjoy the informal effect, or transplant the young seedlings to where you want them to grow. Here are some of the most dependable self sowers:

Agrimony (*Agrimonia eupatoria*)
Borage (*Borago officinalis*)
Caraway (*Carum carvi*)
Chervil (*Anthriscus cerefolium*)
Coriander or cilantro (*Coriandrum sativum*)
Dill (*Anethum graveolens*)
Fennel (*Foeniculum vulgare*)
German chamomile (*Matricaria recutita*)
Lemon basil (*Ocimum basilicum* 'Citriodorum')
Roman chamomile (*Chamaemelum nobile*)
Sweet wormwood (*Artemisia annua*)

KEEP RUBBER BANDS HANDY

Keep small rubber bands looped around the neck of your herb scissors. They'll be easy to find when you're harvesting bunches of herbs in the garden.

Reppert originally used kelp solution primarily as an organic fertilizer to promote blossoming. Outdoors, however, she found that herbs sprayed with kelp also tended to be more tolerant of winter cold. Indoors, kelp-treated container-grown herbs had greater tolerance of dry, low-light conditions. As an added bonus, a spray of kelp solution helped to control pests as they appeared.

To make your own multipurpose spray, start with a bottle of liquid kelp (also sold as seaweed extract); it is available from most garden suppliers. To make a solution, mix 1 tablespoon of liquid kelp with 1 gallon of water. Use the solution for watering, or apply it as a foliar spray. When using it as a spray, add a few drops of liquid dishwashing detergent: It will help make the solution stick to plant leaves.

BLEND BRICKS WITH HERBS

The earthy tones of weathered brick are a perfect complement to the grays and greens of an herb garden. You can use carefully designed patterns and straight angles to

heighten the formal effect, or you can set the bricks in curves for an appealing informal look. Setting bricks on a sand foundation is a good job for do-it-yourselfers. The inevitable irregularities are just part of the charm, especially when herbs make themselves at home in the crevices between the bricks.

Brick pathways meander through the demonstration garden at Well-Sweep Herb Farm in New Jersey. The bricks are set in sand, and thymes have sprung up in nooks and crannies between the bricks, adding a touch of informality to the well-ordered gardens. "Plants won't disturb the bricks," says Louise Hyde, a co-owner of the farm. But bricks can become slippery when wet, she notes. The paths at Well-Sweep's public garden are swept frequently to keep the brickwork clean and prevent slips caused by wet autumn leaves and other debris. Sweeping the leaves off of the path also keeps them from matting down and smothering the plants growing between the bricks.

USE STRAWS TO START STRAIGHT TOPIARIES

Having trouble getting your herbal topiaries off to a good start? Cyrus Hyde, a co-owner of Well-Sweep Herb Farm in New Jersey, suggests enclosing the stem with a clear plastic drinking straw to encourage a straight stem. "This is the most effective method I've found, and beginners find it easy, too," says Hyde. Here's his method:

1. Choose a plant with a straight center stem at least 8 inches tall. Remove the leaves and side branches from the bottom part of the stem where the straw will rest.

2. Slit the straw along its length, rotating it while you cut to create a spiral. Then wrap it around the stem as shown in the illustration on page 250.

3. When suckers form around the base, prune them away. To keep plants upright, Hyde says, "You can support the stem with a stake inserted in the soil, next to the stem. I like to use a long length of twist tie to attach the stem to the stake."

4. When your plant outgrows its straw support, remove the straw and re-place the twist tie as shown in the illustration on page 250. Every six to eight weeks remove the tie, and rewrap it loosely. This prevents marks on the stem as the plant grows.

5. When the top of the plant reaches the height you want, pinch off the growing tip to encourage the stem to

MAKE A TRICOLOR TOPIARY

For something a little different, make a three-colored topiary standard using elfin herb (*Cuphea hyssopifolia*). Start with young seedlings of elfin herb with white, pink, and scarlet blossoms. Plant them closely in the same container; then, braid the stems together as they grow. Support the braided "stem" with a stake inserted in the soil at the base of the plants. Use twist ties to keep the stems upright. The end result will be a topiary with white, pink, and scarlet blooms at the top.

TOP HERBS FOR TOPIARIES

Here are some of the easiest plants to work with for creating charming herbal topiaries:

Basils (*Ocimum* spp.)
Bay (*Laurus nobilis*)
Curry plant (*Helichrysum angustifolia*)
Elfin herb (*Cuphea hyssopifolia*)
Lemon verbena (*Aloysia triphylla*)
Licorice verbena (*Lippia alba*)
Myrtle (*Myrtus communis*)
Rosemary (*Rosmarinus officinalis*)
Scented geraniums (*Pelargonium* spp.)

CHEAP COLOGNE SENDS PESTS PACKING

If you keep potted herbs indoors during winter, keep a small atomizer filled with inexpensive cologne near your plants. Give occasional pests a quick spritz. Alcohol in the cologne will kill common indoor plant pests, and you'll add a pleasant fragrance to the air instead of fouling it with stronger pesticides.

GIVE BUGS THE COLD SHOULDER

Many herb flowers make great salad sprinklings, but you're not the only one to admire edible blossoms—plenty of insects do it, too. If insects are a nuisance in your edible blossoms, freeze them! After harvesting, toss the blossoms in a resealable bag, then partially inflate and seal it. Place the bag in the freezer for several seconds, just long enough to stun the insects without damaging the blossoms. The insects will drop from the blossoms. Take the bag out of the freezer and quickly remove the blossoms, leaving the stunned insects behind.

HERBAL
TOPIARY

branch out. As side branches form, pinch them back lightly to form the shape you want. Hyde suggests that you feed topiaries every three to four weeks with a fish emulsion solution to encourage new growth. To retain the shape as they mature, trim every four to six weeks.

Preserving and Cooking with Herbs

Once your herb plants are established and growing vigorously, you can begin to enjoy the fun of harvesting, storing, and using them to create tasty herbal creations. Here are some suggestions from the experts.

FREEZE HERBS FOR FUTURE FLAVOR

When your herbs are ready to pick but time is short, try the fast freezer method to preserve herbs in a hurry.

"Drying?! I don't dry herbs at all. I don't have time!" exclaims Cathleen Lalicker, a co-owner of Story House Herb Farm in Kentucky. "I freeze them in resealable plastic bags, since it takes only a few minutes of time during the busy growing season. Just about every fresh herb I've tried freezes well, including parsley, dill, oregano, and basil. They retain their green color and flavor much better than dried herbs. When I'm cooking, I'll break off a frozen leaf or two and add them to the pot."

You can pack whole plants into bags or chop the foliage in a food processor first. Don't wash the herbs unless they're gritty with soil. Pat them dry, fill the bags, press out the air, and seal the bags. Use a waterproof marker to label each bag with the date and name of the herb. When a recipe calls for fresh herbs, remove what you need, reseal the bag, and return it to the freezer. If a recipe calls for dried herbs, simply substitute twice as much of the frozen ones.

Lalicker once found a stray bag of basil in her freezer, left over from two years before. "The quality was excellent, although the color was a less vibrant green," she says. "Still, I'd recommend that you only freeze enough to last the winter, until your plants begin producing again the next season."

MICROWAVE MAGIC DRIES HERBS IN A HURRY

For the gardener on the go, microwaving is a fast and easy way to dry a small harvest. "Running an herb business doesn't leave much time for the traditional methods of preserving herbs," points out Judith Merritt, the owner of Squire's Herbary in Pennsylvania. "I like to use an electric food dehydrator to dry large batches of fresh herbs when they're at peak quality. But for small batches, I use the microwave—if I have a handful of fresh herbs left over from a recipe—because it's fast."

Here's how Merritt microwaves herbs:

1. Arrange the herbs in a single layer on a paper towel or piece of waxed paper on the floor of the microwave.

2. Microwave the herbs on high for 2 minutes, check the herbs, then turn the towel or paper.

3. Repeat Step 2 until the herbs are crisp and dry.

4. Store the dry herbs in glass jars labeled with the name of the herb and the date.

FRIDGE-DRIED HERBS

To preserve your leafy green herbs while retaining much of their flavor and color, try drying them in the refrigerator. Harvest as usual, rinse, and pat dry; remove leaves from stems, if desired. Put the leaves or leafy stems in a brown paper bag in the refrigerator. They'll dry in three or four weeks. This technique is particularly effective with tarragon, basil, chervil, savory, parsley, and celery leaves.

Making herbal vinegars is a fast and easy way to preserve your harvest. Just fill a clean glass jar with your favorite fresh culinary herbs, and cover them with warm (not boiling) vinegar. Let the vinegar cool, and then cover the jar. (If you are using a metal cap, line it with plastic wrap first.)

For best results, store the jar in a cool, dark place and use as needed. If you want your vinegars for display, strain out the herbs, pour the vinegar into decorative bottles, and add a few sprigs of fresh herbs. Deeply colored herbs like purple basil can add a beautiful hue to your finished product.

Use herbal vinegars in any recipe that calls for vinegar—they are wonderful in salad dressings or as marinades. Herbal vinegar is also handy as a hair rinse, to make the hair shiny and keep the scalp healthy. Add 1 tablespoon of herbal vinegar per 1 quart of water, and pour it over wet hair after shampooing. Do not rinse.

MAKE "LIQUID BASIL"

Pinching off the growing tips of basil every few weeks will encourage the plants to be bushy and compact. But what do you do with all those leafy tidbits of flavor? Don't waste them on the compost pile! Libby Goldstein, a Pennsylvania food and garden writer, keeps canning jars of olive oil, canola oil, and vinegar on her kitchen counter and drops in any pinched-off leaves that she can't use fresh. The result: delicious herb-flavored condiments. "If the herbs in a jar start looking sort of nasty and pickled," says Goldstein, "I just pour the liquid through a coffee filter [into an empty jar], toss the old leaves out, and add new ones. Then when the oil or vinegar smells and tastes about right to me, I pour it through a filter one last time and bottle it up in a nice-looking container."

Goldstein uses her "liquid basil" in a variety of ways. "The oils are great on salads and for sautéing vegetables or chicken," she says. "And herb vinegar is excellent for deglazing pans, for making vinaigrette, and for seasoning steamed or sautéed vegetables." Goldstein sometimes adds cinnamon-basil vinegar or lemon-basil vinegar to a washbowl of hot water in the morning to make a refreshing facial rinse. "It makes getting out of bed not all that bad," she laughs.

HERBAL COOKING MADE EASY

When beginning herb gardeners enter the kitchen with their first harvest, they'll often try to follow recipe directions and guidelines precisely. "I try to get by with as few rules as possible," says herb grower and author Ellen Spector Platt, the owner of Meadow Lark Flower and Herb Farm in Pennsylvania. Here are Platt's favorite nonrules:

Harvest herbs for cooking when you have the time, no matter what time of day. Platt says, "The big difference in herb flavor is between fresh and dried herbs and not between morning or evening picking." Fresh herbs will always taste better than dried herbs, no matter what time of day you picked them.

Most herbs go with everything. Stand by your favorite combinations, but don't be afraid to try new ones. Remembers Platt, "One winter, the only fresh herb I had was rosemary, and it tasted wonderful in everything I made."

Frozen herbs are the best-flavored alternative to fresh herbs. "But if you have to use dried herbs," says Platt, "crush them before you add them to the pot. Crushing releases the flavor." If you're using a recipe that calls for dried herbs, you can substitute fresh herbs—just use 2 to 3 times more than the recipe calls for. Remember that most herbs don't require cooking: Add them to the pot just before serving. The exceptions are stewing herbs, like bay, that are best when simmered over low heat.

Locate your herb garden near the kitchen. "This is one rule that I advise herb growers to follow! You're most likely to use the plants you've grown if they're located just a few steps away," says Platt.

The Pleasure of Potpourri

Potpourris and herbal essential oils are a wonderful way to enjoy the fragrances of herbs indoors. Try the following tricks to experience the luxury of custom-blended scents.

CUSTOM-BLEND A POTPOURRI

"Making potpourri is a lot like cooking," says Gene Banks, the owner of Catnip Acres Herb Nursery in Connecticut. "In the kitchen, you can create a specially flavored broth by blending the flavors of celery, onions, carrots, and potatoes. To make a pleasing potpourri, you blend aromas instead."

First, select a predominant fragrance (like lavender), then add a complementary fragrance (like cinnamon). These fragrances can come from the herbs and spices themselves or from a few drops of highly concentrated essential oils. You'll also want to include a material known as a fixative, which helps to slow the evaporation of the essential oils and makes your potpourri stay fragrant longer. Common fixatives include dried orris root, dried calamus root, and oak moss. Fixatives and essential oils are generally available in craft shops. You can also add aesthetic ingredients, like colorful home-dried flowers, just for their appearance. See "Potpourri Precautions" on page 255 for information on how to protect your skin and nasal passages while making potpourri. Here is a simple formula for creating a potpourri:

Banks' Basic Potpourri Recipe
1 tbsp. fixative
    Several drops essential oil
1 quart dried flowers, leaves, and stems
    Several tbsp. whole or crushed spices

PICK YOUR FAVORITE PESTO

There's more to pesto than just basil! Try substituting other culinary herbs in your basic pesto recipe, and create a taste sensation that will win over even the most devoted basil lovers. You can, for example, add tender garlic tops in early spring, before other herbs begin producing. Or replace the basil with thyme, coriander (cilantro), or a combination of parsley and rosemary. If the flavors are too strong, replace one-half of the strong herb with the relatively mild-flavored parsley. For an added twist, try substituting ricotta or grated mozzarella for the Parmesan cheese. Here's a basic pesto recipe that will work with any culinary herb:

2–3 c. packed fresh herb leaves
  2 cloves garlic
  ½ c. olive oil
  2 tbsp. pine nuts, walnuts, or
      cashews (optional)
  1 tsp. salt (optional)
  ½ c. finely grated Parmesan
      cheese (optional)

Blend together herb leaves, garlic, and oil with nuts and salt (if using) in a blender or food processor until thoroughly pureed. Transfer to a small bowl, and stir in the cheese (if using). Serve over hot pasta, spread lightly on fresh bread, add to leafy salads, or use in any recipe that lists pesto as an ingredient.

Yield: 1 cup sauce

VARIATIONS ON A THEME

Here are some blends to in-spire you when mixing potpourris:

Spicy scent. Use 2 table-spoons each of whole cloves and broken cinnamon sticks.

Sweet scent. Include 2 cups of lavender and 2 vanilla beans.

Musky scent. Add ½ cup of patchouli leaves and ½ cup of sandalwood chips.

Fruity scent. Add 1 cup each of dried citrus peel, rose- and lemon-scented geranium leaves, and lemon balm or lemon ver-bena leaves.

AROMATHERAPY AT HOME

If you are interested in exper-imenting with aromatherapy, use the lists below to help you choose the ingredients for your custom-blended potpourris:

For a Relaxing Aroma

Juniper
Lavender
Patchouli
Rose geranium
Sandalwood

For a Refreshing and Energizing Aroma

Lemon
Orange
Rosemary

For a Sedating Aroma

Cedar shavings
Cinnamon
Frankincense
Ginger
Rose
Ylang-ylang

Work with a glass or wooden bowl and utensils. (Do not use metal.) Mix the fixative and essential oil, then add the dried materials. (Make sure the dried materials really are dry, or your potpourri may turn moldy.) Add the spices for a richer scent. When you're finished mixing, put the potpourri in a sealed glass jar in a dark spot to "simmer" for several weeks. Check it every few days, and shake it to blend the ingredients. After three to four weeks, your pot-pourri will be ready to use.

CHANGE THE MOOD WITH POTPOURRI

Want to unwind after a stressful day at the office or perk up to enjoy an evening out? Try using essential oils to help change your mood. For thousands of years, herbalists have recognized that some scents, like lavender, promote relaxation, while others, like lemon, have a refreshing effect. New research seems to be confirming the role of essential oils and other herbal constituents in medicinal use. Arlene Kestner, Ph.D., a research psychologist at Southern Univer-sity in Louisiana, is investigating the effects of aromatics on human behavior. Dr. Kestner explains, "Some essen-tial oils and other aromatics react with body chemistry to make you feel a certain mood or emotion. This is such a new area, however, that amateurs should proceed very cautiously."

Dr. Kestner suggests experimenting on your own with small amounts of essential oils or fresh and dried herbs. In a bath, use just a few (no more than six) drops of essential oil or add several sprigs or blossoms of fresh or dried herbs to create a light scent. Use herbal oils for massaging weary muscles, and enjoy the aroma as part of the benefit. Or design your own therapeutic potpourri, using the sugges-tions given in "Aromatherapy at Home" at left. Be sure to use only pure essential oils, not synthetic fragrance oils, which tend to lack the rich blend of aromatic components available in natural oils. See "Potpourri Precautions" on the opposite page for information on how to protect your skin and nasal passages while making potpourri or handling essential oils.

SCENT YOUR HOME FROM TOP TO BOTTOM

Besides using bowls of potpourri to scent the air, there are lots of tricks you can use to bring the delightful fra-grances of herbs into your home. "I like to think about potpourri on a grand scale," claims Gene Banks, the owner of Catnip Acres Herb Nursery in Connecticut. One trick that Banks uses to spread herbal fragrance is dabbing a few drops of herbal essential oil on a dust cloth for cleaning. You can also add several drops of herbal essential oil to a handful of baking soda, spread the baking soda over the rug, and then vacuum it up. Toss herbal sachets into the clothes dryer to scent clothing as it dries. You can even make your own scented drawer liners with old wallpaper. Put a few drops of essential oil on the paper, roll it up with several sprigs of dried herbs, let it sit for several weeks, then remove the herbs. Line your drawers with the scented paper to keep clothing and linens smelling fresh.

THE GARDEN PROFESSIONALS

Gene Banks is the owner and operator of Catnip Acres Herb Nursery in Oxford, Connecticut, which sells over 400 kinds of herb plants and scented geraniums.

Marjie Fortier is a co-owner of Meadowbrook Herb Garden in Wyoming, Rhode Island. This certified organic farm grows and sells fresh and dried herbs, herb teas, and herb seasonings by mail order and in health food stores around the country.

Libby Goldstein is a food and garden writer and is the president of the Philadelphia Food and Agriculture Task Force, a coalition of organizations involved in food and agricultural policy. As a former Philadelphia County extension director, she was a prime force in establishing community gardens in downtown Philadelphia.

Cyrus and Louise Hyde are co-owners and operators of Well-Sweep Herb Farm, which offers a broad selection of herb and perennial plants and is located in Port Murray, New Jersey.

Fairman and Kate Jayne are the owners of the Sandy Mush Herb Nursery in Leicester, North Carolina. They carry over 900 different kinds of plants and specialize in rare and unusual plants, both native and foreign.

Arlene Kestner, Ph.D., is a research psychologist at Southern University in Baton Rouge, Louisiana. She specializes in the effects of aromatics on behavior. She is also the owner of Good Scents, a specialty herb company.

Cathleen Lalicker is a co-owner and operator of Story House Herb Farm in Murray, Kentucky, which specializes in organic herb plants for the kitchen and garden.

Judith Merritt is the owner and operator of Squire's Herbary in Slatington, Pennsylvania. At the herbary, she sells herb plants and products, hosts traditional English teas, and gives tours of her formal gardens.

Ellen Spector Platt is an herb grower and owner of Meadow Lark Flower and Herb Farm in Orwigsburg, Pennsylvania. She is the author of *Flower Crafts.*

Bertha Reppert is the owner of The Rosemary House and Gardens in Mechanicsburg, Pennsylvania. The nursery offers herb seeds, some herb plants, scented geraniums, and saffron bulbs. She is the author of *Herbs with Confidence* and *A Bride's Herbal.*

POTPOURRI PRECAUTIONS

It's a good idea to wear a dust mask and rubber gloves when mixing batches of potpourri. When stirred, dried herbs release clouds of dust that can irritate nasal and bronchial passages. Rubber gloves will protect your hands from concentrated essential oils, which can irritate your skin.

THROW A HANDFUL OF HERBS

Instead of the usual rice, toss a fragrant herbal blend at weddings. Mix equal parts of bird seed and dried herbs or flowers. Be sure to include rosemary for remembrance, roses for love, and lavender for a loyal heart.

HEAT ADDS HEIGHT TO IMPATIENS

Gardeners in hot, humid climates should know that their impatiens will grow taller than the label states. According to Alan Zaeske, the regional product manager for Goldsmith Seeds, impatiens may grow at least 20 percent taller than usual because of warm nights and high rainfall. Keep this point in mind when selecting cultivars by label heights to mix with other plants in beds so your impatiens don't end up dwarfing their companions.

THESE IMPATIENS BEAT THE HEAT

Some impatiens have been bred to keep their short stature even in southern climates. Michael Murgiano, the promotion manager for Sluis & Groot America, a marketing company for a Dutch seed and bedding plant company, recommends the horizontally spreading, 1-foot-high 'Impulse' series for heat- and drought-prone areas. The University of Georgia agrees and has given the 'Impulse' series a gold medal for its performance in heat and drought.

Simon Crawford, a technical services specialist for the Pan-American Seed Company in Illinois, says the extra-dwarf 'Super Elfin' series of impatiens also resists growing rangy in warm climates. For best results with any impatiens, provide them with moist soil and partial shade, especially from afternoon sun.

Flowers

What can brighten a yard like flowers? They will fill your garden or entire landscape with color. Once you watch an ugly wall become a tapestry of clematis stars or a winter-bare bed erupt with purple crocus and golden daffodils, you will be tempted to grow more. You may begin to look for better ways to grow flowers, delightful plant combinations, and new cultivars with outstanding characteristics.

Build from season-long displays of annual flowers to perennials, long-lived but with a shorter bloom season. Bolster your spring bulb display with more color or longer periods of bloom. Plant biennials, a group that contains some of the most beloved cottage garden flowers like foxgloves and violas. Try your hand at roses, the aristocrats of the bunch. There are more easy-care roses now that gardeners are lobbying for lower-maintenance gardens.

In this chapter, you will get the latest scoop straight from American flower experts, the people who are propagating, breeding, distributing, and designing with flowers. You will profit from their new discoveries and enjoy their original ways of using classic flowers.

Annuals

Annuals are the natural starting point in the world of flowers. They're easy to plant and care for, provide quick results and summer-long bloom, and are a source of inexpensive pleasure in the garden. The following tips will help you get the most from your annuals.

COVER UP THOSE ANNUAL BEDS

Annuals grow wonderfully in an organically enriched soil. But the source of the organic matter can make a difference. Jim Nau, the new varieties manager for Ball Seed Company in Illinois, doesn't add manure to annual beds. "People grew annuals in manured flower beds back at the turn of the century. When you see them pictured, the plants look big and bulky from all that nitrogen. They are a little ungainly. So instead of manuring our trial gardens, we plant them with a winter cover crop like winter wheat [*Triticum* spp.] or winter rye [*Secale cereale*]."

Every year, Nau pulls out his old crop of annuals in mid-September. He tills the soil and plants a cover crop. In early spring, he works the cover crop into the soil. His target date is March 15, which allows some time for the crop to decay completely before annual planting time. For instructions on planting cover crops, see "How to Covercrop" on page 94.

"If you try to plant before the greenery is well-rotted, it will tie up nutrients as it decomposes and reduce flower size and potential for growth," Nau says. "People may not realize how long decomposition takes, especially when the weather is cool in spring. If you have to plant early, counteract the nitrogen unavailability by side-dressing with fish emulsion."

VINCAS VANQUISH DROUGHT

Annual vinca cultivars (the new *Catharanthus roseus* hybrids) are becoming hot items in areas where drought strikes frequently. They thrive in sun, heat, and low moisture. However, if you want to start vincas from seed, you'll have to take these special precautions:

Avoid cold feet. Keep the soil warm before and after seed germination. "Young vinca seedlings cannot tolerate cold feet," says Michael Murgiano, the promotion manager for Sluis & Groot America, a marketing company for a Dutch seed and bedding plant company.

Check soil pH. Watch the soil pH and the kind of nitrogen you use when you start vinca in peat-based mixes. Kenneth Peck, a technical advisor for A. H. Hummert Seed Company in Missouri, says, "Vincas are resentful of high-pH [or alkaline] soils and sulk if fed with an ammonia form of nitrate." Of course ammonia isn't usually a problem in organic nitrogen fertilizers, but it could be present in manure.

GO BOLDLY BEYOND BEDDING PLANTS

If you're bored with the same dozen bedding plants featured at your local garden center every year, it may be time to branch out into the world of unusual flowers from seed. "It is so much more exciting to try something different,"

SHORTER SNAPS WON'T RUST

If you live in an area that has humid summers, you may have given up growing rust-prone snapdragons. In humid areas, the old, tall cultivars will discolor and fade early. However, you can put snaps back on your shopping list. Look for the new, more rust-resistant snaps like 'Floral Carpet', says Simon Crawford, a technical services specialist for the Pan-American Seed Company in Illinois.

DOWNSIZING APHID UPSURGE

Tiny aphids cluster on shoot tips, reproducing so quickly that they can do more damage than much larger pests. Plant a diversity of species to deter these soft-bodied pests. Use lots of marigolds, which tend to deter aphids, and fewer aphid favorites such as coleus, nasturtiums, and impatiens. And before you take home greenhouse plants, don't forget to check carefully to be sure they are aphid-free.

PRINCESS VI?

If you like old-fashioned Johnny-jump-up (*Viola tricolor*), try the new 'Princess' viola series. These cool-season annuals bear larger flowers of yellow, cream, blue, or dark purple. They bloom from April to July, but then they usually fade out of flower. Replant in midsummer for a repeat display in fall.

CLASSY CLEOME COMBOS

Cleome (*Cleome hasslerana*) is often the star of the Ball Seed trial gardens. Jim Nau, the new varieties manager for Ball Seed Company in Illinois, plants a medium-tall annual about 15 inches in front of the cleome. It fills in to hide the cleome's lower stems, which may drop leaves in late summer. An edging annual completes the picture. Here are three of Nau's favorite combinations:

1. 'White Queen' cleome combines well with 'White Nicki' flowering tobacco (*Nicotiana alata* 'White Nicki') and a contrasting dark purple ageratum such as 'Royal Delft' or 'Royal Hawaii'.

2. 'Violet Queen' cleome's striking purple color contrasts nicely with cream-colored salvia (*Salvia farinacea*) cultivars, such as 'Victoria White', or 'Century Cream' celosia (*Celosia cristata* 'Century Cream'). 'Grape Cooler' vinca (*Catharanthus* 'Grape Cooler') is a good edging for this combination.

3. Plant 'Rose Queen' cleome with 'Empire Dark Salmon' salvia at its feet and bronze-leaved 'Encore Red/Bronze' begonias as an edging.

says Peter Loewer, a North Carolina garden writer.

Many unusual species are available in extensive seed catalogs, such as Thompson and Morgan, J. L. Hudson Seedsman, and Redwood City Seed Company, or from seed swaps organized by gardening societies and magazines. However, Loewer cautions, don't buy exotic seed just to be exotic. Find one that you think is attractive and that's likely to thrive in your situation.

"I usually don't believe catalog descriptions," says Loewer. "Instead, I pick plants based on other people's recommendations." You can also find information about interesting plants in newsletters from specialized plant societies and associations, such as the the American Rock Garden Society. Loewer also points out that local botanical gardens and horticultural societies are tremendous resources for gardeners.

Loewer recommends two unusual flowers to get you started on your quest for extra garden interest:

Basket flower (*Centaurea americana*) is a relative of the cornflower (*C. cyanus*). This annual bears flower buds that resemble woven straw baskets. The buds open to reveal a lavender asterlike flower. The plant will reach 4 feet tall, blooming in three months if you sow it directly in the garden in spring. However, unlike most common bedding annuals, the basket flower browns and dies after it blooms. Keep sowing the seed so you'll continue to get bloom through the growing season.

Common evening primrose (*Oenothera biennis*) is a biennial wildflower that will reward you with sulfur-yellow blooms the year after planting. "The flowers open at night and release a lovely fragrance that attracts an unbelievable number of beautiful moths," Loewer says. The biennial evening primrose grows about 3 feet tall and is good in a wild garden or the back of a perennial garden. It spends the first year in a low foliar rosette before stretching up to flower the second. It will set seed, so you don't have to keep sowing it. "Once you start growing them, you will have them forever. The plant can get a little weedy, but you can easily pull out the seedlings you don't want while they are in the rosette stage," says Loewer.

OLD-FASHIONED FLOWERS MAKE THE CUT

As cottage gardens become more popular, old-fashioned flowers are coming back into their own. "Old-fashioned flowers leave a glimmer in many people's memories. Or sometimes people see them in contemporary cottage gardens. They are struck by their graceful appearance and fragrance, which are much different than compact bedders or commercial cut flowers," says Wendy Krupnick, the manager of the trial gardens for Shepherd's Garden Seeds in California.

Many old-fashioned flowers have long stems and durable blossoms, so they excel as cut flowers. Here is Krupnick's list of best old-fashioned flowers for cutting, which are illustrated at right. All thrive in full sun.

'Five-Color Mix' cornflower (*Centaurea cyanus* 'Five-Color' mix) brings to mind British cottage gardens. These perky blue, wine, pink, muted red, and white flowers, also known as bachelor's-buttons, have attractive, rounded heads. This mix contains five colors developed for the florist trade about 20 years ago, when cornflowers were popular.

'Satin Cups' farewell-to-spring (*Clarkia amoena* subsp. *whitneyi* 'Satin Cups') produces satiny flowers for cool seasons. It bears open, cup-shaped flowers with contrasting throats or edgings. These can be carmine-rose, lilac, blush pink, salmon-orange, lilac, rose, or white. They grow up to 2 feet tall in light soil.

Rocket larkspur (*Consolida ambigua*) is a 1- to 5-foot-tall spring bloomer with emphatic upswept flower spikes up to 14 inches long. Cultivars are available in dark blue, lilac, carmine, sky blue, rose, salmon, pink, and white.

Canterbury bells (*Campanula medium*) produces dainty, ruffle-edged, bell-shaped flowers that are said to resemble the harness bells on British carriages. They bloom in blue-violet, dusky rose, and white in mid-season on stems up to 2½ feet tall. Because they are biennials, plant the seedlings one season for blooms the following year.

AMERICAN ANNUALS FOR ARID AREAS

Somewhere in the United States, somebody is facing a drought. If that somebody is you, you don't have to skip planting annual flowers. Just pick some of the new and improved natives that can take dry feet. Nona Wolfram-Koivula, the executive director of the National Garden Bureau, has seen a half-dozen of these homespun heroes thrive in trial gardens nationwide. "There is a trend toward people looking for natives that are easy to grow and tolerant of heat and drought. Most of them have been bred in foreign countries and then returned to us as annual cultivars,"

Canterbury Bells

Rocket Larkspur

Farewell-to-Spring

Cornflower

Calliopsis

Blanket
Flower

California
Poppy

Prairie Gentian

ANNUALS FOR
DRY CONDITIONS

Wolfram-Koivula says. The following annuals (illustrated at left) are some she recommends:

'Lady in Red' Texas sage (*Salvia coccinea* 'Lady in Red') is a native of the southern United States with long, graceful spikes of red flowers that hummingbirds and butterflies love. This cultivar was developed in Holland and has won an All-America Selections Award for its American performance.

Prairie gentian (*Eustoma grandiflorum*), a Texas native, was developed in Japan as a long-lasting cut flower before returning as a star to the United States. A tender perennial, this waxy-flowered lavender-, pink-, or white-blooming beauty will tolerate heat and, when established, also holds up in drought.

Blanket flower (*Gaillardia pulchella*) is a 2-foot-tall plant with red, yellow, or mixed red-and-yellow daisy flowers. A native of the arid western United States, it withstands heat and drought better than most annuals.

Marigolds (*Tagetes* spp.) include the petite French and bold American and African cultivars. Despite their exotic names, all are native to the New World, from Arizona south to Argentina. Marigolds thrive in sun and tolerate dry soil, although they prefer moister surroundings.

California poppy (*Eschscholzia californica*) will grow in soils too dry for most plants, but it can't take high heat. Grow it if you have dry soil and moderate summers.

Calliopsis (*Coreopsis tinctoria*), the annual counterpart of the popular perennial coreopsis species, bears gold and russet flowers. It is native from Minnesota to California and grows best in dry soils and full sun.

SEPARATE SPARKLING FLOWERS

When you're designing annual beds, consider whether the colors of your flowers are bright and sparkling or soft and muted. Jim Nau, the new varieties manager for Ball Seed Company in Illinois, finds that the two color types look best if they're kept separate. If you must mix them, he suggests planting the muted colors in larger masses so they can hold their own. Flowers with muted colors include annual vinca (*Catharanthus roseus*), celosias (*Celosia* spp.), salvias (*Salvia* spp.), ageratums (*Ageratum* spp.), and asters (*Aster* spp.), while those with sparkling colors include begonias, snapdragons, marigolds, and zinnias.

"You need to be cautious when you combine iridescent, bright colors with dull pastels—the ones that won't sparkle in light. The bright colors will make the muted ones look washed out," says Nau. "Be especially cautious of using white flowers. It is easy to overuse white. Here in Chicago, we get so much white during winter, we get complaints if we put white flowers out in summer."

But an entire bed of muted flowers looks great. "Try 'Century Cream' celosia, 'Victoria' blue salvia ['Victoria' mealy-cup sage], and 'Grape Cooler' vinca," says Nau. Or combine either sparkling or muted flowers with intermediate-tone flowers with glossy petals. These include cleome (*Cleome* spp.), geraniums, impatiens, petunias, zinnias, and begonias.

Perennials

Perennials are the heart of the flower garden—the basis of borders and cottage gardens everywhere. Use these lovely flowers to add life to your garden. We asked the experts to take the guesswork out of growing these sometimes finicky flowers and to give you lots of new ideas for using your perennials wherever you want lasting color.

"POP!" GOES THE BORER

Borers are the bane of bearded irises. They tunnel down flowerstalks or leaves, leaving hollows that can collapse. They can reach the rhizomes and consume them from the inside out. The borer tunnels invite the invasion of rots, which finish off whatever is left of the plant. "When borers attack, they can really devastate irises. We had a severe year recently and were lucky to save enough pieces of one of our own border bearded irises to introduce it two years later," says Dorothy Willott, an iris breeder from Ohio.

To spray for iris borers, you must catch the larvae just as they hatch and before they enter the shelter of the leaf or stalk interior. Or if you just have a few iris plants, follow Willott's three-step hands-on approach:

1. Avoid planting the most susceptible irises.
2. Pull off all dead iris leaves in very early spring. Bag, burn, or otherwise destroy them. This eliminates most borer eggs left over from the previous season.

MULTIFLORAS HAVE MORE TO OFFER

Heather Will-Browne, a bedding plant specialist at Walt Disney World in Florida, manages the flower trials at Disney to test cultivars before they go into the theme park. She suggests that gardeners looking for the toughest cultivars of traditional bedding plants choose the multiflora types. "Multifloras have smaller flowers than grandifloras, but there are so many more of them, and they hold up to the weather so much better than the giant-flowered types," she says. Petunias, gerberas (*Gerbera* spp.), and pansies are three annuals that have multiflora cultivars.

grandiflora

multiflora

SIX EASY PERENNIALS

In his gardens, Mark Viette, the manager of Andre Viette Farm and Nursery in Virginia, tests perennials from around the world. He has found six that stand out as exceptionally handsome but easy to grow:

'New Hampshire' hardy geranium (*Geranium sanguineum* 'New Hampshire') has a larger flower than the species, a strong purple flower color, and a long bloom season.

Lenten rose (*Helleborus orientalis*) remains one of the great early-blooming shade plants. The foliage is handsomely cut and dark, glossy green. The green-purple, often mottled flowers emerge very early and can last for over a month.

'Switzerland' Shasta daisy (*Chrysanthemum × superbum* 'Switzerland') is a 30-inch-tall, single-flowered daisy that stays upright without staking and does not melt out or collapse in heat.

'Viette's Dwarf Form' baby's-breath (*Gypsophila paniculata* 'Viette's Dwarf Form'), bred by Viette's grandfather on the nursery grounds, is more compact and graceful than many cultivars.

Ornamental oregano (*Origanum herrenhausen*) has purple foliage and bright red to violet blue flowers from July to September. It forms 15-inch-tall clumps that don't overrun their space.

'Aphrodite' August lily (*Hosta plantaginea* 'Aphrodite') is a double-flowered hosta with glossy, heart-shaped leaves and upturned flowers.

3. Identify borer leaf trails to find where they are hiding. The trail begins with a tiny opening where the larvae enter the leaf. Pull the leaves apart where the fan folds, and you can see where they have softened the leaf tissues. To kill borers, squeeze them between your finger and thumb while they are still in the leaves. "If you hear a pop, you got the borer," Willott says.

Some borers will tunnel down the bloom stalk into the rhizome. These borers are the easiest to eliminate. Just cut off the flowerstalk at the base as soon as the flowers fade so the borers lose access.

PLANTS AT STAKE

There is no perfect way to hold a floppy perennial plant upright. If you cannot avoid staking, be prepared to compromise the plant's appearance at some point in the growing season. Allan M. Armitage, Ph.D., a professor of horticulture at the University of Georgia, explains, "It seems no option is perfect. If you use pea stakes in spring, it looks bad until the plant fills out. If you wait to pull the plant together after it flops, it loses its natural shape after staking. I really dislike staking. I do my best to avoid it. It is not hard if you site plants properly."

Wendy Krupnick, the manager of the trial gardens for Shepherd's Garden Seeds in California, agrees: "How much you need to stake depends on where tall plants grow. They are more likely to get leggy and weak if you plant them in shade or if they are overcrowded."

But a little crowding may help a floppy perennial. Dr. Armitage likes to let a slightly leggy 'Autumn Joy' sedum (*Sedum* 'Autumn Joy') lean on the strong leaves of yellow flag iris (*Iris pseudacorus*). The dusty meadow rue (*Thalictrum flavum*), which can get 5 feet tall and floppy, will trundle over and through a sturdy, shrubby perennial like a peony.

When you know a plant will need staking, ask yourself what part of the stem is the weak point. Flowers like peonies and lilies have sturdy enough stems but very large blossoms that weigh them down. Dr. Armitage waits until the buds swell to stake these.

Taller plants can fall into two categories: Some, such as tall delphinium cultivars, produce long, flimsy stems that break at the top when in flower. They need support that reaches close to the summit of the spike. Others, including ironweed (*Vernonia* spp.), have long, sturdy stems that break at the bottom from the combined weight of the stem and flower. These will stay upright if you either support the lower stems by wrapping them with jute held fast to 1-foot-tall posts or enclose them in metal plant hoops.

STAKING PERENNIALS

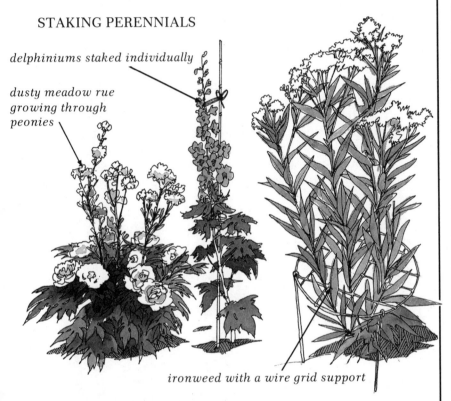

delphiniums staked individually

dusty meadow rue growing through peonies

ironweed with a wire grid support

PILLARS FOR A PRETTIER BORDER

A perennial border is most appealing when you blend plants with different shapes and sizes. However, the tall, vertical spires of plants such as hollyhocks or delphiniums seldom last longer than a month. Their lofty flower shoots fulfill your appetite for height. But when the bloom is through, the tall stem flops, dies back, or needs trimming, and your upright accent is gone.

For vertical interest that you can count on during both summer and winter, Landon Winchester, a staff horticulturist for White Flower Farm, a nursery in Connecticut,

**MORE PLANTS
FOR PILLAR TOWERS**

Clematis (*Clematis* spp.)
makes a choice cover for vertical
towers, but Landon Winchester, a
staff horticulturist for White Flower
Farm, a nursery in Connecticut,
says other vines will do a nice job
as well. Try the perennial trumpet
vine (*Campsis radicans*), silver
lace vine (*Polygonum aubertii*),
and, for a more fleeting but equally
spectacular show, the annual
moonflower (*Ipomoea alba*).

recommends training flowering vines onto columns, pillars, or posts. "When covered with woody vines, they take the winter curse off the herbaceous border," Winchester says. He recommends clematis vines for perennial pillars, as shown in the illustration below. Here's how to make one:

1. Select wire fencing with openings wide enough for the foliage to slip through. For clematis (*Clematis* spp.), Winchester recommends grids that have 2 to 4 inches between the vertical and horizontal wires. If you intend to use the pillar in the back of the border, start with a piece of fencing 5 to 6 feet tall and 6¼ to 9½ feet wide. For smaller gardens or midborder locations, start with a 3 × 3-foot piece. Bend the fencing to form a column, and use pieces of heavy aluminum wire to tie it closed. Space the wire ties every 6 to 8 inches from top to bottom along the seam. "The wire ties will stay there forever," says Winchester.

2. Pound a metal fence post deeply into the soil beside the location you have chosen for the pillar. With more

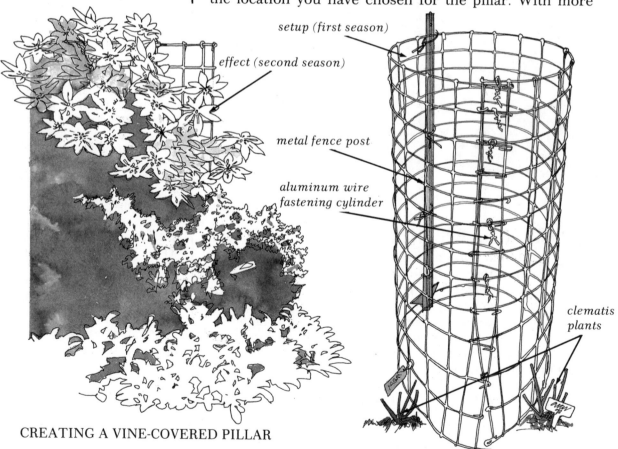

effect (second season)

setup (first season)

metal fence post

aluminum wire
fastening cylinder

clematis
plants

CREATING A VINE-COVERED PILLAR

aluminum wire, tie the cage to the fence post in several locations.

3. Plant one or several clematis vines to wind through and cover the cage. With the 5- to 6-foot pillar described above, you would need to plant two clematis on the open face of the pillar. If the pillar is in the center of the rear of the border, both could go toward the front. If it is closer to the end of the garden edging the patio, put one plant in the front. Set the second plant so it faces the patio and gives the pillar depth.

Choose the clematis cultivars with care. They should be long enough to drape the tower but not so long that they bury it. Stick with more-compact cultivars on smaller pillars. Expand to the longer vining cultivars for taller pillars at the back of the border. Then, guide the flexible young stems, if necessary, so they will fill in open areas and create a solid cover.

PUT A STOP TO ROOT ROT

If you have perennials that have mysteriously died off, chances are they were victims of root rots. These diseases attack from the bottom up, so you may not notice their presence until it is too late for the plant. Yet you can easily avoid situations that predispose perennials to root rots, says Jim Brady, the owner of Sunbeam Gardens in Ohio.

If you grow perennials in heavy clay or poorly drained soil, the roots could be swamped with water for days or weeks. Most of these plants eventually will fall prey to rots. However, it's easy to keep perennial roots safe, says Brady. When you dig a hole for a new perennial, put some gravel or coarse sand in the bottom and plant on top of it. "I use a bucketful of gravel in a 2-foot-diameter hole and top it with a little soil. I have yet to find any root rot after this treatment," Brady says.

Brady also uses composted pine bark fines (shredded pine bark). This fine-textured organic matter will fight the water mold fungi that cause rots. Pine bark releases turtanical acid, a natural fungus fighter. "Add pine bark fines to peat-based soil mixes when you grow perennials in containers," Brady suggests. "And use it to mulch perennial beds instead of hardwood bark. Put on 1 inch in spring, and it will work down into the earth as you pull weeds."

MINIMIZE MILDEW

Powdery mildew is one of the most common fungal diseases that affect perennials. The telltale symptoms are a dusty white coating on the leaves, especially young leaves. Fortunately, some species and cultivars are resistant.

Phlox That Knock Out Mildew

If mildew has destroyed your garden phlox (*Phlox paniculata*), try 'Sternhimmel' ('Starry Sky'), one of the new German cultivars, says Mark Viette, the manager of Andre Viette Farm and Nursery in Virginia. This plant suffers less mildew and blooms much longer than most garden phlox cultivars.

Jim Brady, the owner of Sunbeam Gardens in Ohio, recommends the new cultivars of early-summer-blooming phlox including 'Alpha', 'Omega', and 'Delta' (*P. maculata*), as well as the older 'Rosalinde' and 'Miss Lingard' (*P. carolina*).

Asters That Ax Mildew

For asters that are not susceptible to mildew, Brady recommends compact 'Purple Dome' New England aster (*Aster novae-angliae* 'Purple Dome') and 'Alma Potschke', and the Opal series of New York aster (*A. novi-belgii*), including ice blue 'Royal Opal'.

These Bee Balms Beat Mildew

Bee balm (*Monarda didyma*) is another mildew-susceptible perennial. Viette recommends these mildew-resistant cultivars: mahogany-colored 'Sunset' and orchid pink 'Beauty of Cobham'. Brady suggests 'Gardenview Scarlet'.

GRAVEL MIX GIVES GREAT DRAINAGE

Gardeners with heavy clay soil can make an ideal home for their perennials by digging out a bed at least 1 foot deep and replacing the soil with a mix of one-third humus, one-third rotted manure, and one-third pea gravel, says North Carolina garden writer Peter Loewer.

"Perennials may not die in hard, heavy, wet clay, but their fleshy roots will tend to just sit there. This gravel mix allows the roots to go down easily and water to drain away. Not only that, but the crushed stone warms up during the day, causing water to condense on it at night, quenching the thirst of tiny roots and root hairs," says Loewer. Another advantage, Loewer notes, is that the replacement mix won't turn to mud and be splashed on the plants during heavy rains.

SQUARE-FOOT PRAIRIE

If you have been pondering adding a low-maintenance garden of casually meandering prairie perennials, take a few tips from Paul Rudloff, the nursery manager for Prairie Nursery in Wisconsin:

1. Select plants that are hardy and that grow well in your soil type. They can carry on with little effort on your part. "The key here is planting only the plants that will tolerate your soil. You should only need to amend [the soil] in extreme cases," Rudloff says.

2. Prepare and plant the garden with weed fighting in mind. Remove existing vegetation, a big step toward reducing competition from weeds. Strip off sod layers. Pull out fleshy perennial weed roots. Dig out woody plant stumps.

3. In the spring, set one-year-old, transplant-size perennials into the cleared area as close as possible, one in each square foot. They will leave minimal room for weeds. "Although large-scale seeding rates are much denser, our recommended transplanting rate has been quite successful. It gives the mature plant enough soil space for its root system," Rudloff says.

4. When the prairie plants emerge from dormancy, mulch the areas between plants with a thick layer of straw. Don't let the mulch touch the plants. Once the plants have been in place for four to six weeks, you can pull any weeds that emerge—any earlier and you might pull up the perennial as well. An alternative to pulling is to cut off the foliage of annual weeds before they set seed.

"I can weed a new 60-square-foot prairie in 40 minutes," Rudloff says. "And I seldom have to repeat it every week." Once the plants are growing, they maintain their own space by shading out weed seedlings.

LITTLE GARDEN ON THE PRAIRIE

When you picture a prairie, you may think of tall grasses and large meadow flowers blowing in the breeze. But there's no need to limit your prairie or native plantings to the big and brassy. Paul Rudloff, the nursery manager for Prairie Nursery in Wisconsin, explains that spring begins with diminutive bloomers, which are superseded by progressively taller species. An everblooming prairie garden might start its spring show with the following:

- Prairie buttercup (*Ranunculus rhomboideus*), 5 inches tall
- Pasque flower (*Anemone patens*), 8 inches tall
- Prairie smoke (*Geum triflorum*) 1 foot tall
- Shooting-star (*Dodecatheon meadia*), up to 2 feet tall

"These simply don't need to grow as tall because there is no competition around that early in the season," Rudloff says.

STRETCHING YOUR ZONE

If you have been limiting yourself to growing just the perennials that are listed as hardy in your climatic zone, you are in for a pleasant surprise. Perennial hardiness ratings can be a bit flexible, explains Bill Boonstra, a manager of Bluestone Perennials in Ohio: "United States Department of Agriculture zone ratings do not translate to perennials exactly. After all, perennial plants are hiding underground in the winter. How well they survive depends more on whether there is an insulating snow cover, some other source of heat, and good water drainage."

Here, Boonstra details some examples from his own garden:

Snow cover keeps them alive. Japanese anemone (*Anemone × hybrida*) and *Aster × frikartii* 'Monch' will grow reliably in Boonstra's northern Ohio, Zone 5 garden. Yet they often perish in Kentucky's warmer Zone 6 winter. The difference is that Boonstra lives in the snow belt. His gar-

BIG, BOLD FOLIAGE PLANTS

Try a plant with huge or enticingly textured leaves to spice up the perennial garden. Jim Brady, the owner of Sunbeam Gardens in Ohio, recommends the following plants:

Sea kale (*Crambe maritima*) grows 3 feet tall, bearing glossy, blue leaves that make a big splash. You can blanch and eat the tender spring shoots. Or try colewort (*C. cordifolia*), which towers over 5 feet tall with long, hairy leaves. The flowers billow out in a great baby's-breath-like flower head.

Silver sage (*Salvia argentea*) is loved for its shaggy-haired leaves up to 6 inches long. The plant reaches 2 to 4 feet tall, bearing a graceful candelabra of white flowers touched with pink or yellow.

Ornamental rhubarb (*Rheum palmatum*) grows as tall as 6 feet, with mammoth, heavily cut leaves.

den is covered with snow most of the winter. With this insulation, the soil temperature hovers at 30°F within several inches of the surface.

A heated foundation helps. African lilies (*Agapanthus* hybrids), which thrive in California and Florida, survive the winter for Boonstra despite air temperatures as low as −20°F. What's his secret? He planted them 5 inches away from his heated basement's foundation.

Lighter soils boost survival rate. Winter survival will drop, Boonstra warns, where soils remain wet in winter or early spring. Hardy garden mums (*Chrysanthemum* × *morifolium*), for example, fail when they sit in boggy soil. The problem is most perilous in spring. The soil has thawed, but it is not warm enough for growth to begin, so the roots stagnate and suffocate. But you can beat this barrier to hardiness. Encourage water to drain away from often-saturated gardens: Lighten the soil with lots of compost, or add topsoil and organic matter to raise the bed 4 to 8 inches above the surrounding areas.

PINCH AND SAVE

If you are tired of straddling sprawling plants, take this tip from Allan M. Armitage, Ph.D., a professor of horticulture at the University of Georgia: Pinch potential sprawlers or buy compact, self-supporting cultivars.

Potential sprawlers. Dr. Armitage pinches 'Autumn Joy' sedum (*Sedum* 'Autumn Joy') when it gets to be 9 to 12 inches tall. He trims the tip off each shoot, leaving four or five nodes, or leaf junctions, at the bottom of the stem. Several nodes will sprout sturdy, new, and shorter branches.

Dr. Armitage also pinches fall-blooming mums. "I have mums roaming everywhere. I couldn't possibly stake them all," he says. "So I pinch them three or four times through the spring and early summer. Twice is probably enough in northern areas with shorter seasons. The important thing is to stop before the plants set flower buds, or you could delay or stop flowering dead."

Compact cultivars. Many new cultivars are more compact, self-supporting versions of the species. Look for the following favorites of Dr. Armitage: 'Mariesii' or 'Sentimental Blue' balloon flowers (*Platycodon grandiflorus* var. *mariesii* and 'Sentimental Blue'), 'Goblin' blanket flower (*Gaillardia* × *grandiflora* 'Goblin'), blue star (*Amsonia* *tabernaemontana* var. *montana*), 'Goldsturm' black-eyed Susan (*Rudbeckia fulgida* var. *sullivantii* 'Goldsturm').

WINTER MULCH WRECKS WET BEDS

If you have a heavy clay soil and you mulch your perennial beds in winter, you can do more harm than good, says Bill Boonstra, a manager of Bluestone Perennials in Ohio.

"When the ground is frozen, plants are in suspended animation. But when the ground thaws and plants sit in soggy, mulched soil, they get soft. Then diseases attack. You can create this situation by putting winter mulch on too early in the winter or by not taking it off with the first thaw," says Boonstra. "Around northern Ohio, we often have midwinter thaws. Problems can get a start during a thaw if you don't go out and pull the mulch off. In the end, you might find the plants that survived winter best are those you forgot to mulch in the first place."

Bulbs

Bulbs are the bright lights of the garden—the stars of early spring, the fireworks of summer, and the glowing counterpoints to fall mums and asters. Here, the experts tell you their own tricks for growing and storing bulbs and provide plenty of ideas on using interesting bulbs to extend your season, as well as great ways to mix bulbs with other plants.

DON'T PUT YOUR BULBS IN BONDAGE

Foliage feeds your daffodils and tulips, making the bulbs fat and healthy for next year's flowering. To ensure the success of next year's flowers, let the foliage mature naturally, advises Brent Heath, a co-owner of the Daffodil Mart in Virginia. "Please don't strangle your daffodils," pleads Heath. Tying the leaves in knots or bunches cuts off air circulation and reduces the amount of sun that reaches the leaves for food production. Cutting off bulb foliage altogether before it yellows is also bad for bulbs. You can draw attention away from the ripening foliage with other plants, such as hostas or shallow-rooted annuals, but avoid shading the bulb foliage too much. After the leaves turn yellow, they are no longer feeding the bulb, and you can cut them back safely.

YARROWS FOR LONG-TERM BLOOM

If you want color you can count on, look for new yarrow cultivars bred for an extended season of bloom. Jim Brady, the owner of Sunbeam Gardens in Ohio, recommends the 'Galaxy' series yarrows. These include 'Paprika', 'Heidi', 'Hope', 'Salmon Beauty', and 'Appleblossom'. All have large heads of flowers that open in one color and fade on the plant to another complementary color. For instance, 'Hope' opens creamy yellow and fades to gold. 'Appleblossom' opens bright pink and fades to a clear white.

Mark Viette, the manager of Andre Viette Farm and Nursery in Virginia, recommends 'Altgold' fernleaf yarrow (*Achillea filipendulina* 'Altgold'). It bears deep gold flower heads in summer and fall.

KEEP THOSE BARE BULBS COVERED

When Jim Brady, the owner of Sunbeam Gardens in Ohio, plants spring-flowering bulbs in his rock garden, he wants to make sure he doesn't damage them when they're dormant, so he marks their location in one of two ways: Either he sets a 6-inch-long bamboo stake next to the clump when it emerges in spring, or he plants hardy geraniums (*Geranium* spp.) or hostas on top of the bulbs. The perennials fill the area when the bulb leaves are disappearing and keep them safe from the hoe or shovel.

PANSIES DOUBLE BULB BLOOM SHOW

Gardeners in Zones 6 and warmer can plant pansies between tulips, daffodils, and other tall, spring-flowering bulbs. To do this, plant the bulbs first, using toothpicks to mark where the bulbs are planted. Then plant the pansies in the spaces between the bulbs. As the bulbs grow in late winter, they push through the pansies, and you'll have double the show when the weather is mild enough for both to bloom.

LEAVE THOSE TULIP LEAVES!

Since foliage is so important to bulbs, it's a good idea to cut it sparingly or, better yet, not at all when gathering flowers for indoors. Combine other greenery, such as ferns or hosta leaves, with your bouquet of tulips, and let the tulip leaves mature and feed the bulb.

LILIES LIKE DRY FEET

If you like lilies, plant them in a location that drains quickly after a rainstorm. Otherwise, they won't last long. "Lilies can't stand with their feet in water. If they are submerged in water for three to five days, they will rot," says John Vandenberg, the owner of Vandenberg Bulb Company in New York.

BRAZEN LILIES BEAT SUMMER HEAT

Pastel-colored lilies and heat do not make good bedfellows. But the sturdy, hot-colored cultivars can survive a sweltering summer and still put on a good show. John Vandenberg, the owner of Vandenberg Bulb Company in New York, recommends the following heat-tolerant cultivars for steamy summers: orange 'Jolanda', yellow 'Pollyanna', and red 'Red Night'. All mature at 3 feet tall. However, in very hot weather, 'Red Night' and other red-flowered lilies typically fade to shades of orange. "You will only get true reds where summers are cooler," Vandenberg says.

ANNUALS MASK FADING BULB FOLIAGE

Spring-blooming bulbs are beautiful, but their fading foliage isn't. To keep your garden looking spectacular both during and after bulb bloom, plant annuals like marigolds and petunias in gaps between the bulbs. The annual foliage will fill in and cover the dying bulb foliage, and the annual flower show will pick up where the bulbs left off.

TRIPLE-DECKER BULBS

If you go for bulbs in a big way, don't limit yourself to planting a single layer. Kathy Zar Peppler, a public relations consultant for the Professional Plant Growers Association, likes to set three, even four, tiers of bulbs into any given spot in a flower bed. "You will get the maximum amount of bloom in a limited amount of space. The flowers fill in a greater range of heights and continue in sequence for a longer period," says Zar Peppler.

"I plant bulbs by the thousands around my house. To keep everything organized, I begin by planning on paper. I decide where to put the tallest bulbs, which will go the deepest in the soil. I can put shorter and earlier-blooming bulbs on top or beside them. Then I leave empty spaces to plug in the annual flowers. They fill out and hide the fading bulb foliage," Zar Peppler says.

Zar Peppler recommends a foolproof tier for your garden: combine common grape hyacinth (*Muscari botryoides*) and tulips (*Tulipa* spp.). The grape hyacinths are in full bloom when the tulips emerge through them.

STORING BULBS THE LAZY WAY

If you love tender bulbs but hate the bother of digging, packing, and storing them indoors through winter, try this simple technique from Ray Rothenberger, Ph.D., a professor of ornamental horticulture at the University of Missouri at Columbia. Dr. Rothenberger digs his big hybrid glads, Aztec lily (*Sprekelia formosissima*), Peruvian daffodil (*Hymenocallis narcissiflora*), and dahlias in the fall before freezing weather arrives. After digging the bulbs, he spreads them on the ground to dry in the shade or, if it's going to rain, indoors in the garage. "I leave soil on the ones that dry out easily such as some of the dahlias—that way I don't have to fuss with storing them in vermiculite. The only dahlias I pack in vermiculite are those with very thin roots," Dr. Rothenberger says.

When the bulbs dry, he places them in plastic garbage bags, leaving the bags open. As he places the bulbs inside, Dr. Rothenberger makes absolutely sure that any soil clinging to the bulbs is dry, and he looks carefully for sow bugs. Later (when time allows), he checks them again. He flops the tops of the bags over loosely, never tying them shut, and inspects the bulbs periodically throughout the winter, throwing away any that begin to rot.

A QUICK WAY TO PLANT BULBS

You can make quick work of planting bulbs without lifting the first spadeful of soil. "This technique will only work in deeply worked, well-amended, loose soil," says

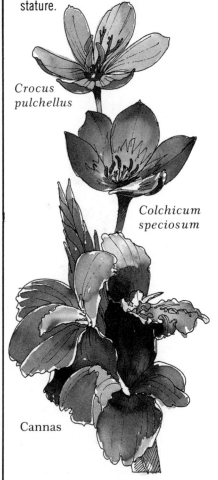

BROADEN YOUR BULB SEASON

Expand your bulb choices to include bulbs that flower in summer and fall, says John Elsley, the vice president of product development with Geo. W. Park Seed Company. He recommends fall-blooming crocuses such as *Crocus pulchellus*, *Colchicum autumnale*, and *Colchicum speciosum* and the new summer-blooming cannas (*Canna* spp.) with softer colors, bronze leaves, and shorter stature.

Crocus pulchellus

Colchicum speciosum

Cannas

QUICK PLANTING
BULBS

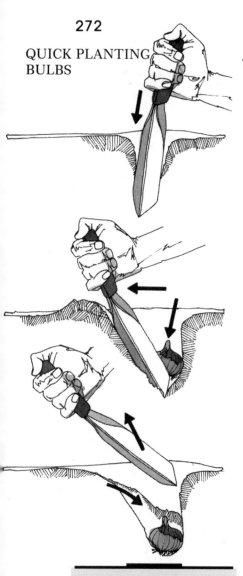

DON'T BISECT BULBS

When you dig bulbs to store for winter, point your shovel straight down into the soil. This guarantees you'll miss the bulb (unless you're standing right over it, of course). Loosen the soil and scoop up the bulb as you dig. If you push the shovel or fork into the soil at an angle toward the bulb, you may gash it or cut right through it.

Ray Rothenberger, Ph.D., a professor of ornamental horticulture at the University of Missouri at Columbia, who likes the following technique for planting big bulbs such as Aztec lily (*Sprekelia formosissima*), Peruvian daffodil (*Hymenocallis narcissiflora*), dahlias, and hybrid gladiolus:

"The easiest way to do this is to throw down a 2 × 6 in the bed to make it easy to walk on," says Dr. Rothenberger. "Go along the edge of the board, push your spade straight down into the soil, and push it away from you to part the soil. Then you drop the bulb in behind the spade. When you pull the spade straight back out, the hole fills itself." The method (illustrated at left) works for smaller bulbs planted with a trowel, too. Dr. Rothenberger adds that you should never do this when the soil is wet, especially in clay soil, or you'll end up with a wad of concrete.

Roses

Our favorite flowers—roses—have a reputation for fussiness. And they do have their share of pests and problems. But most gardeners can't resist the lure of these heavenly flowers, so they struggle to cope with the difficulties of growing roses. Now you can have the flowers without the fuss. Try the following expert tips for growing great roses.

A CREEPY TRICK FOR CLIMBING ROSES

Try a new approach to growing roses—use them as a groundcover. Landon Winchester, a staff horticulturist for White Flower Farm, a nursery in Connecticut, suggests pegging long-limbed roses down on the ground. They become a groundcover that can bloom the entire growing season and an excellent edging for perennial beds. "This is a more radical approach to the old idea of pegging roses," says Winchester. "It is especially valuable in windswept areas, where roses are not too happy." Here's Winchester's secret:

1. Begin with any robust climbing rose or a shrub type with gracefully drooping branches. Look for cultivars with long stems. The hybrid teas and perpetuals tend to be too short and stiff for the job. Winchester particularly likes the climber 'New Dawn', as well as rugosa rose (*Rosa rugosa*), the old-fashioned and early-summer-blooming alba roses

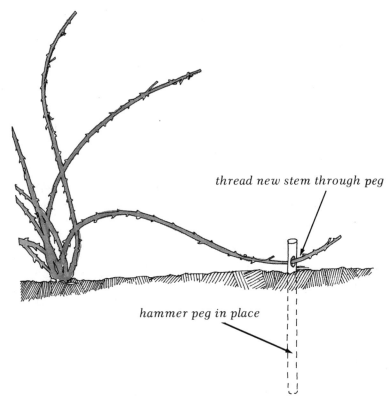

thread new stem through peg

hammer peg in place

(*Rosa* × *alba* cultivars), and repeat-blooming cultivars of moss rose (*Rosa centifolia*).

2. Plant the rose toward the front of a border in full sun. Most of the suitable types will radiate out to fill an area 6 to 8 feet across.

3. As new branches emerge or extend, spread them outward to open areas of soil. Pin the flexible green shoots to the ground using wooden pegs. "Broom handles or tomato stakes that have a diameter of ¾ inch will do fine," says Winchester. "Make each one about 1½ feet long. Then drill a hole through the top. Slide the new branch through the hole, then stick the peg into the ground. This way, you won't have to bother with tying the branch to anything."

4. Do not prune back the growth every year as you would on a hybrid tea rose. Let the existing stems continue to spread until they deteriorate with age. Eventually, they will lose their vigor and floriferous habit or be stricken with disease. When this happens, cut the old branch back to its origin or to a healthy sideshoot. The shrub will generate new, vigorous growth, and you can repeat the technique on it.

DISEASE-RESISTANT ROSES

Thinking of adding roses to your yard? According to a survey by the American Rose Society, the following cultivars are among the best for disease resistance:

Miniatures

'Baby Betsy McCall'
'Gourmet Popcorn'
'Little Artist'
'Rainbow's End'
'Rose Gilardi'

Grandiflora

'Queen Elizabeth'

Floribundas

'Impatient'
'Sunsprite'

Shrub Roses

'All That Jazz'
'Carefree Wonder'

Hybrid Teas

'Duet'
'Olympiad'
'Smooth Lady'

ROSE HELP HOTLINE

Ann Hooper, a certified Consulting Rosarian in Massachusetts, wants you to know that the answers to your rose questions are a phone call away. The American Rose Society (ARS) can get you in touch with Consulting Rosarians in your neighborhood. Consulting Rosarians will come to your house, diagnose your rose problems, and offer solutions—free. Just call (318) 938-5402 to ask the ARS for the phone number of a Consulting Rosarian near you.

BAKING SODA BATTLES BLACKSPOT

At last, there's an organic control for blackspot and powdery mildew, those banes of rose growers. Researchers at Cornell University have found that a solution of 1 tablespoon of baking soda and 2½ tablespoons of horticultural oil in 1 gallon of water, applied when symptoms appear and every two weeks thereafter, helps control these fungal diseases. For more information on spraying baking soda for disease control, see "Give Plants a Bicarb" on page 139.

◆ SHRUB ROSES STEAL THE SHOW

Hardy shrub roses are making a comeback in modern gardens. They tolerate colder weather and are less prone to disease than many hybrid tea roses. Among the best are the Austin roses from England, says John Elsley, the vice president of product development with Geo. W. Park Seed Company. "These are similar to the old species, but many will rebloom throughout the summer," says Elsley. "They grow in a natural shrub form, which I find especially pleasing compared to the hybrid teas."

Unlike teas, shrubby roses also are well-suited for combining with other sorts of flowers. Elsley recommends the following combinations:

1. Plant clematis (*Clematis* spp.) at the rose's feet. The vine will grow up through the shrub, catching sun at the top and adding to the wealth of flowers.

2. Underplant with compact perennials that will fill out around the woody stem bases. Try low-growing pinks (*Dianthus* spp.) beneath a rose with a fully foliated base. Where there is more barren stem showing, use compact daylily cultivars.

MINI MADNESS

If you think your yard is too small or your time is too limited to grow roses, think again. There are scores of new cultivars of miniature roses, only 16 to 18 inches tall, that can grow anywhere it's sunny. Put them in a gallon pot on the patio. Use them to edge a flower border or to give summer-long color to a perennial garden.

Miniatures are like perfect replicas of larger roses. Yet, unlike hybrid teas, you don't have to cut them back hard. In spring before the buds break, cut out the old, brown wood. Through the summer, prune as you pick some blooms to bring indoors. "Cut your roses and deadhead old blooms with a good, long stem. This makes strong, new growth come from deeper in the plant. You see, the new stem is always smaller than the one it arises from. If it comes from a small cane, it will be scrawny and floppy," says Ann Hooper, a certified Consulting Rosarian in Massachusetts. "So prune hard. Don't be bashful."

Miniature roses are not heavy feeders. Hooper fertilizes them in spring and midsummer with half-strength fish emulsion fertilizer. Alternatively, you can top-dress with small doses of composted or well-rotted manure. Be sure to slash the dosage to half of what you would feed full-size roses. Keep the soil in rose beds slightly alkaline so the plants can use the nutrients efficiently. Test your soil pH, and follow recommendations from the soil-testing laboratory or from Cooperative Extension on adding limestone if your soil is acidic.

"Miniatures have fewer insect and disease problems than hybrid tea roses," says Hooper. "I have grown hundreds and almost never seen blackspot. However, they will get red spider mites, especially if you let the soil dry out. Try to never let this happen or you can lose the plants fast. You also can eliminate these pests by washing the plants with a hose every day."

Watch out for powdery mildew, the one fungal disease that can become a problem. It moves in when nights are cool and days are warm. To reduce the incidence of mildew, pick up infected fallen leaves. Then they will not spread disease spores to healthy foliage. Also, space plants at least 18 inches apart so the air can move through freely.

If you grow miniatures in containers, plan to protect them over winter. Set the pots in the garage, and wrap them in burlap or some other insulation. When warmer weather arrives in spring, bring the plant out.

EPSOM SALTS ARE GOOD FOR ROSE FEET, TOO

Epsom salts have an almost magical effect on sore human feet and rundown rose soil. The secret ingredient in both cases is magnesium sulfate, which contains two minor plant nutrients. Ann Hooper, a certified Consulting Rosarian in Massachusetts, says, "I just love it for my roses and houseplants. The magnesium sulfate cleans away accumulated salts that can tie up nutrients. It also starts new basal shoots growing from the bud union."

Here is Hooper's recipe: In the spring, pull back a ½-inch layer of soil from underneath the rose branches to make a saucer-shaped depression. Sprinkle 4 tablespoons of epsom salts in a circle beneath the end of the branches. Scratch the salts lightly into the soil. As you water, the magnesium sulfate will sink down near the root tips. In the fall, pull the soil back close to the plant to protect the susceptible bud union at the base of the trunk.

TOP TWO MINIATURES

If you are intrigued by miniature roses, you may want to check out Ann Hooper's favorites. Hooper, a certified Consulting Rosarian in Massachusetts, grows about 200 miniatures in her suburban Boston backyard. When pressed to pick the two best, she quickly decided on the following:

'Jeanne LaJoie'. This climbing miniature grows 8-foot-long canes laden with tiny pink flowers. "In my garden, 'Jeanne LaJoie' has been totally winter-hardy, never troubled with spider mites or mildew, and exceptionally floriferous," says Hooper.

'Whoopi'. For a perfect teardrop-shaped hybrid tea flower in miniature, look for red-and-white 'Whoopi', named for actress Whoopi Goldberg. It bears one beautifully refined flower per stem.

TUBS PREFER SHADE

Tubs and small pools heat up fast and cool off slowly, points out Charles B. Thomas, the president of Lilypons Water Gardens in Maryland. To keep your miniature water garden healthy, put it in a shady spot. Ponds can handle small swings in temperature, says Thomas, but not the extremes that result when a tub of water is placed on a sunny patio. Decide where you want the garden before filling the tub with water, he advises.

Water Gardens

Gardeners don't often think of water gardens and flower gardens together. But if you've ever seen a pool of breathtaking water lilies or lotuses in bloom, you've probably dreamed of trying your own. Making a water garden isn't hard if you understand the basics and start small. These expert tips will start you off right and keep you going strong.

GET YOUR FEET WET GRADUALLY

"The happiest water gardeners we work with start small," says William C. Uber, the owner of Van Ness Water Gardens in California. "This lets you get a feel for balancing all of the aquatic elements before you spend time and money on a big pond or lily pool." Uber recommends that you experiment with water gardening in a half barrel, horse trough, cauldron, or wash tub. The container should be large enough to hold 25 to 50 gallons of water. Plan to line it with a 4×5-foot sheet of PVC plastic if it is not watertight or if it is porous and might house bacteria. Here's how to set up:

1. Set the container in its permanent home in a sunny location, or put it on a wooden tray on wheels if you want to move it around during the summer.

2. Fill the container halfway up with sandy loam soil (but no compost, manure, or peat moss, which will make the water cloudy).

3. Fill the tub slightly over half full with gently trickling water. Soften the flow by capping the end of the hose with an old sock.

4. Add plants. Plant a water lily in the center. Toward the edges, add two bunches of oxygenating grasses such as waterweed (*Elodea* spp.), arrowhead (*Sagittaria graminea*), or water milfoil (*Myriophyllum* spp.). All grow at least partly submerged beneath the water. They compete with algae for carbon dioxide and release oxygen that is used by other plant roots and fish.

5. When you've added the plants, you can finish filling the tub with water in the same manner as described in Step 3.

6. Fish help make the tub more fun. They also have a job to do. They eat insects and nibble on foliage, keeping it pruned down. For tubs, stick with the hardiest fish, such as

mosquito fish or guppies, which can survive extreme temperature changes.

7. You probably won't need to fertilize for the first three months after planting. After that, you can feed water plants organically by wrapping a small handful of well-leached cow manure or nitrohumus (processed sewage sludge, such as Milorganite) in newspaper. Bury it deep in the soil so it will release nutrients slowly to the plant roots, not the water.

Once your water garden is set up, the trick is to keep it in balance. "If you grow too few plants, your weeds—which are algae—will increase. If there are too many plants, they will crowd each other out and squeeze out the submerged oxygenators," Uber says. "Also, get away from the urge to keep a sterile, swimming-pool-like environment. You may be able to make the water look clear if you use enough filters, but you cannot correct unseen imbalances, like too much fish urine and not enough plants to absorb it all. You don't need a lot of troublesome chemicals, pumps, and filters. You need the right balance of flora and fauna to make a pond really work."

FISH DON'T GO FOR GRAVEL

Try this hint for growing water lilies in a pond with fish—especially big fish. "You must cover the soil in the top of the pot with gravel," says Ray Rothenberger, Ph.D., a professor of ornamental horticulture at the University of Missouri at Columbia. "If you don't, somehow the fish will grovel around in there until all of the soil is worked out of the pot, and you'll find your plant just floating on the water."

Dr. Rothenberger uses river gravel that is heavy enough to withstand the action of the fish. This is especially important in today's liner pools, which are often cleaned out once a year.

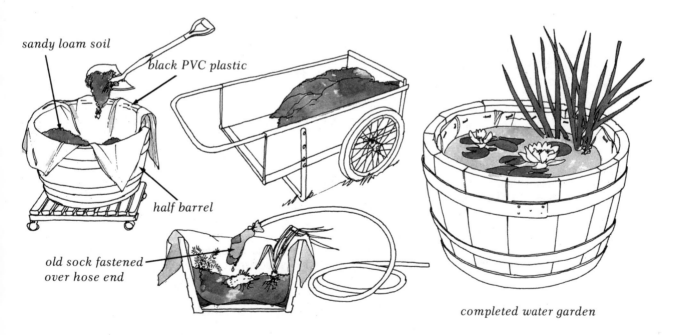

sandy loam soil

black PVC plastic

half barrel

old sock fastened over hose end

completed water garden

CREATING A WATER GARDEN

BLACK IS THE COLOR

A special black dye available from water garden suppliers can make your pond seem endlessly deep. Dyed water looks very clear, and the surface is highly reflective, says Charles B. Thomas, the president of Lilypons Water Gardens in Maryland. The nontoxic dye, often used at public gardens, is sold under the brand name Deep Water. Plants, fish, and snails tolerate it well, and the velvety black color of dyed water hides algae. Be sure to use only dye intended for water gardens to color your garden, and follow label instructions carefully.

PAVLOV'S…FISH?

Still water is a mosquito factory, notes Charles B. Thomas, the president of Lilypons Water Gardens in Maryland. But fish, especially goldfish and koi, eat mosquito eggs and larvae, keeping the water garden pest-free.

Serious koi enthusiasts, who may spend hundreds of dollars for a single fish, want to see that fish every time they visit the pond, observes Thomas. And the fish are easily trained: "You feed your fish, and within a week or two, they come up to be fed, wagging their tails," he says.

THE GOOD, THE BAD, AND THE UGLY ALGAE

The biggest question of first-time water gardeners, says Charles B. Thomas, the president of Lilypons Water Gardens in Maryland, is "What can I do to keep the water clear?" Just because a pond is green doesn't mean it's unhealthy, says Thomas. The green stuff is only algae—natural growth due to warm temperatures, sunlight, and nutrients in the water. You can control algae by adding the right plants and fish.

Submerged plants such as waterweed (*Elodea canadensis*) and Carolina fanwort (*Cabomba caroliniana*) are the key to keeping the water clear or nearly clear, says Thomas. He recommends one bunch of submerged plants for every 1 to 2 square feet of surface area.

Fish are necessary to a healthy pond, since they provide food for the submerged plants. The fish make waste, which is broken down by bacteria that live in the mosslike algae that forms on the sides of the pond. The end product is nitrates that the submerged plants can use. "Some folks go out, pump out the water, and scrub down the sides when they see this algae," says Thomas. "But that only causes another round of algal growth." The moral is: Algae on the side is good, but on the top, it's scum.

THE GARDEN PROFESSIONALS

Allan M. Armitage, Ph.D., is a professor of horticulture at the University of Georgia in Athens. He is the author of *Herbaceous Perennial Plants* and writes a monthly column for *Greenhouse Grower* magazine.

Bill Boonstra is a second-generation manager of Bluestone Perennials in Madison, Ohio. Established in 1972 by Richard Boonstra, the company sells perennials, by mail order only, for spring and fall planting seasons.

Jim Brady is the owner and operator of Sunbeam Gardens in Avon, Ohio. The business specializes in wholesale container-grown perennials, offering approximately 800 cultivars.

Simon Crawford is a technical services specialist for the PanAmerican Seed Company in West Chicago, Illinois. Previously, he was a plant breeder with Asmer Seeds in England.

John Elsley is the vice president of product development with Geo. W. Park Seed Company, Inc., and Wayside Gardens in Greenwood, South Carolina. He is a former botanist for the Royal Horticultural Society in Great Britain, and he trained at the Royal Botanical Gardens at Kew and the University of Leicester.

Ann Hooper is the national publicity chairperson for the American Rose Society and is a certified Consulting Rosarian. She lives in Massachusetts and has written for *The American Rose* magazine and other gardening magazines.

Wendy Krupnick is the manager of the trial gardens and the horticultural advisor for Shepherd's Garden Seeds, a retail mail-order specialty seed company in Felton, California.

Peter Loewer is a garden writer and botanical illustrator from Asheville, North Carolina. He has written *Tough Plants for Tough Places* and other books.

Michael Murgiano is the promotion manager for Sluis & Groot America, Inc., in Fort Wayne, Indiana. The company is the marketing organization for the Dutch company Sluis & Groot, which is a primary seed breeder and producer of F_1 hybrid flowering and bedding plants.

Jim Nau is the new varieties manager for Ball Seed Company in West Chicago, Illinois, a wholesale supplier of annual, perennial, and cut-flower seeds.

Kenneth Peck is a technical advisor for A. H. Hummert Seed Company, which is a wholesale distributor of horticultural products, located in St. Louis, Missouri.

Ray Rothenberger, Ph.D., is a professor of ornamental horticulture at the University of Missouri at Columbia. He also hosts a call-in radio garden show in mid-Missouri.

Paul Rudloff is the nursery manager for Prairie Nursery in Westfield, Wisconsin. The nursery sells prairie plants and seeds, as well as grasses and forbs, wholesale and retail via mail order.

Charles B. Thomas is the president of Lilypons Water Gardens, located in Buckeystown, Maryland. He is the author of *Water Gardens for Plants and Fish* and *Creating a Water Garden*. He founded the International Water Lily Society.

William C. Uber is the owner of Van Ness Water Gardens, a water-garden supply store and mail-order business in Upland, California. He is the author of *Water Gardening Basics*.

John Vandenberg is a bulb importer and the owner of Vandenberg Bulb Company in Chester, New York. He is a fourth-generation wholesale bulb grower and importer.

Mark Viette is the manager of Andre Viette Farm and Nursery in Fishersville, Virginia. The company sells over 3,000 species and cultivars of perennials wholesale and retail via mail order.

Heather Will-Browne is a horticulturist and bedding plant specialist at Walt Disney World in Orlando, Florida.

Dorothy Willott and her husband, Anthony, are award-winning iris breeders from Ohio. They have introduced 208 new cultivars of irises between 1968 and 1992.

Landon Winchester is a staff horticulturist for White Flower Farm, a nursery in Litchfield, Connecticut. Winchester also spent 26 years on the staff of the Brooklyn Botanic Garden.

Nona Wolfram-Koivula is the executuve director of the National Garden Bureau and All-America Selections (AAS). She organizes the AAS trialing program and introduces the AAS winners.

Alan Zaeske is the regional product manager for Goldsmith Seeds, Inc., a multinational company, which is a primary breeder and producer of spring bedding plants.

Kathy Zar Peppler is a public relations consultant for the Professional Plant Growers Association. She is also a garden writer and is the former director of All-America Selections.

SLIME IS NOT FINE

If your pond is harboring more than its share of algae, look closely at the algae to find out its source, says William C. Uber, the owner of Van Ness Water Gardens in California. "Algae tells you that a problem exists. Most likely, you are feeding your fish too much food. Fish food is high in phosphate, a plant nutrient. You also can get algae blooms from excess fish urine or even a few crumbs of lawn fertilizer that fall into the water," Uber says.

Look closely at the algae to get some idea of the severity of the problem. If the algae grows into long, hairlike strands, the water is highly polluted. If it is free-floating greenery that clouds the water, the problem is usually not as severe.

You can solve either problem easily. To limit free-floating algae, add a few additional oxygenating grasses. For the hairlike algae, change how you feed your fish. "Use fish food as an occasional treat for your fish, rather than making fish food their primary food source," Uber says. Scoop out the hairlike algae, which has absorbed many excess nutrients, and compost it. Leave the free-floating algae alone. "It's a basic life source for the garden," Uber says.

Trees, shrubs, and vines form the foundation, framework, and walls of a landscape. They can focus our attention on lovely views or shut out ugly ones. Trees also help to modify the microclimate in our yards by casting shade or serving as a windbreak. They can act as barriers to block the noise and commotion of street traffic.

While trees and shrubs can be expensive, they are true investments that can raise the value of your property. Before you spend money buying trees and shrubs, though, spend time learning about the best plant choices for your site and about how to care for the plants you select. Consult books, local gardening organizations, and county extension agents. Find a reliable nursery, and ask the owner or manager for advice. And for a dose of inspiration, visit public gardens and arboretums.

In this chapter, you'll find expert advice on caring for trees and shrubs, as well as some of the experts' opinions on how to use trees, shrubs, and vines to best effect in the home landscape.

Caring for Trees and Shrubs

The most important thing you can do for your trees and shrubs is plant them in the right spot and with great care. For detailed instructions on choosing healthy plants and starting them out right, refer to "Planning and Shopping Smart," beginning on page 70, and "Planting and Transplanting," beginning on page 13. Here, read on for expert advice on caring for new and existing plants, as well as specific tree, shrub, and vine recommendations.

CHOOSE THE RIGHT TREE

In the market for new trees for your yard? North Carolina garden writer Peter Loewer offers some points to consider before you go tree-shopping. "First," he notes, "make a simplified map of your property that includes the loca-

---

PRESERVE BRANCH COLLARS

Many older gardening texts instruct readers to cut branches flush with the trunk or stem when pruning. The old wisdom was that when pruning trees or shrubs you cut the branch flush with the trunk or stem. Not true, says Alex L. Shigo, the author of *Tree Pruning*. "You should leave a collar, because the plant's defense system resides in the base of the branch. Remove the collar, and you take away the plant's defense system," says Shigo. For instructions on how to properly prune to the collar, see "Corner the Collar" on page 37.

NO FEED IN FALL

As a general rule, don't fertilize trees or shrubs in the late summer or fall. You will only encourage new growth that won't have time to mature before temperatures start to drop. Winter cold can kill such tender growth.

DON'T FORGET FALL MULCH

Too many gardeners fail to refurbish mulch in the fall, says Bonnie Lee Appleton, Ph.D., an associate professor and extension horticulturist at Virginia Polytechnic Institute and State University. "Or they apply new mulch on old mulch, and these too-thick layers don't allow air to get through," says Dr. Appleton. Try raking up old mulch and mixing it with new material, and reapply this mix at the proper thickness.

tions of the septic system and the water lines. Then, think about what purpose you want a tree to serve." You might want a tree in an area where you'd like to grow shade plants.

Consider the plantings on adjoining properties. For example, Loewer says, if there's a grove of trees in your neighbor's yard, continue the planting into your yard to create an inviting space and view between their house and yours. And don't forget about the fall color of a potential tree. "You wouldn't, for instance, want a tree with yellow leaves next to a pink stucco house," says Loewer.

Once you've narrowed your choices, he advises a visit to a local botanical garden. It will help you decide which trees do best in your area and give you a glimpse into the future. You can see how your tree will look in 20 years.

TIPS ON TREE WRAPS

The use of tree wraps is a subject of debate among horticulturists. While some experts feel that most trees should not be wrapped, Ray Rothenberger, Ph.D., a professor of ornamental horticulture at the University of Missouri at Columbia, feels it's necessary for all trees in his part of the country.

"I'm a big believer in wrapping the trunks of newly planted trees for the first year or two because sunscald is such a problem around here," says Dr. Rothenberger. "On a young tree with little canopy to shade itself, the hot sun can kill the bark on the southwest side of the tree. The cambium [layer of living cells] on that side dies. The tree trunk fills out and covers the area, but the damage is still there. It slows development, and worse yet, it's a perfect place for rot to get started." Dr. Rothenberger shares the following tips on specific wraps:

Plastic wrap. "The easiest wraps to work with are the plastic spirals. I don't necessarily like the look or the cost, but they're easy to put on, and they fit loosely enough to reduce the likelihood of creating a home for borers," he says. For best results, remove the spiral at the end of the growing season, inspect the trunk for insects, then put the spiral back in place. As trees grow and expand, the spiral or any wrap can restrict new growth. If you remove the spiral or wrap each season, and then put it back in place, you can avoid girdling trees.

Burlap wrap. For economy, Dr. Rothenberger recom-

GIRDLES CAN KILL TREES

Trees can't die of a broken heart, but they can die of a girdling root. A girdling root is a root that grows in a circling pattern. The root can eventually put so much pressure on a tree trunk that it stops the flow of water and nutrients between the roots and the top, killing the tree.

Symptoms of a root-girdled trunk are weak topgrowth, poor bark development, or a pronounced swelling at the base of the trunk. The leaves on the girdled side may be a lighter green in early fall than the rest of the foliage. Another suspicious condition is a trunk that grows straight up from ground level instead of being flared or buttressed at the soil line. A trunk that is slightly concave on one side can also indicate a girdling root.

What causes girdling roots? Roots can be turned back toward the trunk if they come up against hard, impervious subsoil. Pavement can be the culprit that deflects the roots of street trees. If roots are overcrowded when a tree is first planted, they may interfere with each other's growth and result in a girdling root.

If you suspect a girdling root, do a little detective work, and solve the problem if you uncover one. Gently remove the soil from the roots in the suspect area. Sever any girdling root with a chisel and mallet. Be sure to chop out a gap several inches wide so that the severed root won't rejoin itself. Then cover the area with the soil again.

WRAPPING A TREE WITH BURLAP

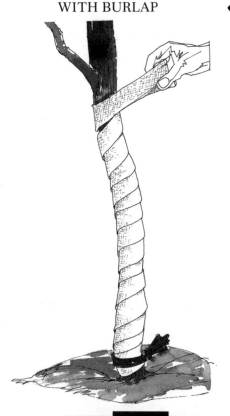

mends cutting long, 3-inch-wide strips of burlap to make your own wrap. Wind the strips around the trunk, as shown at left, spiraling up from the bottom. Keep wrapping until you reach the point where the tree begins to branch. Secure the wrap in place at the bottom and top with electrical tape or panty hose. Don't use wire or any material that binds, because it could girdle the trunk. Even tape can restrict tree growth if left on too long. Adjust the tape and wrap each fall.

Paper wrap. Watch paper tree wraps, warns Dr. Rothenberger, because some have a black interior. This type must be removed as soon as it begins degrading or the black will absorb sunlight. This will actually make the trunk hotter instead of protecting it from sunscald.

TREE WRAPS CAN BE BAD NEWS

Many trees don't need tree wrap. Those that do should have it removed after a year or two. That's the opinion of Bonnie Lee Appleton, Ph.D., an associate professor and extension horticulturist at Virginia Polytechnic Institute and State University. "The use of tree wrap shouldn't be automatic," says Dr. Appleton. "Before you use a tree wrap, evaluate the need."

Wraps are helpful if one or more of the following is true:

◆ The trees came from a nursery where they were grown close together (shading one another).
◆ The trees are thin-barked species such as crab apples (*Malus* spp.), cherries (*Prunus* spp.), peach (*Prunus persica*), pin oak (*Quercus palustris*), birches (*Betula* spp.), and lindens (*Tilia* spp.).
◆ The trees are planted near the street where the heat radiates up off the pavement.
◆ The trees are exposed to fierce north winds or very hot sun.

Even these trees will suffer if the wrap is left in place too long. "We're finding disease, borers, and soggy, peeling bark underneath tree wraps that have been in place two years or longer," Dr. Appleton warns.

TURN SHRUBS INTO TREES

Streets and large trees don't make good companions. Branches tangle with utility lines, and large roots growing

WATER IN WINTER

Trees and shrubs need extra water during hot summer dry spells, but they also need supplemental water during dry periods in the winter or early spring. Cold, windy weather dries out soil and plants just as it dries and cracks your skin. Unfortunately, plants show less injury from lack of moisture in winter and are more likely to be neglected. Evergreens, which transpire water continuously, are particularly susceptible to winter droughts. It may not be much fun, but if you've had a long stretch without rain or snow, bundle up and haul out the hose or watering can!

near the ground's surface cause sidewalks to crack and heave. But you can create a "tree" that's at home in the confined area along a street, says Bonnie Lee Appleton, Ph.D., an associate professor and extension horticulturist at Virginia Polytechnic Institute and State University. She suggests turning large shrubs into small trees by limbing them up. "Some good candidates for this are crape myrtles [*Lagerstroemia indica*], lilacs, and viburnums," she says.

"Limbing up is a technique that anyone with basic pruning skills can accomplish," says Richard Hesselein, the president of Princeton Nurseries in New Jersey. Start the limbing up process when the shrub is dormant. To limb up a 5- to 6-foot-tall shrub, select a strong central stem and cut the others away, Hesselein explains. Temporarily tie the remaining stem to a bamboo or plastic stake for support, as shown in the illustration below. Remove all branches growing along the base of the stem up to about 2 feet. Leave at least 3 feet of light branching on top.

The second year, when the shrub is 6 to 8 feet tall, remove lower limbs up to 3½ to 4 feet from the ground. In the next growing season, you will have a small tree with a sturdy central stem and a well-proportioned top.

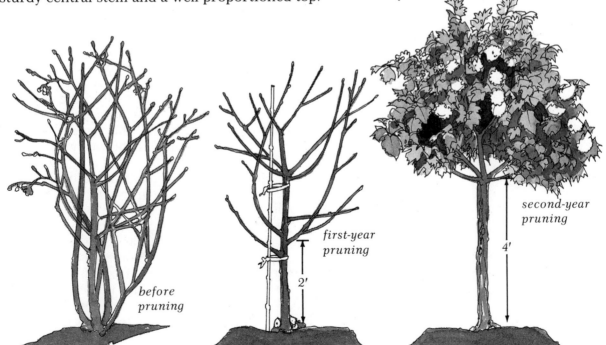

before pruning

first-year pruning

2'

second-year pruning

4'

A pruning technique called limbing up lets you turn a tall shrub into a small tree. You can also limb up low branches on large trees so you can walk underneath them without stooping.

TREES THAT LIGHTNING LIKES

Lone, tall trees growing in moist soil or near water are the most likely trees to be hit by lightning. But lightning also seems to have a particular affinity for certain species of trees, including elms (*Ulmus* spp.), maples (*Acer* spp.), oaks (*Quercus* spp.), pines (*Pinus* spp.), poplars (*Populus* spp.), spruces (*Picea* spp.), and tulip trees (*Liriodendron* spp.). Beeches (*Fagus* spp.), birches (*Betula* spp.), and horse chestnuts (*Aesculus* spp.) are rarely hit.

For information on protecting trees from lightning, write to the Superintendent of Documents, U.S. Government Printing Office, Washington, D.C. 20402. Ask for "Tree Preservation Bulletin No. 5."

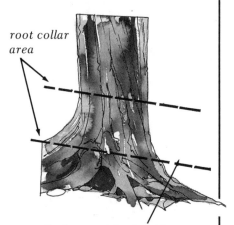

root collar area

Soil or mulch should not extend beyond this level.

MINI-GREENHOUSES FOR TREES

Small trees can benefit greatly from a relatively new product known as a plastic tree shelter. "These 3- to 4-foot-long clear plastic tubes are slipped over the young trees and are tapped into the ground," says W. Gary Smith, an assistant professor of landscape design at the University of Delaware at Newark. "They act just like mini-greenhouses and protect a seedling against sunscald and deer."

To install a plastic tree shelter, position it over the tree, and tap it into the ground using a hammer or the back of a shovel. The shelters come under various trade names such as Tubex and in various sizes, and most are biodegradable. (It will take about three years for the shelters to biodegrade in place.) They cost around $2 each and are available through the Forest Service and the Soil Conservation Service, as well as at local nature centers.

"After about two years, you can simply cut them off the tree," Smith says. "The only drawback is that they attract bluebirds and field nesting birds, which often crawl inside and get trapped. You can solve that problem by putting a mesh net on top of the tubes."

KEEP ROOT COLLARS CLEAR

The solid, imposing trunk of a tree may seem nearly invincible, but it isn't. It's a living organism that can suffer from cuts and scrapes and even from suffocation. The flare at the bottom of a tree where the roots join the trunk is called the root collar. If air movement to this part of the tree is restricted, the tree will suffer and may even die. It's a good idea to inspect the trees on your property to be sure the root collars are exposed.

E. Thomas Smiley, Ph.D., a plant pathologist at the Bartlett Tree Research Labortories in North Carolina, explains, "Root collars are often buried by dirt or mulch when trees are transplanted or during other landscaping projects." If the root collar is covered, the area stays constantly moist. This can favor invasion by insect borers or disease organisms. Also, air movement in and out of the living cells of the tree's inner bark is restricted. This can cause those cells to die. When they do, water and food can't move between the tree roots and the tree top. As a result, the tree may look sickly or die.

Early symptoms of root collar problems include yellowing foliage, early leaf discoloration and drop, and dieback in the upper crown of the tree. "An affected tree will probably have to be removed," Dr. Smiley notes. "But, if treated early, the tree might be saved."

When you're planting new trees, be sure to plant and mulch properly to avoid root collar problems. See the illustration on page 18 for instructions on how to plant and mulch a tree. If you find an existing tree on your property with a buried root collar, dig away the soil or mulch that covers it. Leave an area at least 6 inches wide around the collar exposed. Be very careful not to injure the roots as you dig. In a situation where the grade of the landscape was changed, removing the soil will create a "well" around the base of the tree, as shown in the illustration at right. Slope the sides of the well up to the level of the surrounding soil, or line the outer edge of it with brick or stone. This will keep the area from filling back in with soil. If practical, leave the dug-out area uncovered. If you must fill in the area, use gravel.

THE TREE-CLUSTERING TRICK

If you'd like a big-tree effect in your yard in a short period of time, start by planting a densely spaced group of young trees. W. Gary Smith, an assistant professor of landscape design at the University of Delaware at Newark, suggests buying 6- to 8-foot-tall, 1-inch-caliper bareroot trees. (Caliper is the diameter of the trunk, measured 6 inches above the ground.) Plant at least five of them from 1½ to 5 or 6 feet apart—depending on the effect you want—in a natural-looking cluster.

"Because of the competition for space and light," Smith explains, "those in the center will grow straight up as the others grow outward, soon developing the effect of one great tree. In other words, you'll have a much larger tree mass in a shorter period of time."

Smith also notes that this technique is great for town houses and small urban yards. "You can take a space the size of a parking spot, put in ten trees, and let them grow. After a few years, as some start to be crowded out, remove those until you are down to two or three trees." Be sure to come back and remove the extra trees. Crowded trees will not have as nice a form as trees with room to grow.

Another tree-cluster trick is to plant two or more ½- to 1-inch-caliper, bareroot trees, like maples (*Acer* spp.), birches (*Betula* spp.), or ash trees (*Fraxinus* spp.), in the same hole,

EXCAVATED ROOT COLLAR

SHRUB COVER-UP

Let's say there's a wonderful shrub that you've always wanted to grow, but your winter climate is a zone or two too cold. Karen Jennings, a senior vice president of Geo. W. Park Seed Company and Wayside Gardens in South Carolina, suggests constructing a wood or metal support around the bush in the fall and draping a row-cover-type cloth over it that lets in air and light. "It can give you at least a zone of extra hardiness," she says. "It's also a good way to protect special shrubs if abnormally cold weather is due to hit your area."

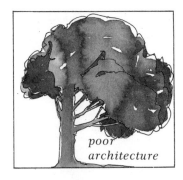

poor
architecture

crotch
crack

crack

rots and
cankers

letting the roots intermingle. This, Smith says, produces an architectural effect—a clump-tree form. Clumps are often seen in open fields where a tree has been grazed down to the ground. Several shoots spring up from the roots to replace the original single trunk.

"Small bareroot trees also have the advantage of being inexpensive," Smith reminds us. "Though not every nursery carries them, they can be found with a little looking. Just keep in mind the real key to successful bareroot planting: *Don't let the roots dry out.*"

Bareroot trees are planted in the late fall or winter. Smith says to get them in the ground immediately after purchasing. If you can't do this, cover the roots with moist mulch or burlap until planting. For directions on how to plant trees, see "Planting the Big Guys" on page 16.

WHAT MAKES A TREE HAZARDOUS?

A tree that topples at the wrong time or in the wrong place can make a mess of your yard. It can also cause significant damage to your house or other structures. In the worst case, it can injure or kill people. Even a structurally sound tree can be a hazard if it obstructs a motorist's vision, raises a sidewalk, attracts lightning, or interferes with utilities. Therefore, inspect trees annually, and don't hesitate to call on an arborist (a tree professional) for advice.

Dangerous trees (such as those illustrated at left and on the opposite page) are more likely to be found bordering wooded areas, roads, drives, and parking areas, where they are exposed to stress during storms or might have experienced root damage during land clearing. In new developments, even native trees frequently have severe root problems. Soil compaction, root wounding, and the root decay that results may not be obvious until it's too late.

Trees that grow on wet sites or that are irrigated frequently can suffer windthrow from ground or root failure; those in shallow, rocky ground are more prone to windthrow from ground failure. Lone, tall trees are more susceptible to lightning strikes; if one is within 10 feet of a building, lightning may jump to the structure and start a fire or even electrocute occupants.

Alex L. Shigo, the author of *Tree Pruning*, says to ask yourself the following questions about each tree:

◆ If the tree falls, will it hit a car, house, power line, or person?

◆ Has the tree lost large branches recently?

◆ Is the tree's top dead?

◆ Does the tree have dead branches?

◆ Is the tree dead?

◆ Are there deep, open cracks in the trunk or branches?

◆ Are there deep, open cracks at the juncture of two branches?

◆ Do living branches bend abruptly upward or downward where tips of large branches were cut off?

◆ Does the tree have heavy new growth sprouting around topping cuts?

◆ Are there broken branches, a split trunk, or injured roots due to storm injury?

◆ Are branches close to power lines?

◆ Are there fungus fruit bodies (mushrooms) on the tree's roots? (This is an indicator of rot.)

◆ Are there hollows or cankers (dead spots) on the trunk, some with fungus fruit bodies?

◆ Is the tree leaning?

◆ Have the roots, trunk, or branches been injured by construction?

◆ Is there a new lawn or garden over injured roots?

If you answer yes to any one—and particularly more than one—of the above questions, it's time to ask an arborist for advice. As with medical advice, you might want a second or third opinion. Also, get more than one cost estimate if your tree needs to be pruned or removed. Prices vary widely.

Shigo emphasizes that homeowners and others who are not qualified tree-care professionals should never do *anything* to a tree that's growing near power lines. He further stresses that you should *never* use a chain saw for cutting or pruning and *never* get on a ladder to prune. "Even if you think you can do the job yourself," Shigo says, "it's better, wiser, and safer to discuss your trees with a tree-care professional first, and be sure that professional is insured. *Don't take chances!*"

BIG-PLANT TRANSPLANTING TRICKS

Gardeners often say that a weed is simply a plant growing in the wrong place. But if you have a small tree or large

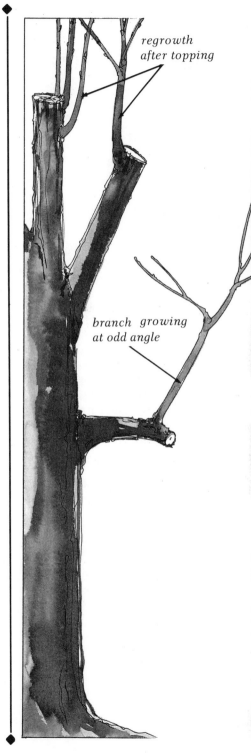

regrowth after topping

branch growing at odd angle

ONE CLUMP, OR TWO?

Mature trees give gardens a finished look and feel, but it may take years. If you can't wait, try bamboo. A clump of bamboo supplies a different kind of shade than the dense coolness of a leafy tree. As its thin leaves and jointed stems stir in the breeze, they produce graceful, moving shadows that make the garden come alive. Clump-forming bamboos are well-behaved, unlike their relatives, the running bamboos. The following two clump-forming bamboos can survive temperatures of −10° to −20°F. They won't take over your yard or the neighborhood.

Umbrella bamboo (*Fargesia murielae*) is a clump-forming but cold-tolerant alpine species. "It's the bamboo the pandas eat," says Albert Adelman, the owner of Burt Associates Bamboo in Massachusetts. It tends to look spindly when young, he notes, but matures into an airy, fountainlike shape, reaching as high as 15 feet. The culms and leaves of umbrella bamboo are a bright apple-green.

Fountain bamboo (*Fargesia nitida*) produces somber-colored stalks that mature to deep purplish black. It grows to 12 feet tall.

shrub in the wrong place, you can't just uproot it with a dandelion fork. And if it's a desirable tree or shrub, chances are you'll want to replant it at a more favorable site. Transplanting a tree or big shrub requires careful advance planning so that you don't put too much stress on the plant. Rich Owings, the horticulturist at The North Carolina Arboretum, explains, "If you want to move a tree in the fall, you should begin preparations a year or more in advance."

The preparation will include gradual severing of the plant's roots, as well as pruning back of topgrowth. Cutting through roots will stimulate regrowth of a network of fibrous roots. The new, contained root system will be easier to dig up and will suffer less damage during transplanting.

First, decide where to prune the roots. Plan for a root ball that is at least 1½ feet wide for each 1 inch of trunk diameter. Measure the trunk diameter 6 inches above the ground. If you want to move a tree with a 2-inch-diameter trunk, for example, plan on a 3-foot-wide root ball. Owings suggests that you map out four quadrants of the root ball. Then, at intervals over several seasons, make one small cut in each quadrant, he explains. Use a shovel to slice straight down into the soil to a depth of 1 foot. Eventually, you will have pruned the entire root system. You can prune roots from early spring to late fall.

It's best to thin the plant's top to reduce the amount of growth that the pruned roots must support and to reduce shock when you move the plant. Remove about one-third of the topgrowth. Begin by cutting out any dead, diseased, or crossing branches, then remove crowded or weak branches. (For information on how to make pruning cuts, see "Corner the Collar" on page 37.)

As you finalize your plans for the actual transplanting of the tree or shrub, be sure to consider how you'll manage the move. Root balls can weigh hundreds of pounds. Two or three people working together can carry small trees. Move large trees on a board fitted with wheels or in the bucket of a front end loader. If you use a front end loader, pad the edges of the bucket and the tree's trunk to avoid scarring the trunk. Follow these steps on transplanting day:

1. Dig a hole of the approximate correct depth at the new location. See "Planting the Big Guys" on page 16 for guidelines on digging planting holes.

2. Dig a trench 1 to 2 feet wide around the plant. Be sure to dig outside the area where you root-pruned, or you will dig through and damage the new fibrous root system.

For each inch of trunk diameter, allow 1 foot of depth for the root ball. At minimum, dig 1 foot deep.

3. When you reach the proper depth, dig under the root ball to "shape" its bottom. Cut through the remaining deep roots that hold the tree in the ground. You may have to tip the tree and ball to make the final cut.

4. Tip the root ball and place a piece of burlap under it. Wrap burlap around the entire root ball. Maneuver the ball carefully, if necessary, to work the burlap around it. Tie the burlap in place with rope.

5. Move the tree to the new planting site. Check the planting hole depth, and correct it, if needed. You'll want to set the tree or shrub slightly higher than it was at its original site. When the disturbed soil settles, the tree will end up at the correct depth.

6. Set the tree or shrub into its new hole. Then remove the ropes and cut away as much of the wrapping as you can: Ropes can girdle the root system, and burlap that sticks up above ground level will wick water away from the roots. Water the plant well, and apply a ring of mulch. For information on mulching around trees, see "Keep Root Collars Clear" on page 284.

HOW MUCH ARE YOUR TREES WORTH?

You may not realize how much you value your trees and shrubs until you lose one. But how valuable are they? The simple answer, of course, is the amount it costs to replace them. But how can you put a cash value on or replace a 100-year-old oak? You can't. There are, however, steps you can take to recoup some of the loss.

"According to its size, species, condition, and location, a tree can be worth thousands of dollars," says Erik Haupt, the chairman of the Council of Tree and Landscape Appraisers, "but it's sometimes difficult to establish the worth. In a recent Southern California case, one arborist put the value of a lost tree at $163,000, while another said it was worth $2,300." For individual plants, insurance companies will pay up to $500 under standard homeowner coverage for some losses. If you have accurate records of planting costs, you may be able to claim a tax loss for the cost of replacing the tree.

"There are two fundamental approaches," Haupt says. "One is the objective approach of replacement cost. The other is the formula method, which is subjective and has more to do with aesthetics and the function of the tree.

THE SUMACADE TREE

Smooth sumac (*Rhus glabra*), sometimes called scarlet sumac, is a tough, adaptable native tree. "Though this is considered a 'trash tree,' it has lovely serrated leaves that turn vermilion-red in autumn, and its fruit makes a fine lemony-tasting 'sumacade,'" says Peter Loewer, a North Carolina garden writer. Sumac is easy to grow from seed and easy to maintain once established. Choose your site carefully, though, because smooth sumac suckers will spread.

If you don't have enough space for a tree, Loewer recommends turning the smooth sumac into an annual shrub. Just cut it down to the ground each year in late fall or early winter, and it will come back as a lower, hedge-type plant.

MAGNOLIA SHADE GARDENS

Southern magnolia (*Magnolia grandiflora*) has shallow roots and large, dense leaves that cast deep shade. This combination makes it a difficult plant companion, and many gardeners believe that nothing will grow well under a southern magnolia tree. However, Roger Gossler, a co-owner of Gossler Farms Nursery, an Oregon nursery that specializes in magnolias, has great success in growing hostas and other shade-garden plants beneath southern magnolias. To avoid harming the shallow, sensitive magnolia roots, Gossler cautions gardeners not to cultivate deeply when planting under the trees.

TOUGH TREES FOR WINDBREAKS

If you need a tree that will stand up to extreme cold, heat, and wind, try one of these three. They were tested over several decades in the Great Plains and will make excellent windbreaks:

Box elder (*Acer negundo*) is a fast-growing, rounded tree that grows 30 to 50 feet tall. Zones 2 to 9.

Green ash (*Fraxinus pennsylvanica*) is a large tree that grows up to 60 feet tall. Its green leaves may turn a nice yellow in fall but not reliably. Zones 3 to 9.

Silver buffalo berry (*Shepherdia argentea*) is a thorny shrub or tree with silvery leaves and red or yellow edible fruit. It grows to 18 feet tall. Zones 2 to 6.

Does it provide shade? Does it act as a sound barrier? Does it define a property line? Is it used for passive recreation? This latter approach has been accepted with some limitations by the IRS."

To help make your case, have a professional real-estate appraiser tell you what a similar house would sell for without your landscaping. Keep all records of landscape expenses. Take pictures of your plants, and list their purpose for being where they are. Once a landscape disaster occurs—whether from storms, lightning, or vandalism—contact your insurance company immediately and hire a horticultural expert familiar with the formulas developed by the Council of Tree and Landscape Appraisers for appraising plants in your region.

To get a free pamphlet on this subject, write to the Council of Tree and Landscape Appraisers at 1250 I Street NW, Suite 500, Washington, DC 20005.

Trees and Shrubs to Try

With trees and shrubs, you may face the delightful dilemma of having planting sites aplenty and so many plants you'd like to try that you can't make up your mind. These tips may help you make choices—or may just make the decision more devilishly difficult.

TRY THESE STREET TREES

Are you looking for some handsome, relatively problem-free trees that will stand up to modern urban stresses? Bonnie Lee Appleton, Ph.D., an associate professor and extension horticulturist at Virginia Polytechnic Institute and State University, thinks the Chinese or lacebark elm (*Ulmus parvifolia*) and Chinese pistache (*Pistacia chinensis*) have great potential. Both are widely available.

"At 35 to 45 feet tall, the lacebark elm is a small version of the American elm [*U. americana*] with smaller leaves," Dr. Appleton says. "But it's resistant to Dutch elm disease and isn't bothered by borers and elm leaf beetles. It grows into a lovely vase shape and has one of the prettiest, exfoliating barks you'll ever see. Small pieces of the tan outer bark pop off showing gray underneath, giving it a mosaic look." It will grow in Zones 5 to 8.

As for the very tough Chinese pistache, Dr. Appleton feels it's "a real sleeper." This relative of the pistachio tree (*P. vera*) grows from 35 to 40 feet tall and is resistant to pests and urban pollution. Its leaves, which turn a brilliant orange in autumn, are similar to those of a walnut or pecan. Female Chinese pistache trees also adorn themselves with big clusters of small fruit in shades of pink, magenta, and robin's-egg blue, but they won't self-seed. It will grow in Zones 6 to 9.

SIMPLY MARVELOUS MAGNOLIAS

Good drainage is essential for magnolia trees, with the exception of the sweet bay, or swamp magnolia, (*Magnolia virginiana*), which likes wet soil. Roger Gossler, a co-owner of Gossler Farms Nursery, an Oregon nursery that specializes in magnolias, ensures good drainage for his plants by placing the top of the root ball an inch or so above the ground. He advises that although "magnolias don't like wet feet, they also dislike droughts, so water frequently if it doesn't rain and use around 3 inches of mulch to conserve moisture." Prune magnolias in the spring, cutting back any frost or freeze damage to the fresh cambium (healthy living tissue).

Gossler points out that magnolias are basically woodland trees that prefer sunlight on their foliage and shaded roots. "Both their tops and fleshy roots need plenty of room to spread freely. And remember," Gossler continues, "some of these trees can grow very large and can be quite brittle, so they are easily damaged by whipping winds."

For areas with late frosts, Gossler likes *M. sieboldii*. "Its 3- to 4-inch, pure white flowers with red stamens normally don't bloom until late May," Gossler says, "and it keeps flowering until late July and, in some areas like the Northwest, right on into August." The flowers are then followed by yellow seedpods that turn a brilliant pink in late summer or early fall.

For very cold climates, James W. Kelly, a New York plant taxonomist, recommends *M. kobus* var. *borealis,* which produces masses of 6-inch white flowers. "It's very close to the ideal ornamental tree," he explains. "It's extremely hardy, surviving temperatures of 30°F below zero, and it's long-lived and disease- and pest-resistant. This magnolia also naturalizes [self-sows], very well, particularly in the Northeast."

Magnolia kobus var. *borealis*

TROUBLED TREES

You may want to avoid planting these weak-wooded trees:

Acer saccharinum (silver maple)
Ailanthus altissima (tree-of-heaven)
Populus spp. (poplars)
Salix spp. (willows)
Ulmus pumila (Siberian elm)

GROW A BEAUTIFUL BACKDROP

Do you need a small, quick-growing shrub as a backdrop for your flowers? North Carolina garden writer Peter Loewer highly recommends white forsythia (*Abeliophyllum distichum*), a Korean native. "In very early March or April, it puts out a profusion of honey-smelling, white, drooping flowers, followed by extremely attractive green foliage," says Loewer. Plant white forsythia in well-drained soil in full sun. It likes the same conditions as the more common yellow-flowered forsythia (*Forsythia* spp.). It will eventually reach a height of around 6 feet.

BUY A BETTER BIRCH

Birches (*Betula* spp.) are a popular choice for the home landscape because of their graceful branches, attractive bark, and magnificent fall color. Be sure to choose a birch that is appropriate to your site, says Tom Ranney, Ph.D., an assistant professor at the Mountain Horticultural Crops Research and Extension Center of North Carolina State University at Raleigh.

"Birches are popular landscape trees with vastly different growing requirements," Dr. Ranney explains. "For example, 'Whitespire' Japanese birch [*B. platyphylla* 'Whitespire'], a native of Japan, does quite well in very dry sites. River birch [*B. nigra*] and paper or canoe birch [*B. papyrifera*], on the other hand, are extremely drought-sensitive. If you choose the wrong species for your site, you'll have greater maintenance worries and possibly a dead tree." Dr. Ranney and other botanists are now grafting a Japanese birch to a river birch. "This produces a stress-tolerant tree that's adaptable to many urban environments and to areas with poor drainage or flooding," he explains.

Dr. Ranney advises gardeners to go on a scouting trip in their area before selecting birches or any other species of tree or shrub. Observe plants in similar native environments. The trees and shrubs that are thriving will probably do well in your yard.

DEFEAT DOGWOOD BLIGHT

Dogwood trees up and down the East Coast and also in the Pacific Northwest can suffer from a serious fungal disease called dogwood anthracnose. The disease has infected and killed native flowering dogwoods (*Cornus florida*) in an area that extends from Massachusetts to the Georgia mountains. It has also killed Pacific dogwoods (*C. nuttallii*) in Washington, Oregon, Idaho, and British Columbia.

The first symptoms of anthracnose are small, reddish purple leaf spots or larger, tan, irregular blotches where water has accumulated on the leaf tips or margins. (Spot anthracnose and other foliage diseases can cause similar symptoms, but they don't result in significant damage to the tree.) As the blight progresses, leaves shrivel up in summer and stay on the tree until the following spring. From infected leaves, the disease can spread to the twigs, resulting in cankers and twig dieback. From twigs, it sometimes moves into the tree's branches or trunk.

"There are things you can do to prevent this blight and to save trees that are already infected," says Glen R. Davis, a North Carolina extension agent. "Keeping a tree healthy is your first defense." To do this, he advises applying 4 inches of mulch around dogwoods starting 3 to 4 inches from the trunk and extending out to the drip line. The mulch conserves soil moisture and and precludes the need to mow or trim near the trunk. The wounds caused by lawn mowers and string trimmers provide entry points for diseases and insects.

During dry spells, water once a week in the morning to a depth of 6 inches, but don't wet the foliage. In the late spring or early summer, feed moderately with an organic fertilizer that's low in nitrogen and high in phosphorus. The latter will help growth to harden off and encourage flowering. Prune mature dogwoods so that they get good light and air movement.

"Don't transplant dogwoods from the wild, and don't plant nursery-grown ones in deep shade," Davis advises. "The ideal spot is a place that gets full morning sun and afternoon shade." Make sure that the soil is well-drained and that the planting hole is at least 3 feet in diameter, regardless of the size of the tree. Prune only broken or damaged branches on young dogwoods.

"Once the disease attacks," Davis says, "wait until winter to prune back canker-ridden branches or twigs to healthy growth. To keep the blight from spreading, remove this infected material from the property. Don't burn it, and don't let infected leaves fall to the ground."

Kousa Dogwood

BLIGHT-RESISTANT DOGWOODS

Even if you live in an area where dogwood anthracnose is a problem, you can still enjoy the pleasure of seeing dogwood trees in flower. Try planting dogwood species that are more resistant to anthracnose than native flowering dogwood (*Cornus florida*). John L. Creech, Ph.D., the former director of the U.S. National Arboretum, recommends using the kousa dogwood (*C. kousa*). It flowers about a month later than native dogwoods, so it is less apt to get nipped by frost. The flower bracts are pointed, making the blossoms look like white or pink stars, and *C. kousa*'s red, raspberry-like fruits are almost as big as a cherry. Its bark is also interesting; it tends to flake off, creating shades of green, brown, and gray. "If you can afford to buy only one tree," Dr. Creech says, "make it this one."

The Stellar Dogwood series (*C. × rutgersensis*) is a cross between *C. florida* and *C. kousa* and is a favorite of Karen Jennings, a senior vice president of Geo. W. Park Seed Company and Wayside Gardens in South Carolina. As might be expected, it presents its floral display midway between the early-blooming *C. florida* and the late-blooming *C. kousa.* These trees are literally coated with either white ('Aurora' and 'Constellation') or pink ('Stellar Pink') flowers with huge bracts. Autumn foliage is a brilliant red.

ATTACK OF THE NORWAY MAPLES

The Norway maple (*Acer platanoides*) is a popular street tree because it tolerates difficult urban growing conditions. But according to W. Gary Smith, an assistant professor of landscape design at the University of Delaware at Newark, the Norway maple is creating an ecological disaster in the northeastern United States. "Therefore," he says, "I use every opportunity to strongly discourage people from planting this tree and to remove it when they have a chance."

What has happened, he explains, is that the seeds of this maple have blown through the native forest and taken root. The trees grow, eventually producing heavy canopies that cast very deep shade. And they are also allelopathic, which means they suppress the growth of plants around them. These two factors mean that nothing other than more Norway maples will grow beneath them. "The result," Smith fears, "is that forests in some regions are in danger of becoming monocultures." He recommends using a weed wrench to pry up any young Norway maples that you find.

TAKE ANOTHER LOOK AT SHRUB ROSES

Hedges make good neighbors, and shrub roses make good hedges. They are attractive, and they keep kids, dogs, and other intruders from trampling across lawns and prized plants. These minimum-maintenance, disease-tolerant bushes are also a good choice for the gardener lacking the time or patience to cultivate more-demanding roses.

Old-fashioned shrub roses have one drawback: a short-lived burst of blooms that only lasts through spring. "Now some of the new everblooming shrub roses are worthy of a focal point in the landscape," says Richard Hutton, the chairman of the board at the Conard-Pyle Company, a whole-sale nursery in Pennsylvania. "They produce masses of flowers in the spring and many scattered blossoms throughout the summer and fall. They are also handsome mixed into a regular shrub border."

Space these trouble-free roses 3 or 4 feet apart to create a beautiful hedge. Since many grow to only 4 or 5 feet high, you won't have to prune them. "However, I like to cut the stems back to the ground every four years or so to rejuvenate them from their bases," Hutton says.

There's a wide variety of new everblooming shrub roses to select from. 'Alba Meidiland' has white flowers and a spreading habit. If you favor pink roses, try double-flowered 'Bonica', which is good for hedge plantings, or single-flowered 'Pink Meidiland', which develops orange-red hips. 'Pearl Meidiland' has light pink blossoms. 'Scarlet Meidiland' has a mounding habit and scarlet flowers. For double, red flowers and scarlet fruit, select 'Sevillana'.

THE CASE OF THE ACID-SICK AZALEA

When plants don't grow or flower properly and the foliage is off-color, a natural response is to doctor them with a fertilizer. When azaleas (*Rhododendron* spp.) and rhododendrons exhibit these symptoms, gardeners usually apply fertilizer formulated for acid-loving plants. But sometimes this only results in plants that look worse. Yellowish leaves develop reddish purple blotches and turn brown at the tips and margins—a sign of a magnesium deficiency.

The problem, according to Glen R. Davis, a North Carolina extension agent, may be that the soil is simply *too* acid. While azaleas and rhododendrons will grow at a pH of between 5.0 and 6.0, they generally do best at a pH between 5.2 and 5.4. But in many areas, including a great deal of the Southeast, the soil has a natural pH of about 4.0. Adding an azalea-rhododendron fertilizer to such a soil could lower the pH to 3.5. "That's about the same pH as vinegar or sulphuric acid," Davis points out. "And when soil is *too* acid," he adds, "the needed calcium and magnesium will be tightly bound to the soil and unavailable to the plants."

So before you fertilize those sick-looking azaleas, take a soil sample and have it tested. See "Take Your Best Soil Test" on page 89 for more information on soil sampling and testing. When you receive the results from your soil

DAPHNES BY THE DOOR

Daphnes (*Daphne* spp.) are among the most fragrant of all shrubs. Unfortunately, they have a reputation for being so difficult to grow that one disappointed gardener has labeled them "annual evergreens." But Karen Jennings, a senior vice president of Geo. W. Park Seed Company and Wayside Gardens in South Carolina, contends that these small, scent-loaded shrubs are just picky about where they're planted. Once they're established, daphnes don't like to be moved.

"They must have good drainage," she says, "and like clematis [*Clematis* spp.], they need mulch to keep their roots cool and to conserve moisture. Give them an annual topdressing of leaf mold or well-decomposed compost in spring. In the North, plant in full sun, and cover them with evergreen boughs in the winter for freeze protection. In hot climates, plant them in light shade. *Daphne odora* [winter daphne], which is only hardy through Zone 7, needs even heavier shade. And always offer daphnes protection from winter winds, such as in the lee of the house."

Jennings offers this hint: If you can find the right spot near a door or window, plant daphnes there. Their powerful springtime fragrance will fill the house.

DON'T SHADE OUT RHODYS

Too much sun will burn the foliage of azaleas and rhododendrons. But give them too little sunlight and they won't set flower buds for the following spring. The best site for these plants is under trees, like pines, that offer filtered shade. If your plants seem healthy but won't bloom, the shade may be too dense. Try moving them to a sunnier spot, but be prepared to wait. Once moved, a young, nonblooming plant will spend its first few years putting down roots and creating branches rather than producing prolific blossoms.

test, ask for advice on liming individual plants. Test results are often listed as pounds of lime needed per acre.

PROPAGATE AZALEAS FROM SEED

Many azaleas (*Rhododendron* spp.) are easy to start from seed if the right conditions are available. John L. Creech, Ph.D., the former director of the U.S. National Arboretum, discovered a perfect growing medium for azalea seeds when he planted moss around his home's small, acid-loving foundation plants. He created a lovely, emerald-green groundcover for his shrubs and got a bonus as well.

"Each spring, a liberal crop of azalea seedlings pop up in the moss. I allow them to grow until the following spring, when I carefully transplant them," he says. This natural little nursery has been so successful that Dr. Creech sows azalea seeds in small designated spots in his moss garden. He says the seedlings require no care other than the normal waterings necessary for moss to thrive.

If you have moss growing in your yard, it's easy to move some underneath your azaleas. If not, you can pur-

Azalea seedlings may sprout in moss around your azalea bushes. You can transplant the seedlings, and with a little tender loving care, grow them into new full-size plants.

chase moss from specialized nurseries. Make sure the nursery can guarantee that it raises its own moss and does not collect it from the wild.

If moss is not readily available in your area, a fine organic mulch may work as well. Do not disturb the mulch around your azaleas in the fall, and check carefully for seedlings in the spring.

GROW MOUNTAIN LAURELS IN MINIATURE

Miniature mountain laurels (*Kalmia latifolia*) can be perfect choices for flowering foundation plants. "But don't be distressed if your little dwarf takes off in a big spurt of growth during the first three to five years," says Richard Jaynes, the owner of Broken Arrow Nursery in Connecticut, which specializes in laurels and rhododendrons. "Once they start to flower, the growth will slow down to half that of regular laurels." In other words, a normal laurel will grow 3 to 5 feet in ten years, while a miniature will only grow 2 to 2½ feet in the same amount of time.

Like other laurels, miniatures require good drainage and aeration and a pH of 5.0 to 5.5. They generally languish and die off if planted in heavy soil.

Try these lower-growing versions of mountain laurel: 'Minuet' has pink flowers with a bold burgundy band inside the petals. 'Elf' has very light pink buds that become white blossoms. 'Little Linda' has red buds that become pinkish blossoms.

Mountain Laurel

THE MOUNTAIN LAUREL MYSTERY

When mountain laurel (*Kalmia latifolia*) puts on a magnificent pink-and-white floral display one year and barely blooms the next, who or what is to blame? Usually the weather—too warm, too wet, or too cold a winter—stands accused, but the real answer is elementary. Richard Jaynes, the owner of Broken Arrow Nursery in Connecticut, which specializes in laurels and rhododendrons, explains: "Though individual plants vary a bit, basically, every terminal [stem] has a flower bud which, if left alone, develops into seed capsules. The plant puts its energy into seed production, so you get very little new growth that year. Since laurel flowers form on new growth, without it, there will be few blossoms the next spring." Jaynes says that if you deadhead

white pine

clematis

the flowers as soon as they are spent, you'll increase the odds of having prolific blooms the following season.

Leggy, older plants that have ceased to bloom can be cut almost to the ground, though it will take them two or three years to recover. Prune mountain laurels while plants are still dormant but just before spring growth begins.

Venture into Vines

You may not realize how versatile and useful vines can be in the home landscape. Train them up walls and trellises to provide shade or a privacy screen, or use them as groundcovers in difficult sites. For more tips on using vines as groundcovers, refer to "Groundcovers," beginning on page 319.

USE NATURAL TRELLISES

Vines make a great cover-up for some of those less-attractive features of a yard, such as a chain-link fence. They can also add an extra-special touch of beauty to the trees and shrubs in your landscape. Simply choose a shrub or tree in your yard, and plant a favorite climbing vine at its base. The vine will climb up and through the plant's branches as shown in the illustration at left. When you plant the vine, be careful not to damage the roots of the tree or shrub. Try these experts' suggestions for easy natural trellises.

Richard Hutton, the chairman of the board at the Conard-Pyle Company, a wholesale nursery in Pennsylvania, recommends growing a clematis (*Clematis* spp.) vine up a large yew tree (*Taxus* spp.). "Because of the dark green of the yew, it's a most effective display!" says Hutton. Roger Gossler, a co-owner of Gossler Farms Nursery, an Oregon nursery that specializes in magnolias, gets a similar effect by combining clematis with the dark green of magnolias (*Magnolia* spp.). He particularly likes to combine pink clematis flowers with the hot pink seedpods of *M. sieboldii.*

Karen Jennings, a senior vice president of Geo. W. Park Seed Company and Wayside Gardens in South Carolina, likes her clematis supported by viburnum (*Viburnum* spp.) bushes and dogwood (*Cornus* spp.) trees. Dark blue clematis flowers particularly provide a lovely contrast when mixed with the white viburnum or dogwood blossoms.

North Carolina garden writer Peter Loewer admires

pest-resistant Virginia creeper (*Parthenocissus quinquefolia*) growing in old apple trees or gnarled, dead trees. The vine's magnificent red fall color lights up leafless branches. "If it starts to choke a living tree or if you simply decide you don't want it, unhook the Virginia creeper and spread it on the ground where it makes an excellent groundcover," he says. Loewer also uses a clematis such as 'Madame Bruchard' with eastern white pine (*Pinus strobus*). The pine provides the base shade needed by clematis roots and shows off the clematis's purple-blue flowers. Try this clematis cultivar with camellias (*Camellia* spp.), too.

James W. Kelly, a New York plant taxonomist, finds climbing hydrangea (*Hydrangea anomala* subsp. *petiolaris*) particularly attractive in sugar maples (*Acer saccharum*). It is pest-free, has beautiful flowers, prefers light shade, and won't harm trees.

However, rampant vines such as wisteria (*Wisteria* spp.), bittersweet (*Celastrus* spp.), wild grape (*Vitis* spp.), and honeysuckle (*Lonicera* spp.) can kill trees. So can poison ivy (*Rhus radicans*). These vines reach high into the tree and spiral around branches, blocking light and reducing the tree's food supply. The best way to get rid of these overexuberant climbers is to cut them off at the roots. But don't rip down the vines; let them wither and fall off naturally. Otherwise the tree trunk will undergo a sudden change from being shaded to being exposed to the sun and may suffer sunscald damage.

TURN OLD VINES INTO TRELLISES

For an unusual trellis, try training a vine over old vine prunings. If you have a brick garage or outbuilding, use mortar nails to create a pattern on one of its walls, suggests Bonnie Lee Appleton, Ph.D., an associate professor and extension horticulturist at Virginia Polytechnic Institute and State University. Garden centers carry special nails, called wall anchors or vine nails, that also work well. They have a strip of soft metal that can be bent around a vine's stem to hold it in place. After the nails are in place, weave prunings from grape or kiwi vines around them, then plant a flowering vine at the base of the trellis. As the flowering vine grows, train it to climb over the woody prunings. "The trellis looks nice even before a vine covers it," says Dr. Appleton.

You can also make a rustic-looking free-standing trel-

A TRELLIS AS A CHIMNEY

A vine-covered trellis set 2 to 4 feet in front of the wall of a house can provide natural air-conditioning. It not only will cool the wall by shading it from the sun but also will circulate the air. The trellis creates a chimney effect, sucking cooler air along the bottom of the trellis and exhausting hotter air out the top. This design also allows space for wall maintenance and keeps the vine away from siding or shingles.

FROM SEED TO VINE

You can have beautiful vines for the cost of a seed packet. Try the following five beauties for color from spring until fall. For information on how to grow plants from seeds, see "Growing from Seed," beginning on page 2.

Black-eyed Susan vine (*Thunbergia alata*) produces 1- to 2-inch-wide orange, yellow, or white blooms with black eyes. Try planting them in hanging baskets, window boxes, and trellises.

Moonflower (*Ipomoea alba*) grows 8 to 10 feet long and has fragrant, white, night-blooming flowers. Soak seeds overnight or notch them with a knife or file to break through the seed coat and encourage germination.

Morning glories (*Ipomoea* spp.) will grow up to 25 feet long. They produce red, purple, pink, white, or blue flowers. Treat seeds as you would moonflower seeds for best germination.

Ornamental gourds (*Lagenaria siceraria, Cucurbita pepo* var. *ovifera,* and *Luffa aegyptiaca*) grown on a trellis will produce straight gourds in a variety of colors and sizes. Soak seeds overnight to promote germination.

Sweet pea (*Lathyrus odoratus*) bears fragrant pea-shaped flowers in every color but yellow in spring and early summer.

---

lis by tying and weaving—and even stapling—vine prunings around two or more large, straight branches stuck in the ground. For lightweight vines like clematis (*Clematis* spp.), two branches set 1 foot deep in the ground should be sufficient. For heavy vines like wisteria (*Wisteria* spp.) or grape (*Vitis* spp.), add more straight branches for support, and set the branches 1½ to 2 feet deep or deeper if you have sandy soil.

CLIMBING HYDRANGEAS START SLOWLY

Don't become discouraged if you plant a climbing hydrangea (*Hydrangea anomala* subsp. *petiolaris*) and it seems just to sit there for a couple of years. After a slow start, climbing hydrangea will "take off like a house afire, growing from 12 to 20 feet," says Bonnie Lee Appleton, Ph.D., an associate professor and extension horticulturist at Virginia Polytechnic Institute and State University. "The wait is worth it. This vine has exfoliating bark, which makes it extremely pretty, even when naked." Make sure, though, Dr. Appleton warns, that you put climbing hydrangea where you intend to keep it, because this clinger will really latch onto whatever support you give it, and it won't let go easily.

Climbing hydrangea, which is hardy to Zone 4, likes a rich, moist but well-drained soil. It can tolerate semishade but blooms best in full sun, except in extremely hot climates.

ENCOURAGE CLINGERS TO CLING

An occasional overhead watering will encourage a clinging vine, like climbing hydrangea (*Hydrangea anomala* subsp. *petiolaris*), smilax (*Smilax* spp.), coral vine (*Antigonon leptopus*), or trumpet vine (*Campsis radicans*), to cling by its roots, says Karen Jennings, a senior vice president of Geo. W. Park Seed Company and Wayside Gardens in South Carolina. "Once clingers are established, pinch off the tips just above the uppermost buds to make their growth denser, and prune out dead and weak wood before it blooms," says Jennings. "Cut back any over-long tendrils to two or three leaves."

MAKE RECYCLED TRELLISES

A tuteur is a fancy plant support for vines that's sometimes found in old French gardens. Tuteurs are elegant but expensive—unless you create your own. "You can make your own version of a tuteur. Just stick a long metal or plastic pipe in the ground and insert the framework of an umbrella into it," says North Carolina garden writer Peter Loewer. You can use any old umbrella that no longer has any fabric covering it. This umbrella trellis, shown at right, is particularly good for vines that grow by twining.

And if you're hooked up to a cable service, consider using that unneeded television antenna as a space-age-looking trellis. Stick it in the ground and train a flowering vine up and around it. Or try growing gourds or pole beans up it for an easy harvest.

THE GARDEN PROFESSIONALS

Albert Adelman is the owner of Burt Associates Bamboo in Westford, Massachusetts, a mail-order nursery specializing in bamboo and other Asian plants for indoor and outdoor use.

Bonnie Lee Appleton, Ph.D., is an associate professor of horticulture, researcher, and extension nursery specialist at Hampton Roads Agricultural Experiment Station, Virginia Polytechnic Institute and State University, in Virginia Beach. She is the author of *Landscape Rejuvenation*.

John L. Creech, Ph.D., is the former director of the U.S. National Arboretum in Washington, D.C. Among many other activities, he has also served as the program director for the conservation of plant genetic materials in the International Biology Program at the National Academy of Sciences.

Glen R. Davis is an extension agent for the North Carolina Cooperative Extension Service in Hendersonville, North Carolina. His responsibilities lie in ornamentals, turf, forestry, and urban horticulture.

Roger Gossler and his mother, Marjorie Gossler, are co-owners of Gossler Farms Nursery in Springfield, Oregon. The nursery specializes in magnolias and unusual woody plants, selling both wholesale and retail through mail order.

Erik Haupt is the chairman of the Council of Tree and Landscape Appraisers, headquartered in Washington, D.C. He is also the vice president for environmental and regulatory affairs for Bartlett Tree Expert Company in Danbury, Connecticut.

Richard Hesselein is the president of Princeton Nurseries, a wholesale grower of shade and ornamental trees and shrubs, in Allentown, New Jersey.

Richard Hutton is the chairman of the board at the Conard-Pyle Company, a wholesale nursery in West Grove, Pennsylvania. He received a meritorious award in 1992 from the American Horticulture Society for outstanding service to the industry.

Richard Jaynes is the owner of Broken Arrow Nursery in Hamden, Connecticut. The nursery specializes in woodland trees and shrubs, particularly laurels and rhododendrons, and sells wholesale, retail, and through mail order.

Karen Jennings is a senior vice president of Geo. W. Park Seed Company, Inc., and Wayside Gardens in Greenwood, South Carolina. Wayside Gardens specializes in perennials, ornamental trees and shrubs, vines, and roses.

James W. Kelly is a plant taxonomist, specializing in lilacs, who works for Micha Tree and Landscape Consultants in Rochester, New York.

FRUITS OF THE VINES

Don't limit your imagination when selecting plants to grow on a trellis. Vines that produce edible fruits and seeds can be just as beautiful climbing a trellis as a strictly ornamental vine would be. Try growing cucumbers or pole beans, such as 'Scarlet Runner' beans, or even winter squash vines up a trellis. If you live in Zones 9 or 10, you can also try growing tropical or semitropical fruiting vines, such as chayote (*Sechium edule*), evergreen grape (*Rhoicissus capensis*), hyacinth bean (*Dolichos lablab*), and passion fruit (*Passiflora edulis*). Keep in mind that these plants grow rampantly in good conditions and will need strong supports.

Peter Loewer is a garden writer and botanical illustrator from Asheville, North Carolina. He has written *Tough Plants for Tough Places* and other books.

Rich Owings is the horticulturist at The North Carolina Arboretum in Asheville, North Carolina. He is working to establish a national native azalea repository at the arboretum.

Tom Ranney, Ph.D., is an assistant professor at the Mountain Horticultural Crops Research and Extension Center of North Carolina State University at Raleigh, Department of Horticultural Science.

Ray Rothenberger, Ph.D., is a professor of ornamental horticulture at the University of Missouri at Columbia. He also hosts a call-in radio garden show in mid-Missouri.

Alex L. Shigo is the owner of Shigo and Trees Associates in Durham, New Hampshire, and a former chief scientist for the U.S. Forest Service. He is the author of *Tree Pruning, A New Tree Biology,* and *A New Tree Biology Dictionary.*

E. Thomas Smiley, Ph.D., is a plant pathologist at the Bartlett Tree Research Labortories in Charlotte, North Carolina. The laboratories provide technical support to Bartlett Tree Expert Company, a national tree-care company.

W. Gary Smith is an assistant professor of landscape design in the Department of Plant and Soil Sciences at the University of Delaware at Newark. He is also a practicing registered landscape architect.

Lawns and Groundcovers

More gardeners ask about lawn care than any other topic. Perhaps that's because so many of us live in one of those neighborhoods where all of the topsoil was hauled away when the homes were constructed. Our houses have a strong foundation, but our lawns are struggling with a poor one of undernourished, compacted subsoil.

Many homeowners are now questioning how much lawn they really need and are thinking of converting some of that monotonous green into a richly textured bed of groundcovers. So whether you're looking for ways to make your lawn healthier, solutions to lawn problems, or alternatives to lawns, peruse the following tips and techniques from experts who deal daily with the concerns of caring for a lawn.

Lawn Care Basics

When to water, when to mow, and when to feed our lawns are decisions that seem to puzzle us more than they should. Following some simple guidelines for organic lawn care will help you keep your lawn looking its best.

SPREAD COMPOST ON THE LAWN?

We all know that adding compost to soil helps to enrich and revitalize it, but did you know that the same thing applies to adding compost to your lawn? Michael Talbot, the owner of Michael Talbot and Associates, a Massachusetts ecological landscape design and maintenance company, recommends compost as a topdressing to help restore lawns. "The importance here is the soil-building organic material as well as nitrogen and other nutrients," says Talbot. He suggests using a compost that contains manure or another nitrogen source like a fertilizer, applied in late summer or early fall for cool-season grasses and in spring and early summer for warm-season ones. How much to apply? About

---

WARM OR COOL?

Lawn grasses are broadly divided into two types: cool-season grasses and warm-season grasses. It's good to know which kind you have and how to manage that type of grass properly.

Cool-Season Grasses

Cool-season grasses grow best in cool weather and cool climates. They are green from fall through spring, and they tend to slow down and even turn brown in the heat of summer. These grasses are predominant in the northern half of the country. They include:

Fescue
Kentucky bluegrass
Perennial ryegrass

Warm-Season Grasses

Warm-season grasses grow best in warm weather—spring and summer—and will turn brown and go dormant after fall frost. They are suited to the South and Southwest regions of the country. They include:

Bahia grass
Bermuda grass
Centipede grass
St. Augustine grass
Zoysia grass

CHOOSE THE RIGHT CUT

Just how short should you cut your lawn? That depends on the season and the type of lawn grass you have. In some cases, some cultivars of a particular grass need higher mowing than others, so it helps to know which cultivar you have, too. For example, 'Bonsai', a dwarf type of tall fescue, grows only half the height of standard 'Kentucky 31' tall fescue: Obviously, it can't be mowed to the same height.

The best place to go for specific information on the height to mow your grass is your local extension office. But as a rule of thumb, remember this: If your lawn looks brown after you mow it, you're cutting too low. And if you leave scalped spots where the ground is bumpy, that's another signal to raise the mower blade height.

COUNT THE EARTHWORMS

Use earthworms to gauge the health of the soil under your lawn, says Michael Talbot, the owner of Michael Talbot and Associates, a Massachusetts ecological landscape design and maintenance company. Talbot likes to see at least five earthworms per square foot in the soil; ten is ideal. Any less than five, and it's time to add organic matter. For more information on how to do an earthworm count, see "Conduct an Earthworm Survey" on page 92.

¼ to ½ inch evenly distributed over the top of the lawn. Just toss it out by the shovelful, and smooth it out with a rake. To compute how much compost you'll need to cover your lawn, see "Compost Calculations" on page 93.

THE TRUTH ABOUT THATCH

Because you can't see thatch—that layer of undecomposed organic matter that builds up between your grass and the soil—you don't think about it. But if it gets too thick, it can cause problems such as shallow rooting, and it can provide a haven for insects and disease. What causes thatch? "Many people think that thatch is a buildup of grass clippings, but it's not," says Daniel A. Potter, Ph.D., an entomology professor at the University of Kentucky. It's made up of undecomposed roots, stems, and rhizomes. "If you over-fertilize and overwater, you often end up with thatch problems," says Dr. Potter.

THE GOLDEN RULE OF MOWING

Giving your lawn a close shave saves mowing time, but it can lead to other lawn headaches. "Never remove more than one-third of the height of the leaf blade," says David Marshall, a Florida extension agent specializing in environmental horticulture. This rule applies to both warm-season and cool-season grasses. Jack Hall, Ph.D., a professor of turfgrass management at Virginia Polytechnic Institute and State University, explains: "Mowing a lot at one time shocks the root system. In tests done by the USDA in Maryland on bluegrass, roots actually stopped growing when 60 percent of the green tissue was removed."

In Pennsylvania, Thomas L. Watschke, Ph.D., a professor of turfgrass science at the Pennsylvania State University at University Park, concurs. "A lawn responds to close mowing by thinning out," he says, "creating spaces for weeds."

"I bought my last mower based on how high it would adjust," Marshall adds. Adjusting the height of your mower so the grass grows taller in summer helps grass through drought. The taller grass shades itself and the ground. There is also a correlation between root depth and grass height. Taller grass grows deeper roots, meaning less need to water.

LET CLIPPINGS FALL WHERE THEY MAY

When you mow the lawn, leave the clippings in place. "Lawn clippings are about 80 percent water. The rest is very rapidly decomposed by soil microbes," says Thomas L. Watschke, Ph.D., a professor of turfgrass science at the Pennsylvania State University at University Park. According to Dr. Watschke, leaving clippings on the lawn translates to recycling as much as 15 to 18 percent of the nitrogen fertilizer you apply.

Are there any instances in which you should remove clippings? According to Dr. Watschke, it's best to remove clippings if you have a bona fide problem with thatch—a dense mat of organic matter at the root level that can prevent water and nutrients from penetrating to your lawn grasses' roots. "Clippings don't cause thatch," he says, "but they can contribute to it if it's there. That's an important distinction." A thatch layer separates the clippings from the soil bacteria that would otherwise quickly break them down.

A mowing strip of closely set bricks laid flat makes trimming along the edges of flower beds easier and helps slow grasses intent on creeping into your beds. One wheel of the lawn mower can ride on the bricks as you mow.

LET THE LAWN BREATHE

Don't let fallen leaves stay on the lawn all winter. They mat down and smother the grass below. Shred the leaves, and then add them to the compost pile. If you don't have a shredder, you can chop dried leaves with your lawn mower instead. Just rake the leaves into a pile, and run your mower over them in a criss-cross pattern until they're cut into small pieces.

KEEP TWO MOWER BLADES ON HAND

We all love the convenience of rotary mowers, but beware: They'll chew up your grass if the blades aren't kept sharp. "We like rotary mowers because they're idiotproof, myself included," says Thomas L. Watschke, Ph.D., a professor of turfgrass science at the Pennsylvania State University at University Park.

Dr. Watschke says he's on a crusade to get everyone to keep the blades of their rotary mowers sharp. "All you've got to do is have two sharp blades and be able to take off a nut," says Dr. Watschke. "Put a nail in the garage, and hang one blade there. Put the other on the mower. When it gets dull, swap it with the sharp blade in the garage and take the dull one to the garden center or dealer to be sharpened. Then hang it on the nail in the garage until you need to swap blades again. It's no big deal," he says.

CHOOSE A SENSIBLE LAWN SHAPE

The shape of your lawn will dictate whether you can water it efficiently. That's the observation of Jerry L. Tanner, a landscape architect from Ohio. "Limit the size of your open lawn," says Tanner, "and don't break it up into little bits and pieces by putting paths and planting beds throughout the property." It's hard to water bits and pieces of lawn efficiently because it requires more zones of spray. Tanner suggests the most water-efficient lawn design: an oval of grass toward the center (or off-center) of the property with a periphery of mulched areas or planting beds.

ABOUT AUTOMATIC IRRIGATION

Poorly designed or do-it-yourself automatic irrigation systems are a no-no in areas where watering is restricted. Most automatic systems can't really know if the lawn needs water; they just come on when the timer says so, even if it happens to be raining at the time.

"The most critical thing about an irrigation system is that it needs to be supervised or installed by a professional," says Jerry L. Tanner, a landscape architect from Ohio, "someone who understands and uses proper equipment and irrigation layout." Sprinkler heads should apply water only to areas where it's needed. Also, the system should be programmable so that zones of irrigation run individually where needed. Many systems also have sensors that shut the system off if it starts to rain.

If you've inherited a system that is less than perfect, Tanner suggests that you have a professional assess its capabilities and recommend simple changes that can increase efficiency. He also suggests running the system in the very early morning (from 5:00 to 8:00 A.M.) to reduce evaporation. If you can program the heads independently, reduce water to areas protected from the hot afternoon sun by shade from trees.

Robert Peek, an information specialist in water conservation and management from Florida, suggests that homeowners consider systems that come with a tensiometer — a device that measures moisture in the soil. Rather than working by timer, the tensiometer triggers the irrigation system based on the amount of moisture available in the soil. Peek also says, "Check into a meter permanently installed in the irrigation line to measure the number of gallons applied per minute." Then you can determine how soon to turn the sprinklers off. How much water you need depends on your soil type and the slope of the soil. Contact your local extension office for information about your soil and its slope.

WHEN SHOULD YOU WATER?

"The best way to schedule watering is to look at your grass and let it tell you it's time to water," says Robert Peek, an information specialist in water conservation and management from Florida. What should you look for? These signals say that your lawn needs water:

- The grass has a bluish gray cast, rather than its normal green.
- Your footprints remain imprinted as you walk across the lawn. (The grass doesn't spring back.)
- The leaf blades curl from the sides.

LOOK FOR AN ORGANIC LAWN SERVICE

Many homeowners consider themselves organic gardeners and aren't aware that their lawn care service isn't. This is the experience of Jack Siebenthaler, a registered landscape architect from Florida who has worked with trees on public and private properties for over 50 years. "Many times I'm called to a problem where the top of a tree

---

WHAT ABOUT DROUGHT?

If a drought strikes in your area, one of the first uses of water you'll try to save on is watering the lawn. If water rationing is necessary, chances are you won't have the choice. Here are some tips you can take to help preserve your lawn during a drought:

Allow the grass to go dormant. This is the grass's natural defense against drought. If you suspect you're in for a drought, don't water. Let your grass begin the natural preparation in case the situation worsens.

Mow high or don't mow. You'll want to leave the dried grass because it helps insulate the crowns so they'll retain more moisture.

Water sparingly after the grass goes dormant. Provide ½ inch of water every two weeks. This will keep some roots and buds alive but won't bring the grass out of its dormant state. If your water use is restricted, choose priority lawn areas, and only water those areas.

FINDING ORGANIC LAWN FOOD

We all know that most of those brightly packaged lawn foods at the garden center *aren't* organic. But how can you tell which ones really are? One way to know a natural, organic lawn fertilizer is to look at how much nitrogen it contains. "Most fertilizers from truly natural, organic sources will contain only a fraction of the amount of nitrogen found in a synthetic fertilizer," says Phil Aaronson, the business manager for The Organic Landscape Company in Rhode Island. "And you'll want to look at the percentage of Water Insoluble Nitrogen [WIN] because that is its slow-release component. In a fertilizer with a low WIN [less than 50 percent], much of the nitrogen dissolves immediately and ends up in the gutter." For other clues on recognizing organic fertilizers, see "What's in the Bag?" on page 95.

is suffering, and the lawn below is a weed-free bright green," he says. "One of the first things I ask is whether they use a lawn service." Siebenthaler says that regular applications of weed-and-feed-type products (routine in some contracts) that contain synthetic postemergent herbicides can injure or even kill trees. The moral: If you use a lawn service, be sure that their approach is as organic as yours.

 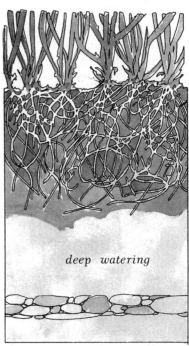

shallow watering

deep watering

Frequent shallow watering leads to shallow rooting. The shallow roots have less of the soil's reserve of nutrients and water to draw from. Frequent heavy watering can waterlog the soil, also suppressing root growth. Your lawn will be healthiest if you give it occasional deep waterings. The grass roots will penetrate to the depth the soil is wet and can draw water and dissolved nutrients from a larger volume of the soil.

Revitalizing Lawns

While a poor-looking lawn doesn't rank as a life crisis, it does drag down the appearance of your whole home landscape. In some cases, you can renovate or repair your lawn without taking the drastic plunge of tilling in the grass and starting over.

CORRECT COMPACTION

Lawn areas that are walked on or used as a playground get pounded, and that means the soil gets compacted. So what do you do? "Core cultivate," says Thomas L. Watschke, Ph.D., a professor of turfgrass science at the Pennsylvania State University at University Park. That's the professional term for using an aerator, which is a piece of equipment that literally takes little cores of soil from the ground to help alleviate compaction. You can rent an aerator from a rent-all-type business. The open cores allow water and air into the soil to help grass roots compete with weeds that don't mind compaction. "If the soil is compacted, that's going to favor anything but grass," says Dr. Watschke.

According to Dr. Watschke, you may need to make more than one pass over the area, and if it's walked or played on regularly, you'll want to aerate at least once a year. The ideal time to do this is when the grasses are in active growth—fall for cool-season grasses and spring or summer for warm-season grasses. If the soil is extremely compacted, you may need to do it three or four times a year, timing treatments about eight to ten weeks apart. "On cool-season grasses, do it in fall. Aerating creates holes in the ground that water will go into," says Dr. Watschke. "Then in winter, the alternate freezing and thawing of water in the holes helps break up the soil even more."

According to Dr. Watschke, you can leave the cores on the lawn if you don't mind their appearance, and the rain will eventually disperse them. An alternative is to rake them up and add them to the compost.

REDO OR START ANEW?

How do you know if your lawn is so far gone that you need to start anew? Michael Talbot, the owner of Michael Talbot and Associates, a Massachusetts ecological landscape design and maintenance company, says, "Remember the 50 percent rule." If 50 percent of the area is covered with healthy turf, then chances are it can be restored. If the amount of healthy grass is less than 50 percent, there may be a serious problem such as poor drainage that needs to be

---

KEEP THESE TREES OFF THE LAWN

Some trees are nearly impossible to grow grass under because they have many surface roots that compete with grass for root space, water, and nutrients. Here is a list of some that you'll want to avoid planting in a prime lawn area:

Acer platanoides (Norway maple)
Acer saccharinum (silver maple)
Betula spp. (birches)
Fagus spp. (beeches)
Ulmus spp. (elms)

solved. You need to correct the underlying problem and then re-establish the grass, or try an alternative groundcover.

Planting grass plugs can restore a damaged lawn area. Begin by raking the area to level it and remove debris. Water thoroughly the night before you plan to plant. Use a plugger, auger, or spade to make 3-inch-diameter planting holes in a checkerboard pattern. For good establishment, place 1 teaspoon of blended organic fertilizer in each hole before planting. Plant a plug in each hole. The spacing you use will determine how long it takes for the grass to fill in and form continuous cover. Water again after planting and regularly for the first few weeks. Fertilize six to eight weeks after planting.

ZOYSIA BEATS THE SUMMER BLUES

"I took out my bluegrass lawn and replaced it with zoysia grass," says Ray Rothenberger, Ph.D., a professor of ornamental horticulture at the University of Missouri at Columbia. "I was tired of a bluegrass lawn that looked green in winter when my flowers were dead and looked dead in summer when my flowers were up and blooming. Now it's all on the same cycle." *Zoysia japonica* 'Meyer' is the most cold-hardy zoysia grass. "It's a good, thick turf that competes well with weeds," he adds, "and it has a nice golden color in winter." Note that zoysia grass is not available as seed because it will not come true to type. If you want a new zoysia grass lawn, you'll have to plant sod or small plugs of grass, known as sprigs.

UN-TILL WE MEET AGAIN, WEEDS!

If you decide to till under your weedy lawn and start from scratch, make sure you deal with perennial weed problems before you reseed. Michael Talbot, the owner of Michael Talbot and Associates, a Massachusetts ecological landscape design and maintenance company, recommends a repeated series of attacks that will eventually weaken and kill out the weeds. Begin by tilling in the weedy area, watering, and letting it sit for a week. "In that time, those grasses capable of growing back will do so. Then you simply till again," he says. Forcing the weeds to start growth afresh each time uses up the food reserves stored in their roots, weakening the plants overall, says Talbot.

After two or three tillings, the area should be ready for reseeding. Add nutrients and lime (as recommended by a soil test) and 1 inch of organic matter. Grade the soil and seed a new lawn. This technique works for perennial grasses such as Bermuda grass, Dallis grass, various pasture grasses, and some broad-leaved weeds such as ground ivy and dichondra.

A FITNESS PROGRAM FOR WEAK LAWNS

If your lawn is weak and sparse, it may take more than adjusting your mowing and watering practices to renew it. Here are a series of steps recommended by Michael Talbot, the owner of Michael Talbot and Associates, a Massachusetts ecological landscape design and maintenance company:

1. Collect soil samples from the yard for a laboratory analysis. Take samples from several locations that have different soil type, conditions, or turf quality. Talbot suggests that homeowners test for pH, key plant nutrients and minerals, and percentage of organic matter. "I like to see at least a 6 percent level of organic matter in a soil test, especially in one from a lawn, because it's always going to be skewed upward from all of the roots, thatch, and other decomposing bits of grass in the soil," says Talbot. For hints on collecting soil samples, see "Take Your Best Soil Test" on page 89.

LAYING SOD

When laying sod, fit the strips as close together as possible. Be sure to stagger the seams between strips so that they do not line up from row to row. Use a sharp knife to cut sod to fit around walks, edgings, or other obstacles. Rolling sod after laying it improves contact between the roots and the underlying soil and gets the sod off to a good start.

Here are some do-it-right tips on how to lay sod from Pratt Brown, the owner of Pratt Brown Landscapes, an Alabama landscape maintenance and design company:

Laying the blocks. Stagger the blocks of sod so they lay in a checkerboard fashion. The turf will knit together more neatly and quickly. Brown suggests the natural way to do this is to start your second row with a half-block of sod.

Sodding a slope. On a slope, always lay the rows of sod across the slope, not up and down.

Patching up bare spots. Do any patching on the inside. Pieces along the periphery should be whole. Brown also suggests that if you're patching here and there as part of a renovation (perhaps to cover where a tree has come down or to re-sod a patch lost to weeds), you should use whole blocks of sod, even if the spot in need is smaller than that. "The smaller the piece, the harder it is to keep alive," he says. So cut out a spot big enough for an entire block of sod to lay in.

2. Mow the lawn close. "That may be 1 to 1½ inches," says Talbot. "I mow as close as I can without scalping or hitting the ground." Collect the clippings for your compost pile.

3. Do an aeration test. Try to force a large screwdriver into the soil in different areas of your lawn. If you have trouble, your soil is compacted. Rent an aerator to break up the soil. See "Correct Compaction" on page 309 for details on soil aeration.

4. Rent a dethatcher. Use it to dig up weeds and open channels through the turf. Before dethatching, Talbot spreads 50 to 100 pounds of rock phosphate per 1,000 square feet over the existing lawn. "Phosphate is most needed in the early stages of growth," says Talbot. Rake up all of the thatch debris brought to the surface by the machine, and compost it separately.

5. Broadcast seed. Talbot recommends sowing 25 to 50 percent more seed than you would for starting a new lawn because some seeds won't penetrate the existing turf, so the germination percentage will be lower. Drag a lawn rake across the seeded area to help scratch the seed in.

6. Fertilize. Spread an all-organic lawn fertilizer as well as lime or any other amendments that the soil test indicated.

7. Add a topdressing. Top-dress with ¼ to ½ inch of compost. "It acts like a mulch to improve germination, the soil, and the turf," says Talbot.

8. Rent a lawn roller. Fill it one-third full, and roll the lawn.

9. Keep the lawn watered. Water lightly twice daily to keep the top ½ inch of soil moist while the seeds sprout.

Coping with Pest Problems

As if mowing and watering the lawn weren't enough of a chore, we find ourselves having to face occasional problems with insects and diseases. Fortunately, there are some effective organic controls and some new types of grasses with built-in protection against pests.

GRASSES WITH BUILT-IN PEST CONTROL

One way to avoid insect problems in lawns is to plant grasses that the insects won't feed on. They're called endophyte-enhanced grasses, which means that they contain endophytes—fungi that produce toxins that kill many grass-eating insects. Initially discovered because they made livestock sick, endophytic grasses are obviously for lawns only—not for pasture. These cultivars not only escape damage of major pests such as chinch bugs, billbugs, and sod webworms, but also are more tolerant of cultural stresses such as drought.

"Unfortunately, much of the seed [for endophytic grasses] common in the marketplace is not necessarily the best," says David J. Shetlar, Ph.D., a landscape entomologist for the Ohio Cooperative Extension Service. Also, keep in mind that endophyte-enhanced grasses can lose their fungal infection if the seed is stored too long, especially at high temperatures. So always be sure you're getting the freshest seed, and store it in a cool, dry place until you're ready to use it.

Dr. Shetlar says that homeowners need a mix that contains at least 50 percent endophyte-enhanced cultivars, and he recommends that they ask for two- and three-way blends of seed mixes that contain endophytic fescues and ryegrass. (So far, endophytes are known only to these two groups of grasses, which would omit them from the Deep South and other areas too warm for certain tall fescues and perennial ryegrass.) See "Endophyte-Enhanced Grasses" at right for a list of endophytic cultivars.

ORGANIC NEMESIS

The good news for homeowners is that in an organically managed lawn most pests are kept in check by their natural predators and parasites. "In the Northeast, we have only two major insect pests that create any kind of problems in an organically maintained lawn. Because we're not applying insecticides, we get natural control of most pests, except for hairy chinch bugs and white grubs," says Michael Talbot, the owner of Michael Talbot and Associates, a Massachusetts ecological landscape design and maintenance company. (For more about white grubs, see "White Grubs Like Wet Lawns" on page 315.)

Talbot has a simple treatment regimen for chinch bugs. First, he does a chinch bug count. If he counts 20 or more chinch bugs per square foot or if he sees damage, he begins to water that section of the lawn and applies fish emulsion or other soluble nitrogen fertilizer and liquid seaweed. "The idea is to stimulate enough growth to outgrow the damage," Talbot explains. Usually chinch bugs

ENDOPHYTE-ENHANCED GRASSES

If you'd like to plant endophyte-enhanced grasses, look for cultivars on this list compiled by David J. Shetlar, Ph.D., a landscape entomologist for the Ohio Cooperative Extension Service and Richard Hurley, Ph.D., the director of research for Lofts Seed in New Jersey:

Perennial Ryegrass

'Accolade'	'Pennant'
'Advent'	'Pinnacle'
'Assure'	'Pleasure'
'Commander'	'Prelude II'
'Competitor'	'Regal'
'Dandy'	'Repell'
'Duet'	'Repell II'
'Express'	'Riviera'
'Gen-90'	'Saturn'
'Gettysburg'	'Seville'
'Legacy'	'SR 4200'
'Manhattan II'	'Target'
'Palmer II'	'Yorktown III'

Fine Fescue

'Jamestown II'	'SR 5000'
'Reliant'	'Warwick'
'Southport'	

Tall Fescue

'Mesa'	'Titan'
'Shenandoah'	'Tribute'

CHECK FOR CHINCH BUGS

Chinch bugs and their larvae are a common lawn pest virtually everywhere except the Northwest and Plains states. Both the bugs and the larvae are about 1½ inches long. The bugs have a distinctive inverted-V pattern on their wings. The larvae are whitish with black spots or stripes on their sides.

If your lawn shows ragged yellow or brown patches, you may have a chinch bug problem. Here's an easy way to find out for sure:

1. Cut both ends from an empty coffee can, and push the can halfway into your lawn.

2. Pour soapy water into the container, and wait 10 to 15 minutes.

3. Count the number of chinch bugs and/or larvae that float to the top. If you see more than 12, you need to take steps to control the pest. Treating problem areas with insecticidal soap is generally effective.

prefer hot, dry areas, so the watering discourages them, too. If chinch bug damage continues, Talbot recommends overseeding the area with a mixture of endophytic grasses. (For more information on endophytic grasses, see "Grasses with Built-In Pest Control" on page 312.)

DON'T LET GRUBS GET YOUR GOAT

If you spot a few grubs in the soil under your lawn, don't overreact. If your lawn is in good basic health, it can withstand some grub feeding. Lawn professionals have what they call a threshold level for the number of grubs a lawn can tolerate before the damage becomes unacceptable. Many professionals believe that a healthy lawn can tolerate 10 to 15 grubs per square foot. Daniel A. Potter, Ph.D., an entomology professor at the University of Kentucky, says, "The conventional wisdom that 3 to 6 grubs per square foot warrants treatment is nonsense. Almost any lawn in decent condition can tolerate 10 white grubs per square foot and possibly twice that if the turf is vigorous." If you want to check for grubs under your lawn, refer to the illustration on the opposite page for instructions.

HOW TO BEAT BEETLE GRUBS

White grubs—the larval stage of Japanese beetles and other beetles—can be tough lawn pests. Michael Talbot, the owner of Michael Talbot and Associates, a Massachusetts ecological landscape design and maintenance company, outlines six things you should do to battle them:

1. Maintain a healthy mix of turf that contains endophytic cultivars of tall fescue. "There is some research that indicates that these grasses are avoided by some white grubs," says Talbot.

2. Keep the lawn healthy. Good culture will help the grass tolerate grubs and outgrow their damage.

3. Monitor the grubs to find out how many are present and when in summer they first appear. See the illustration on the opposite page for information on monitoring grubs.

4. Apply extra water and liquid seaweed to help the grass outgrow the damage.

5. Apply milky disease spores in early July for long-term control. "There is a question about how effective milky spore [milky disease] really is in Massachusetts," says Talbot, "but south of here, where soils are warmer, it seems to work very well." Its success varies throughout the country, but the bottom line is that any control it provides is another tool in an integrated program of grub control. You can read more about this control method in "A Milky Menace for Grubs" on this page.

6. Treat with entomogenous (predatory) nematodes for serious grub problems as a short-term control. For more information about this control method, see "Nematodes That Kill Grubs" on page 316. Talbot recommends only the *Heterorhabditis* species for grub control.

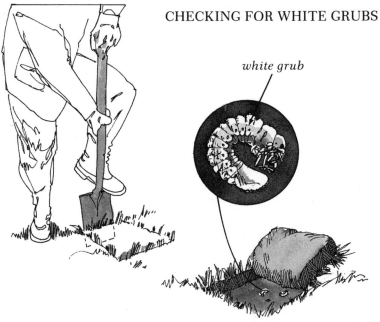

CHECKING FOR WHITE GRUBS

white grub

To check for white grubs, use a blunt-ended spade to cut through three sides of a square-foot-size flap of lawn. Gently pry up the roots, and roll the flap back to look underneath. Count the grubs in that square foot of ground, and then tamp the turf back down. Give it a little extra water for a week or two to be sure it reroots.

WHITE GRUBS LIKE WET LAWNS

Japanese beetles and other white-grub-type beetles may prefer to lay their eggs in lawns that are well-irrigated. "If it's dry in July when most of these beetles are making their mating and egg-laying flights, the adults are going to look for lawns where the soil is nice and moist because the survival of their eggs depends on moisture," says Daniel A.

WHAT IS A WHITE GRUB?

White grubs are the larvae of a certain family of beetles called scarab beetles. This group includes the infamous Japanese beetle and green June beetles. Other common beetles in the group are the May beetle and the masked chafer, which is a small, brown beetle often attracted to porch lights at night. You can identify white grubs by their greasy white color and brown head and by the fact that they rest on their sides in a characteristic C-shape in the soil.

A MILKY MENACE FOR GRUBS

Milky disease spores (also known as milky spore) are spores of a bacterium that attacks white grubs. The grubs become infected with the bacteria while feeding on the treated grass. When the grubs die, they release millions of spores back into the soil. These spores will infect future generations of grubs and new grubs that move in from afar. However, it may take two or three years for the disease to become established enough to get consistent control. You can tell if a grub is infected because its body fluid looks milky rather than clear.

For the best results, team up with neighbors to treat as many lawns as possible. If you live in the country, control is most effective if surrounding pastures and even orchard floors are treated at the same time. Milky disease doesn't kill beneficial insects or earthworms, only white grubs.

NEMATODES THAT KILL GRUBS

Entomophagous nematodes are *helpful* nematodes that feed on insect pests such as grubs. They are applied by the billions as a living pesticide that travels through moist soil to find its host. Beneficial nematodes will control cutworms and many other soft-bodied, soil-dwelling insects, and not just grubs. Unfortunately, they will not kill slugs.

The nematodes are shipped in a gel-like substance and then mixed with water for application with a sprayer or watering can. Be sure to follow the application instructions that come with the nematodes.

These nematodes are very sensitive to dry soil, so it is essential to water the area to be treated before applying and once again afterward. They're also sensitive to ultraviolet light, so apply them in the evening. This gives the nematodes all night to enter the soil. The soil should be between 60° and 85°F for the best results. The nematodes will be active for two weeks and gradually dwindle thereafter.

Thatch acts as a barrier between the nematodes and the soil. Bill Wolf, the president of Necessary Trading Company, a Virginia company that manufactures and sells organic fertilizers, recommends doubling the concentration of the nematode solution when applying it on lawns to ensure penetration of sufficient nematodes to provide control.

Potter, Ph.D., an entomology professor at the University of Kentucky. Dr. Potter suggests keeping your lawn on the dry side during the beetles' egg-laying period (late June to early August). After the eggs have hatched and the grubs are feeding (late August to September), resume watering to help your lawn tolerate and outgrow injury from their feeding.

DON'T MAKE YOUR YARD A BEETLE FEAST

One commonsense way to help prevent problems with the adults and grubs of Japanese beetles is to avoid landscape plants that the adult beetles love. "I know you can't ask a rose lover not to grow roses, but there are certain plants that Japanese beetles just devour that surely one can find a substitute for," says Daniel A. Potter, Ph.D., an entomology professor at the University of Kentucky. Among Japanese beetles' favorites are sassafras (*Sassafras* spp.), linden (*Tilia* spp.), purple-leaf plum (*Prunus* × *cistena*), 'Crimson King' Norway maple (*Acer platanoides* 'Crimson King'), and many crab apples (*Malus* spp.). If you live in an area where Japanese beetles are a problem, Dr. Potter suggests that you ask your local Cooperative Extension Service office for a list of local plants preferred by the pests. Obviously, these are the plants you'll want to avoid.

Lawn Alternatives

How much lawn do you really need? In many cases, less than you have. You can add interest and challenge to your garden by turning some of that lawn into a berry patch or a flower border. If you prefer a low-maintenance alternative to lawns, you may want to try planting a wildflower meadow or a bed of groundcovers.

MAKE YOUR LAWN A WILD MEADOW

You can create a small sanctuary for butterflies and songbirds by converting your lawn to a wildflower meadow. Jim Wilson, a cohost of public television's "The Victory Garden," says he feels that a real breakthrough in meadow gardening is coming as wildflowers are more widely propagated and are available inexpensively in small pots.

However, if started wildflower plants aren't available in your area, you can start your wildflower meadow from seed. "If you try starting a meadow with a seed mix," says Wilson, "you absolutely have to start with a clean bed of soil or the wildflowers can't compete with the grasses." Wilson recommends solarizing the soil before planting. For directions on solarizing soil, see "The Sun as Weed Killer" on page 120. "Solarizing does a remarkable job of cleaning out weed seeds and stoloniferous grasses," says Wilson.

Once you have finished the solarization process, which may take as long as eight weeks, you'll be ready to plant. With as little soil disturbance as possible, cut shallow furrows in the planting area with the corner of a hoe. Drop your wildflower seeds into the furrows, but don't cover them. They will sprout between August and the following spring.

Wilson suggests starting with a small area and establishing a nursery bed. Once those plants have matured, you can save the seeds, solarize new areas, and establish them from your own homegrown seeds. "What that does is let you learn the wildflowers and how they're going to look under garden conditions. They grow better and tend to bush out more than they do in the wild because they're not competing with grasses," he says. Except for extremely poor soils, Wilson suggests growing the wildflowers without fertilizer so as not to encourage weeds.

WILDFLOWER TIPS FROM DOT

Few people have more-difficult planting sites to tackle than the Department of Transportation (DOT). Landowners with large lots often have to deal with similar difficult roadside sites, which may have steep slopes or poor soil or may be difficult to water. It's hardly an area to try a lawn. What to do? Gary L. Henry, a staff coordinator for the Florida Highway Beautification Council, suggests planting native wildflowers. Henry offers the following tips for establishing wildflowers on a difficult site:

Select just one species. "If you look around at the showiest native wildflower stands, they aren't a mix. They're usually just more and more of the same flower," says Henry. Planting a mix just adds competition, and one type will usually predominate and choke out the others anyway.

Henry suggests looking at wildflower stands in your area and selecting the most common species blooming. Identify it, and then see if you can find seed for it in a catalog. "Bringing in something that's pretty but not native to your area isn't going to give you the best results. If you

---

DON'T BE FOOLED BY FILLER

When buying wildflower seeds, Ed Hume, the owner of Ed Hume Seeds in Washington State, suggests you look carefully at the contents of the package. "Some 4-ounce packages may end up being only 1 ounce of seed and 3 ounces of vermiculite or other filler," he says. Filler isn't necessarily bad, because it makes it easier to distribute the seeds. Just be sure you're not overpaying for fancy packaging and what appears to be lots of seed. If you buy wildflower seeds in bulk, Hume suggests that you mix them with sand or vermiculite and scatter them with a drop-type spreader.

EVERGREEN FERNS

If you're planting ferns, you may want to choose ferns that will add color and structure to your garden year-round. You can select from these evergreen types:

Asplenium spp. (spleenworts)
Botrychium spp. (grape ferns)
Cryptogramma crispa var. *acrostichoides* (parsley fern)
Dryopteris spp. (wood ferns)
Phylli'tis scolopendrium (hart's-tongue fern)
Polypodium spp. (polypody ferns)
Polystichum spp. (shield ferns)
Woodwardia spp. (chain ferns)

can't find the native species, then at least order one in the same genus," says Henry.

Plant in late summer or early fall. Your goal is to mimic the plants' natural cycle and to seed at the time that the seed would naturally be ripening and falling in the wild, Henry says.

If you're planting into established turf, be sure the seed makes contact with soil. Broadcasting seed over the area is not enough. Henry suggests the following technique for working seeds into an existing turf: Roughen the ground surface by dragging the area with a pine tree or a section of fence (such as chain-link or livestock fence) hitched behind a tractor or pick-up truck. Then broadcast the seed. Drag the area again to push the seed through the turf cover.

Henry calls DOT's technique "Seed and Run." There is no extra water or fertilizer provided. "We choose the toughest, most prolific local species and let it go," he says.

Once the stand is established, mow as little as possible. Only mow to keep down competing vegetation, such as seedling trees or other invasive plants that you don't want. Never mow between the time the wildflowers come up and the time they set seed. If you mow before they bloom, you'll probably lose the first year's flowers. If you mow after they bloom but before they ripen seed, you'll be cutting off the source of next year's plants.

Check with local sources on what's noxious. "Butterfly weed is a really popular plant in many areas, but it will kill cows," says Henry. "We plant Shasta daisy here, but it's against the law in Ohio."

FIDDLING WITH FERNS

For a shaded area, a bed of ferns is a pleasant alternative to lawn grass. And you might be surprised to learn how easy it is to transplant ferns. If you dig up the entire root system and keep it constantly moist, you can move just about any fern, anytime, says John Mickel, Ph.D., the fern curator at the New York Botanical Garden.

"If you move a fern in early spring, dig it before the shoots begin to arise or after they are fully expanded. Avoid disturbing the plant while the fiddleheads, or curled leaf fronds, are stretching upward. They may wilt if you do. Although the plants usually have a second set of dormant shoots that can take their place, recovery is much slower, sometimes impossible," says Dr. Mickel. Yet once you have a fern like the ostrich fern (*Matteuccia* spp.) in place and growing strongly, you may be able to cut a few fiddleheads to eat.

While you should never transplant ferns from the wild, you may be able to move ferns from a neighbor's yard or rescue them from a construction site. Select small to medium-size plants for transplanting. They are more vigorous growers with less foliage to support than the bigger, more mature ones. To find the edges of the root system, dig in the area below the farthest extent of the frond tips. You'll find the roots about 6 to 8 inches deep. Dig all the way around the plant, and slip a broad shovel under the root clump. Slide the soil-encased roots into moist burlap in a box or wheelbarrow. Then promptly take the fern to a new site.

The fern will need a soil that is moist and light but rich. Since Dr. Mickel's landscape is sandy, he adds a couple of shovelfuls of compost to each planting hole. Loosen heavier soils with extra sand as well as the compost. Mulch with compost or fallen leaves every year or two to maintain soil fertility and texture.

Don't plant ferns in single holes at the bases of trees. "Ferns do not compete well with other roots," explains Dr. Mickel. You'll need to prepare cultivated beds for the ferns and keep them free of woody roots. Hoe or spade around the bed perimeter occasionally, and dig out any roots that invade near the soil surface.

Keep your fern areas moist throughout the growing season. If the area is not naturally damp, use a soaker hose or sprinkler whenever the weather turns dry.

Groundcovers

Groundcovers can be a beautiful and easy-care solution to a troublesome area of lawn. There are groundcovers that spread rapidly and tenaciously to cover steep slopes and groundcovers that thrive in the dense shade under trees. You can select groundcovers that thrive in wet soil. Groundcovers are also great for combining with other ornamentals in mixed beds.

RESPECT TREE ROOTS WHEN PLANTING

One of the worst things you can do when planting groundcovers under trees is slice through tree roots. "Try

SAVE TIME, MULCH FIRST

Trying to lay mulch between plants in a newly planted expanse of groundcover can be a long, tedious task. You can save yourself some time by laying the mulch first. This is especially helpful when planting groundcover plugs or plants in small pots. After laying the mulch, you can easily plant through it with a trowel without pulling up too much soil on top of the clean mulch.

STICK TO SMALL MULCH

In a planting of groundcovers that root along their stems, the size of the mulch you lay affects how quickly the groundcovers spread. "Stay away from large chunks of bark," says Glenn Morris, a landscape designer in North Carolina. "When mulch is big enough to Frisbee, you're in trouble," he laughs. Plants that send roots down as they spread need a finer mulch in order for rooting to occur. Big chunks of bark and stone will slow the rooting process. Morris suggests spreading a mulch of shredded bark or finely ground bark or pine straw.

SAVE MONEY WITH SMALL PLANTS

Starting groundcovers in a large area can be expensive because you must buy many plants. You can reduce the cost by starting with young plants. Groundcovers such as English ivy, Japanese pachysandra (*Pachysandra terminalis*), and common periwinkle (*Vinca minor*) are often sold in flats of rooted cuttings (also called plugs). They will take a little more pampering than those grown in 4-inch pots but may cut your costs by half or more. You can also start mondo grass (*Ophiopogon japonicus*), blue lilyturf (*Liriope muscari*), and many perennial groundcovers from plugs. Another shortcut is to pull apart large clumps of blue lilyturf or mondo grass either from an established planting or from plants purchased in larger pots.

to avoid tilling under a tree," says Jack Siebenthaler, a registered landscape architect from Florida. "It tears up the tree's feeder roots. Most people think tree roots grow deeply into the soil, but the truth is that most roots are within the top 18 inches of soil." So if you're breaking new ground for groundcovers (or any other planting) and must open the soil to help establish the new planting, Siebenthaler suggests this alternative: Rent an aerator like the type used for lawns. Its vertical action is easier on roots than the churning of a tiller.

He also suggests that when choosing a groundcover you select those such as Japanese pachysandra (*Pachysandra terminalis*), blue lilyturf (*Liriope muscari*), yellow starjasmine (*Trachelospermum asiaticum*), or mondo grass (*Ophiopogon japonicus*), which are easily started from plugs or plants grown in 2-inch pots. That way, you can plant with a trowel or a bulb planter. You'll disturb roots less than if you plant larger groundcovers grown in 1- to 3-gallon nursery containers that require a larger hole.

Are there any trees that aren't disturbed by tilling? According to Siebenthaler, pines are most tolerant to soil disturbance, but it's a matter of degree. Some pines have a central taproot, but those growing on a low water table would not. If you must till under any tree, Siebenthaler suggests that you try not to disturb the soil any deeper than 3 inches.

DABBLE IN DIBBLE BARS

Planting groundcovers such as English ivy, euonymus, or pachysandra can be tiresome labor. Each rooted cutting or plant plug needs its own little hole, and often dozens of plants are required to cover a relatively small space. On top of that, sites intended for groundcovers are often rocky or otherwise difficult to work. "The best tool I've found for planting groundcovers is a tree-planting device called a dibble bar," says Bonnie Lee Appleton, Ph.D., an associate professor and extension horticulturist at Virginia Polytechnic Institute and State University. Used by foresters and tree farmers, a dibble bar resembles a treaded garden spade—except that the entire tool is a single piece of heavy-duty cast steel with a blade that's either wedge- or triangle-shaped.

To use a dibble bar, push the tool into the ground with your foot, and lever it back and forth to open up a hole. Then put the plant in place. Now shove the dibble bar into the ground again, about 1 inch back from the original hole, and wiggle the bar back and forth to close the first hole. "Then just use your heel to close up that second hole," says Dr. Appleton, "and move on to the next planting spot. The work goes really fast, and you can do all the digging while standing up, as opposed to crawling around on your hands and knees with a trowel."

Dibble bars are available from forestry equipment companies. (One source is Forestry Suppliers, P.O. Box 8397, Jackson, MS 39284-8397.) They're also available from some tool-rental outlets. "Or you can ask to borrow one if there's a state forestry office near you," suggests Dr. Appleton.

GOOD GROUND RULES FOR GROUNDCOVERS

For best success with groundcovers, heed the warning from Mary Ann McGourty, who, with her husband, Fred, owns Hillside Gardens, a Connecticut nursery that specializes in uncommon perennials. "When you say groundcovers, people think low-maintenance, which they really consider as no-maintenance," says McGourty, "and there is no such thing." However, McGourty says here are things you can do to make your planting as maintenance-free and healthy as possible:

Prepare, prepare, prepare the soil! "We see gardeners make the same mistakes over and over again by skimping on soil prep when starting a planting of groundcover," says McGourty. "The plants must be given a fair chance, and we recommend incorporating at least 4 inches of compost or other organic matter into the soil before planting. If the soil is extra-heavy or extra-light, add even more."

Match the plant to the site. McGourty says pachysandra is one of the plants she sees misplaced most frequently. "It's a shade plant," she says. "It burns when the sun shines on it, especially in winter in frozen soil."

Always mulch to keep weeds down. "Many times, people expect groundcovers to suppress weeds that are already present. That's impossible," she says. McGourty suggests keeping a 1-inch layer of mulch between plants until they've grown together completely.

Choose a groundcover whose vigor fits the area to be planted. "There are several plants we call mile-a-minute plants because they grow so fast. They don't stop just because they reach the boundary of the area you want in ground-

LIVEN GROUNDCOVER WITH BULBS

Spring bulbs also make a nice contrast planted among common groundcovers like English ivy and Japanese pachysandra (*Pachysandra terminalis*). Daffodils work best because they naturalize easily, bloom in light shade, and grow tall enough to reach through the mat of groundcover. However, you may have to thin around the bulbs every two or three years to keep them from being choked out. Common periwinkle (*Vinca minor*) has a light root system, and daffodils do well planted among it without a lot of thinning.

You can also consider interplanting bulbs with perennial groundcovers that emerge later in spring such as hostas, Siberian bugloss (*Brunnera macrophylla*), and daylilies. As the perennials come up, their expanding foliage hides the yellowing leaves of the bulbs.

MOWING ZIPS MAINTENANCE

Make quick work of trimming back certain groundcovers by mowing them with a lawn mower in late winter just before they begin new spring growth. Raise your mower blades as high as possible, and mow as you normally would. To avoid tearing the foliage, be sure your mower blades are sharp.

Groundcovers that respond well to this method include blue lilyturf (*Liriope muscari*), yellow star-jasmine (*Trachelospermum asiaticum*), mondo grass (*Ophiopogon japonicus*), Japanese pachysandra (*Pachysandra terminalis*), and wintercreeper (*Euonymus fortunei*). Wait to mow spring-flowering groundcovers such as moss pink (*Phlox subulata*) after they bloom.

cover," says McGourty. These are lamiums (*Lamium* spp.), English ivy, and evening primroses (*Oenothera spp.*). McGourty says that goutweed (*Aegopodium podagraria*) is another highly invasive groundcover.

Use evergreen groundcovers in places on display year-round. Unless these areas are subject to winter burn, spots that are seen year-round, such as at the front door, should be planted with evergreen groundcovers. For these, McGourty recommends European wild ginger (*Asarum europaeum*), English ivy, Japanese pachysandra (*Pachysandra terminalis*), or wintercreeper (*Euonymus fortunei*).

ADD FERN FANFARE TO GROUNDCOVERS

One way to add pizzazz to a mass of utilitarian mondo grass (*Ophiopogon japonicus*) or Japanese pachysandra (*Pachysandra terminalis*) is to break the planting with punctuation of contrasting perennials. The key is choosing those that are compatible with the groundcover. Mary Ann McGourty, a co-owner of Hillside Gardens, a Connecticut nursery that specializes in uncommon perennials, sug-

gests larger-leaved hostas and big daylilies for a coarse contrast. "Certain ferns also work well," she says. They include cinnamon fern (*Osmunda cinnamomea*), ostrich ferns (*Matteuccia* spp.), and interrupted fern (*Osmunda claytoniana*). "You'll probably need to spend about 15 minutes per year rescuing your treasures [from encroaching mondo or pachysandra]," adds McGourty.

LEAFING OUT IN THE LEAVES

In mountains, foothills, and other areas where the soil is rocky, there's an easy way to encourage groundcovers to spread without doing backbreaking soil preparation. "This works for groundcovers that spread by runners," says Glenn Morris, a landscape designer in North Carolina who learned the technique from his mother. "Every fall, Mother would stretch a little wire flower-bed fence to surround her ferns, and behind it we'd dump all of the leaves we'd raked. Each year, she would move the fence a little farther out." The ferns sent their rhizomes right into the leaves, and they spread much more quickly than they would have in the rocky soil. "Eventually, Mother covered half of the front yard that way," says Morris. Popular plants in the mountainous areas of the mid-Atlantic and New England that respond to this technique include hay-scented fern (*Dennstaedtia punctilobula*), New York fern (*Thelypteris noveboracensis*), and English ivy.

SAVE THE SOIL ON SLOPES

If you want to replace grass with groundcover on a slope, don't till the soil. Norman Kent Johnson, an Alabama garden designer, suggests that you kill the grass and plant right through it. "If you break up the ground, you're going to have problems with erosion," says Johnson. He advises killing the grass by covering the area with clear plastic for a few weeks. Be absolutely sure that all of the grass is dead before you remove the plastic, or it will come back as weeds in your groundcover. After taking up the plastic, dig planting holes through the dead mat of vegetation. "It's harder to dig through the mat than it would be to dig through open ground, but it's worth the effort," says Johnson. The mat keeps the soil in place. As the mat deteriorates, your groundcover spreads to take its place and the area has been converted to groundcover without erosion.

DISCOVER A DAINTIER STRAWBERRY

A new hybrid strawberry makes a beautiful groundcover that also bears fruit. *Fragaria frel* 'Pink Panda' bears large pink flowers and small but tasty fruit. Robert M. Mramor, the head grower for Mikkelsen's, an Ohio company that breeds and propagates new cultivars for the greenhouse industry, says that 'Pink Panda' fills in vigorously as a groundcover. (It's also wonderful for planting in hanging baskets.)

'Pink Panda' is versatile in every requirement but one: It must have soil that is constantly moist, not overly rich. " 'Pink Panda' will droop and fry with dry roots," Mramor says. The plant thrives in full sun or light shade. The plants are hardy to Zone 4 but do best if covered with a straw mulch in winter.

Only about 40 percent of the flowers on 'Pink Panda' bear fruit, but that's still a bonus compared to the 0 percent of edible fruit you'd expect from your typical groundcover bed. The fruits that do form are less prone to fungal diseases than are those from standard strawberry cultivars.

*soil covering
leaf axil*

ROOTING
GROUNDCOVERS

**LOW WINDOW?
USE GROUNDCOVER!**

Tall shrubs in front of windows block the view, but low shrubs and groundcovers let the sun shine in. Choose plants according to the height of windows, making sure their mature height size won't top the sill.

◆ BURY RUNNERS FOR FAST COVERAGE

Make your groundcovers cover ground faster by encouraging rooting along their stems. Glenn Morris, a landscape designer in North Carolina, suggests this: "Pick out plants with the longest shoots you can find. Set a plant in place, and then take each runner and cover a leaf axil with a little soil." It will root and start a new plantlet, so the area fills in more quickly. This technique (illustrated at left) does not work with all groundcovers, so ask your supplier or check a reference text before you try it. Morris uses this technique with two cultivars of creeping juniper (*Juniperus horizontalis* 'Plumosa' and 'Wiltonii'), periwinkles (*Vinca minor* and *V. major*), rockspray cotoneaster (*Cotoneaster horizontalis*), wintercreeper (*Euonymus fortunei*), and English ivy.

PLANTING POINTERS FOR JUNIPERS

Junipers are one of the most common groundcovers for full sun because they grow fast, cover well, and are inexpensive. Glenn Morris, a landscape designer in North Carolina, shares the following tips for using them successfully:

Don't start a competition. Be wary of planting groundcover-type junipers by a Bermuda grass lawn. "If the Bermuda creeps into the juniper, the grass competes with the plants, and its seed heads poke up through the junipers," says Morris. "The whole thing just looks terrible, and you may never get the grass out." If you must combine Bermuda grass and junipers, Morris suggests 'Blue Pacific' shore juniper (*Juniperus conferta* 'Blue Pacific'). It forms a dense cover and has the best chance for competing.

Space plants properly. "Planting most junipers any less than 30 to 36 inches apart is wasting money and plant material," says Morris. "If the soil is decent, they'll grow so fast. Andorra [*J. horizontalis* 'Plumosa'] will get 4 feet across in its third year here." Morris explains that if you space plants 18 inches on center, you'll need one plant for every 1.76 square feet of bed. If you space the plants 36 inches on center, you use only one plant for every 7 square feet.

Stagger plantings on slopes. When planting junipers on a slope, try a staggered planting, as shown in the illustration on the opposite page. "If you're planting junipers on a slope, they're going to spread in the shape of a water droplet," says Morris. Because they spread less across the slope than they do down the slope, Morris recommends spacing them

12 to 18 inches apart in rows and allowing a minimum of 30 to 36 inches between the rows. Stagger the rows so they aren't in a soldier-like symmetry. "What you'll have is a pattern of isosceles triangles," says Morris.

newly planted plants

plants spreading down the slope

THERE'S A BAMBOO FOR YOU

One groundcover you may not have considered planting is bamboo. While bamboo has a reputation as a rampant spreader, some species are easier to control. Albert Adelman, the owner of Burt Associates Bamboo in Massachusetts, is just as concerned about out-of-control bamboos as gardeners are. "We preach responsibility," he says. "It is ecologically and environmentally sound to contain these plants." Most bamboos are easy to contain without barriers, says Adelman. One of his favorites for use as a groundcover is *Sasa veitchii*, a low-growing running bamboo that is popular in Japan. In fall, the edges of the leaves turn tan but the center remains green. This coloring remains all winter long.

Like other ornamental grasses, bamboos are classified as either running or clumping, according to their habit of growth. Running bamboos grow from far-reaching underground runners. Some aggressive running bamboos spread rapidly and pop up in expected places, dismaying the gardener who planted them. Other species, however, are easily controlled. Most cold-hardy bamboos are running types.

Adelman recommends an annual routine to keep your running bamboo in its place. Most species send up culms (new stems) only in spring, and you can easily break them off. Or tug at the new culm, and find the rhizomes. Then clip the root, severing the new plant.

Some of the variegated bamboos make effective accents in perennial beds. To control a border plant, says Adelman, lift the clump each spring, snip off rhizomes, and return it to its place. The snipping and transplanting slow down its growth enough to keep it in bounds.

THE GARDEN PROFESSIONALS

Phil Aaronson is the business manager and **Michael Merner** is the owner of The Organic Landscape Company at Earth Care Farm in Charlestown, Rhode Island. The company is a certified organic farm and includes a farm-scale agricultural composting operation and a natural organic lawn-care treatment service.

Albert Adelman is the owner of Burt Associates Bamboo in Westford, Massachusetts, a mail-order nursery specializing in bamboo and other Asian plants for indoor and outdoor use.

Bonnie Lee Appleton, Ph.D., is an associate professor of horticulture, researcher, and extension nursery specialist at Hampton Roads Agricultural Experiment Station, Virginia Polytechnic Institute and State University, in Virginia Beach. She is the author of *Landscape Rejuvenation*.

Pratt Brown is the owner of Pratt Brown Landscapes, a landscape installation, maintenance, and design company in Birmingham, Alabama.

Jack Hall, Ph.D., is a professor of turfgrass management at Virginia Polytechnic Institute and State University in Blacksburg, Virginia, and an extension specialist with responsibilities for education and support of extension agents and turfgrass professionals.

Gary L. Henry is a registered landscape architect and staff coordinator for the Florida Highway Beautification Council. He is also on the executive board of the Florida Urban Forestry Council.

Ed Hume is the owner of Ed Hume Seeds, Inc., in Kent, Washington, a company that specializes in untreated vegetable seeds. He also hosts "Gardening in America," a nationally syndicated gardening television program.

Richard Hurley, Ph.D., is a vice president and the director of research, specializing in turfgrass breeding, for Lofts Seed, Inc., which is a family-owned, wholesale supplier of cool-season grasses and wildflower mixes and is located in Bound Brook, New Jersey.

Norman Kent Johnson is an independent garden designer in Birmingham, Alabama. He was the garden design editor at *Southern Living* and was the founding editor of *Garden Design*.

Mary Ann McGourty is a co-owner of Hillside Gardens in Norfolk, Connecticut. The nursery specializes in uncommon perennials and perennial garden design. McGourty was a major contributor to *Taylor's Guide to Ground Covers, Vines, and Grasses*.

Cynthia McKenney is an ornamental horticulturist and instructor of horticulture at Texas Tech University in Lubbock.

David Marshall is a Leon County extension agent for the University of Florida in Tallahassee. His area of responsibility is environmental horticulture.

John Mickel, Ph.D., is the fern curator at the New York Botanical Garden in Bronx, New York. He has written *How to Know the Ferns and Fern Allies* and *The Home Gardener's Book of Ferns*.

Glenn Morris is a free-lance landscape designer and garden writer in Greensboro, North Carolina. He is a former landscape editor for *Southern Living* magazine.

Robert M. Mramor is the head grower for Mikkelsen's, Inc., in Ashtabula, Ohio. The company breeds and propagates potted plants and new cultivars for the greenhouse industry.

Robert Peek is an information specialist in water conservation and management for the St. John's River Water Management District in Palatka, Florida. He is the author of the district's *Xeriscape Plant Guide*.

Daniel A. Potter, Ph.D., is a professor of entomology at the University of Kentucky in Lexington. His research specialty is insects of ornamental trees, shrubs, and turf.

Ray Rothenberger, Ph.D., is a professor of ornamental horticulture at the University of Missouri at Columbia. He also hosts a call-in radio garden show in mid-Missouri.

David J. Shetlar, Ph.D., is a landscape entomologist for the Ohio Cooperative Extension Service and an assistant professor at Ohio State University at Columbus. He is the author of *Turfgrass Insect and Mite Manual*, published by the Pennsylvania Turfgrass Council.

Jack Siebenthaler is a registered landscape architect and a consulting arborist in Clearwater, Florida. He is also a former executive director of the American Society of Consulting Arborists.

Michael Talbot is the owner of Michael Talbot and Associates in Dorchester, Massachusetts, an ecological landscape design and maintenance company, providing natural organic lawn care, landscape design and construction, and maintenance of woody plants.

Jerry L. Tanner is a landscape architect, an environmental planner, and the owner of Tanner Associates in Columbus, Ohio.

Thomas L. Watschke, Ph.D., is a professor of turfgrass science at the Pennsylvania State University at University Park. He conducts research on weed control, plant growth regulators, and water control.

Jim Wilson is a cohost of public television's "The Victory Garden." He is the author of *Landscaping with Container Plants*, *Masters of the Victory Garden*, and *Landscaping with Wildflowers*.

Bill Wolf is the founder and president of Necessary Trading Company of New Castle, Virginia. The company manufactures Necessary Organics growing supplies and sells organic fertilizers and pest controls via mail order.

GROUNDCOVERS THAT BACKFIRE

In the moist, mild climate of the Pacific Northwest, some groundcovers can outgrow their bounds rather quickly. Ed Hume, the owner of Ed Hume Seeds in Washington State, cautions homeowners with small lots to avoid these groundcovers:

Galium odoratum (sweet woodruff)
Hedera helix (English ivy)
Hypericum spp. (St.-John's-worts)
Pachysandra terminalis (Japanese pachysandra)

If you must use them, Hume suggests installing a commercial-type steel or plastic edging buried 6 to 8 inches deep to keep the groundcover from creeping into the lawn, flower beds, or other places where it is not welcome.

Sources

SEEDS AND PLANTS

The following companies range from large businesses that offer a wide range of seeds and plants to small nurseries that specialize in a particular type of plant.

Adams County Nursery, Inc.
P.O. Box 108
Aspers, PA 17304
Fruit trees

Andre Viette Farm and Nursery
Route 1, Box 16
Fishersville, VA 22939
Perennials; specializes in daylilies

B & D Lilies
330 P St.
Port Townsend, WA 98368
Hybrid and species lilies

Bear Creek Nursery
P.O. Box 411
Northport, WA 99157
*Fruit trees: scion wood, bud wood, budded
    trees, and rootstocks*

Bluestone Perennials
7211 Middle Ridge Rd.
Madison, OH 44057

Broken Arrow Nursery
13 Broken Arrow Rd.
Hamden, CT 06518
*Specializes in mountain laurels and
    rhododendrons*

Burt Associates Bamboo
P.O. Box 719
Westford, MA 01886

C & O Nursery
P.O. Box 116
Wenatchee, WA 98801
Fruit trees

Champlain Isle Agro Associates
Isle LaMotte, VT 05463
Specializes in disease-tested bramble plants

Clyde Robin Seed Co.
3670 Enterprise Ave.
Hayward, CA 94545
Flower and wildflower seeds

Coenosium Gardens
6642 S. Lone Elder Rd.
Aurora, OR 97002
Specializes in unusual conifers

The Cook's Garden
P.O. Box 535
Londonderry, VT 05148

Country Heritage Nursery
P.O. Box 536
Hartford, MI 49057
Mainly small fruits; some trees

Cumberland Valley Nurseries, Inc.
P.O. Box 471
McMinnville, TN 37110
Fruit trees

The Daffodil Mart
Route 3, Box 794
Gloucester, VA 23061
Specializes in bulbs

Ed Hume Seeds, Inc.
P.O. Box 1450
Kent, WA 98035
Specializes in untreated vegetable seeds

Edible Landscaping
P.O. Box 77
Afton, VA 22920

Farmer Seed and Nursery Co.
818 N.W. 4th St.
Faribault, MN 55021

Foster Nursery Co., Inc.
P.O. Box 150
Fredonia, NY 14063

Gardens of the Blue Ridge
P.O. Box 10
U.S. 221 N
Pineola, NC 28662
Trees, shrubs, ferns, and wildflowers

Gossler Farms Nursery
1200 Weaver Rd.
Springfield, OR 97478
Specializes in magnolias

Gurney Seed & Nursery Co.
Yankton, SD 57079

Harris Seeds
P.O. Box 22960
Rochester, NY 14692

Hastings
P.O. Box 115535
Atlanta, GA 30302
Specializes in plants for southern climates

Henry Field Seed & Nursery Co.
P.O. Box 700
Shenandoah, IA 51601

Henry Leuthardt Nurseries, Inc.
P.O. Box 666
East Moriches, NY 11940
*Specializes in small fruits and espalier
fruit trees*

HollyDale Nursery
P.O. Box 26
Pelham, TN 37366

J. E. Miller Nurseries, Inc.
5060 W. Lake Rd.
Canandaigua, NY 14424
Fruits and ornamentals

J. L. Hudson, Seedsman
P.O. Box 1058
Redwood City, CA 94064

J. W. Jung Seed Co.
335 S. High St.
Randolph, WI 53957

Johnny's Selected Seeds
2580 Foss Hill Rd.
Albion, ME 04910
Vegetables, herbs, and flowers

Kelly Nurseries
Hwy. 54
Louisiana, MO 63353
Fruits and ornamentals

Kurt Bluemel, Inc.
2740 Greene Ln.
Baldwin, MD 21013
Specializes in ornamental grasses

Liberty Seed Co.
P.O. Box 806
New Philadelphia, OH 44663
Vegetable and flower seeds

Lilypons Water Gardens
6800 Lilypons Rd.
P.O. Box 10
Buckeystown, MD 21717-0010

Logee's Greenhouses
141 North St.
Danielson, CT 06239
Exotic flowering plants, herbs, and vines

Long Island Seed Co.
1368 Flanders Rd.
Flanders, NY 11901
*Specializes in open-pollinated tomato
cultivars*

Meadowbrook Herb Garden Catalog
P.O. Box 578
Fairfield, CT 06430

Nichols Garden Nursery
1190 N. Pacific Hwy.
Albany, OR 97321
Herbs, vegetables, and flowers

North Star Gardens
19060 Manning Trail N
Marine on St. Croix, MN 55047
Specializes in raspberries

Orol Ledden & Sons, Inc.
P.O. Box 7
Sewell, NJ 08080

Owens Nursery
P.O. Box 193
Gay, GA 30218
*Specializes in hostas and muscadine
    grapes*

Park Seed Co.
P.O. Box 31
Greenwood, SC 29647

Pinetree Garden Seeds
Route 100
New Gloucester, ME 04260

Prairie Nursery
P.O. Box 306
Westfield, WI 53964
Specializes in prairie plants and seeds

Raintree Nursery
391 Butts Rd.
Morton, WA 98356
Fruits, nuts, and edible plants

Rayner Bros., Inc.
P.O. Box 1617
Salisbury, MD 21802

Redwood City Seed Co.
P.O. Box 361
Redwood City, CA 94064

St. Lawrence Nurseries
R.R. 5, Box 324
Potsdam, NY 13676
Northern hardy fruits and nuts

Sandy Mush Herb Nursery
Route 2, Surrett Cove Rd.
Leicester, NC 28748
Specializes in rare and unusual plants

Seeds Trust High Altitude Gardens
P.O. Box 4619
Ketchum, ID 83340
Seeds for high altitudes and cold climates

Shepherd's Garden Seeds
6116 Hwy. 9
Felton, CA 95018

Southern Exposure Seed Exchange
P.O. Box 158
North Garden, VA 22959

Stark Bro's Nurseries & Orchards Co.
Hwy. 54
Louisiana, MO 63353
Fruits and ornamental trees and shrubs

Stokes Seeds, Inc.
Box 548
Buffalo, NY 14240

Territorial Seed Co.
P.O. Box 157
Cottage Grove, OR 97424
*Vegetable seeds for the maritime climates
    of the Pacific Northwest*

Thompson & Morgan, Inc.
P.O. Box 1308
Jackson, NJ 08527

Vandenberg
3 Black Meadow Rd.
Chester, NY 10918
Bulbs

Van Ness Water Gardens
2460 N. Euclid Ave.
Upland, CA 91786-1199

W. Atlee Burpee & Co.
300 Park Ave.
Warminster, PA 18974

Wayside Gardens
1 Garden Ln.
Hodges, SC 29695

Well-Sweep Herb Farm
317 Mt. Bethel Rd.
Port Murray, NJ 07865
Herbs and perennials

White Flower Farm
Litchfield, CT 06759-0050
Bulbs, perennials, and woody plants

GARDENING EQUIPMENT AND SUPPLIES

The following companies offer merchandise such as organic fertilizers, composting equipment, composting worms, animal repellents and traps, beneficial insects and microbes, shredders, sprayers, tillers, row covers and shading materials, irrigation equipment, hand tools, and carts.

A. M. Leonard, Inc.
P.O. Box 816
Piqua, OH 45356

Bountiful Gardens
19550 Walker Rd.
Willits, CA 95490
*Also offers organically grown herb and
    vegetable seed*

Bricker's Organic Farm
824 Sandbar Ferry Rd.
Augusta, GA 30901
Organic mulches, fertilizer, and compost

Flowerfield Enterprises
10332 Shaver Rd.
Kalamazoo, MI 49002
Books and supplies for worm composting

Gardener's Supply Co.
128 Intervale Rd.
Burlington, VT 05401

Gardens Alive!
5100 Schenley Place
Lawrenceburg, IN 47025

Garden-Ville of Austin
8648 Old Bee Cave Rd.
Austin, TX 78735

Green Earth Organics
9422 144th St. E
Puyallup, WA 98373

Harmony Farm Supply
P.O. Box 460
Graton, CA 95444

Highland Hardware
1045 N. Highland Ave. NE
Atlanta, GA 30306
Fine gardening tools

The Kinsman Co., Inc.
River Rd.
Point Pleasant, PA 18950

The Natural Gardening Co.
217 San Anselmo Ave.
San Anselmo, CA 94960

Necessary Trading Co.
P.O. Box 305
422 Salem Ave.
New Castle, VA 24127

Ohio Earth Food
13737 Duquette Ave. NE
Hartville, OH 44632

Peaceful Valley Farm Supply Co.
P.O. Box 2209
Grass Valley, CA 95945

Smith & Hawken
25 Corte Madera
Mill Valley, CA 94941

The Urban Farmer Store
2833 Vicente St.
San Francisco, CA 94116
*Water-conserving irrigation systems and
    other supplies*

SOIL-TESTING LABORATORIES

The following companies will test soil samples from home gardens. Some companies also make recommendations for adding soil amendments based on test results.

A & L Agricultural Labs
7621 White Pine Rd.
Richmond, VA 23237

Biosystem Consultants
P.O. Box 43
Lorane, OR 97451

Cook's Consulting
R.D. 2, Box 13
Lowville, NY 13367

Erth-Rite
R.D. 1, Box 243
Gap, PA 17527

Peaceful Valley Farm Supply
P.O. Box 2209
Grass Valley, CA 95945

Timberleaf
5569 State St.
Albany, OH 45710

Wallace Labs
365 Coral Circle
El Segundo, CA 90245

Recommended Reading

Appelhof, Mary. *Worms Eat My Garbage.* Kalamazoo, Mich.: Flower Press, 1982.

Appleton, Bonnie Lee. *Landscape Rejuvenation: Remodeling the Home Landscape.* Pownal, Vt.: Garden Way Publishing, 1988.

Armitage, Allan M. *Herbaceous Perennial Plants: A Treatise on Their Identification, Culture, and Garden Attributes.* Athens, Ga.: Varsity Press, 1989.

Ashworth, Suzanne. *Seed to Seed.* Decorah, Iowa: Seed Savers Exchange, 1991.

Bradley, Fern Marshall, ed. *Rodale's Chemical-Free Yard and Garden.* Emmaus, Pa.: Rodale Press, 1991.

Bradley, Fern Marshall, and Barbara W. Ellis, eds. *Rodale's All-New Encyclopedia of Organic Gardening.* Emmaus, Pa.: Rodale Press, 1992.

Brickell, Christopher. *Pruning.* New York: Simon and Schuster, 1988.

Bubel, Nancy. *52 Weekend Garden Projects.* Emmaus, Pa.: Rodale Press, 1992.

————. *The New Seed-Starters Handbook.* Emmaus, Pa.: Rodale Press, 1988.

Coleman, Eliot. *Four-Season Harvest: How to Harvest Fresh, Organic Vegetables from Your Home Garden All Year Long.* Post Mills, Vt.: Chelsea Green Publishing Co., 1993.

————. *The New Organic Grower: A Master's Manual of Tools and Techniques for the Home and Market Gardener.* Post Mills, Vt.: Chelsea Green Publishing Co., 1989.

Ellis, Barbara W., and Fern Marshall Bradley, eds. *The Organic Gardener's Handbook of Natural Insect and Disease Control.* Emmaus, Pa.: Rodale Press, 1992.

Frey, Susan Rademacher, and Barbara W. Ellis. *Outdoor Living Spaces: How to Create a Landscape You Can Use and Enjoy.* Emmaus, Pa.: Rodale Press, 1992.

Gershuny, Grace. *Start with the Soil.* Emmaus, Pa.: Rodale Press, 1993.

Halpin, Anne Moyer, and the Editors of Rodale Press. *Foolproof Planting: How to Successfully Start and Propagate More Than 250 Vegetables, Flowers, Trees, and Shrubs.* Emmaus, Pa.: Rodale Press, 1990.

Heriteau, Jacqueline, et al. *The National Arboretum Book of Outstanding Garden Plants.* New York: Simon and Schuster, 1990.

Hill, Lewis. *Fruits and Berries for the Home Garden.* Rev. ed. Pownal, Vt.: Garden Way Publishing, 1992.

Horst, R. Kenneth. *Westcott's Plant Disease Handbook.* 5th ed. New York: Van Nostrand Reinhold Co., 1990.

Jeavons, John. *How to Grow More Vegetables Than You Ever Thought Possible on Less Land Than You Can Imagine.* Rev. ed. Berkeley, Calif.: Ten Speed Press, 1991.

Kourik, Robert. *Designing and Maintaining Your Edible Landscape Naturally.* Santa Rosa, Calif.: Metamorphic Press, 1986.

Kowalchik, Claire, and William H. Hylton, eds. *Rodale's Illustrated Encyclopedia of Herbs.* Emmaus, Pa.: Rodale Press, 1987.

Loewer, Peter. *Tough Plants for Tough Places: How to Grow 101 Easy-Care Plants for Every Part of Your Yard.* Emmaus, Pa.: Rodale Press, 1992.

McGourty, Frederick. *The Perennial Gardener.* Boston: Houghton Mifflin Co., 1989.

Martin, Deborah L., and Grace Gershuny, eds. *The Rodale Book of Composting: Easy Methods for Every Gardener.* Emmaus, Pa.: Rodale Press, 1992.

Martin, Tovah. *Essence of Paradise: Fragrant Plants for Indoor Gardens.* Boston: Little, Brown, and Company, 1991.

Ogden, Shepherd. *Step by Step Organic Vegetable Gardening: The Gardening Classic.* Rev. & updated ed. New York: HarperCollins Publishers, 1992.

Parnes, Robert. *Fertile Soil: A Grower's Guide to Organic and Inorganic Fertilizers.* Davis, Calif.: agAccess, 1990. (Available from agAccess, P.O. Box 2008, Davis, CA 95617.)

Peirce, Pam. *Environmentally Friendly Gardening: Controlling Vegetable Pests.* San Ramon, Calif.: Ortho Information Services, 1991. (Available from Ortho Information Services, P.O. Box 5047, San Ramon, CA 94583-0947.)

————. *Golden Gate Gardening: The Complete Guide to Year-Round Food Gardening in the San Francisco Bay Area and Coastal California.* Davis, Calif.: agAccess, 1993. (Available from agAccess, P.O. Box 2008, Davis, CA 95617.)

Phillips, Ellen, and C. Colston Burrell. *Rodale's Illustrated Encyclopedia of Perennials.* Emmaus, Pa.: Rodale Press, 1993.

Platt, Ellen Spector. *Flower Crafts.* Emmaus, Pa.: Rodale Press, 1993.

Pleasant, Barbara. *Warm-Climate Gardening: Tips — Techniques — Plans — Projects for Humid or Dry Conditions.* Pownal, Vt.: Storey Communications, 1993.

Roth, Susan A. *The Four-Season Landscape.* Emmaus, Pa.: Rodale Press, 1993.

————. *The Weekend Garden Guide.* Emmaus, Pa.: Rodale Press, 1991.

Schultz, Warren. *The Chemical-Free Lawn: The Newest Varieties and Techniques to Grow Lush, Hardy Grass.* Emmaus, Pa.: Rodale Press, 1989.

Shigo, Alex L. *Tree Pruning: A Worldwide Photo Guide.* Durham, N.H.: Shigo and Trees Assoc., 1989. (Available from Shigo and Trees Assoc., 4 Denbow Rd., Durham, NH 03824.)

Smith, Marny, and Nancy DuBrule. *A Country Garden for Your Backyard: Projects, Plans, and Plantings for a Country Look.* Emmaus, Pa.: Rodale Press, 1993.

Smith, Miranda, and Anna Carr. *Rodale's Garden Insect, Disease, and Weed Identification Guide.* Emmaus, Pa.: Rodale Press, 1988.

Taylor's Guides Staff. *Taylor's Guide to Ground Covers, Vines, and Grasses.* (Taylor's Guides to Gardening Series.) Boston: Houghton Mifflin Co., 1987.

Uber, William C. *Water Gardening Basics.* Upland, Calif.: Dragonflyer Press, 1988.

Wilson, Jim. *Landscaping with Container Plants.* Boston: Houghton Mifflin Co., 1990.

————. *Landscaping with Wildflowers.* Boston: Houghton Mifflin Company, 1992.

Contributors

Fern Marshall Bradley is an editor of garden books for Rodale Press. She has a master's degree in horticulture from Rutgers University and has managed an organic market garden. Currently, she experiments with the experts' gardening hints in her home garden in eastern Pennsylvania.

Lois Trigg Chaplin is a free-lance garden writer from Alabama. She is a former garden editor for *Southern Living* magazine and has a bachelor's degree in horticulture and entomology from the University of Florida. She is the author of *A Garden's Blessings* and a coauthor of both *Trees and Shrubs* and *Growing Vegetables and Herbs*.

George DeVault is the U.S. editor of *Novii Fermer,* a Russian-language farming magazine, and the former editor of *The New Farm.* He also manages an organic market garden near Emmaus, Pennsylvania, where he specializes in peas, garlic, and leeks.

Terry Krautwurst is a free-lance writer from North Carolina. He is the editor of *BackHome* magazine and former senior editor of *Mother Earth News* magazine.

Susan McClure is a free-lance garden writer from Ohio. She has a master's degree in botany from Miami University. She is the author of *The Harvest Gardener,* a coauthor of *All About Pruning,* and a frequent contributor to Rodale garden books.

Lynn McGowan is a free-lance writer from Pennsylvania. She is a former associate editor for *American Horticulturist* magazine and was a contributor to *Gardening in Small Spaces.*

Patricia S. Michalak is a free-lance garden writer from Pennsylvania and has a master's degree in entomology from Michigan State University. She is the author of *Rodale's*
Successful Organic Gardening: Herbs. She markets herbs and gourmet vegetables organically grown at her farm, Long and Winding Row Farm, in Kempton, Pennsylvania.

Jean M. A. Nick is an associate editor of garden books for Rodale Press. She has a master's degree in horticulture from Rutgers University and extensive experience in the commercial greenhouse industry. Her 1-acre home garden in eastern Pennsylvania includes a wide variety of blackberries and raspberries.

Nancy J. Ondra is an associate editor of garden books for Rodale Press. She has a bachelor's degree in agronomy from Delaware Valley College. She collects and propagates perennials and trees and maintains a large composting area on her home farm near Pennsburg, Pennsylvania.

Sara Pacher is a free-lance writer from North Carolina. She is a former senior editor for *Mother Earth News* magazine.

Sally Roth is a free-lance garden writer and editor in New Harmony, Indiana. She publishes a nature and gardening newsletter called *A Letter from the Country* and is a frequent contributor to Rodale garden books.

Miranda Smith is an agriculture writer and organic market gardener from Belchertown, Massachusetts. She is the editor and writer of *The Farmer Speaks: Organic and Low-Input Farming in the Northeast* for the federal Low-Input Sustainable Agriculture (LISA) program. She is a coauthor of *Rodale's Chemical-Free Yard and Garden.*

Heidi A. Stonehill is a senior research associate and photo editor for Rodale Press. She has a bachelor's degree in biology from Colby College.

USDA PLANT HARDINESS ZONE MAP

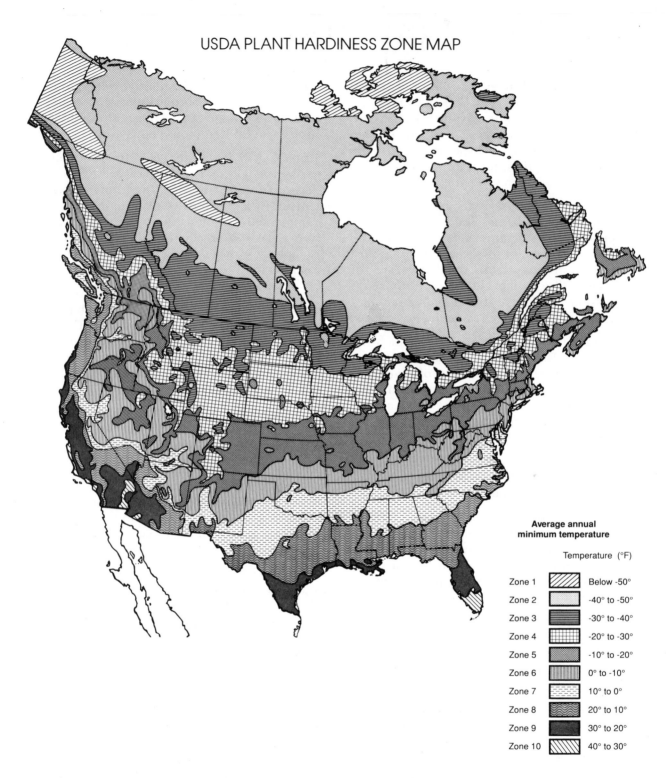

Average annual minimum temperature

Temperature (°F)

Zone 1	Below -50°
Zone 2	-40° to -50°
Zone 3	-30° to -40°
Zone 4	-20° to -30°
Zone 5	-10° to -20°
Zone 6	0° to -10°
Zone 7	10° to 0°
Zone 8	20° to 10°
Zone 9	30° to 20°
Zone 10	40° to 30°

Index

Note: Page references in *italic* indicate illustrations and captions. **Boldface** references indicate tables.